ARABY THE BLEST

MARGARET GOLDING

IN MEMORIAM

JUNE 18, 1922 – JANUARY 16, 1985

'Off at sea north-east winds blow
Sabaean odours from the spicy shore
Of Araby the blest'.

JOHN MILTON, *PARADISE LOST,* BOOK IV, 161

CNI PUBLICATIONS 7

ARABY THE BLEST

STUDIES IN ARABIAN ARCHAEOLOGY

EDITED BY D.T. POTTS

THE CARSTEN NIEBUHR INSTITUTE OF ANCIENT NEAR EASTERN STUDIES

UNIVERSITY OF COPENHAGEN 1988 · MUSEUM TUSCULANUM PRESS

D.T. POTTS, EDITOR, ARABY THE BLEST
The publication of this book was made possible
by grants from Carlsbergfondet, Dronning Margrethes og prins Henriks fond,
Kong Christian den Tiendes fond, and Københavns Universitets Publikationskonto.

Designed by Thora Fisker.

Set in Garamond by TR Sats, Køge,
and printed by Special-Trykkeriet Viborg a/s, 1988.

Published and distributed by Museum Tusculanum Press,
University of Copenhagen, Njalsgade 94
DK-2300 Copenhagen S.

ISBN 87-7289-051-7
ISSN 0902-5499

Contents

Editor's Preface

Archaeological exploration in the Arabian peninsula is not a new phenomenon, but over the course of the past decade Arabia has finally been given the kind of concerted scholarly attention it deserves, and begun to emerge from the relative and, it must be stressed, artificially imposed obscurity that has made it a kind of poor relation in the field of Near Eastern archaeology for far too long. Surveys and new excavations are taking place now in every country in the peninsula, and more and more publications dealing with Arabia's past appear each year. We hope that the collection of studies presented here will take its place among them, and contribute both material and ideas to the field of Arabian studies. The topics covered range from the palaeogeography and prehistory of the Rub' Al Khali, to the history and archaeology of Aden and the Hadhramaut since the Islamic conquest. There are contributions on the early second millennium in the northern Oman peninsula; the Late Bronze and Early Iron Age in the Hijaz; and the first millennium B.C. in al-Hasa. Recent work along part of the 'Incense Route' in the Yemen Arab Republic is discussed; two new inscriptions from Qaryat al-Faw are published here for the first time; and Arabia's relations with the kingdom of Characene during the first and second centuries A.D. are examined.

It is my hope that this collection of essays will be of interest to all scholars with a desire to better understand Arabia in antiquity. Although many worthy topics and important sites are not represented, I believe that this volume represents an important new generation of studies and serves in some measure as an index of the rapid growth of scholarship and archaeological research in the Arabian peninsula in recent years.

It is entirely fitting that a volume dedicated to Arabia should appear in the series of an institute named after one of the immortal explorers of that country, Carsten Niebuhr. It is also fitting that a certain portion of the studies published here concern the countries of the Arabian Gulf, the archaeological investigation of which has been furthered immeasurably by a large number of Danish archaeologists.

Finally, it is my great pleasure to acknowledge with thanks the generous financial contributions made towards the publication of this volume by King Christian X's Fund, Queen Margrethe's and Prince Henrik's Fund, the Carlsberg Foundation, and the Faculty of the Humanities of the University of Copenhagen.

Late Quaternary Palaeogeography and Landscape Evolution of the Rub' Al Khali

BY H.A. McCLURE

Introduction

Though other deserts of the world had been studied and described to varying extents by the end of the 19th century, the great Rub' al Khali desert of the Arabian Peninsula remained, until recent decades, virtually unknown. St. John Philby (1933) first reliably described general geographic aspects of it in his traverses of the 1930's. Oil company operations resulted in detailed geologic and geographic mapping in the 1950's and 1960's. Holm (1950) described the geomorphology of the sand dune terrain. McClure (1976, 1978) reported radiocarbon dates and a chronology for some lake beds of the Rub' al Khali and presented a discussion of the general Quaternary context in which they occur. McClure and Swain (1980) discussed microfossils of some of the lake beds. McClure (1984), in a doctoral thesis, presented a detailed analysis of Late Quaternary palaeoenvironments and palaeogeography of the Rub' al Khali.

The Rub' al Khali desert of the Arabian Peninsula is a structural basin which had filled with alluvium by the end of the Pliocene. During the late Quaternary, intense arid wind activity transformed it into a vast area of sand dunes. Occasional, brief rainfall periods gave rise to shallow lakes scattered among the dunes. Stratigraphic examination of the lake bed sites, combined with radiocarbon, sedimentary, geochemical, geomorphological, and biological data, provides a framework for interpreting late Quaternary climatic and geologic events in the region.

The classic sediments of the lakes were derived by runoff from surrounding sand dunes. Two distinct types of sand furnished the substratum on which lakes were deposited. Carbonate precipitation resulted from high rates of plant fixation and subsequent evaporation and concentration. Gypsum was the usual end product of the evaporative phase of the geochemical process, but dolomite was deposited in some cases.

Radiocarbon dates on lake molluscs and marls indicate that rainfall, probably of monsoon nature, filled the lakes during two intervals of about 32,000-20,000 and 10,000-6,000 years B.P. Lakes lasted from a few years to hundreds of years, and their depths ranged from about 2 meters to 10 meters. Temperatures were probably very warm throughout most of the Pleistocene, and hot in the latest Pleistocene and Holocene, with seasonality similar to that of today.

The evidence of geology, geomorphology, and flora and fauna suggests that the Rub' al Khali evolved from a relatively subdued Pleistocene landscape of longitudinally furrowed and gently rounded dunes with lush grassland vegetation into a Holocene landscape of highly crested longitudinal dunes and prominent interdunes with sparse grass cover. The wind directions that prevailed throughout the Pleistocene probably persist today, but their intensities may have varied.

The evidence from the Rub' al Khali is consistent with evidence from other parts of the Arabian Peninsula and the Near East and complements the low latitude record of other parts of the world, notably Australia and East Africa.

Discussion

During the period of about 32,000 to 20,000 years B.P., and perhaps in earlier times of the Pleistocene, the Rub' al Khali, especially in the southwest part, was a landscape of longitudinal, wind-furrowed (wind-rift) dunes and interdunes, the ancestors of the modern crested, longitudinal dunes and interdunes. Crests of dunes were gently rounded and subdued, slopes probably gentle, and interdune furrows probably not as deep as today. Intermittent and sporadically scattered, moderately heavy summer monsoon rainfall in places filled some of the interdune depressions with lakes. In many cases, these bodies of standing water, during at least initial fresh water fill-up stage, took the shape of long, narrow, 'Shoe-string' lakes, extending for several kilometers or more along the elongate interdune furrows. Further to the NE, sand sheets of a more rolling nature and zibar dunes prevailed with scattered irregular hollows in which lakes occurred. During this time, the Rub' al Khali was an immense grassland with perhaps a considerable amount of low scrub and shrub vegetation of type similar to but much more abundant and lush than today's. Vertebrate fauna included large beasts such as water buffalo, hippopotamus, cattle, oryx, and gazelle, which required a considerable vegetation cover of grass, herbs and bushes for grazing and fairly substantial bodies of standing water. Lakes were fringed with water plants such as *Phragmites* and *Typha* as well as tamarisk and probably low scrub bushes. Though bird bones have not been identified in the fossil state, many different kinds were without doubt present in this environment of grassland and lakes.

Though the wind may have been of moderate intensity, seasonal, probably summer, rainfall was locally often sufficient enough to keep dune crests of a

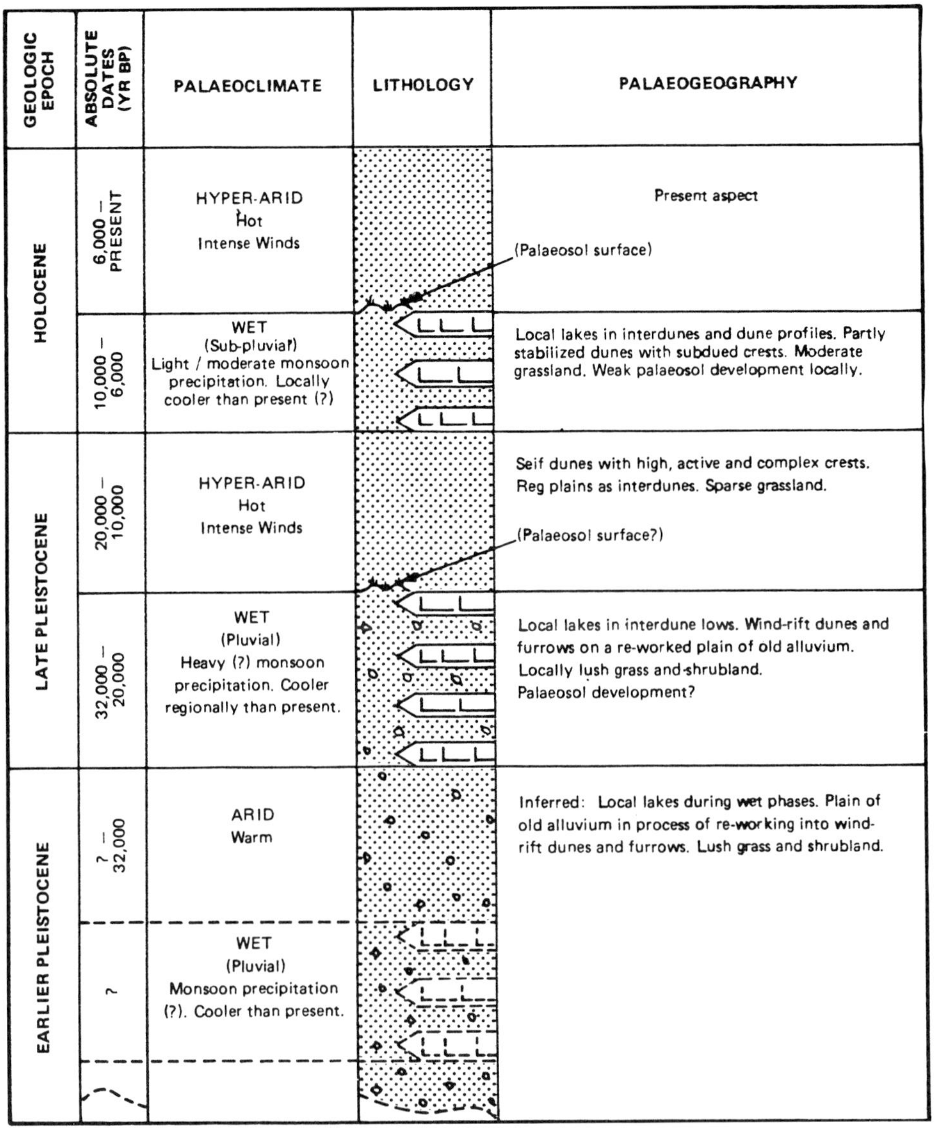

Fig. 1. Composite time-stratigraphic column of Quaternary sediments of the Rub' al Khali and aspects of generalized palaeoclimate and palaeogeography. (Modified after McClure, 1978.)

gently rounded nature and maintain a subdued rolling elevation. In places rainfall was intense enough to fill the lakes.

About 20,000 years B.P., the last late Pleistocene lakes dried up. Aridity of an intense nature set in and the Rub' al Khali took on an aspect similar to that of today. Arid wind regimes that were possibly stronger than previously instituted more intense shaping of the dunes into higher, sharply cresting features and deeper interdune areas, the whole superimposed on and with the same lineations as the former furrowed sand terrain of the 32,000-20,000 years B.P. lacustrine and earlier periods. Hyper-aridity with just enough moisture to leach and concentrate iron from the heavy mineral fraction of the old alluvial sand and coat grains with the iron oxide resulted in the landscape taking on a reddish-tan aspect. Vegetation cover became sparse, perhaps similar in type and distribution to that of today.

Dry wind began to erode the lake beds of the previous period into their present topographic occurence of irregularly scattered mesas and discontinuous low benches. What little rainfall occurred was apparently not substantial enough to result in many standing bodies of water, a few exceptions being at several times in the interval when brief 'respites' of rainfall may have occurred.

In early Holocene time, about 10,000 years B.P., as a northerly displacement returned monsoon rainfall to the Rub' al Khali, dune topography and terrain again took on a more gentle aspect as crests and high areas were locally rounded off (by sporadic seasonal rainfall), and light vegetation cover, in the form of grassland, probably very similar to but not as lush as the former lake period, returned. The Rub' al Khali was in general again a grassland watered by sporadic seasonal (summer) monsoon rainfall. The general aspect may have been similar to that of the Nebraska Sand Hills of today or the present pan area of Rhodesia, both relict longitudinal dune systems (Flint and Bond, 1968; Warren, 1976). Scattered small playa lakes were local features of the terrain, occurring in hollows up in the dune complex and in large hollows toward bases of the dunes. These lakes were not nearly as extensive as those of earlier times, possibly in many cases lasting little more than a few months or a year and in many cases not preserved at all. Others lasted long enough or were extensive enough so that they were preserved in fossil form. In areas such as the Mundafan and Wadi Ghiran however, more extensive accumulations occurred because of more extensive catchment areas and basins. Water plants such as *Phragmites* and *Typha* probably thrived around some of the lakes of longer duration, but duration was probably not long enough for lush growth around most. Large mammals at this time very likely included only bovid populations of *Bos primigenius*, oryx, gazelle, possibly wild ass and questionably camel, other large grazers such as *Bubalus* (water buffalo) and hippo having died off during the preceding hyper-arid period as lusher lakes and climate of the earlier lacustrine period disappeared.

At the end of this lake period, about 6,000 years B.P., as the summer monsoon retreated once more to its present zone of occurrence to the south, conditions of today, probably very similar to the inter-lacustrine period of 20,000-

10,000 years B.P., came into being. The last Holocene lake dried up. Dune crests were re-activated and the old vegetation surface of grass and low shrubs became the almost barren surface of today. Large bovids, such as *Bos primigenius*, that required more substantial vegetation, disappeared, leaving only the oryx and gazelle, capable of existence on the most meagre of grass cover. There appear to have been no standing bodies of water present in the Rub' al Khali since that time when the present landscape came into being.

Human hunter-gatherer populations periodically exploited optimum palaeoenvironmental and palaeoecological conditions of the Rub' al Khali in late Pleistocene and Holocene times (Edens, 1982; Field, 1960, 1961; Gramly, 1971; Sordinas, 1973). This discussion provides background analysis for further study of these populations.

Figure 1 is a composite time-stratigraphic column summarizing the palaeogeographic and palaeoclimatic features discussed above.

Bibliography

Edens, C. (1982), 'Toward a definition of the Western Rub' al Khali "Neolithic",' *Atlal*, vol.6, p.109.

Field, H. (1960), 'Stone implements from the Rub' al Khali,' *Man*, vol.60, p.25.

Field, H. (1961), 'Paleolithic implements from the Rub' al Khali, *Man*, vol.61, p.22.

Flint, R.F. and Bond, J. (1968), 'Pleistocene sand ridges and pans in western Rhodesia,' *Bull. geol. Soc. Am.*, vol.79, pp.299-314.

Gramly, R.M. (1971), 'Neolithic flint implement assemblage from Saudi Arabia,' *Jour. of Near Eastern Studies*, vol.30, p.177.

Holm, D.A. (1960), 'Desert geomorphology in the Arabian Peninsula,' *Science*, vol.132, pp.1360-1379.

McClure, H.A. (1976), 'Radiocarbon chronology of late Quaternary lakes in the Arabian desert,' *Nature*, vol.263, pp.755-756.

McClure, H.A. (1978), 'The Rub' al Khali,' in S.A. Al-Sayyari, and J.G. Zötl, (eds.), *Quaternary Period in Saudi Arabia*, Vienna, Springer-Verlag, pp.252-263.

McClure, H.A. (1984), *Late Quaternary Palaeoenvironments of the Rub'al Khali*. Doctoral thesis, Univ. of London.

McClure, H.A. and Swain, F.M. (1980), 'Fresh water and brackish water fossil Quaternary Ostracoda from the Rub' al Khali, Saudi Arabia, [Actes du VIe Colloque Africaine de Micropaléontologie, Tunis, 1974] *Annales des Mines et de la Géologie*, Tunis, III, pp.427-441.

Philby, H. St. J. (1933), *The Empty Quarter*, London, Constable and Co.

Sordinas, A. (1973), *Contributions to the prehistory of Saudi Arabia, II*, Field Research Projects, Coconut Grove, 28 pp.

Warren, A. (1976), 'Morphology and sediments of the Nebraska Sand Hills in relation to Pleistocene winds and the development of aeolian bedforms, *Jour. Geol.*, vol.84, pp.685-700.

The Rub al-Khali 'Neolithic' Revisited: the View from Nadqan

BY CHRISTOPHER EDENS

In 1974 Marny Golding's paper on pre-Seleucid occupation of eastern Arabia appeared in the *Proceedings of the Seminar for Arabian Studies* (Golding, 1974). In that summary review of the results of amateur archaeologists, notably Grace Burkholder and herself, in the Eastern Province, Golding used her collections from the localities at Nadqan to illustrate the aceramic occupation of the region. She later donated these materials, along with the rest of her collection, to the National Museum in Riyadh. In 1978 the present author obtained the permission of Abdallah Masry, the Director of Antiquities of Saudi Arabia, to make a study of collections from aceramic sites in the Rub al-Khali then housed in the museum. The study, completed late in 1979, focused on four collections from the western Rub al-Khali, namely from Jiladah, Mundafin, Janub al-Mutabthat and Sharorah (Edens, 1982). By original intent, Golding's collections from Nadqan were to have been included in the broader study, and accordingly her collection was examined in conjunction with the others. Due, however, to some typological differences and to geographical distance, Nadqan was excluded from the published version of the study, except by allusion to certain comparative aspects of the material.

On the present occasion, the author would like to rectify this omission. The present paper first offers a typological description of Golding's Nadqan collection. Next, using the Nadqan and the previously described western Rub al-Khali collections as a springboard, the issue of geographical variability (or identification of industrial facies) within the bifacial lithic tradition found throughout the Arabian peninsula will be re-opened. The Arabian bifacial lithic tradition is commonly typified by the pressure-flaked stemmed and barbed point, though these are not universally present, and is commonly judged to date roughly 5000-2500 B.C. largely by analogy with the Levantine sequence (Moore, 1973 and 1982 is usually cited at this point; now also see Zarins, n.d.), by the presence of Ubaid sherds in sites with this industry along the Gulf coast (cf. Oates, 1982, pp. 362-66; Potts, n.d.), and by a presumed correlation with the mid-Holocene moister climatic phase (McClure, 1976, 1978; Larsen, 1983, pp. 142-49; Hötzl *et al.*, 1984)[(1)]. Northern Arabia will be ignored in this analysis of regional facies. Finally, various aspects of behavior which were addressed in the western Rub al-Khali study will similarly be reexamined in light of more recently published evidence.

Nadqan

Nadqan lies some 110 km. east of Jabrin, on the edge of playa lake deposits probably dating to the mid-Holocene. Lithic material occurs scattered somewhat diffusely along the lake front, this being the main site of Nadqan proper, while several kilometers away a smaller scatter yielded a second colletion, Nadqan West. The present report concerns only Nadqan proper, except where otherwise stated. The Nadqan material will be presented in two sections, chipped stone and ground stone. No faunal material (other than a few fragments of ostrich egg shell) is contained in the collections.

TABLE 1: **General Components of the Nadqan Collection**

tools:	123
debitage:	39
cores:	5
chunks & nodules:	6
total	173

TABLE 2: **Tool Types**

		total	%
1)	stemmed bifacial points	14	11.4
2)	miscellaneous small points	6	4.9
3)	rhomboidal points	0	0.0
4)	narrow foliates	1	0.8
5)	broad foliates	7	5.7
6)	lanceolates	1	0.8
7)	unidentified broken bifaces	*15	12.2
8)	unfinished bifaces	43	35.0
9)	end scraper on flake	0	0.0
10)	end scraper on lamellar flake	1	0,8
11)	peripheral scraper	0	0.0
12)	simple side scraper	1	0.8
13)	miscellaneous scraper	1	0.8
14)	trihedral drill	1	0.8
15)	drill on flake	1	0.8
16)	miscellaneous small tool	1	0.8
17)	retouched flakes	27	22.0
18)	axe/adze	3	2.4
19)	chopping tool	0	0.0
20)	disc	0	0.0
	total	123	(*=133)

*=MNI; total pieces=25

Chipped Stone

The chipped stone inventory of the Nadqan collection is summarized in tables 1 and 2. The collection consists of 173 pieces of chipped stone, almost three quarters of which are tools (formally defined as pieces exhibiting retouch) and the rest being debitage, cores, and other waste. Given that Nadqan shows various indications of being a general habitation site (a wide variety of tool forms, presence of grinding stones, evidence of on-site knapping), the ratio of tools to debitage is much too high to be a random sample. Recent work at sites in the Arabian Gulf and the western Rub al-Khali makes this point most effectively. The combined totals for surface collections from two sites in the western Rub al-Khali show that less than 8% of the chipped stone (n=2581) are formal tools (Zarins *et al.*, 1981, p. 20), while no more than 2% of the excavated assemblages at the 'Ubaid sites Khor F.B. in Qatar and al-Markh in Bahrain are retouched (Inizan, 1980, pp. 67-70; Roaf, 1976, p. 151). While these sites are not strictly comparable with such localities as Jilidah or Nadqan in terms of topographic setting or range of activities represented, the relative amount of debitage in them is more representative of habitation sites in general than is the Nadqan collection. The collection is therefore probably biased toward tools; a corresponding bias toward larger sizes and bifacial pieces probably also exists but cannot be measured. These same biases are also present, *mutatis mutandis*, in the western Rub al-Khali sites reported by the present author.

The raw material of the Nadqan collection is predominantly cherts, which vary considerably in color though less so in texture. A small number of tools in quarzites also appear, and will be identified in the typological summary below; none of the debitage is quartzite, though one split and battered quartzite pebble does occur.

The following discussion present first the tools using the typology erected for the western Rub al-Khali study as far as possible. Then the cores and debitage will be presented in a technological analysis.

Formal Typology

1) **stemmed bifacial points**: Both varieties of this category, i.e. barbed or shouldered, occur in the Nadqan collection. The examples of the barbed variety (n=10) are extremely typical of the mid-Holocene bifacial industry throughout the Arabian peninsula, a form that provides the standard leitmotiv for this horizon (fig. 1: 1-5; Golding, 1974, fig. 2: 4). Examples of the shouldered variety are fewer in number (n=4) than those with barbs, an inversion of the usual situation in the western Rub al-Khali. These shouldered points

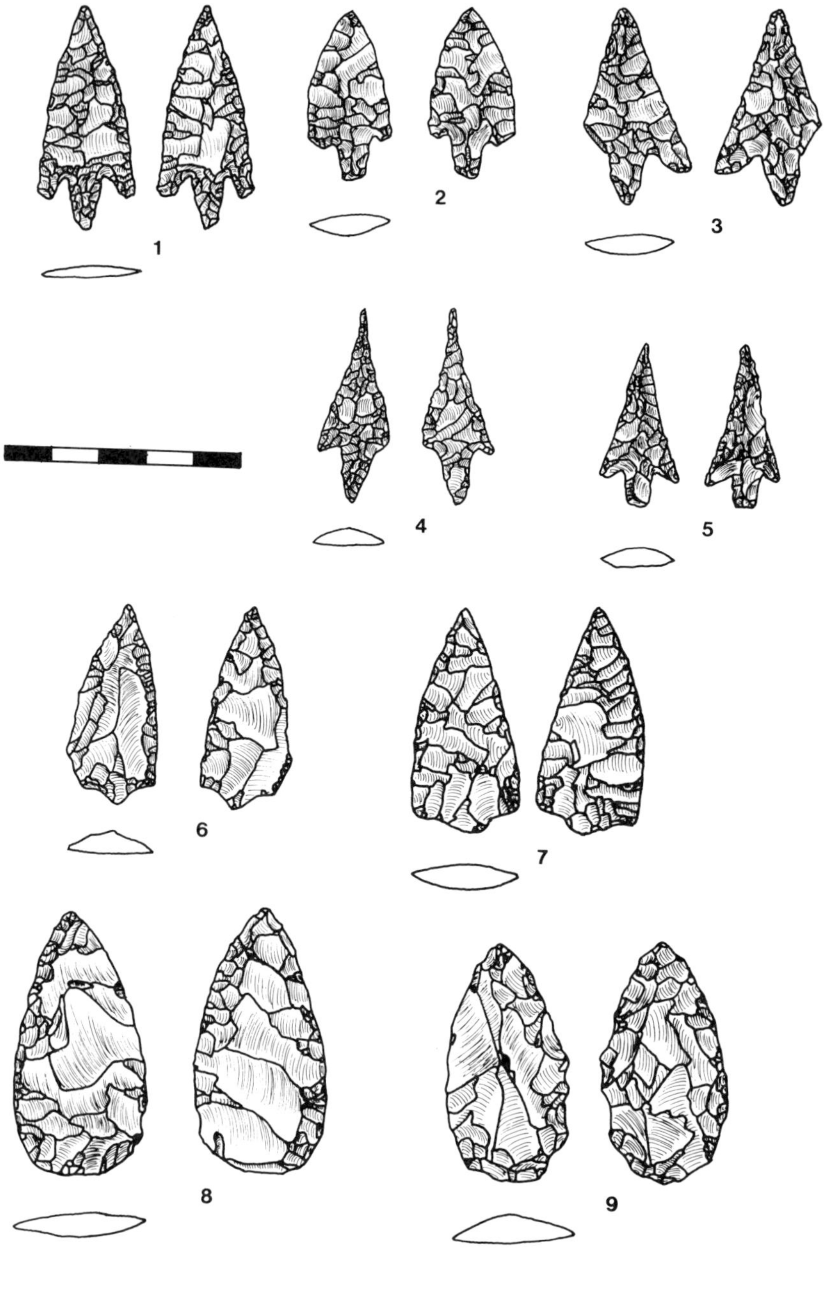

Fig. 1. Nadqan collection: bifacial points

tend to be formally less typical of these Arabian bifacial industries, particularly in details of the shoulder and stem (compare the poorly delineated stem in Golding, 1974, fig. 2: 3, 5 with Edens, 1982, fig. 101A: 13, 15). One of the shouldered points is in quartzite. The size of both these varieties at Nadqan conforms entirely with that of the western Rub al-Khali, being c. 35-45 mm. long, 14-20 mm. wide and 3-5 mm. thick. Both vareties tend to exhibit pointed rather than rounded stem bases, and are technologically identical with the pressure flaking technique found throughout the peninsula.

2) **miscellaneous small projectile points**: Three minor types found in the western Rub al-Khali sites also occur at Nadqan. Bifacial points with small rudimentary and obtuse stems appear in the collection from all four sites in the western Rub al-Khali and four examples also occur in the Nadqan sample (fig. 1: 6-7, compare Edens, 1982, pl. 101A: 22-23). Although this formal type is listed among the finished tools, such a procedure is probably erroneous – the form is more likely simply a stage in the reduction sequence from initial piece of raw material to stemmed point. This conclusion derives from the observation both at Nadqan and in the western Rub al-Khali sites that these points with obtuse stems are 'finished' largely with soft hammer and are larger in size (including thickness) than the putatively finished product. According to these observations, these pieces should logically be included among the unfinished bifacial pieces (type 8). The latter category contains larger pieces, however, and represents either earlier stages in the reduction sequence or stages on a reduction sequence toward an alternative final product (e.g. foliates). Thus the form will provisionally be retained in the category of miscellaneous bifacial point.

Two other pieces also fit into this miscellaneous category. The first is an oversized (but broken) stemmed and barbed point which is formally similar to the corresponding variety of type 1 but which is too large comfortably to be accommodated in that type. A similar point occurs in one of the western Rub al-Khali sites (Edens, 1982, fig. 101A: 21). The second piece is a lamellar flake shaped into a stemmed point by bifacial but marginal retouch (fig. 2: 10). This production technique also occurs, rarely, in the western Rub al-Khali sites and regularly appears in collections from sites belonging to the bifacial horizon of Arabia.

3) **rhomboidal points**: None occurs at Nadqan. Rhomboidal points have been reported from Qatar (Inizan, 1980, fig. 43) and the Eastern Province (Potts *et al.*, 1978, pl. 18A: 8; cf. Sordinas, 1973, fig. 9: 18), but the type seems to be very rare throughout eastern Arabia.

4) **narrow foliates:** Only one example of this type, so characteristic of the western Rub al-Khali sites, appears at Nadqan. Even so, and although falling at the small end of the range established for this type in the Rub al-Khali (here at 36 mm. long, 11 mm. wide, and 4 mm. thick), the form and technique of the Nadqan example is entirely typical (cf. Edens, 1982, pl. 101B: 12). Narrow foliates occasionally appear in assemblages from the Eastern Province (e.g. Sordinas, 1973, pl. 47, 54) but are much less frequent than in western Rub al-Khali assemblages.

5) **broad foliates:** Of the seven broad foliates recorded in the Nadqan collection, six are comparable (in form and size) with variations found in the western Rub al-Khali sites. Three of these are very similar to the large cordiform to amygdaloid variation (fig. 1: 8-9; compare with Edens, 1982, pl. 102A: 5-9), and the other three to the narrower and more elongate triangular form (cf. Edens, 1982, pl. 102A: 4). The remaining specimen is a small elongate ovate with a rudimentary and pointed stem. As with the western Rub al-Khali sites (Edens, 1982, p. 111) and elsewhere in eastern Arabia (e.g. Madsen, 1962, p. 199), some or all of these broad foliates were probably blanks, at the stage just prior to pressure flaking into finished form.

6) **lanceolates:** Only one example, broken, occurs in the Nadqan collection. This example is comparable to the smaller and cruder rather than the larger and finer variety (i.e. Edens, 1982, pl. 101A: 14-15 rather than pl. 102A: 12-13).

7) **unidentified broken bifaces:** As became apparent during the Rub al-Khali study, many fragments of bifaces cannot be assigned certainly to a given type, due to the morphological ambiguity of various portions such as butts or tips of foliates and lanceolates. The procedure for calculating a minimum number of individuals from these fragments is explained in the earlier study (Edens, 1982, pp. 111-12). This calculation shows that the 25 broken pieces in the Nadqan collection represent at least 15 additional bifacial points. Six of the foliate fragments are in quartzite.

8) **unfinished bifacial pieces:** According to the original definition, unfinished bifaces are characterized by irregular and non-linear edges, relatively thick and often irregularly lenticular or non-lenticular cross-sections, and extensive evidence of hard or soft hammer technique but little or no pressure flaking. This understanding of the state of being unfinished was designed to cover the beginning stages of the reduction sequence, when the form has only been roughed out. By the same token, however, various pieces classified as miscellaneous bi-

facial points or broad foliates have been suggested to be equally unfinished but at a later point in the reduction sequence (see above). Roughly speaking, the present type corresponds to Madsen's 'blanks, early stage' and the broad foliates/miscellaneous points just mentioned to his 'blanks, late stage' (Madsen, 1962,p. 199). Of 43 pieces included in the present category, three are quartzite.

9) **end scraper on flake**: None is present in the Nadqan collection. This type occurs elsewhere in eastern Arabia (e.g. Sordinas, 1973, fig. 3: 1-2. fig. 4: 6; Masry, 1974, fig. 29: 2).

10) **end scraper on lamellar flake**: The one Nadqan example of this type is entirely comparable to materials from the western Rub al-Khali (fig. 2: 12; compare with Edens, 1982, pl. 102B: 15, 17).

11) **peripheral scraper**: None is present at Nadqan. The analogous form in the Eastern Province is the common side scraper on tabular flint tile.

12) **simple side scraper**: Only one piece may belong in this category, this being a bifacially worked flake possessing an almost denticulated steeply retouched right and a blunted left margin (fig. 2: 16). This piece does not unambiguously belong in the scraper category, since it might equally have been arranged with the unfinished bifacial pieces, and none of the examples of the present type in the western Rub al-Khali is worked so extensively on the ventral surface.

13) **miscellaneous scraper**: The only instance in the Nadqan collection is a convergent double sided scraper (fig. 2: 15) which finds parallels in the western Rub al-Khali sites (Edens, 1982, pl. 103B: 10).

14) **trihedral drill**: Only one instance from Nadqan may fit into this type, the fragment of a blade with blunting retouch along both margins and some squamous ventral retouch along one margin. This piece does not match the fully formed 'mèche de foret' (cf. Edens, 1982, pl. 103A: 13-16), and may more properly belong in the next category. Trihedral drills are generally rare in eastern Arabia (cf. Sordinas, 1973, fig. 9: 8).

15) **drill on flake**: The single instance of this category present in the Nadqan collection consists of a snapped or broken lamellar flake which has been trimmed into a sharp point by retouch on dorsal and, to a lesser degree, ventral aspects (fig. 2: 11).

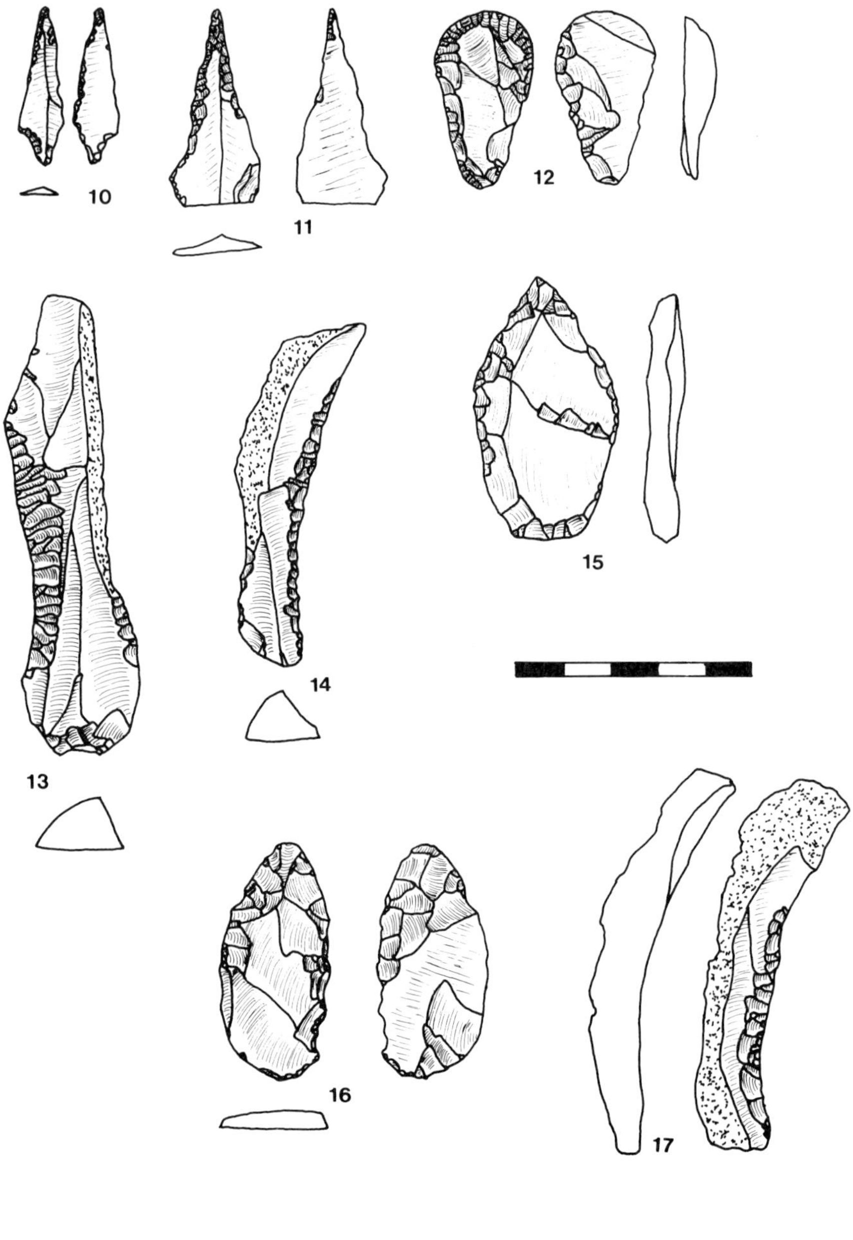

Fig. 2. Nadqan collection: various light tool types

16) **miscellaneous small tools**: Belonging to this type is the fragment of a partially cortical lamellar flake which has been blunted by steep retouch along one margin. A large series of lamellar flakes trimmed by (semi-) invasive sub-parallel or squamous retouch along one or both margins is included in the next category.

17) **retouched flakes**: A total of 27 retouched flakes occur in the Nadqan collection. As just mentioned, a series of these flakes, lamellar and trimmed by sub-parallel to squamous (semi-) invasive retouch, might have been included in the category of miscellaneous small tools, or even, in some instances, of side scraper (type 12), given the care evident in the retouch (e.g. fig. 2: 13-14 and cf. fig. 2: 17, fig. 4: 24-25; compare Edens, 1982, pl. 103A: 8); such specimens, extremely distinctive of the Nadqan collection, total 19 in the present collection. Cortical lamellar flakes with invasive sub-parallel retouch are reported elsewhere in eastern Arabia (e.g. Sordinas, 1973, fig. 3: 7). However, this group of material grades smoothly into the minimally retouched flakes, without admitting any easy discrimination between the distinctive sub-parallel retouch of fig. 2: 13 and the light marginal retouch of type 17 as a whole. Thus the entire range of variation has been enclosed in type 17. All of these retouched flakes exhibit only modest alteration of the original flake, and tend to be on flakes produced early in core reduction or as errors in that reduction. Thus, of the 27 retouched flakes, ten are cortical, two are plunging, four are both plunging and cortical, one is hinged out, and one is both hinged out and cortical, i.e. a total of 18 of the 27 retouched flakes or 68% (see below for further discussion).

18) **axe/adze**: Three examples of this type appear in the Nadqan collection. Two of these are unifacial (fig. 3: 19), the other bifacial (fig. 3: 18), and all three are entirely typical of the Arabian bifacial industry (Edens, 1982, pl. 103B: 4, 6; for eastern Arabia see Madsen, 1962, fig. 11, 16b; Kapel, 1967, pl. 45, 52; Field, 1971, pl. 10). Two of the three at Nadqan are of quarzite.

19) **chopping tool**: None appears at Nadqan. Chopping tools are relatively common on bifacial industry sites elsewhere in the Eastern Province (e.g. Masry, 1974, fig. 29: 3) and Qatar (e.g. Smith, 1977, fig. 5: 9-10, fig. 11: 1, and fig. 12: 1).

20) **disc**: None appears at Nadqan. Discs seem not to appear in eastern Arabia (for a possible exception, see Smith, 1977a, fig. 5: 1).

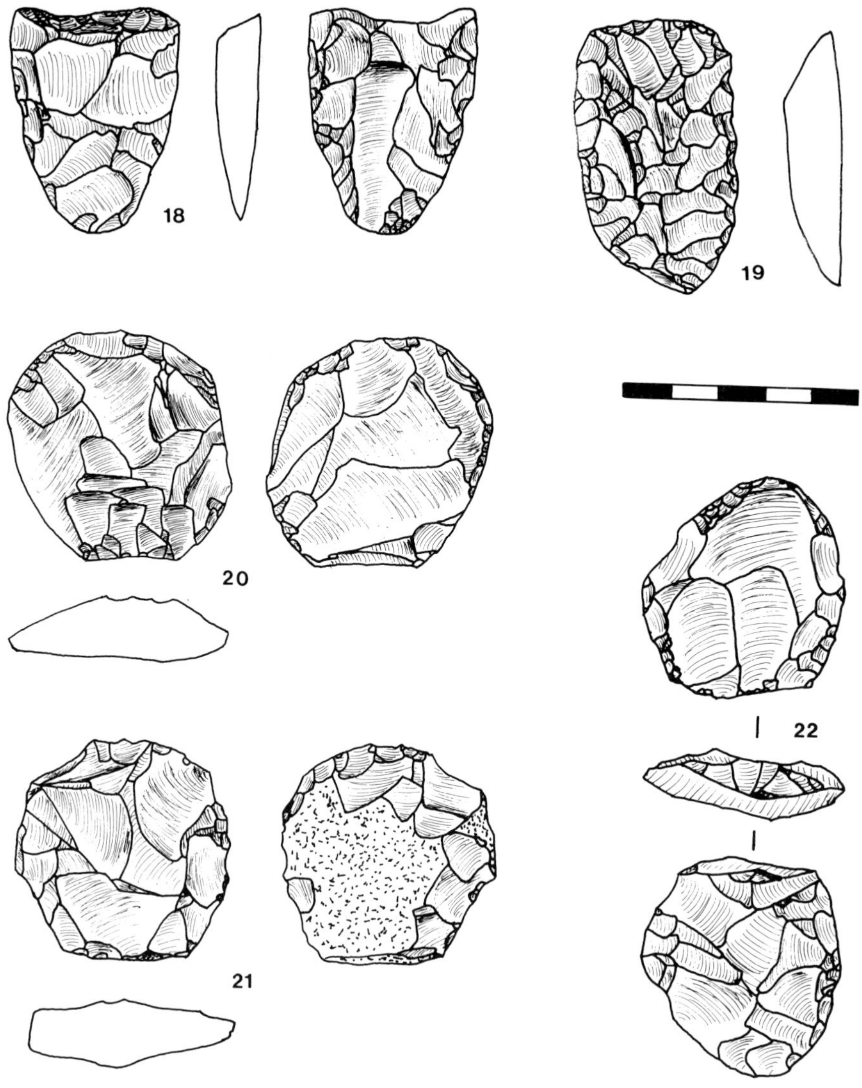

Fig. 3. Nadqan collection; heavy tools and discoidal cores

In the concluding section of the original study, the formal characteristics of the four western Rub al-Khali collections were contrasted with those of Nadqan and site LX in Qatar (Edens, 1982, p. 120). This comparison showed in particular that the rhomboidal bifacial points, fine lanceolates and narrow foliates characteristic of the western Rub al-Khali facies are absent or very infrequent in the other two collections. Further, the morphology of the stemmed bifacial points tends to distinguish the two sets of sites (though with considerable overlap) and, a detail not remarked in the original study, stemmed and barbed points outnumber stemmed and shouldered points in the Nadqan and site LX collections whereas the reverse is true in the western Rub al-Khali. Other differences, particularly among the scrapers, were also observed but these distinctions are less easily defined for want of adequate sample size or description. Such specific comparisons show the existence of a lithic tradition, typologically and technologically nearly homogeneous, extending from Qatar and the Eastern Province of Saudi Arabia into the western fringes of the Rub al-Khali. The various reports of Field (1961, 1971) and Sordinas (1971, 1973, 1978) indicate that various sites elsewhere around the northwestern, northern, and southwestern fringes of the Rub al-Khali contain essentially the same industry, though in most cases detailed comparison is made impossible by the brevity of these reports. The description of sites in the Wadi Dawasir made by the present author (Zarins *et al.*, 1979, pp. 19-21) indicates that this same industry, though with some salient typological differences, exists here as well. The recently published site from the Ramlet es Sahmah in Oman (Gotoh, 1981; cf. Pullar, 1974, p. 41) shows a very similar or identical industry that includes the fine lanceolates so characteristic of the western Rub al-Khali facies.

Technological aspects

In general the technology of knapping stone evident in the Nadqan collection is comparable to that seen in the western Rub al-Khali. Technological aspects of the Nadqan material may be discussed under two headings: a) cores and flake production and b) bifacial reduction. These two aspects will be presented in that order.

Five cores appear in the collection, one being an exhausted lamellar flake core (fig. 4: 23) and the other four flat discoidal cores (fig. 3: 20-22). The latter form is common in the western Rub al-Khali (Edens, 1982, p.116). The Nadqan examples may be carefully shaped by radial trimming on both dorsal and ventral aspects and by the forming of a facetted striking platform. In one instance the core approaches a Levallois technique in the preparation of the flake

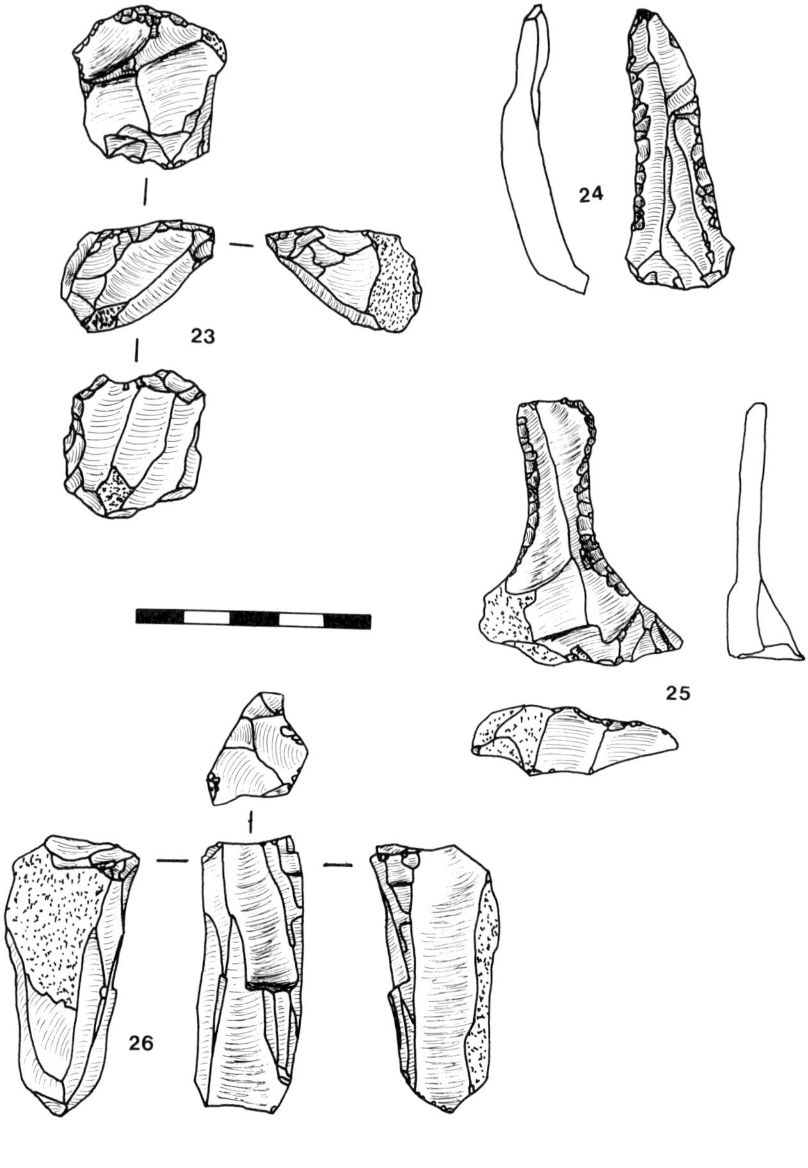

Fig. 4. Blade cores and plunging flakes

release surface and of the striking platform (fig. 3: 22); one may recall the similarly careful preparation seen in a flake core from Hili 8 (in the Buraimi area, fig. 5: L), associated with the 3rd millennium B.C. occupation there (Inizan and Tixier, 1980, fig. 1). In other instances the core preparation is desultory, leaving the original cobble readily apparent and showing no effort closely to control the striking platform (e.g. fig. 3: 21),

Blade cores are uncommon in southern Arabian assemblages except those typologically and technologically related to the Qatar B-group of the 7th millennium B.C. A blade core which Golding collected at Nadqan West probably belongs to such a blade industry (fig. 4: 26). This core is virtually identical in form of raw material, preparation, striking platform and blade removals to examples from the B-Group in Qatar, and differs from the core at Nadqan proper (fig. 4: 23) in many respects. The presence of the core at Nadqan West in the midst of an assemblage clearly related to that of Nadqan proper,[2] combined with the distinctly lamellar bias found in the debitage at Nadqan (see below) urges caution in unhesitatingly assigning the Nadqan West core to the earlier industry. The question of a blade technology in the context of the Nadqan bifacial industry must be examined more deeply.

The debitage and retouched flakes where little overall modification has occurred (n=47 complete flakes; almost all of these show hard hammer, some soft hammer, bulbar characteristics; sizes up to 95 mm. long and 57 mm. wide) display several salient characteristics. In the first place, this material tends to be lamellar, with roughly 65% of the flakes being at least twice as long as wide; almost 10% of the flakes are four times as long as wide. The implication of a blade technology is contradicted, however, by two other aspects of the debitage, expressed in tables 3 and 4. Table 3 indicates a very strong preference for plain (i.e. unfacetted, unground) striking platforms, with a sizeable minority having no formal striking platform at all (i.e. cortical). In total, over three quarters (and probably more, given the indeterminacy of the splintered and point categories) of the flakes were struck from minimally or unprepared platforms. This aspect is entirely incompatible with a blade technology of the sort implied by the Nadqan West core, where careful control of striking platform and flake release surface is essential. Table 4 shows that 45% of the flakes are cortical (cf. fig. 2: 13-14, 17; fig. 4: 25) and that 21% are plunging (i.e. the error of running completely through the flake release surface to remove the bottom of the core; cf. fig. 2: 17; fig. 4: 24-25). These attributes imply a very low ratio of cores to flakes produced and, again, a poor control over the mechanics of flake removal, both aspects being inconsistent with a blade technology *sensu stricto*.

All three attributes just discussed – remaining cortex on the dorsal aspect, cortical or plain striking platform remnants, and mistaken plunging – are related to the form of the raw material used. The cherts which constitute the bulk of the collection take the form of cobbles or angular nodules. Frequently these cobbles present flattened surfaces which might serve, unprepared, as a striking platform. In other cases the nodule might be split to produce the same effect, but now as a plain striking platform (the Nadqan collection contains an instance of a nodule which has been treated in this fashion). In the same spirit, a given cobble may be flaked from several different striking platforms, which may form a single flake release surface (cf. fig. 2: 13; fig. 4: 24; cf. Copeland and Bergne, 1976, p. 50 for a similar situation at Buraimi) or several intersecting ones (cf. fig. 4: 25). Further, these same angularities of the cobbles provide a ridge that substitutes (with loss of control) for the crest prepared for the first removal in a blade industry (again several flakes at Nadqan illustrate this procedure). Finally, since the cobbles are usually small, and since the core is not carefully prepared or maintained, the flakes tend to run through the cobble, removing its bottom; no fewer than 15 (of the total debitage, including flake fragments, n=66) flakes show exactly this mistake of plunging through the core. In another instance, the inverse error appears on a flake, where the flake was terminated prematurely by a natural ridge which had been left on the cobble. These various observations all indicate a very opportunistic production of flakes, which procedure was related directly to the nature of the raw material at hand in combination with a disregard for the standardized blanks made available by a blade technology. Opportunistic lithic technologies are known elsewhere in the Arabian peninsula (e.g. Gebel *apud* Weisgerber, 1981, p. 255). In such an opportunistic technology, the carefully prepared discoidal cores of the sort discussed above are anomalous. The Nadqan West blade core and the technical process it represents is therefore irrelevant to the Nadqan industry.

The second technological aspect of the Nadqan collection, bifacial reduction sequences, need not be detailed *in extenso* here, both because the conclusions would largely mirror those of the western Rub al-Khali study and because crucial categories of information (notably that provided by soft hammer thinning flakes and by pressure flakes) are unavailable. Comments will be confined to the following two observations. 1) The original support piece may be either a thin cobble (of tabular chert) or a thick flake; in the few instances where these two categories may be distinguished, cobbles are far more frequent than flakes. 2) In at least one instance, a thinning flake plunged across the biface, removing a section of the opposite margin. This sort of accident produces a 'winged flake' in Kapel's (1965, p. 150; 1967, p. 20) terminology, even though none is included in the collection. Inizan and Tixier (1978) sug-

TABLE 3: **Flake characteristics**

	retouched	not retouched	total	%
cortical	10	5	15	31.9
plunging	2	4	6	12.8
hinged	1	0	1	2.1
plunging & cortical	4	0	4	8.6
hinged & cortical	1	1	2	4.3
standard	9	10	19	40.4
totals	27	20	47	

TABLE 4: **Striking Platforms**

	total	%
cortical	8	17.0
plain	26	55.2
facetted*	9	19.1
splintered	3	6.4
point	1	2.1
total	47	

* includes 'pseudo-facetted'

gest that the production of winged flakes during bifacial reduction represents an intentional and characteristic method of reduction in the Qatar assemblages. Winged flakes also occur, infrequently, in the Wadi Dawasir (Zarins *et al.*, 1979, p. 20) but are not included in materials from the Rub al-Khali or further west. Given the infrequency of this type of plunging bifacial trimming flake outside Qatar, the Nadqan and Wadi Dawasir cases are, in all likelihood, simply accidental.

Ground Stone

As commonly occurs in other sites of the Arabian bifacial tradition, ground stone equipment constitutes a prominent element of the Nadqan material (10 pieces). The inventory may be summarized as follows:

- three fragments of a wide and very shallow sandstone dish;
- one broken slab of grey granite ? with a ground convexity on each face;
- two small sandstone slabs, each ground on one face (one slightly concave, the other slightly convex);

– two limestone nodules, flattened on one side;
– one quartzite pebble ground on one side and possessing battered edges;
– one quartzose sandstone slab ground on one face.

Aside from the dish, this ground stone equipment is essentially amorphous (Golding, 1974, p. 19, described them as 'amoeba-shaped'), but represents both upper and lower elements (i.e. mano and metate in Americanist terms) required for grinding activities. The sandstone dish, even if not simply a more formally made grinding stone, is unusual but not unprecedented in Arabian bifacial sites, as shown by the chlorite bowls from Janub al-Mutabthat and elsewhere (see discussion below)

Discussion

In his previous study of the western Rub al-Khali, the present author attempted to define the formal and technological characteristics of that lithic facies, supplemented by perceptible behavioral aspects such as inter-site variability, subsistence, and inter-regional exchange. The goal of this exercise was to distinguish, insofar as then possible, a western Rub al-Khali facies of the wider Arabian lithic tradition whose 'fossile directeur' is the stemmed and barbed bifacial point and whose technological leitmotiv is bifacial pressure flaking, often in combination with production of lamellar flakes as support pieces.

Since that writing, only a little new information on Rub al-Khali sites and industries has been published, notably the brief report on collections from two sites (fig. 5: 24) near Shaqqat al Kharyta, mentioned above (Zarins *et al.*, 1981, p. 20), and the fuller report of a collection from a locality (fig. 5: 41) in the southeastern reaches of the Rub al-Khali (Gotoh, 1981). New information from regions surrounding the Rub al-Khali, on the other hand, has been accumulating at a much faster rate. The continuing Saudi Arabian Comprehensive Survey has added important comparative material from areas to the west (Zarins *et al.*, 1981), northwest (Zarins *et al.*, 1980) and north (Zarins *et al.*, 1980, 1982) of the western Rub al-Khali. Reporting of new material from southeastern Arabia continues with almost every issue of *The Journal of Oman Studies* (Smith, 1976, 1977; Pullar, 1985; Pullar and Jäckli, 1978). And to the southwest in the Yemen, the Italian mission has reported an extremely important site at Jebel Qutran (Zarattini, 1984). These new data permit a sharper delineation of differences between regional facies at the lithic industrial level, as well as at broader behavioral levels, even while re-affirming the basic unity of the Arabian bifacial lithic tradition.

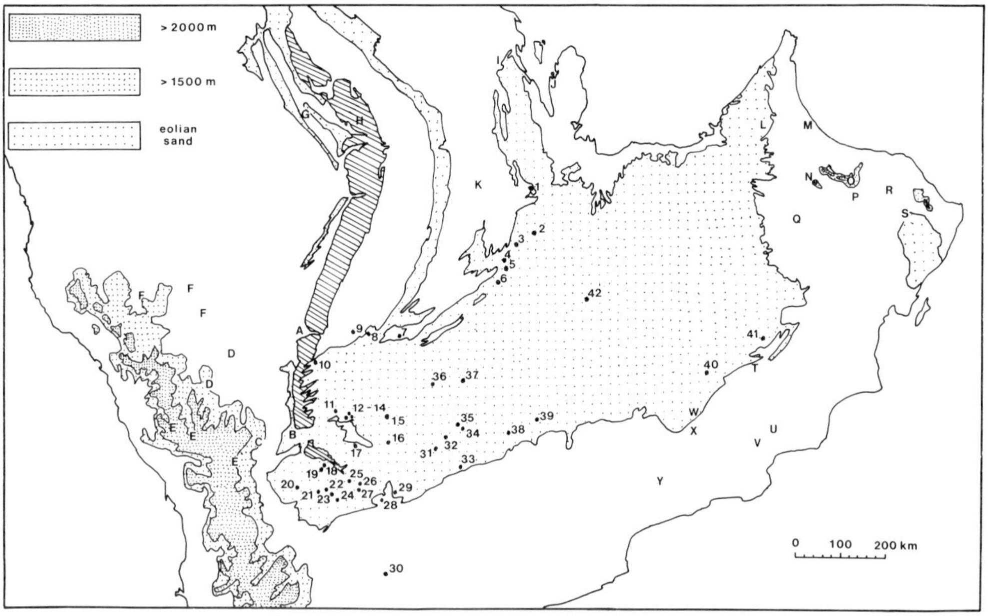

Fig. 5. Site Distributions (numbered sites Nadqan and Rub al-Khali, lettered sites circum-Rub al-Khali)

A Wadi Dawasir
B Mundafin
C Bir Hima
D Wadi Tathlith
E 'Asir
F southern Hejaz
G Nefud as-Sirr
H Riyadh
I Hofuf/Ayn Dar
J Qatar site LX
K Jabrin
L Buraimi
M Wadi Suq
N Amlah
O Sayq (Jebel Akhdar)
P Wadi Halfayn
Q Natih and Fahud
R Wadi Samad/Lizq area
S Wahiba sands border
T Mughshin
U Bir Khasfa
V Qaharir
W Fasad
X Shisur
Y Habarut

1 Nadqan
2 Field, 1971, p.47
3 Philby, 1933, p.138; Field, 1971, p.47
4 Ash-Shalfa: Field, 1956 map 24, p.53; Marshall, 1962, site 14
5 Field, 1971, p.47
6 Field, 1971, p.47
7 Abu Bahr ar-Raida: Field, 1961, p.34; Marshall, 1962, sites 2 and 3
8 Qawnasat ibn Ghudayyan: Field, 1961, p.34; Marshall, 1962, site 1; Sordinas, 1971
9 Field 1956 map 24, p.71
10 Irq al Kudnah: Field, 1956, p.98; Marshall, 1962, site 8
11 Jiladah: Field, 1956, map 24, p.69
12 Field, 1961, p.32
13 Jiladah: Field, 1961, p.32-34
14 station 6: Field, 1958; Marshall, 1962, site 10
15 Marshall, 1962, site 11
16 station 13: Field, 1958
17 Jilidah (218-6): Edens, 1982
18 K-20: Gramly, 1971
19 Madbathat (218-7): Edens, 1982
20 K-13: Gramly, 1971
21 K-17: Gramly, 1971
22 K-20a: Gramly, 1971
23 Shaqqat al Kharyta: Zeuner, 1954; Field, 1956, map 24, p.64
24 218-4, 218-5: Zarins *et al.*, 1981, p.20
25 K-18: Gramly, 1971
26 Field, 1961, p.30-31
27 Harding, 1964, p.50
28 Sharorah, station 7: Field, 1958; Smith and Maranjian, 1962
29 K-14: Gramly, 1971; Marshall, 1962, site 9
30 K-16 (near Shabwah): Gramly, 1971
31 ARAMCO camp: Field, 1956, map 24, p.56
32 Marshall, 1962, site 5
33 Hairat al Ul: Field, 1961, p.34
34 Field, 1971, p.46
35 station 14: Field, 1961, p.34
36 Field, 1961, p.34
37 Field, 1961, pl.26; Marshall, 1962, site 4
38 G-2554: Field, 1956, map 24, p.55; Marshall, 1962, site 12
39 Field, 1960a; Marshall, 1962, site 6
40 Field, 1971, p.46; Marshall, 1962, site 7
41 Ramlet as-Sahmah: Gotoh, 1981; cf. Pullar, 1974, p.41
42 Thomas, 1932, p.207

In the Rub al-Khali study the observation was made that the industries from the Rub al-Khali, the Eastern Province and Qatar, and from the Wadi Dawasir area are all highly comparable not withstanding the formal typological differences that distinguish these three areas; this point was repeated above. A further observation in the Rub al-Khali study pointed to more strongly marked differences with materials from southeastern Arabia. This last conclusion is reinforced and expanded by the more recent publications just mentioned.

The Omani comparative material may be reviewed briefly as follows. In the original study of the western Rub al-Khali facies, the present author contrasted typologically this facies with materials from Jebel Huwaya in Buraimi (Copeland and Bergne, 1976) and from Habarut (Payne and Hawkins, 1963; see also Harding, 1964, pp. 49-50; Pullar, 1974,p. 44; Smith, 1977, pp. 72-74 for other collections from Habarut), concluding that significant differences existed between these two collections and the western Rub al-Khali facies, even while the Habarut corpus is generally more similar (and geographically closer) to the latter than is the Jebel Huwaya material. The more recently published materials from Oman have confirmed both these conclusions.

While in some instances forms morphologically identical to the western Rub al-Khali types occur in Oman,[3] on the whole these assemblages are highly bifacial in character without being similar to the western Rub al-Khali facies. The characteristics that separate these lithic zones may be summarized as follows. The stemmed point, so prominent in the Rub al-Khali, is largely absent from greater Oman, and those points that do occur tend to be *sui generis*. This contrast is clearly illustrated by a comparison of the Rub al-Khali site in the Ramlet es Sahmah (Gotoh, 1981) with Fasad or Habarut. The Ramlet es Sahmah stemmed points belong unambiguously in the Rub al-Khali/Eastern Province/Qatar tradition both formally and technologically, whereas at Fasad and especially at Habarut the stemmed points tend to be narrow, with body not much wider than stem, lacking a barb, and with a pronounced triangular cross-section (Pullar, 1974, fig. 9F; Payne and Hawkins, 1963, fig. 2: 3-5; Harding, 1964, pl. 51: 20). These points do not occur further east in Oman, where stemmed points of any form are rare.[4] The eastern Omani assemblages, therefore, only barely qualify for inclusion in the Arabian bifacial tradition *qua* prominent array of stemmed (and often barbed) points.

These Omani collections rarely display in their bifacial component the formal sense of symmetry and the achievement of elegance found in the Rub al-Khali facies or in the Eastern Province and Qatar materials. In Oman bifaces tend to be large, often asymmetrical, with irregular margins and thick cross-sections, i.e. correspond to the definition of unfinished bifacial pieces in the

Rub al-Khali and the Eastern Province/Qatar facies, a fact remarked upon by several authors. Here again a difference between sites in the Dhofar region and eastern Oman is preceptible, where bifacial reduction is carried more consistently to a finer level in the former area, but even here without rivalling the Rub al-Khali production. Thus in Oman at least two general geographical facies seem to be present, neither identical with the Rub al-Khali 'Neolithic' despite the close proximity in space of the Dhofar sites to the easternmost of the Rub al-Khali sites (see fig. 5: T-Y).

In the areas to the west of the Rub al-Khali, especially in the Wadi Dawasir (Zarins *et al.*, 1979, pp. 19-21), Bi'r Hima, the Wadi Tathlith, and the 'Asir highlands (Zarins *et al.*, 1981, pp. 20-22; Drechou *et al.*, 1968), sites belonging to the Arabian bifacial lithic tradition bear strong resemblance to the western Rub al-Khali facies. These resemblances extend to many point and scraper forms and to elements of heavy equipment such as axes/adzes, as well as to basic technological procedures. Notable qualitative differences include a virtual absence of rhomboidal bifacial points (two poorly formed examples are reported from the Wadi Tathlith, Zarins *et al.*, 1981, pl. 19: 13 and Drechou *et al.*, 1968, fig. 4: 4) and fine lanceolates from these sites to the west, where are present ground stone axes and high backed unifacial narrow foliates not common in the Rub al-Khali (celts are reported only for Qawnasad ibn Ghuddayyan and Abu Bahr in the Rub al-Khali; Field, 1961, pl. 1971, p. 46; Sordinas, 1971, p. 20). Quantative differences cannot readily be adduced, due to the nature of reporting, except in noting the higher proportion of stemmed and barbed points in the Wadi Dawasir (Zarins *et al.*, 1979, p. 19; by contrast, more of the shouldered than barbed variety are illustrated in Zarins *et al.*, 1981). In sum, then, a very strong family resemblance unites these sites in the southwest of Saudi Arabia with those in the Rub al-Khali and in the Eastern Province and Qatar. One may add that the family resemblance grows somewhat attenuated with distance from the Rub al-Khali – the Wadi Dawasir and Bi'r Hima materials are more similar to the western Rub al-Khali facies, that of the upland 'Asir less so.

The attenuation of family resemblance continues to the northwest and north into the southern Hejaz and the central Nejd (Zarins *et al.*, 1980, 1982), where occur not only the diagnostic stemmed bifacial point (though usually of smaller size and often replaced with parti-bifacially trimmed lamellar flakes), but also narrow and broad foliates, oversized stemmed points, typical scraper forms and axes/adzes, but where the bifacial component is generally less dominant than further south and often less well made. These more generic similarities extend further north into the northern portions of the Arabian peninsula, where the assemblages in which occur stemmed points take on a much more pronounced Levantine flavor (cf. the review of Arabian bifacial 'Neolithic' sites in Zarins n.d.). Further south, in North Yemen, the lithic industry at Jebel Qutran is described as being very similar to the western Rub al-Khali facies, containing bifacial foliates and rhomboidal points, various scrapers, trihedral drills and axes/adzes (Zarattini, 1984).

The regional variation exhibited across the industrial family resemblance just discussed probably correponds to industrial facies comparable to that previously defined for the western Rub al-Khali. As Zarins notes in connection with the 'Asir, 'the al-Rub al-Khali Neolithic shows a number of different traits... mainly concerning the finer points in knapping technique' (Zarins *et al.*, 1981, p. 22). In addition to the formal typological and quantitative differences mentioned above, the Rub al-Khali facies is distinguished qualitatively by the greater extent and finer control of soft hammer and pressure flaking exhibited in all aspects of given assemblages. Precise definition of these regional facies of the bifacial lithic tradition in southwestern and central Arabia awaits systematic study of site collections already in hand.

Such regional facies are almost certainly representative of local populations adapted to different regional environments of the mid-Holocene, ranging from playa lakes in the Rub al-Khali to the cooler and much wetter uplands of the 'Asir and the Yemen. Recent paleo-environmental studies suggest that the mid-Holocene climate in southern Arabia was an extension of that in northern Africa (Hötzl *et al.*, 1984, pp. 312-14). During the altithermal (peaking at c. 8000 b.p.) the inter-tropical convergence zone shifted well to the north, bringing a regime of equatorial summer rain to most of the peninsula, and an overall increase in precipitation on the order of 100-400 mm (decreasing from south to north). Thus even though average annual temperatures were higher (by 1°-1.5°C), the general effect was to promote formation of playa lakes (notably in the Rub al-Khali and the Eastern Province, McClure, 1976, 1978, Larsen, 1983, pp. 142-49) and greater run-off through wadis draining the uplands (Hötzl *et al.*, 1984, pp. 307-308). The Rub al-Khali was thus semi-arid to arid rather than hyperarid, and supported a dry steppe vegetation. The uplands to the west were proportionately better watered by virtue of the orographic effects of the 'Asir and Hejaz mountain range.

Despite general climatic amelioration, the local populations in the Rub al-Khali were very closely tied to water sources. This dependence is evident in the distribution of occupation within the aeolian sands of the Rub al-Khali (fig. 5)[(5)]. Sites are concentrated in the extreme southwest of the Rub al-Khali, within a 250 km. arc of Mundafin (fig. 5: B), with lesser numbers of localities extending along the margins of the sands to the northeast and east. Two of the three major exceptions to this pattern (fig. 4: 36-37, 42) are in fact only single flint points, representative either of a transient prehistoric presence (e.g. a hunting trip) or more recent re-use of an older flint as a strike-a-light by a nomad (on this practice, see Thomas, 1932, p. 207; Philby, 1933, p.51).[6] Thus even though playa lake deposits are known from interior stretches of the Rub al-Khali, these seem to have been little frequented (cf. Philby, 1933, p. 51). The reason for the site distribution may be related not so much to the distribution of playa lakes as to subsurface water. Zötl argues that the Arabian paleodrainage system of the plio-Pleistocene (for which see Anton 1984: 281) was partially reactivated during the Late Pleistocene, at least in the Wadi Dawasir portion of this system, and cites as supporting evidence the observation that 'even in the current period of extreme aridity, there is the probability of a groundwater stream through the Rub al-Khali, running in the direction of the old wadi system' (Hötzl *et al.*, 1984, p. 322). The increased amount of run-off and of local precipitation in the mid-Holocene can only have augmented this groundwater stream, though scarcely to the point of reactivating the drainage network. In this regard, the location of sites shown in fig. 5 coincides with the proximal segments of the Wadi Dawasir and Wadi Najran drainages, together with lesser sources along the northwestern and southern fringes of the Rub al-Khali. The ground water conducted along these channels provided the opportunity of more dense and permanent occupation of the western Rub al-Khali than did the more ephemeral playa lakes away from this groundwater (see McClure, 1978, p. 256 on sheet-flooding as well); the predominant topography in the southwest of the Rub al-Khali, that of linear dunes spaced 2 km. apart and stretching 200 km. (Anton, 1984, p. 291), also promoted the pooling of this water in interdunal lakes. By contrast the higher elevations and different topographies to the west, northwest, and southwest were wetter and contained more topographic settings conducive to open or immediately subsurface water, especially in wadis (cf. Hötzl *et al.*, 1984, pp. 308). Hence location of occupation was not as restricted as in the Rub al-Khali and sites in these regions are found in strikingly variable topographic settings (see discussion in Zarin *et al.*, 1982, pp. 31-32 as well as other field reports). These different mid-Holocene environmental regions encouraged differently adaptive social behaviors.

Such regionally differentiated adaptations are expressed by structuring of space on sites. In the Rub al-Khali and areas immediately to the west, sites display no formal structuring beyond presence of hearths, often dispersed as a scatter of fire-cracked rock (Zarins *et al.*, 1979, p. 22; 1981, p. 21); small stone circles also occur in the Bi'r Hima and Wadi Tathlith regions (Zarins *et al.*, 1981, p. 21). In the Wadi Dawasir one site (211-24) was found to be composed of small clusters of fire-cracked rock, lithics and calcined bone, probably representative of separate (simultaneous and/or serial) encampments; this sort of site structuring, common enough in other desert areas (cf. the description of Bordj Mellala in Algeria, Tixier *et al.*, 1976), is probably more frequent in southwestern Arabia than has been reported. In contrast to these open situations, formal stone structures occur in the uplands of the 'Asir and the southern Hejaz (stone circles and platforms, Zarins *et al.*,1980, p. 19; 1981, p. 21) and in the Yemen (stone circles, Zarattini, 1984), as well as in northern Arabia (see Zarins, n.d., for a review) and Qatar (Inizan, 1982; cf. also structures in 'Ubaid sites generally in the Arabian Gulf). Such stone circles, likely the footings for superstructures of different materials, reflect the cooler temperatures, greater moisture and generally higher biomass of higher altitudes, and probably also a greater degree of sedentism promoted by these factors.

No new information on subsistence patterns is available except for Jebel Qutran in the Yemen, where domesticated (*Bos taurus*, *Ovis aries*, *Capra hircus*) as well as wild species (*Bos* cf. *primigenius*, *Capra ibex*, *Equus* sp.) are reported (Zarattini, 1984). This first report of domesticated animals for southwestern Arabia implies major social difference between the pastoralism in the highlands – proven for the Yemen and probably also for parts of the 'Asir and southern Hejaz – and the purely hunting/gathering focus of the Rub al-Khali. This range of economic orientation also exists in the Eastern Province, Bahrain and Qatar, where the range of lithic variability (not always adequately) observable disguises great subsistence variability, *viz.* hunting away from the littoral zone, mixed hunting and fishing on the littoral (e.g. the Khor sites in Qatar, 'Ubaid al-Markh), and hunting, fishing and herding on a few sites (e.g. post- 'Ubaid al-Markh and probably the Eastern Province 'Ubaid sites). A similar range was also present in Oman, where domesticated animals in small numbers occur in mid-4th millennium littoral occupations at Ras al-Hamra near Muscat (cf. Biagi *et al.*, 1984, p. 48) but are probably absent in environmentally more marginal settings of the interior (unfortunately the investigations in such important habitations as Lizq 2 in the Wadi Samad area have produced no direct evidence of subsistence patterns due to absence of relevant organic material (Gebel *apud* Weisgerber, 1981, p. 256).

The general prevalence of hunting as the dominant, if not exclusive, man-animal [7] relationship in southwestern Arabia is confirmed by the indirect evidence of the rock art, especially in the Wadi Dawasir and at Bi'r Hima where the rock art seems associated with bifacial industry sites. At these sites the rock art, variants of the 'Jubba style' or earlier products, portrays a variety of animals (long and short horned bovids, gazelle, oryx, ibex, camel, onager, fat-tailed sheep) being hunted, with the only domesticate being the dog (Zarins *et al.*, 1979, p. 30); Zarins *et al.*, 1980, pp. 30-31; Zarins *et al.*, 1981, pp. 34-36;

Zarins, 1982; and n.d.). The variety of animals far exceeds the list of species occuring osteologically in Rub al-Khali sites (Edens, 1982, p. 19), and may be taken (cautiously) to reflect the richer and more variable environments in the higher and better watered lands to the west of the Rub al-Khali.

While distinguished by fundamental subsistence orientations (and therefore by the social adaptations built around these orientations), the southwestern Arabian regional facies are united by a different facet of the social economy, inter-regional exchange. Obsidian occurs as an infrequent raw material on a number of sites in the western Rub al-Khali, up the western mountain range well north of Taif and into the central Nejd in the areas of Dawadami and Riyadh (see the distribution map in Zarins *et al.*, 1981, pl. 5C, to which should be added the green obsidian reported for site 207-62 in the Nefud Qunayfidhah [Zarins *et al.*, 1980, pl. 19D. 18], as well as four sites in the Rub al-Khali, fig. 5: 10, 22, 26 and 35, and the unlocated site(s) in the northwest of the Rub al-Khali in the vicinity of sites fig. 5: 7-9 represented in the Zimmerman collection [Sordinas, 1978, p. 21]). Most of this obsidian appears as debitage, usually lamellar flakes, and implements of this material are rarely reported (examples being the bifacial point from the Zalim area of the southern Hejaz [Zarins *et al.*, 1980, pl. 20A: 1]; no formal tools of obsidian, to this author's knowledge, are reported for the western Rub al-Khali, though some flakes do bear retouch, cf. Zarins *et al.*, 1981, pl. 18: 27-28). Further south, particularly in the Yemen, formal tools of obsidian are more common (e.g. Zarattini, 1984; for other obsidian industries, see e.g. Caton-Thompson, 1944; de Bayle des Hermens, 1976). The sources of this obsidian undoubtedly lie in the Yemen, where flows are known at Sana'a and Taiz. The character of the distribution of this obsidian conforms entirely to the 'fall-off model' whereby the sheer amount of material (in proportion to the total assemblage) and the variety of uses to which it was put is inversely related to distance from the source (on this simple model, see Wright 1969, Renfrew 1975 among others). Although close chronological control is entirely absent, the fall-off distribution of obsidian in southwestern Arabia probably represents interaction at the boundaries of local populations in addition to seasonal movements of such populations, both being elements of down-the-line exchange.

Other materials also attest to this kind of exchange network. Chlorite (steatite), usually worked into vessels, is reported from a number of sites in the western Rub al-Khali (Edens, 1982, pp. 118-19), the Wadi Dawasir (Zarins *et al.*, 1979, p. 20), the Wadi Tathlith (Zarins *et al.*, 1981, p. 21), and, further north in the Nefud as-Sirr/'Urayq al-Buldan area (Zarin *et al.*, 1980, p. 20; the last identification is not certain). Although the number of sites for which chlorite has been collected is small (no more than half a dozen reported), making interpretation preliminary, their distribution falls within that of obsidian, and probably reflects the practice of the same exchange network. Chlorite sources are known for the western Nejd and southern Hejaz (Zarins, 1978, p. 67; Bayer, 1984, p. 10). Marine shell is another substance that occasionally appears on these sites, notably in the western Rub al-Khali (*Cypraea* sp., Edens, 1982, p. 119), the Turaba area in the southern Hejaz (species not identified, Zarins *et al.*, 1980, p. 19), and in the environs of Riyadh (*Dentalium* sp. and a ring cut from *Conus* sp., Zarins *et al.*, 1982, p. 32). One may also note the sandstone blocks fashioned into grinding equipment found throughout this region. This material was carried at least 75 km. to sites in the Wadi Tathlith from the nearest source on the Arabian Plateau (Zarins *et al.*, 1981, p. 21), and the similar equipment in the western Rub al-Khali probably derived from sources equally or more distant, such as the sandstone outcrop near Sharorah (Smith and Maranjian, 1962, p. 21) or the island of outcropping Wasia Formation in the Jiladah area (see fig. 5). Some of the grinding equipment made of granite found on a site in the Riyadh area (207-97) derives from a source some 150 km. away (Zarins *et al.*, 1982, p. 32). Distances of this magnitude are well within the size of annual movements of hunters/gatherers in an arid to semi-arid environment.

Golding drew attention to a shouldered point at Nadqan made of a purplish red quartzite whose nearest source is in the vicinity of Riyadh some 500 km. away (Golding, 1974, p. 19 and pers. comm., 1979). Since no quartzite debitage appears on the site, this point was introduced already fashioned, and again may reflect long distance (seasonal) movement of populations, probably in conjunction with exchange across social boundaries.

Conclusions

Field research of the past decade throughout the Arabian peninsula has confirmed the existence of an industry polythetically characterized by small bifacially pressure flaked points, especially stemmed and barbed but also other forms, other bifacially worked forms (large points, 'knives', axe/adzes and other heavy equipment), and opportunistic flake production adapted to the vagaries of local raw materials; the industry also contains grinding equipment, ground stone tools and stone vessels. Within the geographical range covered by this industry, a number of distinctive facies are apparent or suspected, defined by variation in quality, quantity or technique of lithic equipment. Excluding northern Arabia, such facies are notable in the Eastern Province/Qatar region (including Nadqan),the western Rub al-Khali, the Wadi Dawasir/Bi'r

Hima axis, the 'Asir/southern Hejaz uplands, Dhofar, and eastern Oman. Further typological analysis on controlled collections is required to define more closely these facies.

The industry and its facies have meaning only as a technology and a style, while the social activities of the populations they archaeologically represent were enormously varied in terms of site configuration and location, of diet and the social strategies of getting food, of access to exchange networks, and doubtless in many other ways not yet archaeologically perceptible. These variations were in part a response to local adaptive needs, but local social tradition and dynamics also played its major role. Further, different local social behaviors do not correlate perfectly with lithic industrial facies - even at this finer degree of stylistic resolution, behavioral variability is marked.

These conclusions point out the need to move on to the next stage of a long-term inquiry, to excavation of sites, particularly those which show a potential for answering the fundamental questions of local environment, local diet, local seasonal variability, local exchange networks, local occupation patterns, local chronology as well as of local lithic variability. This kind of intensive work in well-defined local settings has begun in some quarters (e.g. at Khor, Inizan 1980; Qurm, Durante and Tosi, 1977; Biagi *et al.*, 1984; Lizq 2 in the Wadi Samad area, Gebel *apud* Weisgerber, 1981, pp. 254-56; Jebel Qutran, Zarattini, 1984), but needs to be conducted in a wide range of environments and topographic circumstances. Such sites as Jiladah, for example, possess a stratigraphic depth of tens of centimeters (Zarins *et al.*, 1979), while others are associated with, and perhaps stratified by, playa lakes (McClure, 1976, 1978) or alluvial sediments in wadis (e.g. Zarins *et al.*, 1979, pp. 21-22; cf. McClure, 1978, p. 262). These sites would greatly repay careful interdisciplinary investigation.

Notes

1. Only one site (fig. 5:39) in the Rub al-Khali has been radiometrically dated, that to the end of the 4th millennium B.C. (5090 ± 200 bp; Field, 1960a). The pre-'Ubaid levels at Ain Qannas, which despite the lamellar emphasis of the debitage (see below), contain this same industry as early as c. 7000 bp (Masry 1974, pp.110-13). Bifacial stemmed points occur on the surface of late 4th and early 3rd millennium B.C. sites (with Late Uruk and Early Dynastic pottery), but these points may not be in genuine association since the excavated assemblage is significantly different (Zarins,

1983). A bifacial industry is said to occur on Umm an-Nar period sites in Oman (cf. Pullar, 1985, p.63; Pullar and Jäckli, 1978, p.61), but this 3rd millennium industry has never systematically been studied. Further afield, lithic industries with formally similar bifacial elements (but differing in major ways otherwise) occur through much of western Asia during the 4th-3rd millennia, as Lechevallier's review indicates (Lechevallier, 1978, p.309); these forms appear from Central Asia (see the various papers in Kohl, 1981) to Mesopotamia (e.g. Mallowan, 1947). These various lines of evidence corroborate the chronological inference based on the paleoclimatic sequence without really strengthening it.

2. At Nadqan West, the lithic assemblage is small (n=28), consisting of several unfinished bifacial foliates, some bifacially worked cobbles (one heavily battered as well), an assortment of flakes, chunks, split cobbles and a hammerstone, and minimally prepared discoidal core as well as the blade core.

3. E.g. the narrow foliates in the Wadi Suq (Pullar, 1985, fig. 6.1), at Miskin near Amlah (Smith, 1976, fig. 3.6), in the Wadi Halfayn (Pullar and Jäckli, 1978, fig. 15B), at Lizq 2 in the Wadi Samad area (Gebel *apud* Weisgerber, 1981, Abb. 99), at the edge of the Wahiba sands (Smith, 1977, fig. 3:17), at Sayq (Smith, 1977, fig. 4:21); broad foliates at Jebel Huwaya (Copeland and Bergne, 1976, fig. 1:1-3), Sayq (Smith, 1977, fig. 4:19, 20, 22), in the Amlah region (Smith, 1976, fig. 2:1, 5), in the Wadi Samad area (Gebel *apud* Weisgerber, 1980, p.99; 1981, p.256 and Abb. 100), Natih (Pullar, 1985, fig. 11:1), Fasad (Pullar, 1974, fig. 2D), Bir Khasfa (Pullar, 1974, fig. 5D), Habarut (Pullar, 1974, fig. 11A); lanceolates at Jebel Huwaya (Copeland and Bergne, 1976, fig. 2:11), in the Wadi Halfayn (Pullar and Jäckli, 1978, fig. 15A), Qaharir (Pullar and Jäckli, 1978, fig. 6F), Mughshin (Pullar, 1985, fig. 15:3), Fasad (Pullar, 1974, fig. 9D) and Habarut (Payne and Hawkins, 1963, fig. 2:6-8; Harding, 1964, pl. 51:21; Smith, 1977, fig. 5:31); some of these same sites also contain coarse lanceolates, trihedral rods, axes/adzes.

4. E.g. one, not illustrated, at Jebel Huwaya (Copeland and Bergne, 1976, p.44); an extremely large unifacial point at Kadusa (Pullar, 1985, fig. 3:7); and another smaller parti-bifacial point at Fahud (Pullar, 1985, fig. 9:4); bifacial points with rudimentary stem similar to that described in type 2 above appear at Sayq (Pullar, 1985, fig. 7:1) and Bir Khasfa (Pullar, 1974, fig. 6B), where markedly asymmetrical stemmed and barbed points and poorly delineated shouldered points (Pullar, 1974, fig. 6A, D-F) also occur .

5. That this distribution map of sites in the Rub al-Khali is incomplete is obvious and basically irrelevant; that the pattern of the distribution of these sites is distorted is less obvious and more curcial to the argument being advanced here. In this circumstance, the negative evidence afforded by travellers and oil geologists of playa lake deposits without cultural associations is important. In the event, the pattern probably does approximate the prehistoric reality, though any active aeolian sedimentation (as appears to be the case in the southeastern margin of the Rub al-Khali, where dunes appear to be migrating northward; McKee, 1979, pp.366-67) introduces a biased distribution of both prehistoric sites and playa lakes.

6. Another probable instance of (sub-) recent nomadic rearrangement of the archaeological record is the arrangement of 20-40 lanceolates in a tight circle, a phenomenon recorded for two sites (fig. 5:38 and W) along the southern fringes of the Rub al-Khali (Field, 1956, p.185 and Pullar, 1974, p.41).

7. The question of the plant component of diet, and the man-plant relations that provided this component, cannot be addressed in any concrete way with present evidence. One may point to the ubiquitous grinding equipment in this respect, but the materials processed with this equipment and the dietary significance (if any) of these materials is entirely speculative. Firm evidence of cultivated plants does not appear until the late 4th millennium (especially at Hili, Cleuziou, 1982), perhaps also at Umm an-Nussi of Late Uruk date, where sickle blade elements with sickle sheen are reported (Zarins, 1983, p.1029); there is no solid suggestion of 'Ubaid period cultivation in the Eastern Province.

Bibliography

Anton D. (1984), 'Aspects of geomorphological evolution: palæosols and dunes in Saudi Arabia', in A. Jado and J. Zötl (eds.), *Quaternary Period in Saudi Arabia*, vol.II, Vienna, Springer-Verlag, pp.275-296.

Bayer, H.-J. (1984), 'General Geology of western Saudi Arabia: the Arabian shield', in A. Jado and J. Zötl (eds.), *Quaternary Period in Saudi Arabia*, vol.II, Vienna, Springer-Verlag, pp.5-13.

de Bayles des Hermens, R. (1976), 'Première mission de recherches préhistoriques en République arabe du Yemen', *L'anthropologie*, vol.80, pp.5-38.

Biagi, P., Torke, W., Tosi, M., and Uerpmann, H.-P. (1984), 'Qurum: a case study of coastal archaeology in northern Oman', *World Archaeology*, vol.16, pp.43-61.

Caton-Thompson, G. (1944), *The Tombs and Moon Temple of Hureidha (Hadhramaut)*, London, Report of the Research Committee of the Society of Antiquaries.

Cleuziou, S. (1982), 'Hili and the beginnings of oasis life in eastern Arabia', *Proceedings of the Seminar for Arabian Studies*, vol.12, pp.15-22.

Copeland, L. and Bergne, P. (1976), 'Flint artifacts from the Buraimi area, eastern Arabia, and their relations with the Near Eastern post-Pleistocene', *Proceedings of the Seminar for Arabian Studies*', vol.3, pp.40-61.

Drechou, H., Hivernel, F., and Karpoff, R. (1968), 'Nouvelle stations préhistoriques dans les reliefs anciens de l'Arabie saoudite', *Bulletin de la Société préhistorique française*, vol.65, pp.817-832.

Durante, S. and Tosi, M. (1977), 'The aceramic shell middens of Ra's al-Ḥamra: a preliminary note', *Journal of Oman Studies*, vol.3, pp.137-162.

Edens, C. (1982), 'Towards a definition of the western Rub al-Khali "Neolithic"', *Atlal*, vol.6, pp.109-124.

Field, H. (1956), *Ancient and Modern Man in Southwestern Asia I*, Coral Gables, University of Miami Press.

Field, H. (1958), 'Stone implements from the Rub' al Khali, Saudi Arabia', *Man*, vol.58, pp.93-94.

Field, H. (1960), 'Stone implements from the Rub' al Khali', *Man*, vol.60, pp.25-26.

Field, H. (1960a), 'Carbon-14 date for a 'neolithic' site in the Rub' al Khali', *Man*, vol.60, p.172.

Field, H. (1971), *Contributions to the Anthropology of Saudi Arabia*, Miami, Field Research Projects.

Golding, M. (1974), 'Evidence for pre-Seleucid occupation of eastern Arabia', *Proceedings of the Seminar for Arabian Studies*, vol.4, pp.19-32.

Gotoh, T. (1981), 'A stone age collection from the Rub' al Khali desert', *Bulletin of the Ancient Orient Museum*, vol.3, pp.1-15.

Gramly, R. (1971), 'Neolithic flint implement assemblages from Saudi Arabia', *Journal of Near Eastern Studies*, vol.30, pp.177-185.

Harding, G.L. (1964), *Archaeology in the Aden Protectorate*, London, H.M. Stationery Office.

Hötzl, H., Jado, A., Moser, H., Rauert, W., and Zötl, J. (1984), 'Climatic fluctuations in the Holocene', in A. Jado and J. Zötl (eds.), *Quaternary Period in Saudi Arabia*, vol.II, Vienna, Springer-Verlag, pp.301-314.

Inizan, M.-L. (1980), 'Premiers résultats des fouilles préhistoriques de la région de Khor', in J. Tixier (ed.) *Mission archéologique française à Qatar I*, Doha, Ministry of Information, pp.51-98.

Inizan, M.-L. (1982), 'Préhistoire' in *Rapport d'Activité 1982*, Paris, CNRS, R.C.P. 476, pp.3-16.

Inizan, M.-L. and Tixier, J. (1978), 'Outrepassage intentionel sur pieces bifaciales néolithiques du Qatar (golfe arabo-persique)' *Quaternaria*, vol.20, pp.29-40.

Inizan, M.-L. and Tixier, J. (1980), 'Industrie lithique taillée de Hili 8', *Archéologie aux Emirats Arabes Unis*, vol.2-3, pp.72-73.

Kapel, H. (1965), 'Stenalderfund fra Qatar', *Kuml 1964*, pp.112-155.

Kapel, H. (1967), *Atlas of the Stone Age Cultures of Qatar*, Copenhagen, Jutland Archaeological Society Publications.

Kohl, P. (1981), *The Bronze Age Civilization of Central Asia*, Armonk, Sharpe.

Larsen, C. (1983), *Life and Land Use on the Bahrain Islands*, Chicago, University of Chicago Press.

Lechevallier, M. (1978), 'L'industrie lithique de Mehrgarh (Pakistan)', *Paléorient*, vol.4, pp.307-318.

McClure, H.A. (1978), 'Ar Rub' al Khali', in S. al-Sayari and J. Zötl (eds.), *Quaternary Period in Saudi Arabia*, vol.I, Vienna, Springer-Verlag, pp.252-263.

McKee, E.D. (1979), *A Study of Global Sand Seas*, Washington, United States Geological Survey Professional Paper 1052.

Madsen, H.J. (1962), 'En flintplads i Qatar', *Kuml 1961*, pp.185-201.

Mallowan, M. (1947), 'Excavations at Tell Brak and Chagar Bazar', *Iraq*, vol.9, pp.1-259.

Marshall, B.H. (1962), *Stone Implements from the Arabian Desert, in the Collections of the University Museum, Philadelphia*, unpublished M.A. thesis, University of Pennsylvania.

Masry, A. (1974), *Prehistory in Northeastern Arabia: The Problem of Interregional Interaction*, Coconut Grove, Field Research Projects.

Moore, A.M.T. (1973), 'The late Neolithic in Palestine', *Levant*, vol.5, pp.36-68.

Moore, A.M.T. (1982), 'A four-stage sequence for the Levantine Neolithic, ca. 8500-3750 B.C.', *Bulletin of the American Schools of Oriental Research*, vol.246, pp.1-34.

Oates, J. (1982), 'Archaeological evidence for settlement patterns in Mesopotamia and eastern Arabia in relation to possible environmental conditions', in J. Bintliff and W. van Zeist (eds.), *Paleoclimate, Paleoenvironments and Human Communities in the Eastern Mediterranean Region in Later Prehistory*, BAR International Series, vol.133 (ii), pp.359-398.

Payne, J.C. and Hawkins, S. (1963), 'A surface collection of flints from Habarut in southern Arabia', *Man*, vol.63, pp.185-188.

Philby, H.St.J.B. (1933), *The Empty Quarter*, London, Constable.

Potts, D. (n.d.), 'The Chronology of the Archaeological Assemblages from the Head of the Arabian Gulf to the Arabian Sea (8000-1750 B.C.)', in R.W. Ehrich (ed.), *Chronologies in Old World Archaeology*, Chicago, University of Chicago Press.

Potts, D.T., Mughannum, A., Frye, J., and Sanders, D. (1977), 'Preliminary report on the second phase of the Eastern Province survey, 1397/1977, *Atlal*, vol.2, pp.7-27.

Pullar, J. (1974), 'Harvard archaeological survey in Oman, 1974: I-flint sites in Oman', *Proceedings of the Seminar for Arabian Studies*, vol.4, pp.33-48.

Pullar, J. (1985), 'A selection of aceramic sites in the Sultanate of Oman', *Journal of Oman Studies*, vol.7, pp.49-87.

Pullar, J. and Jäckli, B. (1978), 'Some aceramic sites in Oman', *Journal of Oman Studies*, vol.4, pp.53-74.

Renfrew, C. (1975), 'Trade as action at a distance: questions of integration and communication', in J. Sabloff and C.C. Lamberg-Karlovsky (eds.), *Ancient Civilization and Trade*, Albuquerque, University of New Mexico Press, pp.3-69.

Roaf, M. (1976), 'Excavations at al-Markh, Bahrain', *Proceedings of the Seminar for Arabian Studies*, vol.6, pp.144-160.

Smith, G. (1976), 'New neolithic sites in Oman', *Journal of Oman Studies*, vol.2, pp.189-198.

Smith, G. (1977), 'New prehistoric sites in Oman', *Journal of Oman Studies*, vol.3, pp.71-81.

Smith, G. (1977a), 'Two prehistoric sites on Ras Abaruk, site 4', in B. deCardi (ed.), *Qatar Archaeological Report, Excavations 1973*, Oxford, Oxford University Press, pp.80-106.

Smith, P.E.L. and Maranjian, G. (1962), 'Two "neolithic" collections from Saudi Arabia', *Man*, vol.62, pp.21-23.

Sordinas, A. (1971), 'Francis collection from al-Qawnasat ibn Ghudayyan', in H. Field (ed.), *Contributions to the Anthropology of Saudi Arabia*, Miami, Field Research Projects, pp.1-24.

Sordinas, A. (1973), *Contributions to the Prehistory of Saudi Arabia* II, Coconut Grove, Field Research Projects.

Sordinas A. (1978), *Contributions to the Archaeology of Saudi Arabia III: The Zimmerman Collection from the Northern Fringe of the Rub' al-Khali*, Miami, Field Research Projects.

Thomas, B. (1932), *Arabia Felix*, New York, Scribner's.

Tixier, J., Marmier, F., and Trecolle, G. (1976), *Le campement préhistorique de Bordj Mellala*. Paris, Editions du Cercle de Recherches et d'Études Préhistoriques.

Weisgerber, G. (1980), '... und Kupfer in Oman', *Der Anschnitt*, vol.32, pp.62-110.

Weisgerber, G. (1981), 'Mehr als Kupfer in Oman', *Der Anschnitt*, vol.33, pp.174-263.

Wright, G. (1969), *Obsidian Analyses and Prehistoric Near Eastern Trade: 7500 to 3500 B.C.*, Ann Arbor, Anthropological

Papers 37, Museum of Anthropology, University of Michigan.

Zarattini, A. (1984), 'Neolithic settlements from North Yemen: data from field excavations (a preliminary report)', paper presented at the International Symposium: Late Prehistory of the Nile Basin and the Sahara, Poznan, 1984.

Zarins, J. (1978), 'Steatite vessels in the Riyadh Museum', *Atlal*, vol.2, pp.65-94.

Zarins, J. (1982), 'Early rock art of Saudi Arabia', *Archaeology*, vol.35, pp.20-27.

Zarins, J. (1983), 'The chipped and ground stone industries of Umm an-Nussi, Tell Ramad and related sites in the Eastern Province of Saudi Arabia', in C. Piesinger, *Legacy of Dilmun: The Roots of Ancient Maritime Trade in Eastern Coastal Arabia in the Fourth/Third Millennium B.C.*, Ph.D. thesis, University of Wisconsin-Madison.

Zarins, J. (n.d.), 'Archaeological and chronological problems within the greater southwest Asian arid zone: 13,000-1,850 B.C.', in R.W. Ehrich (ed.), *Chronologies in Old World Archaeology*, 3rd edition, Chicago, University of Chicago Press.

Zarins, J., Ibrahim, M., Potts, D., and Edens, C. (1979), 'Preliminary report on the survey of the central province 1978', *Atlal*, vol.3, pp.9-42.

Zarins, J., Murad, A., and al-Yaish, K. (1981), 'The second preliminary report on the Southwestern Province', *Atlal*, vol.5, pp.9-42.

Zarins, J., Rahbini, A., and Kamal, M. (1982), 'Preliminary report on the archaeological survey of the Riyadh area', *Atlal*, vol.6, pp.25-38.

Zarins, J., Whalen, N., Ibrahim, M., Jawad, A., and Khan, M. (1980), 'Preliminary report on the central and southwestern provinces survey: 1979', *Atlal*, vol.4, pp.9-36.

Zeuner, F. (1954), '"Neolithic" sites from the Rub-al-Khali, southern Arabia', *Man*, vol.54, pp.133-136.

Fig. 1. Shimal Tomb 6: view from the north showing entrance along west wall

The Grave-Goods from Shimal Tomb 6 in Ras al-Khaimah, U.A.E.

BY BEATRICE DE CARDI

The object of this study is to investigate the circumstances surrounding the deposition of a couple of Harappan objects in an early second millennium B.C. tomb at Shimal near Ras al-Khaimah, the northern-most of the United Arab Emirates.

The tomb, located in a cemetery known since 1968 (de Cardi, 1971, Site 6, f, p.246), was one of two long chambered burial structures excavated by Peter Donaldson on behalf of the Government of Ras al-Khaimah in 1977-78. Both the structure and the contents of Tomb 1 have been described in detail (Donaldson, 1984, pp.196-220) but events beyond the excavator's control precluded his study of the grave-goods from Tomb 6. This might not have mattered unduly had they simply duplicated those of Tomb 1 but Tomb 6 contained some pottery not previously encountered. In that category could be included several beakers with zoomorphic decoration and an Harappan jar which, together with a cubical chert weight of Indus type, were objects of sufficient interest to call for a postscript. Moreover, the advent of the Göttingen Archaeological Mission in 1985 to excavate further tombs in Shimal has emphasised the importance of this extensive cemetery and prompted the compilation of this catalogue of the Tomb 6 finds when the opportunity to revisit Ras al-Khaimah arose in 1986.[(1)]

Because of its position below the hills just north of Wadi Haqil at the opposite end of the re-entrant to Tomb 1 its excavator considered that Tomb 6 might have been among the last to be built there and he regarded it as being transitional between Tombs 1 and 2, the latter a ring-chambered structure excavated at Ghalilah in 1977 (Donaldson, 1984, pp.221-276; 1985, pp.95-96). While Ghalilah 2 can now be recognised as a second millennium structure re-used during the Iron Age, it was virtually impossible in the light of knowledge at that time to distinguish between the plain wares of the first and second millennia. Since much of the pottery could be related to al-Qusais and other Iron Age sites in the Emirates Ghalilah 2 was regarded as being of that date (Donaldson, 1985, p.132) and the error needs to be kept in mind pending closer temporal definition of the various tomb types in the locality as a result of the work currently being carried out by the German team.

Both in size and structural type Tomb 6 (Fig. 1) corresponded closely to Tomb 1. Conditions inside the tombs were also similar with bone fragments and sherds lying beneath collapsed roofing slabs. This state of disorder, due in part to successive interments and possibly later looting, restricts the deductions which can be made regarding burial rites and little can be said about the association of the various objects in the tomb. Nor is it possible without expert examination of the skeletal material to estimate how many individuals were buried in Tomb 6. However, the deposition of some 72 pots and 23 soft stone objects may bear some relation to the 67 pots and 16 stone vessels buried with the remains of at least 28 persons in Tomb 1.

While augmenting the growing corpus of early second millennium material, including the single interments in Wadi Suq (Frifelt, 1975, Figs. 20-23) and the final occupation at Hili 8 (Cleuziou, 1980, Figs. 34-38), the particular interest of the Tomb 6 grave-goods lies in the presence of recognisably Harappan objects, notably a large jar (Fig. 11) and a cubical chert weight (Fig. 14, 22). Those finds and their significance in relation to the date of Tomb 6 have been discussed elsewhere (de Cardi, n.d.). In summary, the high-necked jar with its encircling bands of thin multiple black lines can be matched on Harappan sites in Saurashtra, notably Lothal A and Rangpur IIA, in about 1900 B.C. Cubical weights of cream and buff banded chert were current there at much the same time but were later replaced by truncated spheroid weights during the Late Harappan or Post-Urban period at Rangpur IIB (*c.* 1900-1700 B.C.). The Shimal weight is indubitably an Harappan product and exhibits the slightly convex polished surfaces intended by Indus craftsmen to protect the edges of what was after all a carefully calculated precision object. Despite that precaution the weight has been chipped and that fact must be taken into account when its 26.300 grammes are compared with weights of the Dilmun standard. In that context one may add that the same type of weights occurred in the North Wall Sounding at Qala'at al-Bahrain where they ranged from late City I to early City II, the latter dated to the Isin-Larsa period (Potts, 1983, p.132; 1985, pp. 697-698).

The Harappan finds shed some light not only on Ras al-Khaimah's external relations but on burial customs of the period. Both Tomb 1 and Tomb 6 contained a high incidence of drinking vessels and it is tempting to see the deposition of the jar as appropriate to and possibly owned by a dead Harappan, together with the weight as a tool of this trade if he had been resident in Shimal as a merchant. Until last year one might well ask what a foreign trader would be doing in Shimal, but the German team has now identified a settlement area near the cemetery and other Harappan objects are coming to light.

The contents of Tomb 6 were more varied than those of Tomb 1 but neither the pottery nor the stone objects gave any indication that the structure had been re-used in the Iron Age. Slight differences, particularly in the shape of the beakers and spouted jars may indicate some degree of stylistic development resulting from interments made over a period of several centuries but discussion must await the outcome of current fieldwork.

The Tomb 6 pottery comprised mostly fine wares with a sandy red fabric of variable hardness predominating. Only four examples of a self-slipped creamy-buff ware occurred. No attempt could be made in the time available to relate the various types of fabric to those noted in Tomb 1, but the presence of small inclusions, usually white or larger grey grits, shell and vegetal tempering is referred to in the Catalogue.[2] Apart from the hand-made miniature vessels, most of the pottery had been made on a wheel but rarely reached any level of technical excellence. A number of vessels bore girth grooves and many had been shaved externally to reduce their thickness below the girth. The bases of both cups and beakers were often string-cut but, in the case of large spouted jars, there were signs of spiral coiling inside while the exterior had been deliberately flattened and a number were off-centre.

The forms ranged from goblets, cups and beakers, an arbitrary distinction being made between the latter categories based on rim-diameter, vessels below 8 cm. being regarded as cups. Those three categories together comprised 60% of the total; spouted jars, 20%, miniature pots, 9% and the remainder being made up of five flasks, three bowls and a suspension-vessel.

Features distinguishing many of the beakers and, to a lesser extent, the cups were their strongly everted rims, e.g. Figs. 5-6, 1, 17 and 24, and thin upright or slightly sinuous sides generally shaved around the lower part of the body to produce curved or sometimes carinated walls above either flattened or slightly concave string-cut bases. In some instances, e.g. No. 3, the base sagged to such an extent as to be almost rounded. Most of these features were present on the Tomb 1 beakers but they were decidedly less common on the second millennium pottery of Hili 8 to judge from the examples published to date (Cleuziou, 1981, Fig. 8).

The majority of the beakers were decorated, the four standard designs all occurring in Tomb 1 (Donaldson, 1984, p.200). In most instances the border was set below the rim but No. 3 bore a dark brown band over the rim-edge and No. 20 was decorated with pendant lines in addition to horizontal bands, both slight but abnormal details. Of considerably greater interest were two red ware beakers, Nos. 5 and 8, with a metopic band consisting of opposed swags or concentric semi-circles between multiple vertical dividers. This particular motif had provided a date for the Suq/Sunaysl burials as it had occurred in 'a disturbed level connected with the outer wall of the third Barbar temple' (Frifelt, 1975, p.379), a context now ascribed to the Isin-Larsa period (Potts, 1983, p.133) and a similarly dated grave-mound near A'ali in Bahrain has yielded

Fig. 2. Bird beaker from Tomb 6

other parallels (Frifelt, 1986, p.133). The same design was present in the final occupation at Hili 8 which also produced part of an Indus-inspired offering-stand (Cleuziou, 1980, Figs. 35 and 38, 5), but at the second millennium settlement at Tawi Sa'id in the Sharqiya it was used on vessels different in shape to those of Tomb 6 (de Cardi, Bell and Starling, 1979, Fig. 11, 26, 27).

Another beaker, Fig. 2, Fig. 5, 6 and a cup, Fig. 3, Fig. 6, 21 were exceptional in bearing zoomorphic motifs in addition to the more usual chevron bands. The former is decorated with an upper zone of long necked heavy-bodied birds with large wings – perhaps ostriches – proceeding from right to left; the latter merely has a scorpion set below the main design zone. Close parallels are difficult to cite: bird motifs appear on Kaftari-ware in Fars during the early 2nd millennium B.C. but, that feature apart, the range of forms has little in common with the Shimal pottery.(3) Zoomorphic motifs also occur on a spouted jar from Wadi Suq (Frifelt, 1975, Fig. 20b) and a suspension-vessel from Maysar 9 (Weisgerber, 1981, Abb. 5b) though in neither case is there a close stylistic resemblance to the Tomb 6 vessels.

Fig. 3. Cup with scorpion motif from Tomb 6

Few of the other cups call for comment, most bearing either chevron bands or the vertically extended version of that pattern. Four were in a self-slipped creamy-buf ware, No. 29 bearing traces of an unusual brown painted design incorporating a vertical wavy line not unlike the motif on a larger vessel in one of the Sar burials on Bahrain which has been compared with pottery from Tall-i Zohak in Fars (Potts, 1985, p.694). Two of the cups were unmatched in Tomb 1, Nos. 22 and 23 by reason of their decoration, and two goblets with flat splayed string-cut bases, Nos. 43 and 44, occurred not only in Tomb 2 but also in the Shimal settlement (Donaldson, 1984, Fig. 22, 131).[(4)] Similar splay-based goblets were found in the 'Intermediate' phase (Level III) on Failaka Tell 6 though that context adds nothing to their dating (Calvet and Salles, 1986, Fig. 12, 22 and 24).

Other Tomb 6 vessels matched in Tomb 2 but absent from Tomb 1 included several flasks, Nos. 45-46, in a tan-buff ware found also in the Shimal settlement (Donaldson, 1984, Fig. 22, 131). Flask 47 has no parallels in either Tombs 1 or 2 but like No. 48 was made in a fabric known on the settlement.

Three types of miniature jars occurred in Tomb 6; No. 50, black banded around its neck, Nos. 51-53, and No. 54; they have counterparts in Shimal Tomb 103, a structure of Ghalilah type (Vogt and Franke-Vogt, 1987, Fig. 23, 1-4).

Tomb 6 contained no open bowls of the kind found in the settlement (Vogt and Franke-Vogt, 1987, Fig. 41, 1-6) and only two globular vessels, Nos. 55-56, the latter decorated with one of the standard designs used on beakers. A small disc base belonging to another spherical vessel, No. 57, was the only example of its type in Tomb 6 and is so far unmatched in the Shimal pottery. Also of note was a biconical hole-mouth suspension-vessel, No. 58, with four vertically pierced lugs and standard beaker decoration. It is closer in shape to some of the soft-stone vessels from Tomb 6 (e.g. Fig. 12, No. 9) than another specimen with everted rim from a disturbed layer in a comparable structure, Shimal Tomb 102 (Vogt and Franke-Vogt, 1987, Fig. 13, 11 and p.28). A vessel similar in form and decoration is known from Failaka but is undated (Højlund, 1987, Fig. 176, Type 50, p.54).

Tomb 6 contained three types of spouted vessel: Type 1, a large globular jar with horizontally extended beak-spout joined to the rim; Type 2, a free-standing beak-spout; and Type 3, a short tubular shoulder spout. Types 2 and 3 were present only as single examples but ten jars were included in Type 1. Within that group certain variations were noted but whether they have any chronological significance or stem from vagaries in production cannot be resolved until a larger corpus of material is available.

A distinctive feature of some Type 1 jars was their flattened globular shape with the width at girth exceeding their height, proportions shared by similar jars in Tomb 103 (Vogt and Franke-Vogt, 1987, Fig. 24, 6-7). Rims were often rolled outwards to provide a grip in the absence of any pronounced neck, the only jar with a well-defined short upright neck and broad flat base being No. 59. Spouts were generally raised slightly above rim- level springing upwards from either a wide or narrow outlet pierced through the body of the jar just below the rim. In order to support the spout, the rim was expanded to form a broad band across the top of the narrow trough and at its point of juncture with the body the spout was luted to the exterior, the fabric being occasionally pinched or puckered. Of the few Type 1 bases which had survived, several were flattened (Nos. 60-62 and 67) while No. 66 sagged unevenly. Four of the jars in this category (Nos. 60, 63, 66 and 68) were decorated with a broad zone of black painted vertical zigzags edged by double horizontal bands around the neck and extending over the upper part of the body. Both spouts and rims bore traces of linear ornament and in the case of No. 68, a linking motif below the spout was partially visible. That jar was exceptional in bearing a motif resembling a stick figure on one side below the main design zone. A band of double wavy lines was used in place of zigzags on No. 59, the design being set between lines on the shoulder and dipping below the spout. The zigzag zone was used on most of the Tomb 1 spouted jars but there, as in Tomb 6, the design was replaced in one instance by wavy lines (Donaldson, 1984, Fig. 10, 64).

Four medium-sized jars were of either globular or spherical shape with flattened bases, Nos. 60-62 and 64. They differed from the other Type 1 jars not only in their size and shape, but in having a smaller pouring outlet through the body, in one instance thickened internally. The rim band joining the edges of their spouts gives an impression of angularity particularly when viewed from above. Several of the jars bore irregularly flowing linear decoration carried over the expanded rim band and along the side of the spout in the case of No. 64.

The opposed swags and dividers referred to in connection with a beaker (No. 8 above) added interest to a thin-walled spouted jar of elegant form, No. 61, which should be compared with No. 67 bearing a similar, but more carelessly applied disign. A spouted jar with the same kind of pattern is known from Hili 8 in a context which also produced a beak-spouted vessel with the bold chevron pattern characterising much late third millennium pottery (Cleuziou, 1981, Fig. 3, 1 and 3). No. 65, a jar with an unusual inturned rim, thick walls and sagging base, bore a zone of diagonal cross-hatching, while No. 67, a small much eroded vessel, was decorated with swags and dividers. Nos. 65 and 67 have been grouped together because in each case the rim band joining the sides of their spouts curved elliptically in plan.

Tomb 6 contained only one example of a jar classed as Type 2 by reason of its free-standing spout raised above rim-level and not joined to it in any way, No. 70, though an element of uncertainty exists as both rim and spout have been damaged. Spouts of this kind did not occur in Tombs 1 or 102 but they were present together with Type 1 jars in Tomb 103, a Ghalilah-type structure ascribed to *c.* 1800 B.C. (Vogt and Franke-Vogt, 1987, Fig. 24 and p.43).

The short oval tubular spouted jar, No. 71, regarded as Type 3, is known together with Type 2 on Failaka but their stratigraphical contexts there are ill-defined (Højlund, 1987, Fig. 154-156, p.48; Fig. 152, p.47). On Bahrain, although uncommon, spouted jars 'seem to be a feature which belongs to the late Barbar pottery tradition dating in the second half of Qala'a II, i.e. probably from *c.* 2000 to 1600 B.C. and the beginning of Qala'a III, maybe up to *c.* 1400 B.C.'[5]

A final word on No. 71 relates to the double wavy lines down its sides. The motif is one used not only on a Type 1 jar in Tomb 1 (Donaldson, 1984, Fig. 9, 59) but also on the side of a globular jar in Tomb 102 (Vogt and Franke-Vogt,

1987, Fig. 13, 12). Further afield, it adorns a Harappan sherd from a Period I context on Failaka which is described as similar to a group of sherds from Qala'at al-Bahrain identified as belonging to that culture (Højlund, 1987, Fig. 435, p.100).

In addition to the funerary wares Tomb 6 contained ten stone vessels and thirteen lids. The soft stone used for their manufacture tallied for the most part with the colour range noted in Tomb 1, the material often containing reflective flakes. Both the vessels and the lids ranged from greys with dark green, olive, blue and blackish tones to pale dove grey. In one instance a light grey stone with white veining was used for a shallow bowl (Fig. 12, 2) and a dark brown lid (15) was also unusual in being the only example with a concave base, all the rest being flat. It is matched both as to stone and concavity by a lid in Ghalilah Tomb 4 (Donaldson, 1985, Fig. 2, 2); it may also be compared in shape with one from Tomb 103 (Vogt and Franke-Vogt, 1987, Fig. 26, 7 and p. 43), and with examples from the Sar burials on Bahrain and Hili North Tomb A (Mughal, 1983, Fig. 25, 7, and Vogt, 1985, Pl. 27, 24 respectively).

As in Tomb 1 there were several types of lugged vessels, one (6), decorated with the dot in double ring motif usually associated with third millennium stone vases, had only three vestigial unpierced lugs – a form noted also in Tomb 103 (Vogt and Franke-Vogt, 1987, p.43). Nos. 4 and 5 had four similarly unperforated lugs but each bore the dot in single ring combined with linear incising which is thought to characterise the early second millennium stone vessels of the region. Two other vessels with four vertically pierced lugs were unusual: No. 9 being exceptionally large and relatively deeply incised, while No. 7 bore a middle zone of alternately placed vertical incising below the usual bands of dot and ring decoration. Three different types of bowl were present: Nos. 1 and 2 differed largely in the height of their walls, though the latter also exhibited the incising or slashing of the rim executed rather crudely. The same feature was present on a small but exceptionally well made round based bowl, No. 3, bearing conventional second millennium decoration but carved in a polished greenish-grey stone bearing fine tool-marks on both surfaces. Similarities in the stone, the tooling and the decorative technique suggest that the small vessel with vestigial lugs (No. 4) and the lid (No. 16) may have emanated from the same workshop as No. 3.

All the lids save one bore typical second millennium decoration, the exception being No. 11 with its dot and double rings. In eight instances the dot in single ring was combined with edge slashing and the knob bore some motif on top, either an incised 'tree' design, triple lines or a combination of lines with dot and ring. The 'tree' motif comprising a vertical with branches on either side was used on some of the lids in Tombs 1 and 2 (Donaldson, 1984, Fig. 12,

Fig. 4. Grave-goods from Tomb 6

9; Fig. 25, 21). Knobs varied in height and shape: five could be described as high (Nos. 12, 13, 15, 18 and 23) while four were short (Nos. 14, 19-21). An intermediate type with slightly expanded terminal was also noted (Nos. 11, 15 and 16). In so basic a feature as a knob the distinction may have little significance but it is noted in the present context since work on other tombs in the locality will undoubtedly yield their quota of lids.

The grave-goods included few personal possessions unusual to burials in this locality and period. Four bronze rivets or nails (Fig. 4, 1-2; Fig. 14, 1-4) and a couple of ear or nose-rings with tapered ends (Fig. 4, 3-4; Fig. 14, 5-6) have close parallels in Tombs 1 and 2 (Donaldson, 1984, Fig. 27, 22-23 and Fig. 29, 25-27 respectively). Three celt-like blades (Fig. 4, 5-7) are of greater interest.[7] They are too thin to have served any offensive purpose but similar objects are known from Lothal, Hansi and Rewari (Yule, 1985, Cat. Nos. 23, 540 and 547). Since no analysis of the metal could be carried out it is assumed that the blades were of copper or a copper alloy like the metalwork of Tombs 1 and 2. The largest blade, Fig. 4, 6; Fig. 14, 8, was rectangular with a slightly expanded thin curved cutting edge, a feature also present on the smallest blade, No. 9, which had a thickness of only 1 mm. The socketed spearhead, Fig. 4, 8; Fig. 14, 10, was similar to those from Tombs 1 and 2 (Donaldson, 1984, Fig. 14, 4; Fig. 28, 10) and elsewhere in the Oman peninsula (Cleuziou, 1981, Fig. 11, 288). The Shimal weapons are rather more triangular in shape than the spearheads from the Sar burial complex which appear to have a shorter socket (cf. Ibrahim, 1982, Pl. 55, 1-4, Fig. 47, 1-3; Mughal, 1983, Pl. LIII, 1-3, Fig. 26, 1-4).

Shell objects comprised a conical terminal bead, No. 11, similar to one in Tomb 2, three rings matched in Tombs 1 and 2 (Nos. 12-14), a cowrie pendant and several small shells used as beads in addition to a flat disc and smaller types of shell beads (Nos. 15-21). Time did not allow for a study of the 142 other beads, many of carnelian, sard and sardonys, with 28 in a light green stone, a few in agate, chalcedony and ?basalt, 21 in glass and 9 made of fired clay.

In concluding the list of stone objects it is necessary to refer again to the Indus weight whose dimensions are given below. Had it been found on its own among the Tomb 6 grave-goods it could have been regarded as a chance find prized for its appearance. Combined, however, with the Harappan jar, it assumes greater significance and suggests contact with that culture if not the actual burial of a Harappan resident in the area. The evidence provided by the Harappan objects, together with the swag-decorated pottery comparable to that in Isin-Larsa contexts on Bahrain, gives grounds for thinking that Tomb 6 was probably in use between 1900-1800 B.C. though for how long it continued to serve as a collective burial place cannot at present be estimated.

In conclusion, I would record my indebtedness to His Highness Sheikh Saqr bin Mohammad al-Qasimi, Ruler of Ras al-Khaimah, and to His Highness Sheikh Sultan bin Saqr al-Qasimi, Deputy Ruler and Director of Antiquities and the National Museum. Had His Highness the Ruler not invited me to visit the Emirate on other business I should have had no opportunity of studying the Tomb 6 grave-goods. Most of the material is now on display in the Archaeological Section of the National Museum of Ras al-Khaimah.

Notes

1. I am indebted to Mr. Donaldson for allowing me to publish the Tomb 6 grave-goods. In Ras al-Khaimah I would also record my sincere thanks to Mr. Jay Laxman, who drew the grave-goods in 1978, and to Mr. Ali Omar who has kindly provided the photographic illustrations, which are reproduced by courtesy of Ras al-Khaimah National Museum.

2. Mlle. Sophie Méry was studying the Shimal ceramics and I would thank her for pointing out that the fabric used for nos. 44, 45, 46, 47, 48 and 61 could be identified with Donaldson's Type G, and was the same as the ware in the settlement currently being excavated by the German team.

3. I am indebted to Professor W.M. Sumner for his views.

4. Information kindly provided by Mlle. Méry.

5. I am indebted to Mr. Flemming Højlund for his comments and for telling me that several spouted W. Suq vessels have recently been excavated in Bahrain.

6. Donaldson's field notes, not available when the catalogue was compiled, refer to the use on No. 3 of a ring cutting tool shaped to form a sloping cut leaving a central disc in *bas relief* instead of the more usual groove type ring. It has not been possible to check if the same holds good for Nos. 4 and 16.

7. Identification and reference kindly provided by Dr. P. Yule.

Bibliography

Calvet, Y. and Salles, J-F. (1986), *Failaka. Fouilles Françaises, 1984-1985.* Travaux de la Maison del 'Orient, No. 12, Lyon.

Cleuziou, S. (1980), 'The Second and Third Seasons of Excavations at Hili 8', *Archaeology in the United Arab Emirates*, vol.2-3, pp.30-69.

Cleuziou, S. (1981), 'Oman Peninsula in the Early 2nd Millennium B.C.', in H. Härtel, ed., *South Asian Archaeology 1979*, Berlin, Dietrich Reimer Verlag, pp.279-293.

de Cardi, B. (1971), 'Archaeological Survey in the Northern Trucial States', *East and West*, n.s. 21, pp.225-289.

de Cardi, B. (n.d.), 'Harappan finds from Tomb 6 at Shimal, Ras al-Khaimah, U.A.E.', *South Asian Archaeology 1985*, in press.

de Cardi, B., Bell, R.D., and Starling, N.J. (1979), 'Excavations at Tawi Silaim and Tawi Sa'id in the Sharqiya, 1978', *Journal of Oman Studies*, vol.5, pp.61-94.

Donaldson, P. (1984), 'Prehistoric tombs of Ras al-Khaimah', *Oriens Antiquus*, vol.23, pp.191-312.

Donaldson, P. (1985), 'Prehistoric tombs of Ras al-Khaimah' (continued), *Oriens Antiquus*, vol.24, pp.85-142.

Frifelt, K. (1975), 'On prehistoric settlement and chronology of the Oman Peninsula', *East and West*, n.s. 25, pp.259-424.

Frifelt, K. (1986), 'Burial Mounds near Ali excavated by the Danish Expedition', *Bahrain through the Ages*, pp.125-134.

Højlund, F. (1987), *Failaka/Dilmun. The Second Millennium Settlements. Vol.2. The Bronze Age Pottery.* Jutland Archaeological Society Publications XVII:2.

Ibrahim, M. (1982), *Excavations of the Arab Expedition at Sar el-Jisr, Bahrain*, State of Bahrain.

Mughal, R. (1983), *The Dilmun Burial Complex at Sar. The 1980-82 Excavations in Bahrain*, State of Bahrain.

Potts, D.T. (1983), 'Bārbār Miscellanies', in D.T. Potts, ed. *Dilmun. New studies in the archaeology and early history of Bahrain*, Berliner Beiträge zum Vorderen Orient, 2, pp.127-139.

Potts, D.T. (1985), 'Reflections on the history and archaeology of Bahrain', *Journal of the American Oriental Society*, vol. 105.4, pp.675-710.

Vogt, B. (1985), 'The Umm an Nar Tomb A at Hili North: a preliminary report on three seasons of excavation, 1982-1984', *Archaeology in the United Arab Emirates*, vol.4, pp.20-37.

Vogt, B. and Franke-Vogt, U. (1987), *Shimal 1985/1986. Excavations of the German Archaeological Mission in Ras Al-Khaimah, U.A.E. A Preliminary Report.* Berliner Beiträge zum Vorderen Orient, 8.

Weisgerber, G. (1981), 'Mehr als Kupfer in Oman – Ergebnisse der Expedition 1981', *Der Anschnitt*, vol.33, pp.174-263.

Yule, P. (1985), *Metalwork of the Bronze Age in India.* Prähistorische Bronzefunde 20, 8, Munich, Beck.

Catalogue

With only 3 exceptions all the pottery from Tomb 6 has been illustrated and bases are included in the Catalogue under their appropriate vessel types. All the grave-goods are in the National Museum of Ras al-Khaimah either on display or in the study collections. The following are abbreviations used as follows:–

Ext.	External: Int. Internal	S.	Shell
G.	Grey grits	V.	Vegetal tempering
SC.	String-cut	WI.	Small white inclusions

Pottery

Beakers (Figs. 5-6)

1 Sharply everted rim, diam. 11.50 cm. Thin walls curve towards uneven eroded base with spiralling grooves int. Hard red ware; large and WI. Cat. 23.38

2 Everted rim, diam. 11 cm. Slightly curved walls grooved on both surfaces above flat SC base, diam. 5.50 cm., with small knop. Medium hard sandy red ware, grey core; large and WI, V, pitted surface. Black/dark brown paint. Cat. 24.38

3 Everted tapering rim, diam. 11 cm., thin grooved walls trimmed above sagging base. Medium hard dense cream-buff ware; WI, V. Self-slipped. Brown painted band over rim is unusual, but cf. Tomb 1 (Donaldson, 1984, Fig. 3, 1). Cat. 24.1

4 Flaring rim, diam. 11.80 cm. Medium hard dense sandy red ware, grey core. WI, V. Concave SC base, diam. 5.20 cm. Cat. 22.29 a & b (Note: sherd bag also contained fragments of No. 20)

5 Everted rim, diam. 11 cm. Thin sinuous walls curve towards trimmed sagging base with slight knop int. Hard sandy red ware; WI. Black paint. Cat. 24.13

6 Tapering upright rim, diam. 8 cm. Upper part of walls grooved int., trimmed ext. above flattened base, diam. 3.80 cm., with pronounced knop. Dense sandy red ware; WI, V. Similar form but different base in Tomb 1 (Donaldson, 1984, Fig. 3, 3). Cat. 24.20

7 Thin tapering everted rim, diam. 11 cm., girth grooves int. Fine sandy pink-buff ware; WI. Black paint. Cf. Tomb 1 (Donaldson, 1984, Fig. 5, 32 and Fig. 3, 5). Cat. 23.32

8 Out-turned rim, diam. 11.30 cm., curving walls with girth grooves int., trimmed ext. above flattened base, diam. *c.* 5 cm., with knop int. Dense orange-red ware. Black paint. Cat. 22.32

9 Upright tapering rim, diam. 11.20 cm., walls curved and shaved; slightly SC base diam. 6.50 cm. Dense sandy orange-red ware. S. but few WI. Cat. 22.34

10 Slightly everted rim, diam. 11 cm. Trimmed and unevenly flattened base, diam. *c.* 7.50 cm. not truly concave. Medium hard brownish-red ware, grey core: WI, S, V. Self-slipped on both surfaces. Black paint. Cat. 22.33

11 Strongly everted rim, diam. 12 cm. Thin walls ridged int. and crudely trimmed below girth ext. The SC base, diam. 3 cm., uneven rather than concave. Dense sandy tan ware, grey core. Black paint. Cat. 24.6

12 Tapering rim, diam. 12 cm., straight-sided grooved walls, trimmed. Flattened base, diam. 4 cm. Dense sandy red ware; WI, V and mica specks. Dark brown paint. Cat. 23.36

13 Thin flaring rim, diam. 11.40 cm., straight walls trimmed above slightly concave SC base, diam. 6.20 cm., with knop int. Hard sandy red ware, grey core; many WI, S, V. Black paint. Cat. 23.37

14 Thin flaring rim, diam. 9 cm., straight walls trimmed near carination above slightly concave SC base, diam. 3.60 cm. Dense sandy red ware; WI, V and mica specks. Black paint. Cat. 22.38

15 Everted rim, diam. 9.80 cm. Girth grooves on upper part of body. Hard red ware, grey core; WI, S. ?Self-slipped. Black paint. Cat. 23.8

16 Tapering rim, diam. 11.60 cm. Trimmed above concave SC base, 5.50 cm., heavy for size of vessel. Hard sandy red ware; WI, G. Cat. 24.9

Fig. 5. Beakers from Tomb 6

17 Out-turned tapering rim, diam. 8.40 cm., sinuous sides, SC disc base, diam. 4.80 cm., with grooving and knop int. Medium hard sandy ware unevely fired; many large and WI, V. Black paint. Cat. 24.16

18 Slightly concave SC base, diam. 6 cm., thin upper walls thickening near base. Over-fired red ware, grey core; large G, WI, S, V. Cat. 23.22

19 Slightly concave SC base, diam. 6.10 cm., of thin-walled beaker. Medium hard brownish-red ware; WI, V. Cat. 24.15

20 Thin flaring rim, diam. 10 cm. medium hard fine dense tan ware with metallic ring when struck; WI, S, V and mica specks. Unusual in having black pendant lines over rim as well as dsign ext. Cat. 22.29

- Tapering rim, diam. 11.20 cm. Base trimmed and unevenly flattened rather than concave, diam. *c.* 7.50 cm. Medium hard brownish-red ware, laminating. Cream-slipped ext. Black paint. Cat. 24.39 (Unillus.)

- Slightly concave SC base, diam. 6.20 cm., trimmed below girth. Dense sandy tan-red ware, grey core; WI, V, and mica specks. Cat. 23.31. (Unillus. similar to No. 18)

Cups (Fig. 6)

21 Flared rim, diam. 7.30 cm., straight walls, grooved int., curve inwards to trimmed uneven sagging base. Medium hard dense red ware; G and mica specks. Brown painted geometric design above representation of a scorpion. Cat. 23.3

22 Everted rim, diam. 7 cm., carinated outline due to trimming above flattened base, diam. 3 cm. Medium hard dense sandy pink-buff ware with a few large white grits. Cream-buff slip on both surfaces. Brown paint. Cat. 24.5

23 Tapering rim, diam. 7 cm., sinuous sides and concave SC base, diam. 3.80 cm. Dense sandy red ware; WI. Black paint. Cat. 23.29

24 Everted rim, diam. 7 cm., slightly grooved int. Fine dense sandy tan-red ware, grey core; V and mica specks. Self-slipped on both surfaces. Black paint. Cat. 23.31a

25 Everted rim, diam. 6.30 cm., thick walls and uneven flattened base, diam. 2.30 cm. Hard sandy red ware: flaking. Black paint. Cat. 23.10

26 Everted tapering rim, diam. 7 cm., very thin walls. Powdery red ware, eroded. Black paint. Cat. 23.17a

27 Flattened base, diam. 2.50 cm. Orange-red ware, laminating. Self-slipped on both surfaces. Cat. 23.17b

28 Tapering everted rim, diam. 7 cm., grooved walls, trimmed above SC base with pronounced knop int. Medium hard pink ware; WI. Cream-slipped on both surfaces. Dark brown paint. Cf. base in Tomb 1 (Donaldson, 1984, fig. 5, 36). Cat. 23.21

29 Everted rim, diam. 8 cm., trimmed above sagging base. Thin dense cream ware; small black inclusions, V. Self-slipped. Traces of brown paint. Cat. 23.30

30 Flaring rim, diam. 6.30 cm., sinuous sides grooved int., flattened base, diam. 2.80 cm. Powdery tan-buff ware; WI, V. Self-slipped on both surfaces but eroded. Black paint. Cat. 23.24

31 Everted rim, diam. 8.50 cm. Medium hard dense sandy tan-red ware, grey core; large WI, G, V. Self-slipped on borth surfaces. Black paint. Cat. 24.10

32 Flat base, diam. 4 cm., minimal trimming. Medium hard fine dense cream-buff ware; WI, V. Cream-slipped on both surfaces. Cat. 24.18

33 Base, diam. 2.20 cm., scraped or SC. Soft dense sandy buff ware; WI, G, V. Cat. 24.12

34 Sharply everted rim, diam. 6 cm. Sandy buff ware; V.? Cream-slipped int. Black paint. Cat. 24.8

35 Flattened base, diam. *c.* 3.50 cm. Ware as No. 34. Cat. 24.8 (Note: 34 and 35 are probably two different vessels.)

36 Straight tapered rim, diam. 5.80 cm., thin walls curving to thick flat base, diam. 3.80 cm. (cup not available to describe ware). Cat. 23.5

37 Trimmed sides and base, diam. 3 cm. Soft tan-buff ware; WI, G, S and mica specks. Self-slipped on both surfaces. Cat. 22.35

38 Tapering rim, diam. 6.10 cm., trimmed ext. above small flattened base, diam. 2.30 cm. Dense reddish-buff ware, grey core: WI. Cf. Tomb 1 (Donaldson, 1984, Fig. 4, 11). Cat. 23.1

39 Slightly concave SC base, diam. 3.60 cm., carination above base. Hard red ware, eroded; WI. Cat. 23.27

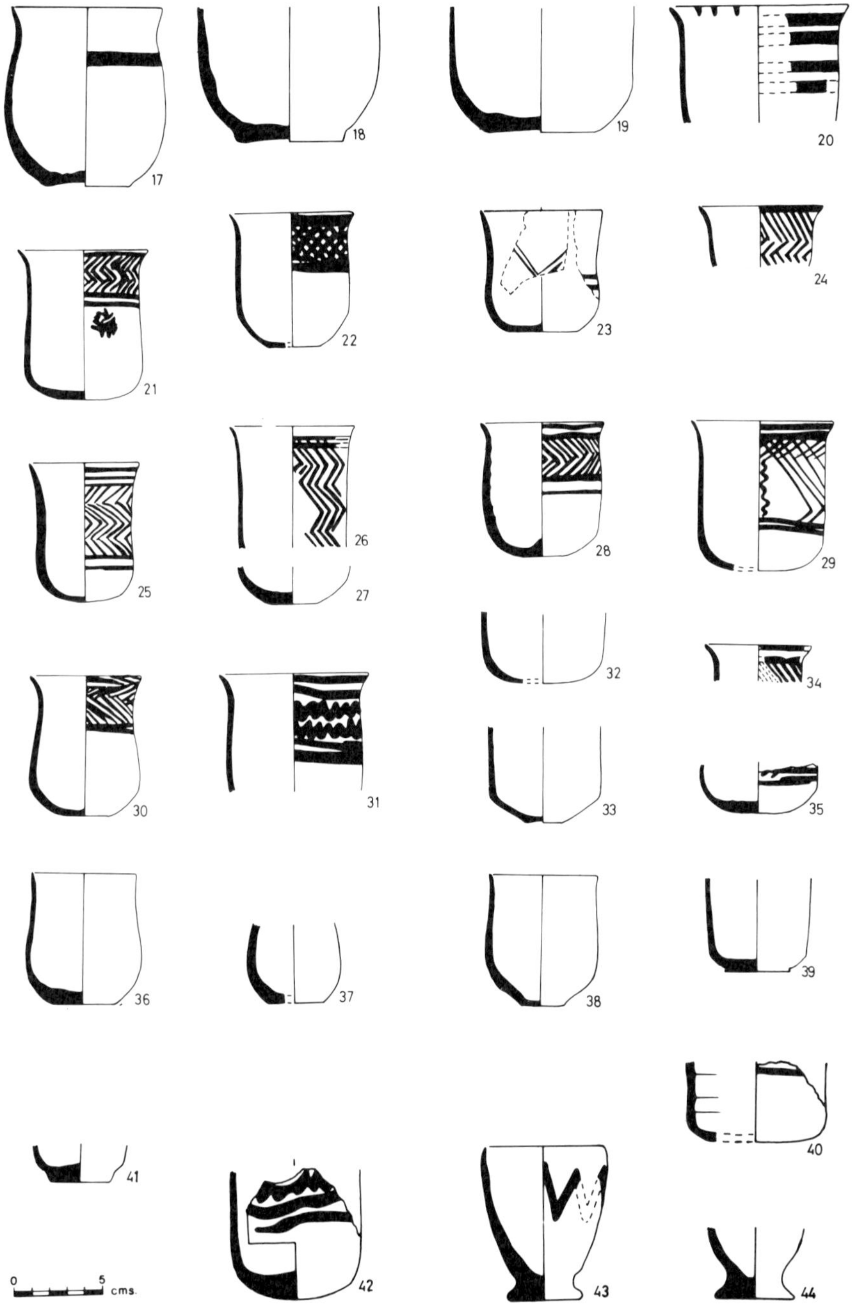

Fig. 6. Beakers, 17-20; cups, 21-42 and goblets, 43-44

40 Fragmentary flat base, diam. *c.* 6 cm., grooved int. of cup or bowl. Sandy red ware; mica specks. Black paint. Cf. Tomb 1 (Donaldson, 1984, Fig. 4, 12; and Fig. 5, 29). Cat. 23.14

41 SC base, diam. 3.30 cm., thin carinated walls. Overfired red ware, grey int.; WI. Cf. Ghalilah Tomb 2 (Donaldson, 1984, Fig. 21, 108). Cat. 23.26

42 Thick sagging base of thin-walled cup. Tan-buff ware; G, V and mica specks. Black paint. Cat. 24.14

43 Tapering rim, diam. 6.70 cm., uneven walls, flat splayed SC base, diam. 4 cm. Medium hard buff ware, grey core; large and small G and WI. Cream-buff slip on both surfaces. Reddish-brown paint. Cf. Ghalilah Tomb 2 (Donaldson, 1984, Fig. 22, 131). Cat. 22.36

44 Flat splayed SC base, diam. 4.50 cm. Soft orange ware; WI, G, V. Self-slipped ext. Cf. Tomb 2, as No. 43 above. Cat. 24.3

Flasks (Fig. 7)

45 Narrow-necked with flaring rim, diam. 6 cm., slight ridging on sloping shoulder. Powdery tan-buff ware, eroded; G and V. Self-slipped ext. Cf. Ghalilah Tomb 2 (Donaldson, 1984, Fig. 21, 63 and 67). Cat. 23.28

46 Thick-walled vessel with slightly concave SC base, diam. 4.50 cm., with central knop int. Tan-buff ware, grey core; WI, V. Self-slipped ext. Cat. 23.23

47 Narrow-necked with upright tapering rim, diam. 4 cm., sloping shoulder. Shape reminiscent of the commoner type of miniature pot, eg. Nos. 51-53. Sandy reddish-buff ware, eroded; G, black and WI, V. Cat. 23.25

48 Small flask with everted rim, diam. 4.50 cm. Sandy red ware; WI, G. Cat. 23.6

49 Everted rim, diam. 4 cm. Sandy tan-buff ware; large WI, smaller G. Traces of cream slip int. but eroded ext. Cat. 23.15

Miniature jars (Fig. 7)

50 Narrow everted rim, diam. 2.50 cm., sloping shoulder. Hand-made red ware, laminating. Surface partly covered by a deposit adhering to cream slip on both surfaces. Black paint. Cat. 23.13

51 Narrow inverted rim, diam. 2.20 cm., sloping shoulder, wide girth. handmade: sandy orange-red ware; WI, V and mica specks. Surfaces eroded. Cat. 24.4.

52 Worn rim, diam. 2.80 cm., wide girth trimmed above very thick uneven flat base, diam. *c.* 2.50 cm. Soft hand-made buff ware with mica specks. Cat. 23.2

53 Tapering rim, diam. 2.40 cm., wide girth and uneven flat base, diam. 3 cm. Fine sandy red ware; WI. Cat. 22.37.

54 Everted rim, diam. 3.20 cm., short neck and globular body with flattened base, diam. *c.* 1.70 cm. Hand-made red ware, grey core, laminating; WI. Traces of cream slip round neck and an incised line below rim ext., possibly an unintentional grit scratch. Cat. 23.9

Bowls (Fig. 7)

55 Thin everted rim, diam. 10 cm., trimmed walls, uneven flattened base. Medium hard sandy brownish-red ware; large and WI, V. Traces of creamy-buff slip over rim and ext. Too worn to say with certainty whether neck encircled by black/dark brown band. Cat. 23.4

56 Tapering rim, diam. 11.60 cm., mis-shapen grooved walls trimmed above flattened base, diam. 5 cm., with spiral grooves and slight knop int. Soft sandy red ware, laminating and eroded; S, V and mica specks. Black paint. Cat. 24.2

57 Globular vessel with small disc base, diam. 4.50 cm. Soft brownish-buff ware; WI, G and mica specks. Surfaces laminated and worn; traces of red slip. Black paint. Cat. 24.17

58 Biconical hole-mouth suspension-vessel, rim diam. 5.50 cm. Thin walls, 4 vertically pierced lugs around the girth, trimmed above flattened base, diam. *c.* 4 cm. Hard smooth red ware, grey core; WI. Black paint. Cat. 23.23.

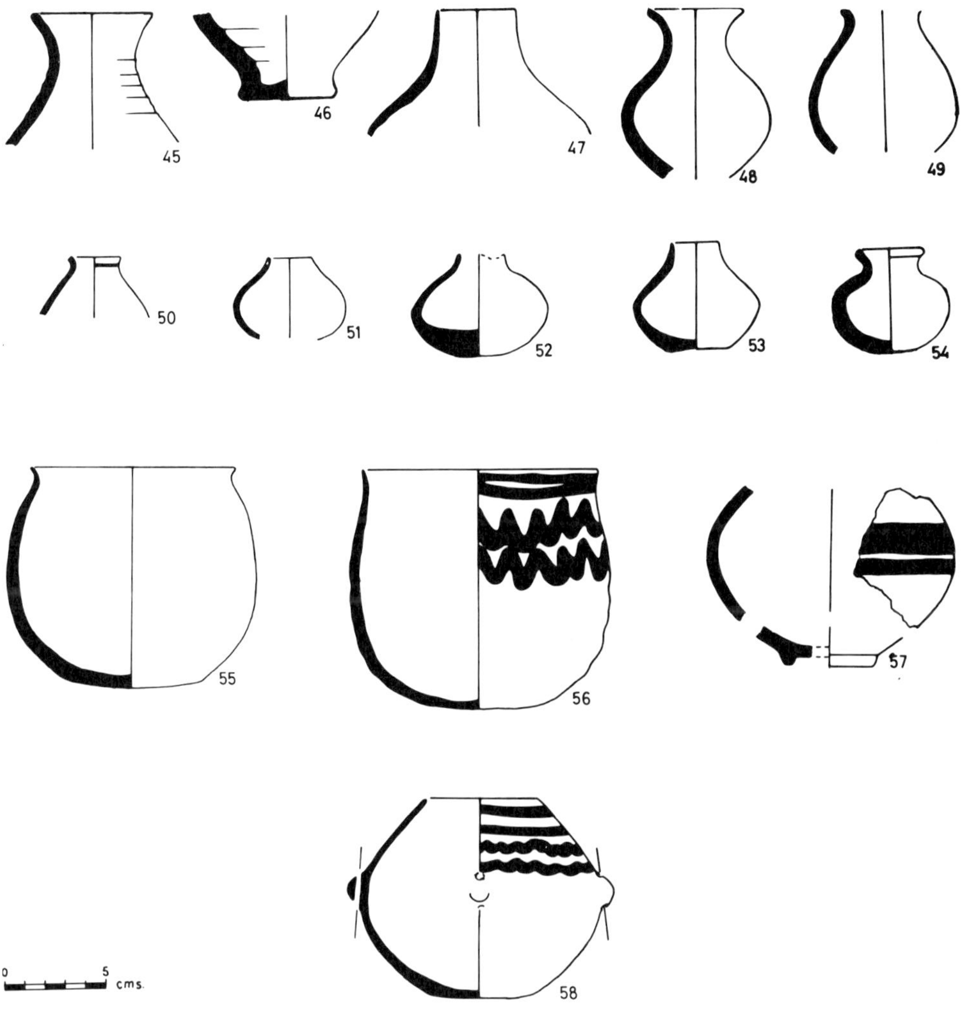

Fig. 7. Flasks, 45-49; miniature jars, 50-54; bowls and suspension vessel, 55-58

Beak-spouted jars: Type 1 (Figs. 8-9)

59 Squat vessel with rolled rim, diam. 9.50 cm., short upright neck. Narrow drooping spout raised above rim and joined to it by broad band. Wide irregular outlet below neck; shoulder strengthened. Flat base, diam. 11 cm. Medium hard dense sandy red ware, grey core, laminating. WI, S, V. Black paint. Cat. 23.34

60 Medium-sized jar with out-curved rim, diam. 9.40 cm., uneven thickness and raised spout. Rectangular expanded band on rim across edge of spout with small outlet through neck; luted to body, thickened int.; pinched ext. Jar shaved and flattened base, diam. 7 cm., scraped. Dense red ware, grey core. Large WI, S, V. Black paint. Cat. 22.30

61 Thin-walled jar with flat everted rim, diam. 10 cm. Spout springs from narrow outlet on shoulder and courves above rim-level. Flat base, diam. *c.* 5.50 cm., of irregular thickness. Thin medium hard dense tan-red ware. V but no inclusions. Red slip. Black paint. Same ware in Tomb 1 (Fabric Type G) and on Shimal settlement. Cat. 22.26

62 Thick-walled spherical jar with out-turned rim, diam. 7.50 cm., shaved and heavily scored below girth with unevenly flattened base, diam. 7.50 cm., grooved int. Slightly drooping spout attached to rim by broad band across edges giving angular shape when viewed from above. Spout narrowly triangular in section with small outlet reinforced below neck. Overfired dense sandy red ware, grey core. Large and WI, S. V. Black paint. Cat. 22.25

63 Everted rolled rim, diam. 8.50 cm., short neck and damaged spout raised above rim, the large outlet tilted upwards and opening from below neck to a point further down the body than the other jars. Spout luted ext. but broken at rim. Medium hard sandy overfired greyish-red ware; WI, G, V. Dark brown paint. Cat. 24.11

64 Medium-sized jar with rolled rim, diam. 11 cm., narrow rectangular down-curved spout with circular outlet just below neck. Medium hard thick sandy red ware. WI, S. V. Black paint. Cat. 23.8

65 Ovoid jar with inturned rim, diam. 8 cm. Raised spout narrowly rectangular with oval outlet below neck. Thickening of its juncture with rim curved, not straight; fabric puckered around base of luted spout ext. Unevenly thick shaved walls grooved near rounded base with spiral coils and central knop int. Medium hard dense sandy red ware, grey core. WI, S, V. Dark brown paint. Cat. 24.21

66 Wide globular jar with rim, diam. *c.* 8 cm., missing from above broken spout. Jar grooved int., lower walls shaved; sagging base uneven with slight knop int. Sandy red ware, grey core. WI, V. Black paint. Cat. 22.31

67 Small spherical vessel with bead rim, diam. 11.20 cm. Ovoid outlet below rim which lacks thickness of heavier jars. Spout curves down from rim-level; narrow rectangular trough rounded at juncture with top of rim. Walls shaved, base flattened, diam. *c.* 4 cm. Medium hard sandy red ware, grey core. WI, S, V. Black paint. Cat. 24.7

68 Expanded rim, diam. 11.20 cm., short vertical neck, narrow spout raised slightly above rim with oval outlet high on shoulder. Spout luted to body, thickened and pinched ext. Hard dense sandy red ware, grey core, laminating. V, mica specks and a small framgent of ?bronze but few WI. Black paint. Cat. 23.19

69 Flattened base, diam. 9.50 cm. Medium hard sandy brownish-red ware, grey core. WI, G, S, V. Cat. 23.7
Flattened base, diam. 9.50 cm., of large globular jar (unillus.); walls shaved to form a flattened SC base with coiled ridges int. Soft sandy brownish-tan ware. Large and WI, G, V. Cat. 22.27

Spouted jar, Type 2 (Fig. 9)

70 Broad globular jar with out-turned rolled rim, diam. 10.60 cm. Free-standing spout raised above rim-level with outlet through shoulder, thickened ext. Medium hard sandy red ware, grey core. Mica specks and V but few Wi. Black paint. Cat. 24.19

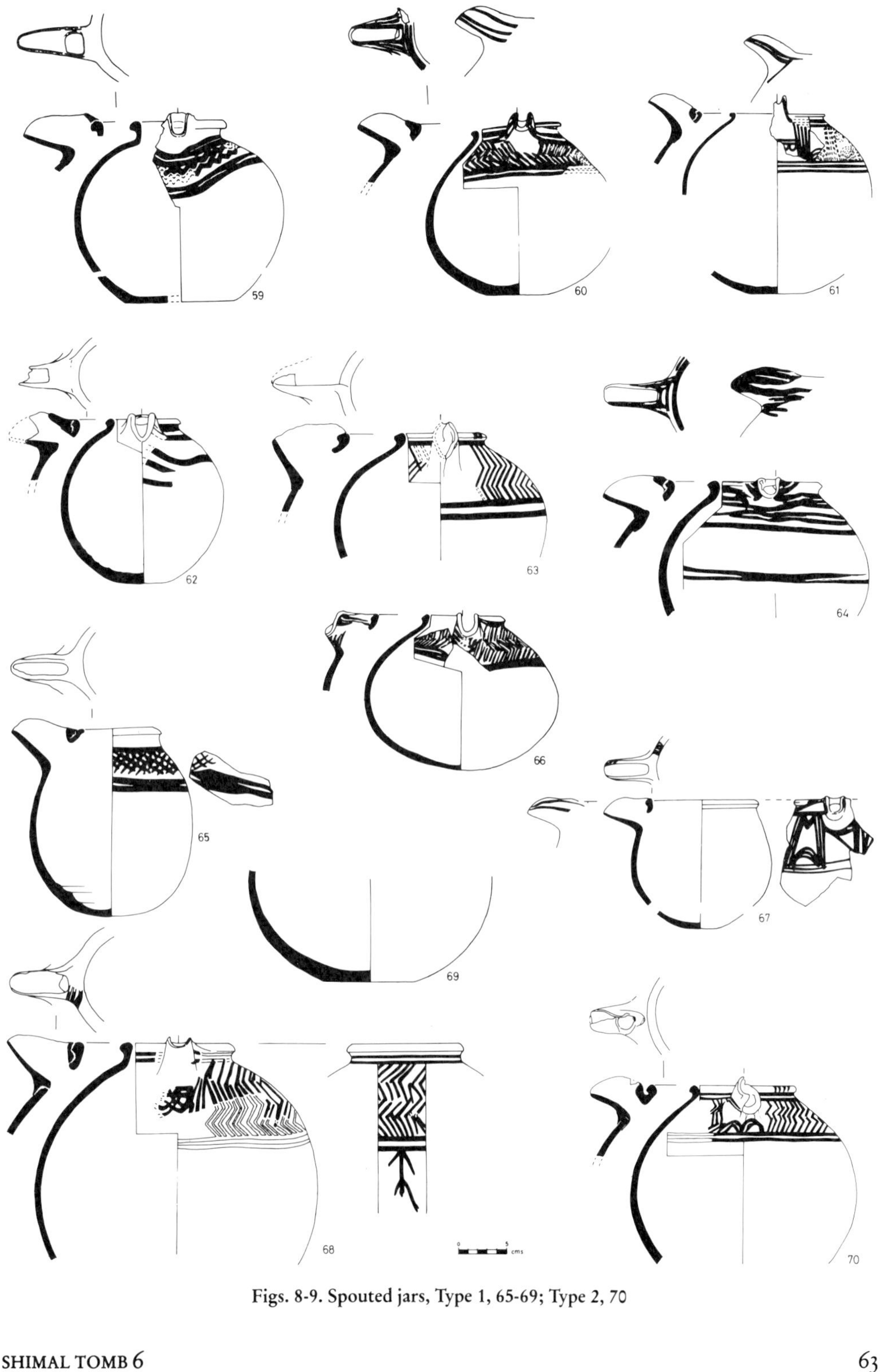

Figs. 8-9. Spouted jars, Type 1, 65-69; Type 2, 70

Spouted jar, Type 3 (Fig. 10)

71 Broad globular jar with out-rolled rim, diam. 10.50 cm. Short oval tubular shoulder spout raised slightly above rim-level; lower portion of jar shaved; flattened base, diam. 12.40. Sandy red ware, laminating. WI, S, V. Black paint. Cat. 23.16

Harappan jar (Fig. 11)

High-necked globular jar with externally squared rim, diam. 8.50 cm. Scored ext. below girth but not shaved. Flat base with spiral marks int. medium hard wheel-made orange-red ware, laminating; mica specks and grey core. Thinly self-slipped and partially covered by whitish deposit. Decorated with black or dark brown bands on outside of rim and five zones of horizontal multiple lines of varying thickness round the neck, shoulder and body. Exact height uncertain owing to two breaks. Cat. 22.28

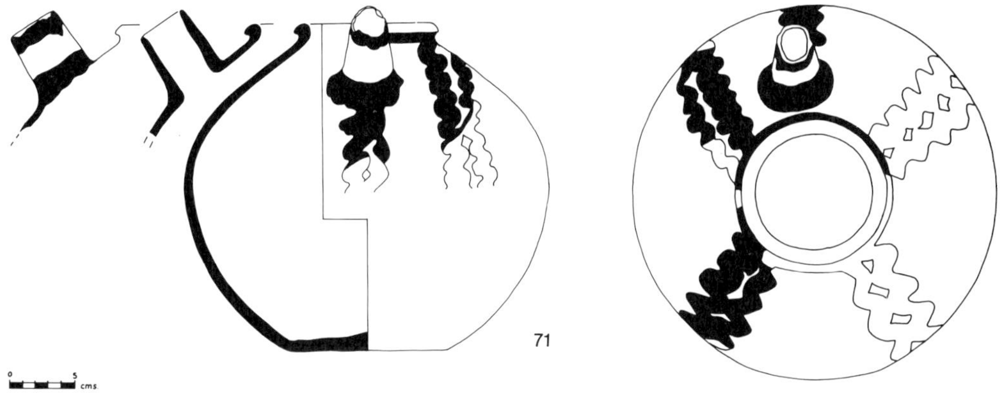

Fig. 10. Spouted jar, Type 3

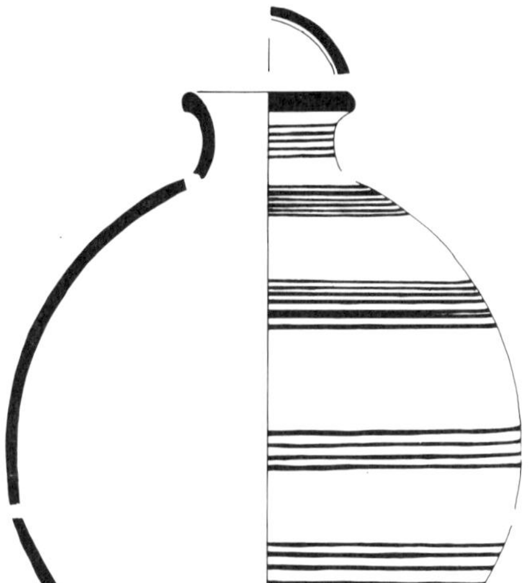

Fig. 11. Harappan jar from Tomb 6

Incised stone vessels (Fig. 12)

Bowls

Decoration: dot and ring with horizontal lines above and below and opposed diagonals on lower part of the body

1 Shallow bowl,.rim diam. 11.20 cm. Greenish-grey with reflective flakes. Cat. 22.4

2 Shallow bowl with rim diam. 9.80 cm., flat uneven base. Light grey with white veining; fine but irregular tooling on both surfaces. Uneven rim slashing. Cat. 21.36

3 Small bowl with rounded base. Greenish-grey. Finely tooled on both surfaces; polished. Fine regular slashing on rim, diam. 6.70 cm. Cat. 21.37

Lugged jars

4 Jar with incurved rim, diam. 4.80. Four vestigial unperforated lugs. Greenish-grey similar to Nos. 3 and 16. Fine tooling inside rim and over body. Polished. Dot and ring with mulitple horizontal lines above diagonals between lugs. Cat. 21.38

5 Jar with incurved rim, diam. 6 cm. Four vestigial unperforated lugs (base damaged). Pale grey-green with reflective flakes. Dot and ring with horizontal lines above opposed diagonals set between lugs. Design crudely incised. Cat. 22.1

6 Jar with incurved rim, diam. 6.60 cm., sagging base; three vestigial unperforated lugs. Brownish-grey. Vertical tool-mars. Polished ext. Two rows of dot and double ring; opposed diagonals in lower zone. Cat. 22.3

7 Jar with thick rim, diam. 6.50 cm., uneven base; four vertically pierced lugs. Grey with reflective flakes. Vertically tooled int., polished ext. Two rows of dot and ring with single horizontal lines above and below and two registers of alternating upper and lower vertical linear decoration. Lid 19 fits. Cat. 22.2

8 Rim, diam. 4 cm., of rhombic vessel. Brownish-grey. Vertical tooling. Cat. 23.11

9 Heavy vessel with incurved rim, diam. 8.30 cm., four vertically pierced lugs (missing and damaged). Pale olive grey. Diagonal and vertical tooling int. Four rows of dot and ring with horizontal lines above and below; opposed diagonals between lugs and horizontal lines below. Cat. 22.5

10 Rhombic vessel, rim diam. 10 cm., base missing. Pale grey with reflective flakes. Tooling ext. and vertically int. Two bands of dot and ring between horizontal lines with multiple lines on lower part of body. Cat. 24.23

Lids: all with flat rebated bases except No. 15

Decoration: dot and double ring

11 Olive greenish-grey; eroded, rough texture. Medium high expanded knob, faint horizontal lines and triple dot in double ring on top. Cat. 21.34

Decoration: dot and ring

12 Greenish-grey, eroded, with reflective flakes; polished base. High knob with fine diagonal incising; quadruple dot and ring motif on top. Cat. 21.33

13 Blue-grey with reflective flakes. High knob with multiple horizontal lines; 'tree' motif on top. Cat. 21.26

14 Pale grey-green with reflective flakes, fragmentary. Short knob with horizontal lines, top broken. Cat. 21.32

15 Dark brown, eroded. High expanded knob with linear quartering and four dot and ring on top. Concave rebated base. Cf. Ghalilah Tomb 4 (Donaldson, 1985, Fig. 2, 2, p. 87); Sar burial (Mughal, 1983, Fig. 25, 7) and Hili North Tomb A (Vogt, 1985, Pl. 27, 24).

Fig. 12. Soft stone bowls, vases and lids

Decoration: dot and ring with edge slashing (Fig. 13)

16 Greenish-grey; very finely tooled. Medium high expanded knob with fine incising radiating from large dot and ring on top. Lid possibly made in same workshop as Nos. 3 and 4. Cat. 21.28

17 Pale grey with reflective flakes. Large lid with medium high knob, multiple horizontal lines and 'tree' motif on top. Well-cut base. Cat. 21.35

18 Blue-grey with reflective flakes; finely tooled. High cylindrical knob with chevrony incising and 'tree' motif on top. Cat. 21.27

19 Blue-grey with reflective flakes, polished. High knob with multiple lines and triple incisions on top. Cat. 21.30

20 Greenish-grey; fragmentary. Cat. 23.12

21 Olive-grey; fine tooling; polished. Small knob with incised horizontal lines; ?damaged. Cat. 21.31

22 Greenish-grey; upper surface polished, laminating below. Horizontal lines around knob, damaged. Cat. 24.22

23 Blackish-grey with reflective flakes, polished. High knob with multiple lines and 'tree' motif on top. Cat. 21.25

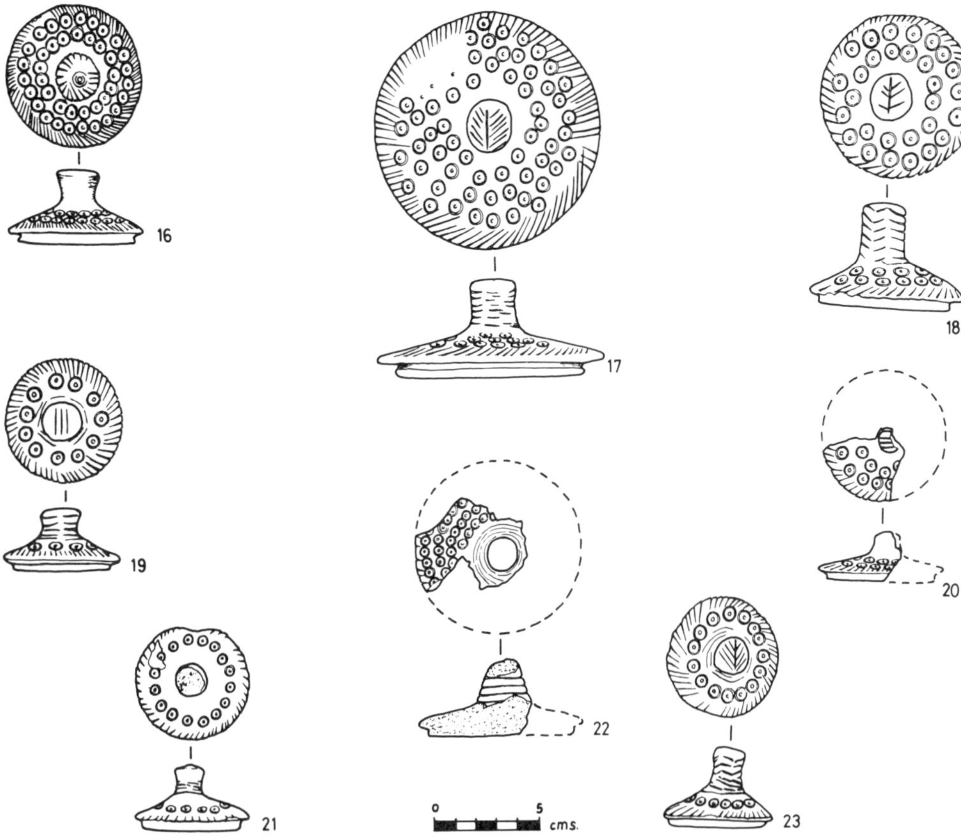

Fig. 13. Soft stone edge-slashed lids

Small finds (Fig. 14)

1-4 Four bronze rivets, three of square section, one rectangular. Cat. 22.7-10

5-6 Two bronze ear or nose-rings, tapered ends. No. 5, round section, No. 6, oval. Cat. 22.11-12

7 Fragment of a rectangular bronze blade, width 3.60 cm., thickness, 0.01 cm. Cat. 22.14

8 Thin rectangular bronze blade, width at base, 4.70 cm., expanded along cutting edge, 5.50 cm., length, 7.20 cm., thickness 0.02 cm. Cat. 22.15

9 Thin rectangular bronze blade, width at base, 2.50 cm., at cutting edge, 3 cm., length, 4.20 cm., thickness, 0.01 cm. Cat. 22.13

10 Spearhead, socketed, central rib, integral rolled socket. Length, 13.70 cm., max. width of blade, 2.70 cm., max. diam, of socket, 1.80 cm. Cat. 22.6

11 Shell terminal, hollow conical, cream coloured, polished. Cf. Ghalilah Tomb 2 (Donaldson, 1984, Fig. 29, 76-77). Cat. 22.16b

12-14 Three shell rings, one cream coloured with polished edges; one fragmentary with smoothed edges; one flaking. Cf. Tombs 1 and 2 (Donaldson, 1984, Figs. 13, 26-27, and 29, 79 respectively). Cat. 22.18

15-18 Cowrie shell pendant and three small shells. Cat. 22.17

19 Perforated shell disc. Cat. 22.16a

20-21 Shell beads. Cf. Tomb 2 (Donaldson, 1984, Fig. 29, 80). Cat. 22.16a

22 Cubical weight of Indus type, cream and buff banded chert. The surfaces of the cube are slightly convex leaving the edge, as opposed to the central axis measurements, approx. 0.05 cm. shorter all round, the max. dimensions being 2.20 - 2.25 cm. Weight 26.300 gr. Cat. 22.20

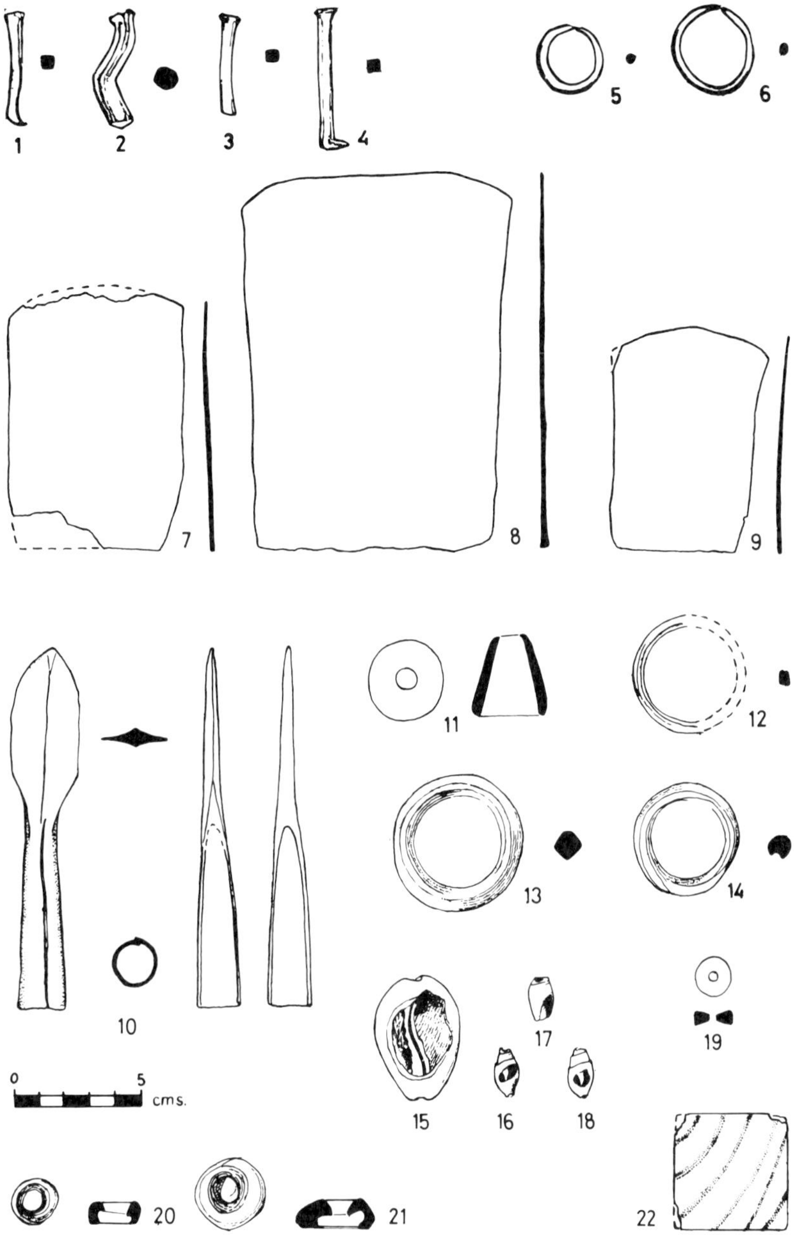

Fig. 14. Small finds from Tomb 6

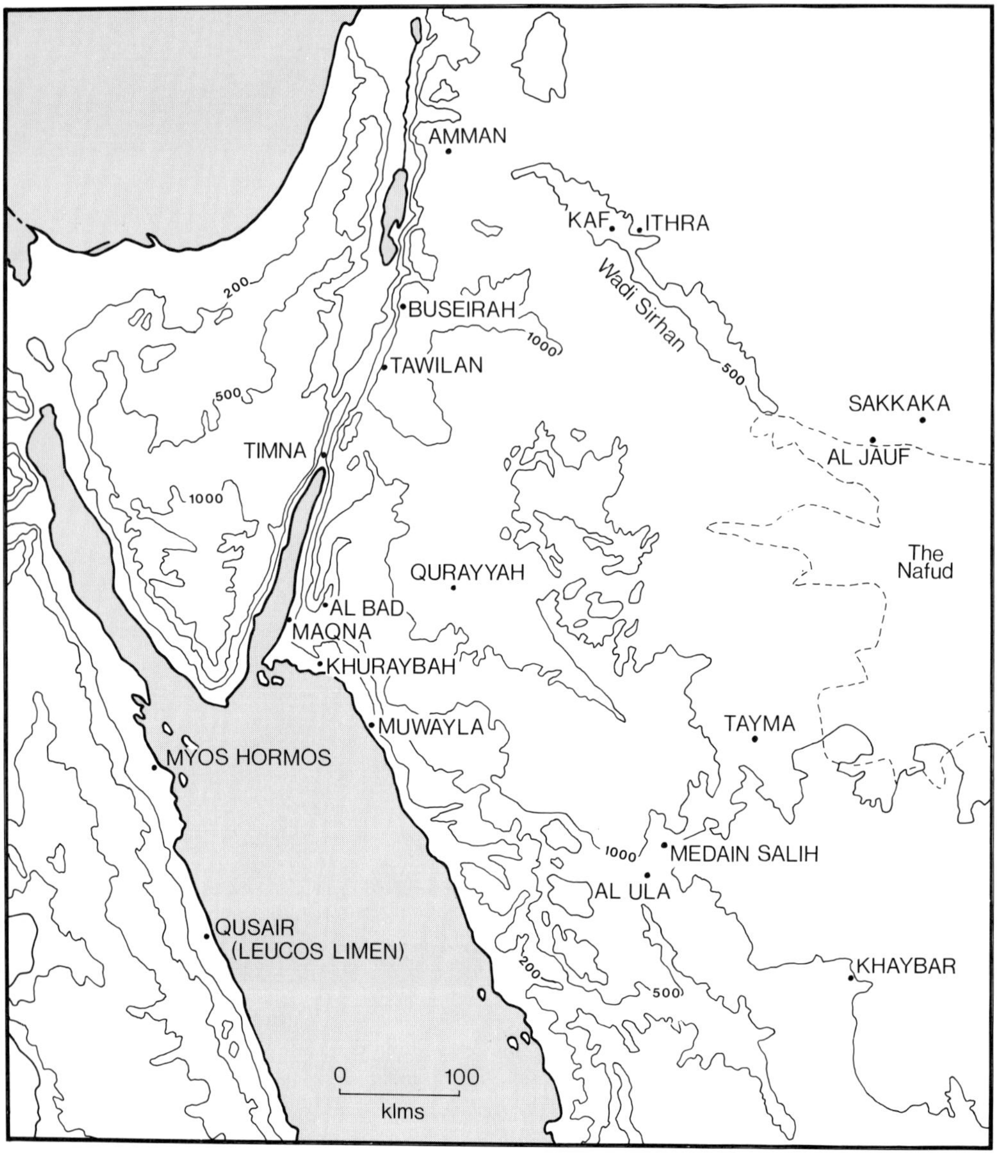
AMMAN
KAF
ITHRA
Wadi Sirhan
BUSEIRAH
1000
TAWILAN
200
500
SAKKAKA
AL JAUF
TIMNA
1000
The Nafud
QURAYYAH
AL BAD
MAQNA
KHURAYBAH
MUWAYLA
TAYMA
MYOS HORMOS
MEDAIN SALIH
AL ULA
QUSAIR
(LEUCOS LIMEN)
KHAYBAR
0
100
klms

Pottery of the Late Second Millennium B.C. from North West Arabia and its Historical Implications

BY PETER J. PARR

It is now almost twenty years since a distinctive painted pottery – characterized by a generally light fabric, a thick slip, and decoration often, though not invariably, in two or more tones on a paler surface – which was then being found at sites in Northwest Arabia and in the Wadi Arabah, was dated to the late 2nd millennium B.C. and called 'Midianite'.[1] Both date and appellation have since been criticised more than once. In 1977, in a discussion at a colloquium in Jerusalem on Temples and High Places, Professor F.M. Cross quoted James Sauer, one of the most highly regarded specialists in Palestinian pottery, as having 'extreme doubts as to whether or not the so-called Midianite ware can be regarded as early as the Late Bronze Age'.[2]

Three years later, in the Tyndale Biblical Archaeology Lecture delivered in Cambridge,[3] John Bimson argued on the basis of evidence from the Wadi Arabah sites that there was a strong possibility that the pottery in question was still in use in the 7th and even the 6th century B.C. More recently still, Professor James Muhly, in a review article devoted to Rothenberg's work at Timna, has written that 'past claims made for the Late Bronze Age, even Aegean, antecedents of this so-called Midianite pottery ... can now be largely, if not entirely, discounted. No Mycenaean pottery has yet been found in Arabia and the suggested stylistic parallels between Mycenaean and Midianite wares cannot withstand close scrutiny'.[4] In a paper delivered at the First International Conference on the History and Archaeology of Jordan, held at Oxford in 1980,[5] the present author conceded that it had perhaps been unwise to term this category of pottery 'Midianite', given the obvious dangers of equating pottery styles with ethnic groups. The term was, in fact, originally intended to be more geographic than ethnic, but it was certainly based on the assumption, generally accepted by biblical scholars, that during the late 2nd millennium the territory east of the Gulf of Aqaba – where the pottery seemed to originate – had been the homeland of the biblical Midianites, whose name survived there into the Islamic period.[6] Recently the view has been argued by Elizabeth Payne that the association of the Midianites with Northwest Arabia begins at a later time, and that in the period of Israel's emergence in Palestine they occupied a wider arc of territory surrounding the northern portion of the lands held by the Canaanites, being found amongst groups living in the Negev, Edom, Moab, the east bank of the Jordan, and even as far north as the hills of Galilee.[7] The argument is not entirely convincing and the present writer prefers the more conventional view. But if there is any doubt, then the painted pottery, which is certainly not found over all of this extended 'Midianite arc', should perhaps not be given an ethnic designation, even though there are well-attested instances where pots can be, and are, equated with peoples, as in the case of the Nabataeans.[8] However, to avoid possible misunderstandings an alternative to 'Midianite ware' should be found. Knauf's suggestion of 'Hejaz Ware'[9] is quite unsuitable and indeed confuses the issue, since it ignores the fact that there are several distinctive ceramic types now recognised in the Hejaz, between which it is vitally important to differentiate, as we have shown elsewhere and will discuss further below. If the term 'Midianite' is to be abandoned then the only alternative is to use a site designation. There are dangers in this as well; terms such as 'Halaf ware' and 'Khirbet Kerak ware' are as loaded with unwarranted overtones of historical interpretation as are ethnic designations. Nevertheless, since all the available evidence points to the fact that much, if not all, of the painted pottery in question was manufactured at the site of Qurayya,[10] the term 'Qurayya painted ware' is now proposed for this distinctive ceramic type, and will be used henceforth in this paper.

Whatever concessions may be made over terminology, there can be none over date. On both stylistic and stratigraphic grounds the evidence is unassailable. The stylistic parallels to the Qurayya painted ware first adduced in 1970 by the author,[11] and developed by J.E. Dayton two years later,[12] are as convincing in general terms today as they were then. Professor Muhly's scepticism is, frankly, astonishing. It is true that, *pace* Dayton, no Mycenaean sherds have been found in Arabia, and it is also obvious that decorative analogies between Aegean and Qurayya ware cannot necessarily be taken to imply direct contact. But the ultimate Aegean inspiration for many of the Qurayya motifs – for example, the running spirals, chevrons and lozenges – surely cannot be doubted, while the birds on some of the vessels have a good eastern Mediterranean ancestry. Recently published material has not only strengthened these general conclusions but has served to support the suggestion, made by the writer at the Jordanian Conference in 1980, that a more immediate source of inspiration for the Qurayya style might be found in Late Bronze Age Egyptian faience vessels.[13] Two sherds of Qurayya ware from Tayma, published by Bawden in *Atlal* 4 (1980) plate 63, nos. 5 and 19, have stylised lotus patterns, very reminiscent of those on faience bowls from Timna.[14] In the light of the closeness of these Aegean and Egyptian Late Bronze Age parallels, it seems to the writer little other than perverse to look elsewhere for comparative material for the Qurayya pottery. For example, the view expressed a number of times verbally, if not in writing, that the Qurayya pottery is medieval, can be dismissed out of hand; enough is known of Islamic pottery in both the Levant and in Arabia to show that there are no analogies. Only in Eastern Arabia is there a painted pottery tradition in the 2nd and 1st millennia B.C. which has decorative features somewhat in common with the Qurayya ware,[15] but the parallels are by no means close or specific, there are no intermediate sites, and a cultural connection between Northwestern and Eastern Arabia at this period seems far less likely than that with the eastern Mediteranean world we have suggested.

Turning now to the stratigraphic evidence for the dating of Qurayya ware, this also seems as conclusive as it was, at least as regards its initial appearance in the 13th-12th centuries B.C., and little need be added to previous discussions.[16] However, in their separate reviews of the history of metallurgy in the Wadi Arabah, both Bimson and Muhly have rightly drawn attention to the unsatisfactory nature of the evidence relating to the end of the pottery's period of use, thereby throwing doubt on its value as an indicator solely of 2nd millennium, as distinct from 1st millennium, settlement. It is true that there is ambiguity over this matter, already discussed by the present author[17], but it is also true that wherever Qurayya painted pottery has been found in secure stratigraphic contexts these all date to the final centuries of the 2nd millenium and not to the 1st. Bimson's argument in favour of a later date derives largely from his somewhat uncritical acceptance of the evidence from Tell el-Kheleifeh, where Nelson Glueck reported the presence of painted sherds of Qurayya type in Level IV, together with clear 7th-6th century material.[18] The data from Kheleifeh are suspect, however, as is well known; the recent re-working of the excavation records by Practico[19] has not only shown how utterly unreliable Glueck's methods and conclusions were but, more pertinently, has indicated that very few sherds of Qurayya style were in fact found (or at least recorded), and these from very doubtful contexts. Even if Glueck did find a little pottery of this type in his Level IV (whatever that means in terms of stratigraphy and architecture) there is nothing to prove that it was not derived from an earlier phase, brought up out of context by the constant building activities to which the site was subjected. These few Qurayya painted sherds at Kheleifeh may well have originated in the earliest attested structural phase there, that of the casemate fortress, the date of which is disputed but which may be of the 11th century – a date compatible with that of the pottery on other grounds[20]. Almost equally plausibly, the sherds could have come from an even earlier phase of less substantial, and therefore unrecognised, occupation, perhaps relating to the Ezion Geber (if, indeed, Tell el-Kheleifeh is to be identified with that site) mentioned in the Exodus narratives. With so many uncertainties it is surely best to ignore this excavation in any discussion of the chronology of the Qurayya painted ware.

The site of Timna, which Bimson and Muhly also discuss, is a different matter, however, since it is the association here of the Qurayya painted pottery with inscribed objects of the 19th and 20th dynasties which has hitherto provided the best evidence for dating the ware. The association has never been doubted and seems certain enough; but Bimson has sought to show that the radiocarbon determinations published from various parts of the mining complex and temple suggest that activities continued at the site later than Rothenberg allows, well into the 1st millennium and perhaps as late as the 6th century B.C.[21] However, if Timna had been occupied as late as this the absence of the very distinctive 8th-6th century pottery of the region – 'Edomite' painted and dentiled ware, 'Assyrian' bowls, perforated cups, etc. – would be very hard to explain, especially in view of the prolixity of these types at Kheleifeh, less than 30 kms. away. In any case, Muhly has drawn attention both to inaccuracies in some of the published C^{14} dates and to inconsistencies in Bimson's use of them, and, after a more rigorous study, has reached the eminently reasonable conclusion that 'given the vagaries of radiocarbon dating and the problems of the contamination of samples at a metallurgical site, these dates present quite a good sequence in support of a Ramesside dating for the main period of copper mining and copper smelting activity at Timna'[22]. He also admits (against Bimson but with Rothenberg) that 'there does seem to be a genuine hiatus in the occupation of the Wadi Arabah in the early centuries of the first millennium B.C.'[23] It is therefore somewhat surprising to find him also arguing that 'at Tayma, and perhaps also at Tell el-Kheleifeh and even Tawilan, Midianite pottery seems to appear in an Iron Age II context dated no earlier than the eighth century B.C.'[24] We have already seen that Kheleifeh can be ignored in this connection, while the single sherd from Tawilan was unstratified.[25] There remains Tayma, in North West Arabia, and since Muhly relies heavily on recent work at this site for his chronology, it is to there that we must now turn.

In 1979 a survey, accompanied by some very limited excavation, was carried out at Tayma by a team headed by Garth Bawden on behalf of the Department of Antiquities and Museums of the Saudi Arabian government. The preliminary results have been published in *Atlal* 4 (1980) 69-106, with a supplementary note on the radiocarbon dating in *Atlal* 5 (1981) 149-153, while a summary, together with a more general review of the painted pottery of N.W. Arabia, was given by Bawden at a colloquium held in London in 1981.[27] In this latter paper Bawden accepts the distinction (first made by the present writer at the Oxford Conference) between the Qurayya painted ware (which he characterises as 'polychrome') and another, different but possibly related, painted ware (called 'bichrome' by Bawden), better known from its prolific occurence at the ruins (Khuraybah) of ancient Dedan near modern al-'Ula, and he seems to accept a Late Bronze Age date for at least some of the Qurayya ware.[27] However, as he perceptively remarks, the 'actual formal and chronological boundaries of the Midianite [Qurayya] wares remain somewhat undefined'. On the basis of his work at Tayma and of the known history of the site from textual sources he finally concludes that, at Tayma at least, painted pottery of one sort or another was in more or less continuous use from the end af the 2nd millennium until at least the middle of the 1st, thus covering the Iron Age I and II periods, in Palestinian terminology, as well as part of the Late Bronze Age.[28] It is presumably largely because of this statement that Muhly believes that 'Midianite' pottery appears in Iron Age II contexts.

The present writer has, on a previous occasion, already discussed the relationship between the Qurayya and al-'Ula painted wares, and between the al-'Ula ware and the painted Edomite ware found in southern Jordan, the latter being now securely dated to between the 8th and 6th centuries B.C. as a result of the excavations of Crystal Bennett at Tawilan and Buseirah.[29] One of several possibilities adumbrated there was that, although the al-'Ula painted ware might well be as early as the 7th or even 8th century on the basis of its analogies with the Edomite pottery, there still appeared to be too long a gap between this date and that of the Late Bronze Age Qurayya ware to substantiate the view that there was a direct connection between these two pottery styles, despite the obvious formal parallels. Dr. Bawden's evidence from Tayma, as summarised by him in the colloquium paper cited above, might be thought to resolve this chronological problem, but before accepting his conclusions it will be wise to consider carefully the data published in his preliminary report.[30]

The excavated pottery from Tayma on which Bawden's conclusion is based comes from three distinct provenances: (i) the upper part of the debris piled against the wall of Compound C, at the western foot of the mound which is probably the site of the original town; (ii) the occupation levels associated with a small cult installation at Qasr al-Hamra, at the N.W. corner of the site; and (iii) the cairn field and long-chambered tombs just outside the north city wall. It should be noted that these three provenances are widely separated in space, Qasr al-Hamra being some 3 kms. from Compound C, while the cairn field stretches for at least 7 kms. south of the town (though the exact location of the cairns and tombs excavated is not given).

The pottery from Tayma is divided by Bawden into three distinct 'Typologies' (I-III) which, by a most extraordinary and hardly comprehensible piece of archaeological methodology, are defined, not by the nature of the material itself, but by the three distinct areas from which it comes. Thus Typology I is the material from the dump against the Compound C wall; Typology II is from the Qasr-al Hamra soundings; and Typology III seems to be both excavated and surface material from the cairns and chambered tombs. The logic of this procedure entirely escapes the present writer, and he fails to see how Bawden can assume that each of the three *corpora* of pottery from three distinct provenances can be 'relatively homogenous' and can 'provide the basis for three formally and ... chronologically distinct typologies.'[31] Rothenberg has already noted that Bawden's 'Typology I' is by no means homogeneous, and that 'Bawden et al. seem to date their pottery groups by historical considerations rather than by straightforward archaeological evidence'.[22] But the critique of Bawden's work needs to be taken further.

In the case of Typology I, it must surely be recognised that material taken from a 'fairly substantial dump located in the upper part of the debris piled up against the outer compound wall of Compound C' cannot be 'treated as a roughly contemporaneous assemblage and as representative of a chronologically confined ceramic tradition,'[33] and that it has as little evidential value for defining the 'actual formal and chronological boundaries' of the varieties of painted pottery from Tayma as has a surface collection. Similarly, with regard to Typology III, material from burial structures of several types and different locations can hardly be treated as homogenous. The vessels and sherds published from both of these provenances show in fact, as is to be expected, a mixture of ceramic and decorative types, including both the Qurayya ('polychrome') and al-'Ula ('bichrome') styles. Nor can any of this material, on the evidence presented, be securely related to any stage in the history of Tayma as known from the textual sources. By any acceptable archaeological methodology and reasoning only the corpus of Typology II, from the Qasr al-Hamra sounding, can be accorded any chronological value.

The discoveries at Qasr al-Hamra were indeed remarkable. They comprised a small shrine, apparently built into the corner of a larger building, consisting of a narrow room with two adjacent stone-paved platforms. Various cult objects were uncovered, including a stone cube, decorated with a low relief of elaborate iconography, and a damaged inscribed stone stela, the latter lying face down across the perimeter wall of one of the platforms and clearly not in its original position.[34] A detailed study of the iconography of the cube led Bawden to assign it to the mid-6th century B.C., when Nabonidus resided at Tayma, and to assume that the installation was a Neo-Babylonian shrine.[35] He further draws attention to similar reliefs on the broken stela and dates this to the same period, quoting a personal communication of the epigraphist Jacques

Ryckmans in support of this. However, in a more definitive publication of the stela, Livingstone states that on epigraphic grounds it 'should be dated to the same period as the Louvre stela [the well-known Tayma Stone], which specialists in Aramaic script have dated to the end of the 5th century B.C. or the beginning of the 4th century B.C. (Naveh) or to the middle of the 5th century B.C. (Gibson).'[36] Livingstone does not, it is true, mention that Assyriologists have tended to place the Louvre stela somewhat earlier on iconographic grounds, dating it also to the time of Nabonidus. As against this, however, Winnett has pointed out that the reference in line 1 of the Louvre stela to 'the 22nd year [of the king]' precludes such a date; Nabonidus only reigned for seventeen years (556-539 B.C.). 'To get a monarch who reigned twenty two years we have to go back to Nebuchadrezzar (604-562 B.C.) or forward to Darius I (522-486 B.C.).'[37] It must be concluded that the dating of all three objects, the Louvre stela, the newly discovered stela, and the carved stone cube, remains uncertain.

A further point needs to be made. Whatever the original date of the new stela, it was in any case not found in its original position, and, moreover, had apparently been damaged prior to its having fallen, since no mention is made by the excavators of the missing fragments having been found nearby, as they would have been had the stone broken in falling. A short Thammudic text, presumably a later addition, had been inscribed on one edge of the stela, though whether on a broken edge or not is not reported.[38] In short, it seems to have had a long history before it ended up in the position in which it was found, and it therefore provides no secure evidence for dating the surface on which it lay, and from which the pottery (which is our main concern) was recovered. Neither are the two radiocarbon determinations published by Bawden particularly helpful.[39] One (GX 7103), from carbonised wood not precisely associated stratigraphically with the structures, has a range of 345-65 B.C. (uncalibrated) at one standard deviation (2155 ± 140 b.p.), while the second (GX 7101), from carbonised bone on the floor of one of the platforms and directly associated with the cultic activities, ranges from 670-410 B.C. (2490 ± 130 b.p.). Since it is from this latter context that the bulk of Bawden's 'Typology II' pottery comes, this date is potentially of some importance, but the large standard deviation renders it of little real use for our present purposes. Calibration of GX 7101, either by the MASCA tables (790-420 B.C. at one standard deviation) or by the more rigorous computations of Klein et al.[40] (875-270 B.C. with 95% certainty), hardly helps. In view of these uncertainties, to refer to the shrine as Neo-Babylonian is no more than an assumption; it could be earlier or later, and in any case it almost certainly had a fairly long life.

Let us now look at the pottery from the shrine, Bawden's 'Typology II'.

This appears to come mostly from a deposit associated with a late use of the cultic installation,[41] though precise loci are not given in the report. The important fact is that in the actual account of the discoveries in the area of the shrine no painted pottery is reported: 'ceramic remains consisted of fragments of rough plainware vessels together with a few unpainted pieces of pottery incised in a distinctive fashion'.[42] This is confirmed by the illustrations of Typology II on Plate 64 of the report, where no painted fragments are shown; although it is true that in the accompanying text[43] one sherd with bands of black paint on a light slip is mentioned, though again without exact provenance.

Regrettably – since Typology II appears to be the only material from Tayma which can justifiably be treated as a homogeneous group – too little has been published to make a comparative discussion profitable at this juncture. Resemblances between the incised decoration and that on some Eastern and Central Arabian wares (from, for example, Thaj and Layla)[44] generally dated to the 'Hellenistic' period are perhaps too superficial to be meaningful. What needs to be stressed is that – with the solitary exception of the one sherd of unknown provenance mentioned above – all of the painted pottery from Tayma, both of Bawden's 'polychrome style' and his 'bichrome' style, comes not from 'Typology II', but from the essentially heterogeneous and unstratified groups called Typologies I and III. As we have said, neither of these two groups can be related to any particular stage in the documented history of the site, except by assumption and guess-work. It is difficult to see, therefore, how Bawden's researches at Tayma can be cited by Muhly as evidence that 'Midianite pottery seems to appear in an Iron Age II context, dated no earlier than the 8th century B.C.'.[45] In fact, all that the Tayma evidence seems to tell us for sure is that 'Midianite' pottery does *not* occur at the period of the Qasr al-Hamra shrine – whatever that may be. As for the al-'Ula 'bichrome' style, its dating and its relationship to the Qurayya ware – to which (it must be stressed) it is similar in some basic aspects of its decoration but from which it is very different in form and technology – remains as obscure as it was in 1980 when the present writer discussed the problem at the Oxford Conference.[46] Bawden's assumption – on the grounds that it is very common at Tayma, being widely distributed over the whole of the site within the walls – that it coincides with the time of Tayma's greatest areal expansion, which he places in the mid-1st millennium B.C., may be correct, but remains an assumption, unsupported by the evidence from the Qasr al-Hamra shrine.[47] In this connection it should also be borne in mind that much of the area within the walls seems to have been given over to agriculture, and that the wide dispersal of painted sherds may well be the result of the later use of domestic refuse as fertiliser, a practice well known in the ancient and modern Near East.[48] Bawden's 'bichrome' pottery may be earlier than this agricultural expansion, therefore. On the other hand, at al-'Ula, where this style is also prolific, it seems to be associated, both on the surface and in soundings, with the latest structural remains which, on the basis of inscriptions and Egyptianising sculptures, have been assumed to date to about the 4th-3rd centuries B.C.[49] There are many assumptions involved in these arguments, however, and any or all could be wrong. The present writer still inclines to the view that there is a relationship of some sort between the al-'Ula painted pottery and the Edomite painted ware of the 7th-6th centuries in southern Jordan, though the precise nature of the relationship is unclear. The al-'Ula pottery could well be, therefore, of the Iron Age II (in Palestinian archaeological terminology), even though the Qurayya painted ware is not. It must be stressed that there is as yet absolutely no stratigraphic evidence for this, however, and no indication that the al-'Ula style follows the Qurayya style without a break. Only careful excavation of the sites concerned will resolve these problems, and it is to be hoped that an appropriate programme of fieldwork will be not too long delayed.

This long discussion of ceramic chronology – much of which may be seen as a plea for more rigorous scholarship in the analysis of such matters – has been necessary in order to correct some misconceptions and to provide an acceptable, if severely limited, basis on which to attempt a preliminary appraisal of the history of N.W. Arabia in the late 2nd and early 1st millennia B.C. The writer last attempted such a review in 1977,[50] but much new information has appeared since, almost entirely as a result of the comprehensive archaeological survey programme initiated by Dr. Abdullah Masry the previous year, and the following account will draw heavily on the preliminary reports of that programme published in the journal *Atlal.*

It seems clear that towards the end of the 2nd millennium a remarkable development took place in the occupational history of N.W. Arabia. Whatever archaeological evidence there is for the preceding periods seems to relate to small encampments and burial grounds, more likely to be associated with pastoralism and seasonal scratch-farming than to any more permanent settlement. The extensive archaeological remains at Qurayya, however, comprising citadel fortifications, a settlement mound, field systems, and kilns for the distinctive painted pottery, point to a more permanent village, if not urban, community in the final centuries of the millennium. Despite the fieldwork of 1968[51] and 1980[52] this site has not yet been at all adequately investigated, even on the surface, and much needs to be done before the precise dating of its various components can be established. As was argued in the writer's original description of the site, however, the abundance of Late Bronze Age painted pottery on the surface in close association with the visible remains, and the absence, except in a few restricted areas, of anything obviously different in character (such as Nabataean pottery) makes it reasonably certain that most of these remains are of that date; and the observations of Ingraham and his colleagues seem to support this conclusion. As we have seen, the Qurayya painted pottery is also found at Tayma, though it is less common there than the al-'Ula 'bichrome' style. Tayma also may thus have been occupied in the Late Bronze Age. If so, it might suggest that the north-south Arabian route, which would have passed through these two sites, was in use by this period, as has been argued previously.(53) The decoration on the Qurayya pottery proves, to the satisfaction of this writer at least, that these newly settled inhabitants of N.W. Arabia were in cultural contact with the Mediterranean world, and more specifically with Egypt, and recent evidence concerning the distribution of the painted pottery tends to confirm this. The dozen or so sites with this pottery which have so far been discovered in Arabia – apart from Tayma and Qurayya itself – occur in two major clusters, one at the head of the Wadi 'Ifal in the area of al-Bad', the other in the lower reaches of the Wadis Sharmah and Aynunah.(54) Khuraybah (not to be confused with the ruins at al-'Ula of the same name), at the mouth of the Wadi Aynunah, is one of the largest and best natural harbours on this part of the Red Sea coast, and has plausibly been identified with Leuke Kome of the classical geographers.(55) On the opposite side of the sea, some 150 kilometres distant, is Myos Hormos, one of the most important of the Egyptian ports. Although no Qurayya painted ware has yet been reported from Khuraybah itself, it seems unlikely that the anchorage was not known to Egyptian navigators of the New Kingdom. From Khuraybah two routes penetrate the mountains to the interior, one north along the Wadi 'Ifal past al-Bad' to Haql and Aqaba, and so to the Arabah and to Timna, the other east along the Wadi Sharmah towards Qurayya. It is reasonable to suppose that the two clusters of sites testify to the utilisation of these routes in the 13th-11th centuries B.C. Rothenberg has already discussed the evidence for trade in copper between Egypt and the Timna mines,(56) and although most of this trade probably went by land across Sinai or by sea down the Aqaba Gulf, an alternative land route along the Wadi 'Ifal to Khuraybah is by no means impossible. The absence of Qurayya painted ware from Sinai might indicate that the Sinai route was controlled directly by the Egyptians, while the route down the 'Ifal was in Arabian hands. As for the eastern route, along the Sharmah, this can best be explained as the link between the coast and the inland route through Tayma and Qurayya, and its utilisation at this time provides some supporting evidence for the view that New Kingdom Egypt obtained part of its aromatics *via* Northern Arabia, a matter which is discussed further below.

Two additional features of the distribution of Qurayya ware in Arabia deserve mention. First, it is noticeably absent from sites along the Hejaz coast and the immediate hinterland between al-Wajh and Muwaylah, where gold, silver and copper deposits and ancient mines are known to exist.[57] Conversely, no deposits of these ores are shown on the mineral locality map in the al-Bad'-Aynunah-Sharmah region, where the 'Qurayya ware' sites cluster (despite Ingraham's statement to the contrary and despite the discovery of copper or nuggets on the surface of one site).[58] In the light of this evidence it may be that both the present writer and Rothenberg have been wrong in suggesting that the Hejaz mines, as well as those of the Arabah, were exploited at this time by the makers of the Qurayya pottery.[59]

Secondly, no sites with the painted ware are reported east of the Qurayya-Tayma route, and in particular its absence from the al-Jawf-Sakaka oasis should be stressed, since this area has been intensively surveyed and sounded in recent years, and the distinctive pottery would certainly have been found had it been present. As is well known, al-Jawf is the site of ancient Adummatu (biblical Dumah, Arabic Dumat al-Jandal) mentioned in the Assyrian records repeatedly after c.700 B.C. as one of the main tribal and religious centres of the Arabs.[60] It controls the southern end of the Wadi Sirhan, and the absence of the Late Bronze Age pottery suggests that this route had not yet acquired the importance it was to achieve in later times.[61]

Whatever the importance of aromatics and copper in the economy of Northwest Arabia in the late 2nd millennium, it seems clear that agriculture also played a major role, and it is, of course, the evidence for irrigation farming at Qurayya that is one of the primary bases for the claim that we are dealing with sedentary occupation. Much more study of the fields and channels around Qurayya is necessary before even elementary questions concerning the technology involved can be answered; although it is already evident (as a result of the observations of Ingraham et al.),[62] that much of the water utilised came from a spring (now dry) at the foot of the citadel hill, rather than from flash floods, as was first postulated. Nonetheless, the system seems to have been essentially similar to those known from South Arabia and from the Palestinian Negev, both of which are not usually dated to before c. 1000 B.C. Whether, and to what extent, these systems are related, and whether they are an indigenous development in one or more of these regions or are derived from the alluvial valley irrigation of Egypt and Mesopotamia, are matters which must remain obscure pending further research. In the present state of knowledge we can only speculate, also, on the relative importance of the discovery, or the introduction from outside, of these farming techniques in the economy and lifestyles of the N.W. Arabian peoples at this time; to what extent they were the cause of sedentarism and prosperity or the consequence of a prosperity already based on trade and/or mining. Cause and effect were probably here, as so often, inextricably entwined.

Despite all the uncertainties, the fact remains that by c. 1300 B.C. sedentary agricultural communities were living in N.W. Arabia, and some of the wider historical implications of this must now be considered, if only briefly. We have already suggested, on the basis of ceramics and site distribution, that Egypt played a part in the economic and cultural development of the region, and we must now ask whether any trace of this can be found in the Egyptian records. Relevant to this is the discussion by Dr. Abdel-Aziz Saleh of Arabian involvement in the Egyptian incense trade during the New Kingdom, in which he argues, amongst other things, that the 'foreign chiefs' mentioned in an incription from Sinai of year 36 of Amenophis III (i.e. c. 1366 B.C.) were from North Arabia and were engaged in both land and sea traffic.[63] Dr. Saleh's interpretation of the inscription is convincing, and his hypothetical reconstruction of the trade across the Red Sea has, in the present writer's view, received striking confirmation from the archaeological evidence. In New Kingdom texts it is the Shoshu, however, who are most commonly associated with the regions to the east of Egypt; they seem most at home in the area of Transjordan, but there is no reason to suppose that Northwestern Arabia was not also within their ambit. The term 'Shoshu' is usually translated 'beduin', and it is clear that they were mostly transhumant pastoralists, though they came into contact with the Egyptians most frequently in less peaceable roles, such as mercenaries, bands of robbers, and prisoners. Giveon's comprehensive study of the relevant texts[64] indicates a significant development in the relations between Egypt and the Shoshu in the early 19th Dynasty. A campaign of Seti I, recorded in a long inscription from Karnak (Giveon's Document 11) and specifically mentioning the Shoshu, appears to have resulted in the pacification of the eastern Delta and to have paved the way for the establishment of forward military bases in this region, as well as for the later building activities there of Rameses II. It is in a text of the latter (Giveon's Document 32) that we find a reference to Shoshu towns. Though the locations of these (whether in Egypt, Canaan or elsewhere) and the exact significance of the references (to existing towns attacked by Rameses, or to new towns founded by him) are matters about which Egyptologists seem not to agree,[65] both Giveon and Ward[66] incline to the view that at least some of the Shoshu were 'urbanised'. If such were the case, and if the Shoshu of N.W. Arabia include the tribal chiefs who acted as intermediaries in the incense trade, is it too fanciful to see in sites such as Qurayya and perhaps Tayma 'Shoshu towns', possibly founded under Egyptian influence in order to settle the tribes and control the trade routes?

At this point we must return to problems of ethnicity, and to the Midianites. To the Egyptians the Shoshu were not an ethnic group but were a class, though a somewhat diverse class, of people. The same can almost certainly be said about the Midianites, though here the name is presumably gentilic in origin. Despite Payne's contrary view, the localisation of the Midianites in N.W. Arabia during the final centuries of the 2nd millennium, accepted by the majority of biblical scholars,(67) has much to commend it, and Gottwald has suggested already that the Midianites were included in the Egyptian cover term Shoshu.(68) In view of the congruence of the Egyptian, biblical and archaeological evidence, the present writer finds it very hard not to believe that Qurayya was a Midianite settlement, one of those Midianite 'cities' which Gottwald (apparently unaware of the site) argues must have existed,(69) even though it cannot be claimed that the archaeological evidence is sufficient to support his further hypothesis of incipient Midianite 'statism' at this time.

It is important to recognise that this Midianite 'urban' development was very localised, being confined to Northwest Arabia. Although the Midianites might well – as Eissfeldt and Albright have argued(70) – have exercised some sort of economic and political control over their neighbours to the north, the archaeological evidence from southern Jordan does not justify Albright's use of the term, 'vassal state' for Edom, if by 'state' is implied the existence of settled communities. Despite much recent fieldwork there are still no real grounds for supposing that Edom was the scene of village, let alone urban, occupation in the late 2nd and early 1st millennia B.C. Lack of space prevents a thorough evaluation of the evidence, and it must suffice to say that, with our present lack of knowledge about such things as regional variations and local typological developments in pottery, arguments based, for example, on the presence of a few sherds of possibly Palestinian Early Iron Age I (i.e. c. 1200-1000 B.C.) type, such as those published by Weippert from sites near the Wadi al-Hesa,(71) are hardly compelling. The most recent relevant survey, that of Hart on the southern Jordanian plateau, provides no indication of settlement prior to about the 8th century at the earliest,(72) thus confirming the results of Bennett's excavations at Buseirah (the Edomite capital), Tawilan and Umm al-Biyara. Further north, in Moab and Ammon, the picture is quite different, but there the settlements of the Early Iron Age are to be most readily understood as a continuation of the urbanism of the region in the Late Bronze Age, when northern Transjordan was culturally a part of Canaan. Edom certainly did not participate in this Late Bronze Age urbanism, and (despite the presence of a single Qurayya sherd from Tawilan) it seems clear that it was not affected by Midianite 'urbanism' either.

If our arguments above concerning the chronology of the Qurayya pottery are correct, Midianite sedentarism was not only localised but was also short-lived. Around 1000 B.C., if not earlier, the economic, social and political systems implied by the archaeological remains seem to have collapsed, for reasons which can only be surmised. If strong commercial links did indeed exist between this part of Arabia and Egypt during the 19th and 20th Dynasties, then the abandonment of Qurayya and related sites is not surprising, however. The weakening of royal power under the 20th Dynasty is well documented, and the effects this would have had on foreign trade – normally vested in pharaoh's hands – are obvious. Royal mining expeditions to Sinai probably ceased after the reign of Rameses VI,[(73)] while the latest dated Egyptian object from Timna dates to that of his predecessor, Rameses V. The disengagement of the Egyptians from the Midianite region could well have led to the collapse of a precocious and precarious 'urbanism' there. Moreover, if climatic deterioration was a contributing factor in the Egyptian decline, as Butzer believes,[(74)] then agricultural production in Northwest Arabia may also have been adversely affected. How all this relates to the exploitation of the camel in northern Arabia is hard to say. Albright wrote of Midianite 'donkey caravans', but the depiction of a camel on a fragment of Qurayya painted pottery[(75)] proves that these animals also were known in the area, and it is at least possible that they were already being used for transport. The fact that camels are nowhere shown or mentioned in connection with the warlike Shoshu presumably indicates that they were not used for raiding as early as the New Kingdom. However, it is well known that they figure in the slightly later (early 11th century) Midianite attack on the Israelites in northern Palestine (Judges 6-8), and it is surely more than just coincidence that this is the date by which, on our reconstruction, sedentary occupation in Midian was collapsing. It is reasonable to suppose that the two developments are related, and that camel nomadism in northern Arabia was at least partly the result of the abandonment of sites such as Qurayya.[(76)] Camel nomads leave few traces in the archaeological record, however, and it is perhaps for this reason that the record in Northwestern Arabia for the next few centuries is at present a blank.

Notes

1. B. Rothenberg, *Illustrated London News* 15 November 1969, 32; P.J. Parr et al., *Bulletin of the Institute of Archaeology*, vol. 8/9, 1970, London, p.240. See also B. Rothenberg and J. Glass, 'The Midianite Pottery' in J. Sawyer and D. Clines, (eds.), *Midian, Moab and Edom*, Sheffield, 1983, pp.68-69.

2. A. Biran, (ed.), *Temples and High Places in Biblical Times*, Jerusalem, 1981, p.9.

3. John J. Bimson, 'King Solomon's Mines? A Reassessment of Finds in the Arabah'. *Tyndale Bulletin*, vol. 32, 1981, pp.123-149.

4. J. Muhly, 'Timna and King Solomon', *Bibliotheca Orientalis*, vol. XLI, 1984, pp.278-9.

5. P.J. Parr, 'Contacts between North West Arabia and Jordan in the Late Bronze and Iron Ages', in A. Hadidi (ed.), *Studies in the History and Archaeology of Jordan*, vol. I, Amman, 1982, pp.127-133.

6. On the Classical and Arab references to Midian see A. Musil, *The Northern Heğaz*, New York, 1926, pp.278-281.

7. E.J. Payne, 'The Midianite Arc in Joshua and Judges', in Sawyer and Clines, op.cit. (note 1), p.163.

8. P.J. Parr, 'Pottery, People and Politics', in P.R.S. Moorey and P.J. Parr (eds.), *Archaeology in the Levant*, Warminister, 1978, pp.202-209.

9. E.A. Knauf, 'Midianites and Ishmaelites', in Sawyer and Clines, op.cit. (note 1), p.156.

10. For the discovery of a kiln at Qurayya, see Parr et al., op.cit. (note 1), p.240. Additional kilns and the probable source of the clay used for the pottery are reported by M.L. Ingraham et al. 'Preliminary Report on a Reconnaissance Survey of the Northwestern Province', *Atlal*, vol. 5, 1981, p.73. A technical study of the pottery, supporting the view that it originated in the Qurayya region, is given by Rothenberg and Glass, op.cit., (note 1).

11. Parr et al., op.cit. (note 1), pp.238-240.

12. J.E. Dayton, *Proceedings of the Fifth Seminar for Arabian Studies*, 1972, pp.25-33.

13. Parr, op.cit. (note 5), pp.129-130.

14. B. Rothenberg, *Timna, Valley of the Biblical Copper Mines*, London, 1972, fig. 52.

15. See, for example, the illustrations of 2nd and 1st millennia pottery from sites in Abu Dhabi published in *Archaeology in the United Arab Emirates*, vol. I, 1977, p.42; and vol. II-III, 1978-79, pp.64-66.

16. Parr, op.cit. (note 5), pp.128-129; Rothenberg and Glass, op.cit. (note 1), p.101.

17. Parr, op.cit. (note 5) pp.128-129.

18. See in particular: N. Glueck, 'Some Edomite Pottery from Tell el-Kheleifeh.' *Bulletin of the American Schools of Oriental Research*, vol. 188, 1967, pp.8-38.

19. G.D. Practico, 'Nelson Glueck's 1938-1940 Excavations at Tell el-Kheleifeh: A Reappraisal', *Bulletin of the American Schools of Oriental Research*, vol. 259, 1985, p.1-32, especially 22.

20. Parr, op.cit. (note 5), p.129.

21. Bimson, op.cit. (note 3), pp.142-145.

22. Muhly, op.cit., (note 4), pp.282-283.

23. Ibid., p.284.

24. Ibid., p.284.

25. Parr et al., op.cit. (note 1), p.239.

26. G. Bawden, 'Painted Pottery of Tayma', in Sawyer and Clines, op.cit. (note 1), pp.37-52.

27. Ibid., p.40-50.

28. Ibid., p.50-51.

29. Parr, op.cit. (note 5), pp.131-133.

30. G. Bawden, C. Edens and R. Miller, 'Preliminary Archaeological Investigations at Tayma', *Atlal*, vol. 4, 1980, pp.69-106.

31. Ibid., p.92.

32. Rothenberg and Glass, op.cit. (note 1), p.73.

33. Bawden, Edens and Miller, op.cit. (note 30), p.93.

34. Ibid., p.84.

35. G. Bawden, op.cit. (note 26), pp.46-47.

36. A. Livingstone et al. 'Taima: Recent Soundings and New Inscribed Material', *Atlal*, vol. 7, 1983, p.111.

37. F.V. Winnett, 'A reconsideration of some inscriptions from the Tayma area', *Proceedings of the 13th Seminar for Arabian Studies*, 1980, p.137.

38. Livingstone et al., op.cit. (note 36), p.109, 112.

39. G. Bawden, 'Recent Radiocarbon Dates from Tayma', *Atlal*, vol. 5, 1981, pp.142-153.

40. J. Klein et al., 'Calibration of Radiocarbon Dates', *Radiocarbon*, vol. 24, 1982, pp.103-150.

41. Bawden, Edens, Miller, op.cit. (note 30), pp.84-85.

42. Ibid, p.85.

43. Ibid, p.96.

44. See, for example, the wares discussed by D. Potts in J. Zarins et al., 'Preliminary Report on the Third Phase of the Comprehensive Archaeological Survey Program - The Central Province', *Atlal*, vol. 3, 1979, pp.31-35.

45. Muhly, op.cit. (note 4), p.284.

46. Parr, op.cit. (note 5), pp.130-131.

47. Bawden, op.cit. (note 26), pp.49-50.

48. See, for example, T.J. Wilkinson, 'The Ancient Landscape of the Tell es-Sweyhat Plain', *Levant*, vol. 8, 1976, pp.67-70.

49. Parr et al., op.cit. (note 1), p.213; G. Bawden, 'Khief el-Zahrah and the nature of the Dedanite Hegemony in the al-'Ula oasis', *Atlal*, vol. 3, 1979, pp.63-72.

50. P.J. Parr, 'Archaeological Sources for the Early History of North-West Arabia', in *Studies in the History of Arabia*, vol. I, Riyadh, 1979, pp.37-4.

51. Parr et al., op.cit. (note 1).

52. M.L. Ingraham et al., 'Preliminary Report on a Reconnaissance Survey of the Northwestern Province', *Atlal*, vol. 5, 1981, pp.71-74.

53. Parr, op.cit. (note 50), pp.40-41, with references to earlier discussions by W.F. Albright, etc. The argument has been accepted and developed by Knauf, op.cit. (note 8). See also note 63, below.

54. Ingraham et al., op.cit. (note 52), pp.7-75.

55. L. Kirwan, 'Where to Search for the Ancient Port of Leuke Kome', in *Studies in the History of Arabia* II: *Pre-Islamic Arabia*, Riyadh, 1984, pp.55-61.

56. Rothenberg, op.cit. (note 14), pp.201-207.

57. *Mineral Locality Map of the Arabian Shield*, Kingdom of Saudi Arabia Ministry of Petroleum and Mineral Resources, Jeddah, 1974.

58. Ingraham et al., op.cit. (note 52), pp.74-75.

59. Parr, op.cit. (note 50), p.41; Rothenberg and Glass, op.cit. (note 1), p.115.

60. For convenience, see the references in E. Eph'al, *The Ancient Arabs*, Jerusalem and Leiden, 1982.

61. The earliest archaeological evidence for the use of the Wadi Sirhan route in the 1st millennium B.C. would appear to be the Iron Age II pottery (c. 8th-6th centuries) found on the surface and in a burial mound at its northern end, in the vicinity of Kaf and Ithra (cf. P.J. Parr, *Atlal*, vol. 1, 1977, p.36). The earliest archaeological evidence so far recorded from the al-Jawf region is of Hellenistic-Nabataean date (ibid., p.38-39),

though rock inscriptions of the 7th century B.C. are known.

62. Ingraham et al., op.cit. (note 52), p.73.

63. A-A. Saleh, 'An Open Question on Intermediaries in the Incense Trade during Pharaonic Times', *Orientalia*, vol. 42, 1973, pp.370-382. In her recent detailed study of *Meccan Trade and the Rise of Islam*, Oxford, 1987, Patricia Crone argues against the existence of a trade in South Arabian aromatics (as distinct from those from Punt and elsewhere), and *a fortiori* against the use of the Arabian land route, before about the 7th. century B.C. The history of the aromatic trade is notoriously difficult to elucidate, not least because of the inconsistencies and ambiguities in the terminology used in the ancient texts for different types of 'incense', and Crone is undoubtedly correct in her view that export of the South Arabian products cannot be attested with certainty prior to that date. Nevertheless, the evidence - slight though it may be - for an earlier trade with South Arabia should not be ignored. Even Groom, who also denies the significance of overland trade through Arabia before the 1st millennium B.C. (and whom Crone cites with approval) admits that some hand-to-hand trading between South Arabia and the Levant may have existed at the time of the 18th Dynasty, when chiefs of Retenu are recorded as having sent 'incense' to Egypt as part of their tribute (N. Groom, *Frankincense and Myrrh*, London and Beirut, 1981, p.29.) Dixon, also, seems happy to accept that the incense from Retenu originated in South Arabia (D.M. Dixon, 'The Transplantation of Punt Incense Trees in Egypt', *Journal of Egyptian Archaeology*, vol. 55, 1969, p.55, note 1). It is important to note also, in this connection, that recent work in South Arabia has proved the existence there already in the 2nd millennium of sedentary occupation, thereby removing one argument against the exploitation of the local aromatics at this time. (See, for example, A. de Maigret, 'A Bronze Age for Southern Arabia', *East and West*, vol. 34, 1984, pp.75-106.)

64. R. Giveon, *Les Bedouins Shoshu des Documents Egyptiens*, Leiden 1971; W.A. Ward, 'The Shoshu "Beduin"', *Journal of the Economic and Social History of the Orient*, vol. XV, 1972, pp.35-60.

65. Giveon, op.cit. (note 64), p.115.

66. Ward, op.cit. (note 64), p.54.

67. See, for example, the discussions by G. Mendenhall, *The Tenth Generation*, Baltimore, 1973, esp. pp.163-173; E.A. Knauf, op.cit. (note 9), pp.147-162.

68. N.K. Gottwald, *The Tribes of Yahweh*, New York, 1979, p.459.

69. Ibid, p.463.

70. O. Eissfeldt, 'Protektorat der Midianiter über ihre Nachbarn im letzen Viertel des 2. Jahrtausends v. Chr.', *Journal of Biblical Literature*, vol. 87, 1968, pp.383-393; W.F. Albright, 'Midianite Donkey Caravans', in H. Frank and W. Reed (eds.), *Translating and Understanding the Old Testament*, Nashville, 1970, pp.197-205.

71. M. Weippert, 'Remarks on the History of Settlement in Southern Jordan during the Early Iron Age', in A. Hadidi (ed.), *Studies in the History and Archaeology of Jordan*, vol. I, Amman, 1982, pp.153-162.

72. S. Hart, 'Some Preliminary Thoughts on Settlement in Southern Edom', *Levant*, vol. 18, 1986, pp.51-58.

73. J. Černy, 'Egypt: From the Death of Ramesses III to the End of the Twenty-First Dynasty', *Cambridge Ancient History*, 3rd edition, vol. II, Part 2, 1975, p.615.

74. K.W. Butzer, *Early Hydraulic Civilization in Egypt*, Chicago, 1976, pp.55-56.

75. Ingraham et al., op.cit. (note 52), plate 79, no.14.

76. See also the discussion by Knauf, op.cit. (note 9), pp.151-152.

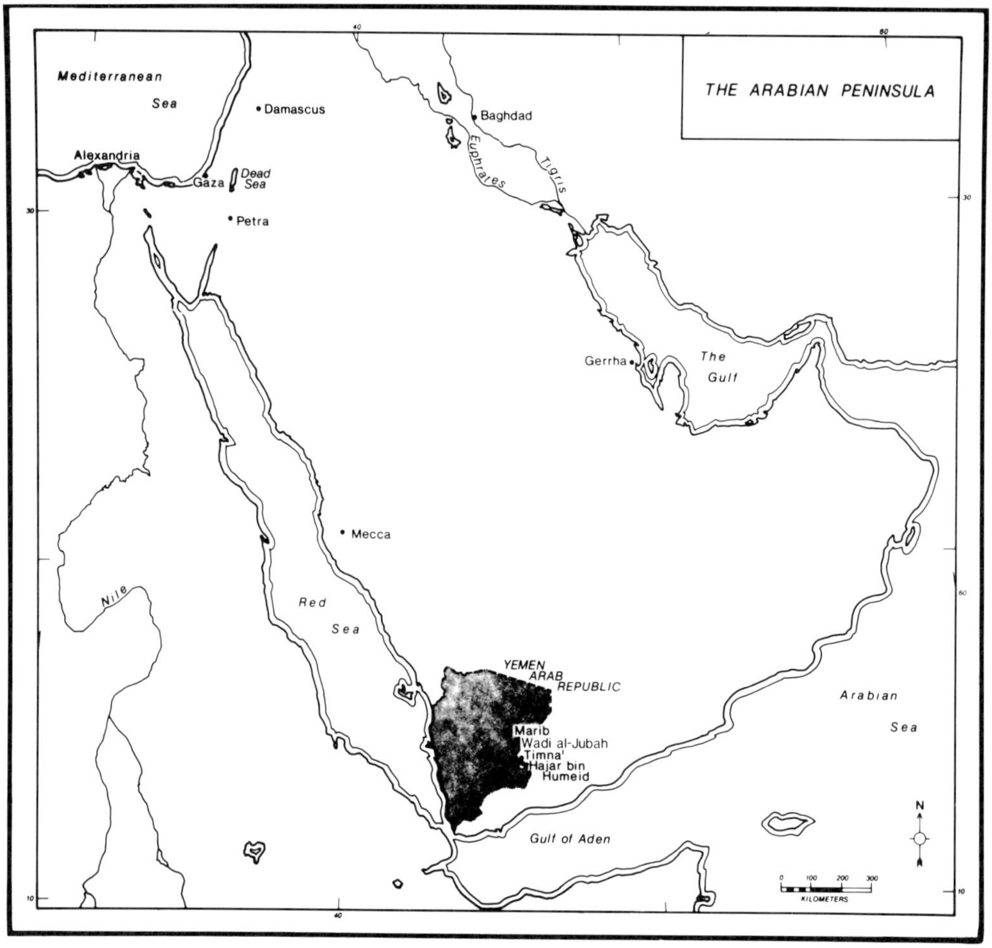

Fig. 1. Map of Arabian peninsula, showing the locations of Timna, Hajar Bin Humeid, Marib, and the Wadi al-Jubah. After Toplyn, 1984, Map 1; drawn by Helen Schenck.

Archaeology along the Spice Route of Yemen

BY JAMES A. SAUER AND JEFFREY A. BLAKELY

With contributions by M.R. Toplyn, W.D. Glanzman, A.O. Ghaleb, M.J. Grolier, W.C. Overstreet, and L.J. Tiede

Starting in the spring of 1950 Wendell Phillips, a young paleontologist turned explorer and archaeologist, led the first American archaeological team that was to excavate major ancient cities along the spice[1] routes of South Arabia. This project was sponsored by the American Foundation for the Study of Man (AFSM), which was founded by Phillips in 1949, and it worked in Yemen, including what is now called the Yemen Arab Republic (North Yemen) and the People's Democratic Republic of Yemen (South Yemen), for about two years. Then circumstances dictated that the project cease and the archaeological staff move to Oman (Phillips, 1955; Cleveland, 1960; F.P. Albright, 1982). After the untimely death of Phillips, the AFSM has been reactivated under the presidency of his sister, Merilyn Phillips Hodgson, and it is in the fifth year of its new archaeological work in the Yemen Arab Republic. As did the teams led by Phillips, the new project is studying a part of the ancient spice routes of Yemen. The subject of our investigations is a small geographical region, the Wadi al-Jubah (Toplyn, 1984; Blakely and Sauer, 1985; Blakely, Sauer, and Toplyn, 1985).

The legends of the Queen of Sheba (Saba) and the wealth of South Arabia were well known to the Mediterranean and later Western worlds from the time of Solomon in the 10th century B.C. I Kings 10:1-13 describes the visit of the Queen of Sheba (Saba) and the gifts she brought by camel to the court of King Solomon, '... 120 talents of gold, spices in great abundance, and precious stones.' Although some scholars have disputed this tradition (e.g., Pirenne, see dating discussion below; see also Groom, 1981, pp.38-54; Doe, 1983, p.252), our project in Yemen so far supports the presence of South Arabian cultures as early as ca. 1300 B.C. (see below). Assyrian annals describe the precious stones, gold, camels, and spices which came from Arabia to the north; Babylonia and Persia also took a keen interest in Arabia (Pritchard, 1969, pp.274-317). Alexander was planning the conquest of this rich country of frankincense, myrrh, cinnamon, and nard at the time of his death (Robson, 1929-33). Knowledge of Sabaean wealth was common in the Hellenistic and Roman world, as today we have reports concerning its splendor written by Herodotus (Godley, 1921-

24), Strabo (Jones, 1967), Pliny the Elder (Rackham, 1969), and the author of *The Periplus of the Erythraean Sea* (Huntingford, 1980), among others. A Roman army under Aelius Gallus failed in its attempted conquest in 25/24 B.C. (von Wissmann, 1976, pp.426-29, 467-74). It was at about this time, however, that the prosperity of South Arabia began to wane and the spice routes suffer as transshipment was shifted from land to sea. The later advent of Islam further closed this period of inland international commerce in Yemen (for discussions of these sources, see Hourani, 1952; Van Beek, 1960; Harding, 1964; von Wissmann, 1964, 1968; Montgomery, 1969; Van Beek, 1969b; Doe, 1971; Pritchard, 1974; Faris, 1981; Groom, 1981; Robin, 1982; Doe, 1983).

The memory of this period was not lost to the Western world during the Christian era. The Queen of Sheba (Saba) became a legendary figure portrayed in literature and art. In Arabia the memory and legends were recorded in the Koranic book Saba. Even in modern times, the recent kings of Ethiopia bore the title 'The Lion of Judah,' commemorating their belief that they were direct descendants of the Queen of Sheba and King Solomon (for these legends see Pritchard, 1974).

When the world was opened to Western explorers starting in the 15th century, the region of South Arabia remained largely closed. The Danish Expedition of 1761-67 was the first to explore parts of the interior of Yemen, and only Carsten Niebuhr survived from this work to describe what was found in Yemen (Niebuhr, 1792; Hansen, 1964). Various explorers visited Yemen in the 19th century, and of these Eduard Glaser was among the most productive. In a series of campaigns in the 1870s and 1880s he traveled the country and gathered copies of thousands of ancient inscriptions (e.g., see Glaser, 1890). With the decipherment and translation of the inscriptions much was learned of ancient South Arabia. Early archaeological excavations in Yemen were carried out at al-Huqqa in 1928 by Rathjens and von Wissmann (1932, 1934), at the Moon Temple in the Hadhramaut in 1937-38 by Caton-Thompson (1944), and at Shabwa in 1938 by Hamilton (1942), but these projects left unanswered many questions of chronology and history which had to be dealt with before the culture of the region could be understood.

This was the basic state of knowledge of the area in 1950, when Wendell Phillips brought his archaeological team to the Aden Protectorate (now South Yemen) and negotiated a contract to survey and excavate in the Wadi Beihan. Qataban, with its capital at Timna, was the ancient kingdom located just to the southeast of Saba and was a major staging ground for the caravan traffic that went northwest along the Arabian desert to end in Egypt, the Levant, Mesopotamia, and the Gulf. Qataban had rivaled Saba in wealth and power from the beginnings of the caravan traffic (probably in the Late Bronze/Early Iron

Age, ca. 1300 B.C.; see below) until Saba finally subdued this neighbor within the first half-century of this era, or ca. A.D. 30-45 (Jamme, 1962, pp.358-59; Müller, 1984, p.125).

From 1950 until 1951 the AFSM, under archaeological director William F. Albright, excavated at four locations in and around Timna (fig.1). In Timna itself (Hajar Kohlan) part of the city gate complex and some of the structures interior to that gate were uncovered. Work here set the date of the final destruction of Timna at ca. A.D. 10 (Comfort in Bowen and Albright, 1958, p.200), and established much of the chronology for the late period of Qataban (Bowen and Albright, 1958). Near Timna, at the necropolis of Heid Bin Aqil, part of the cemetery was excavated and many artifacts illustrative of life in Qataban were discovered (Cleveland, 1965). Along the Wadi Beihan, a study was made of the ancient dam, canal, and irrigation systems, showing how the city supported itself in its otherwise desolate surroundings (Bowen and Albright, 1958). Finally, a deep cut was made through the large stratified mound of Hajar Bin Humeid (see fig.1). The publication of this excavation by Van Beek (1969a) provided the first stratified ceramic corpus with which archaeologists could obtain a relative chronology of Qataban, back to about the 11th century B.C.

Late in 1951 Phillips and his AFSM expedition team were invited by the Imam of Yemen to come and work at Marib (see fig.1), the ancient capital of Saba, and they conducted excavations at the Mahram Bilqis (the so-called 'Scared Place of the Queen of Saba'). This work was interrupted after a few months, with only the peristyle entrance hall having been exposed before the project was terminated (F.P. Albright, 1952; Phillips, 1955). Numerous works of art and inscriptions were discovered during the excavation which helped clarify the history and high culture of the region. At the same time, epigraphic studies at the Marib Dam and its immediate vicinity allowed epigrapher Albert Jamme to begin to piece together a history of the area and to clarify numerous chronological problems (Jamme, 1962). With the termination of this work in 1952, much more of the history and material culture of Qataban and Saba was known than only two years before.

Between 1952 and 1982 the political climate of the area changed dramatically, and archaeological research was renewed. A major French excavation at Shabwa in South Yemen (see Pirenne, 1975, 1976, 1978) and a major Saudi Arabian excavation at Qaryat al-Fau (al-Ansary, 1981), as well as numerous archaeological, epigraphical, and historical-geographical surveys (e.g., Benardelli and Parrinello, 1970; Garbini, 1970; Benardelli and Parrinello, 1971; Costa, 1973; Bayle des Hermens, 1976; Costa, 1976; Robin, 1976; Robin, 1979; Bayle des Hermens and Grebenart, 1980; Breton, 1980; Robin, 1981; Robin, 1982;

Fig. 2. Photo of the Wadi al-Jubah with Marny Golding in foreground. View to southwest.

Robin and Breton, 1982; Schmidt, 1982; Brunner, 1983; Keall, 1983; Tindel, 1984), have been conducted by teams from many nations. It is now possible to study the archaeology of a discrete area in Yemen and then compare and contrast it with findings from elsewhere in greater Arabia.

In 1982 the AFSM, through an agreement with the government of North Yemen, initiated a new archaeological project in Yemen located along the caravan route about halfway between Qatabanian Timna and Sabaean Marib (see fig.1). This project, the Wadi al-Jubah Archaeological Project, is studying the archaeologically unknown region of the Wadi al-Jubah, attempting to discover sites of all periods, place them in chronological sequence, and discern human uses of the area from the evidence of early man to modern times. As a result, geology, geomorphology, botany, malacology, and epigraphy are playing major roles in the current work in addition to archaeology.

During our first campaign, in 1982, the team concentrated on site reconnaissance and epigraphic survey, and a total of 61 archaeological sites (occupation sites, hydraulic sites, wells, funerary sites, agricultural zone sites, sites of secondary context, sites of questionable context) were recorded (Toplyn, 1984). In 1983, 41 archaeological sites were recorded during the continuing reconnaissance in the wadi (see fig.3); the new category of baetylic sites was added. A small (less than 4 sq. m.) probe was excavated to completion at the small, eroded occupation site of Hajar at-Tamrah (HT12; figs.3, 4) (Blakely, Sauer, and Toplyn, 1985). Site reconnaissance continued in 1984, and a small (less

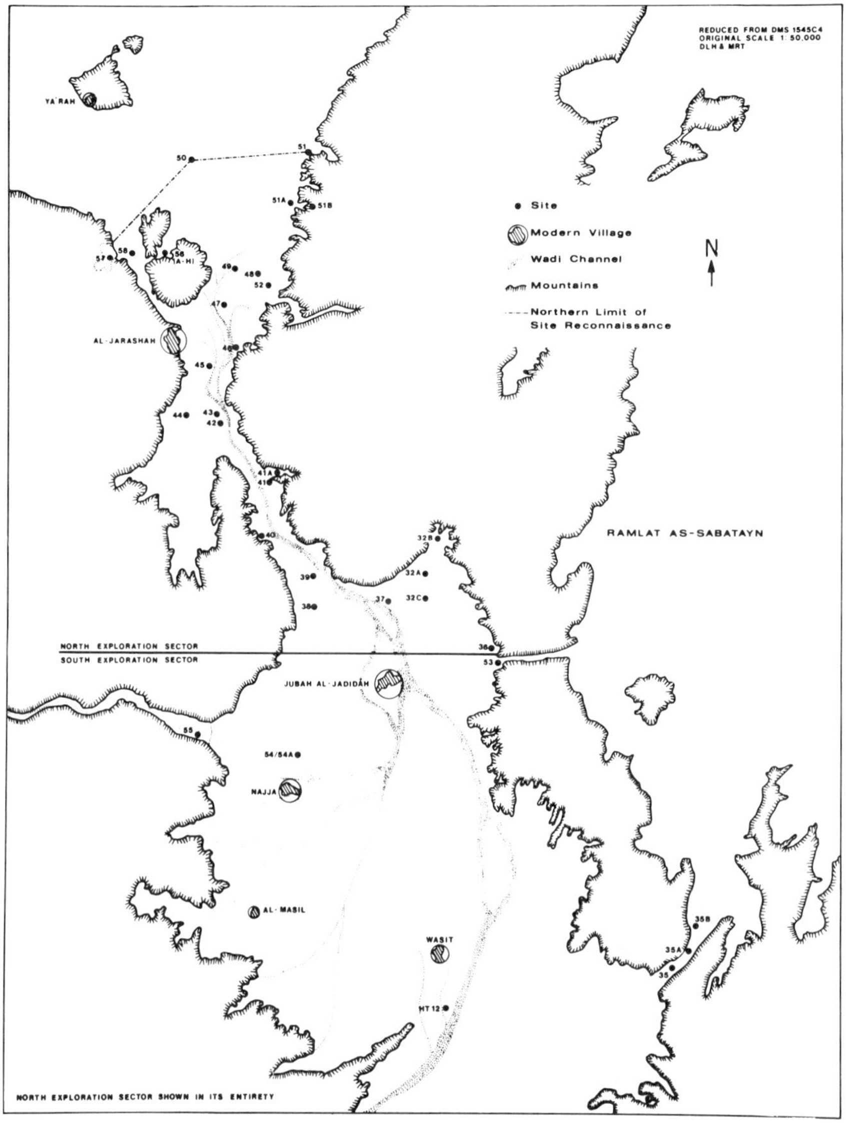

Fig. 3. Map of the northern portion of the Wadi al-Jubah, showing the locations of sites Hajar at-Tamrah (HT12), Hajar ar-Rayhani (Jubah al-Jadidah, HR3), al-Faraah (F56A-H), and Hajar al-Husn (HJR45). After Toplyn in Blakely, Sauer, and Toplyn, 1985, Map 1; drawn by Michael R. Toplyn and Denise L. Hoffman.

than 4 sq. m.) probe was started on the eroded western face of the large fortified site of Hajar ar-Rayhani (HR3; see figs.3, 5, 6), also known as (Jubah) al-Jadidah (Glanzman et al., in preparation for vol.3 of our preliminary report series; von Wissmann and Höfner, 1952, pp.36-37; Groom, 1976, p.75). During the 1985 campaign, geologists W.C. Overstreet and M.J. Grolier con-

Fig. 4. Photo of Hajar at-Tamrah (HT12), prior to excavation of 1983 probe. View to northeast.

ducted an invaluable geological and hydrological study of the wadi. They were accompanied by R.B. Stewart, who completed a comprehensive botanical survey. The reconnaissance team carried out the partial excavation of a burial cairn (F56C; see fig.3, site no.56). The results of these investigations will be published in vol. 4 of our preliminary report series. Only a limited campaign was conducted in 1986, when additional epigraphic data were gathered from throughout the wadi, and ceramic analysis was carried out in Sanaa. In 1987, the probe at Hajar ar-Rayhani will be expanded to ca. 25 square meters, and it will be continued until the earliest occupational remains are recovered. Some additional reconnaissance work will also be carried out in 1987. After the completion of that campaign, the team will devote its energy to the complete publication of this material.

The Wadi al-Jubah is a basin eroded into the edge of the Precambrian schists and gneisses which form the bedrock for Yemen, but at a point where a later, softer Precambrian dioritic rock intruded. With the erosion of the dioritic rock, the Wadi al-Jubah basin was created and cliffs of the schists and gneisses were exposed. These cliffs have been the source for the stone used by the various human communities of the Wadi al-Jubah over the past half-million years.

The basin of the Wadi al-Jubah is surrounded by mountains, but to the east, just across one narrow mountain range, is a blowing sand desert, the Ramlat as-Sabatayn. With the prevailing winds blowing southwest, the Wadi al-Jubah has accumulated substantial amounts of fine, windborne silt, or loess, which forms the basic soil for the region. As this is being deposited in the wadi by wind and wash from the mountains, it is also being eroded by flash floods which begin high up in the mountains. These floods cut into the silt and carry it back into the desert. There exists a delicate balance between accumulation and erosion in the wadi, and any change in rainfall or water-use patterns can have dramatic consequences.

The climate of the region allows only marginal agricultural activities. The rain fall is limited to a few centimeters a year, but this is augmented by the seasonal flash floods from the central Yemen mountains and by nightly dew accumulation. Periods of greater rainfall in the Arabian peninsula are known, however (e.g., Dayton, 1975; McClure, 1976; al-Sayari and Zötl, 1978; Jado and Zötl, 1984), and evidence from the Wadi al-Jubah suggests areas of standing water that survived throughout the year. One such period may be as recent as the 5th-4th millennia B.C. (see below).

Only meager evidence for human habitation of the Wadi al-Jubah region prior to the 'Neolithic' (Chalcolithic) period is known. A few handaxes, apparently of Lower Paleolithic type, have been found in wash contexts at the edges of the wadi. Possible Middle and Upper Paleolithic flakes and tools have been found in similar locations, but no primary deposits of this material have been discovered within the wadi (cf. Caton-Thompson and Gardner, 1939, for primary Paleolithic deposits in Hadhramaut). It seems that the primary deposits, if they still exist, will be located in the nearby hills and mountains. Some could be covered by silt on the floor of the basin proper. Thus, although these artifacts attest to human presence in the Wadi al-Jubah region during the Paleolithic Period, they do not allow for much further interpretation at this time.

The apparently oldest *in situ* remains in the Wadi al-Jubah seem to belong to the 'Neolithic'/Chalcolithic, ca. 5th-4th millennia B.C.[2] These consist mainly of small circular structures, but to date they have produced few clearly associated artifacts (Blakely, Sauer, and Toplyn, 1985, p.49). Many sites of this type have been found by our surface reconnaissance, and they usually are to be found on top of or in association with thick (up to ca. 5 m.) gray-black native soil layers, at the points where those layers touch the hillsides surrounding the wadi. The gray-black soil layers evidently were formed when the environment was wetter, when grasslands and swamps covered the wadi floor. An uncalibrated radiocarbon date of 3320 ± 90 B.C. (CRD date of 4530-3970

Fig. 5. Photo of Hajar ar-Rayhani (HR3), prior to excavation of 1984 probe. View to northeast.

B.C.)[3] came from an ash/carbon deposit (F56G) near one of these sites at al-Faraah. Two other uncalibrated radiocarbon dates, 4610 ± 120 B.C. and 3820 ± 110 B.C. (CRD dates of 5940-5390 B.C. and 5090-4560 B.C., respectively), came from the upper parts of two exposures of the gray-black soil layers (to be published in vol. 4 of our preliminary report series).

These dates from the Wadi al-Jubah agree in general with those from evidence of a wetter phase found elsewhere in Arabia (e.g., Field, 1960; McClure, 1976). In central and western Arabia, including the Wadi al-Jubah and other sites in Yemen to the southwest (Bayle des Hermens, 1976; Bayle des Hermens and Grebenart, 1980), the 'Neolithic'/Chalcolithic sites seem to reflect a hunting population, contemporary with the wetter grassland setting. In the Levant the locations of some Chalcolithic period sites, especially Tuleilat al-Ghassul and Beersheba, can be explained by a postulated wetter climatic phase (e.g., Horowitz, 1979, pp.319-20).

The 'Neolithic'/Chalcolithic period in eastern and central Arabia is defined by the presence of burial tumuli, Ubaid pottery, and/or short, pressure-flaked, tanged arrowheads (e.g., Zeuner, 1954; Field, 1958, 1960; Burkholder and Golding, 1971; Masry, 1974, pp.96-142, 150-205; Masry, 1975, pp.129-30,

Fig. 6. Photo of southern balk in HR3 probe, with Abdu Ghaleb pointing to radiocarbon sample that yielded uncalibrated date of 260 ± 60 B.C. (CRD date of 405-155 B.C.). Coin was found stratified above sample.

140-41; Copeland and Bergne, 1976; Roaf, 1976; Smith, 1976; Masry, 1977, pp.10-12; Adams et al., 1977, pp.27, 34-35; de Cardi, 1978, pp.36-116; Parr et al., 1978, pp.36-42; Potts et al., 1978, p.8; Zarins et al., 1979, pp.19-22; Zarins et al., 1980, pp.17-26; Ingraham et al., 1981, pp.66-71; Whalen et al., 1981, pp.49-51; Zarins, Murad, and al-Yish, 1981, pp.19-22). No sherds or lithics of these types, however, have been found in our wadi. The generally 'Neolithic' appearance of the burial cairns in Yemen and central Arabia presents special dating problems (e.g., Bayle des Hermens, 1976; Wade, 1979; Bayle des Hermens and Grebenart, 1980; Doe, 1983, pp.40-62; Bayle des Hermens, 1984). This is further emphasized by the 1985 season's excavation of the burial cairn F56C (see below), which produced a burial whose bones yielded an uncalibrated radiocarbon date of A.D. 570 ± 70 (CRD date of A.D. 590-790).

The Wadi al-Jubah so far lacks any trace of occupation between the 'Neolithic'/Chalcolithic and Pre-Islamic Arabian periods (to be discussed below). This general gap also characterizes the rest of Yemen as well as western Arabia. To the east, around the shores of the Arabian/Persian Gulf, very rich remains typify the 3rd-2nd millennia B.C. (Bronze Age) deposits (e.g., Bibby, 1970; Masry, 1974; pp.143-49; Hastings, Humphries, and Meadow, 1975; Adams et al., 1977, p.27; Masry, 1977, p.13; Potts et al., 1978, pp.8-9; Ibrahim, 1982). These sites near the Gulf benefited from sea-based subsistence and trade, in the favorable region between Mesopotamia, Persia, and India. On the other side of the Fertile Crescent, Egypt was at its peak through much of the 3rd and 2nd millennia B.C. This was due in part, at least, to the fact that Egypt had direct overland and Red Sea access to the incense-producing regions of East Africa (but apparently not to distant South Arabia). Even more important, it is widely held that donkey caravans linked Egypt, the Levant, and Mesopotamia, but that they could not negotiate the arid distances of western and southern Arabia. Thus, the trade routes of the 3rd and 2nd millennia B.C. apparently did not normally reach South Arabia, and they favored Egypt, the Levant, Mesopotamia, and the Gulf.

Only in the Late Bronze or Early Iron Age, ca. 1300 B.C., did western and southern Arabia begin to be populated extensively again, as can be argued from the new evidence from our wadi. Some (e.g., Pirenne, 1955, 1956, 1961, 1969, 1974, 1975) have maintained, largely on the basis of epigraphic evidence, that the Pre-Islamic Arabian cultures of South Arabia did not come into existence until very late, ca. 550-500 B.C. A 'high' chronology, ca. 1300-1100 B.C., for the South Arabians' adoption of the alphabetic script is maintained by W.F. Albright (1955), Van Beek (1952, 1956, 1960, 1969a, 1969b), and Jamme (see Phillips, 1955, p.42), who draw on epigraphic, stratigraphic, ceramic, radiocarbon, and historical evidence. The Wadi al-Jubah project has had as one of its chief goals the testing of these dating theories by excavating single small vertical probes at two different occupation sites in the wadi. From the bottommost occupational layer in the 1983 probe at Hajar at-Tamrah (HT12) came a large wood sample that produced an uncalibrated radiocarbon date of 1330 ± 110 B.C. (CRD date of 1850-1385 B.C.). Although at the moment this constitutes only a single piece of evidence, it clearly supports the 'high' chronology of W.F. Albright, Van Beek, and Jamme, and perhaps pushes it back even further.

With a starting date of ca. 1300 B.C., it seems most likely that the rise in occupation in South Arabia should be connected with the domestication and widespread use of the dromedary camel as a beast of burden (for a discussion of this complex issue, see esp. Wapnish, 1981; cf. Bulliet, 1975;

Ripinsky, 1975; Zarins, 1978). Only with the use of the camel in this way could the interior parts of western and southern Arabia have been opened up for extensive urban occupation and trade, because these 'remote' arid regions could now be reached for the first time on a regular commercial basis. The land routes in Arabia would have essentially bypassed Egypt, and the Levant would have benefited from the trade in such Arabian resources as incense, precious stones, and metals (cf. I Kings 10:15). Since Egypt went into decline in the 1st millennium B.C., it is possible that these economic factors may have been involved. Assyria, Babylonia, and Persia rose in power in that millennium, and they fought for control of the Levant and its caravan routes.

This shift in trading patterns must have had a very significant impact on the Fertile Crescent to the north, as well as on Arabia itself, which now flourished in both the west (including South Arabia) and the east (the Gulf). In northwest Arabia, the still undated 'Midianite' pottery may have begun to appear in the Late Bronze or early Iron Age (Parr, Harding, and Dayton, 1968-69; Dayton, 1972; Masry, 1977, p.13; Parr et al., 1978; Bawden, 1979; Bawden, Edens, and Miller, 1980; Bawden, 1981; Ingraham et al., 1981, pp.71-75; Parr, 1982; Bawden, 1983; Rothenberg and Glass, 1983). Literary, epigraphic, and archaeological lines of evidence all bear witness to the presence of a vigorous high culture in Arabia before the mid-1st millennium B.C. (see, e.g., Pritchard, 1969, pp.305-6, 562-63 and Lambert, 1972, for Nabonidus' removal of the Babylonian court to Teima, a North Arabian oasis). That camel-borne trade continued to benefit Pre-Islamic culture in the Arabian peninsula well into the Hellenistic and Roman periods is clear from the Classical authors and from many sites in the east (e.g., Adams et al., 1977, p.27; Potts et al., 1978, pp.10-13; During Caspers, 1980; Hannestad, 1983; Lombard and Salles, 1984), and in the south (e.g., Bowen and Albright, 1958; Jamme, 1962; Cleveland, 1965; Pirenne, 1975; al-Ansary, 1981; Zarins, Murad, and al-Yish, 1981, pp.23-28; Tindel, 1984).

By far the greatest quantity of visible remains in the Wadi al-Jubah date to this Pre-Islamic Arabian period, when Marib to the north was the capital of Saba, and Timna to the south was the capital of Qataban. This is the period when human efforts drastically changed the local environment. As at Marib (e.g., Dayton, 1979; Schmidt, 1982; Brunner, 1983) and in the Wadi Beihan (Bowen and Albright, 1958), the Sabaean/Qatabanian hydraulic engineers constructed water-diversionary devices and canals in the Wadi al-Jubah, enabling them to irrigate substantial field plots (above the thick gray-black native soil layers described above). The water trapped during the seasonal floods, which normally would have been lost into the neighboring deserts, was instead channeled into the field plots. This system did impose substantial costs on the society. It was very labor-intensive, both in operation of the system and in the farming of the land, as well as in the continuing need to rebuild the system as the fields rose from the silt that no longer escaped back to the desert (Van Beek, 1969, p.368), but instead was trapped in the agricultural fields (see fig.7). The economic gain, however, was considerable. It seems from excavated samples (Blakely, Sauer, and Toplyn, 1985, pp.126-28) that wheat and barley were grown in the fields and that date and lotus, or *'alb* (*Zizyphus spina christi*), were cultivated, crops impossible without irrigation and ones which along with animal products (from, e.g., sheep/goat, camel, cattle) and vegetables would provide the basic foodstuffs needed in an economic system.

In conjunction with this irrigation system in the Wadi al-Jubah, numerous ancient wells were excavated down about 15-30 meters to the dioritic bedrock; these captured water that had percolated through the soil, allowing it to be recycled (see fig.8). Usually mounds containing much silt and broken pottery surround these wells, and many times structures are found nearby (for details, see Toplyn, 1984, pp.22, 47; Blakely, Sauer, and Toplyn, 1985, pp.42-43, 48). It is assumed that these structures were the houses and farmsteads of the farmers who ran the irrigation/farming system. At Hajar at-Tamrah (HT12), broken storage vessels, cooking pots, and bowls were found; these items sup-

Fig. 7. Photo of silt beds at Hajran al-Kanus (HK25), after excavation of geological probe (behind M.R. Toplyn). Note silts' horizontal bedding planes. View to west.

Fig. 8. Photo of ancient well being used by epigrapher Albert Jamme at Jubah al-Jadidah. View to south.

port the idea of habitation on such mound sites. Artifacts typical of this period in the wadi include handmade organic-tempered pottery with burnished red slip (see figs.9, 10), obsidian microliths, vessels carved from steatite, and inscribed materials (Toplyn 1984; Blakely, Sauer, and Toplyn, 1985).

Other contemporary occupied sites have been found in the Wadi al-Jubah region. A major (ca. 10-acre) fortified site, Hajar ar-Rayhani (HR3; figs.3, 5), occupies a position at the north end of the Wadi al-Jubah basin. To the north of it, in the narrow pass leading into the wadi, some additional but smaller (ca. 1-2 acres) walled sites appear (e.g., HJR45, F56H). The positioning of these sites might suggest a military function. Both Marib and Timna, as well as two large sites near modern Harib (one of which was visited by team members), were fortified and situated amid large agricultural tracts. Smaller agricultural areas were found in conjunction with small walled sites, one (Hajar Ayanah) found east of the Wadi al-Jubah on the road to modern Harib and ancient Timna, and one (Hajar Ramis) found north of the Wadi al-Jubah on the road to Marib. All of these sites are found along the mountain edges, where the seasonal flash flood runoff could be collected and used for irrigation.

A satellite picture of the spice caravan route between Timna and Marib during the Qatabanian and Sabaean period would show two major fortified cities,

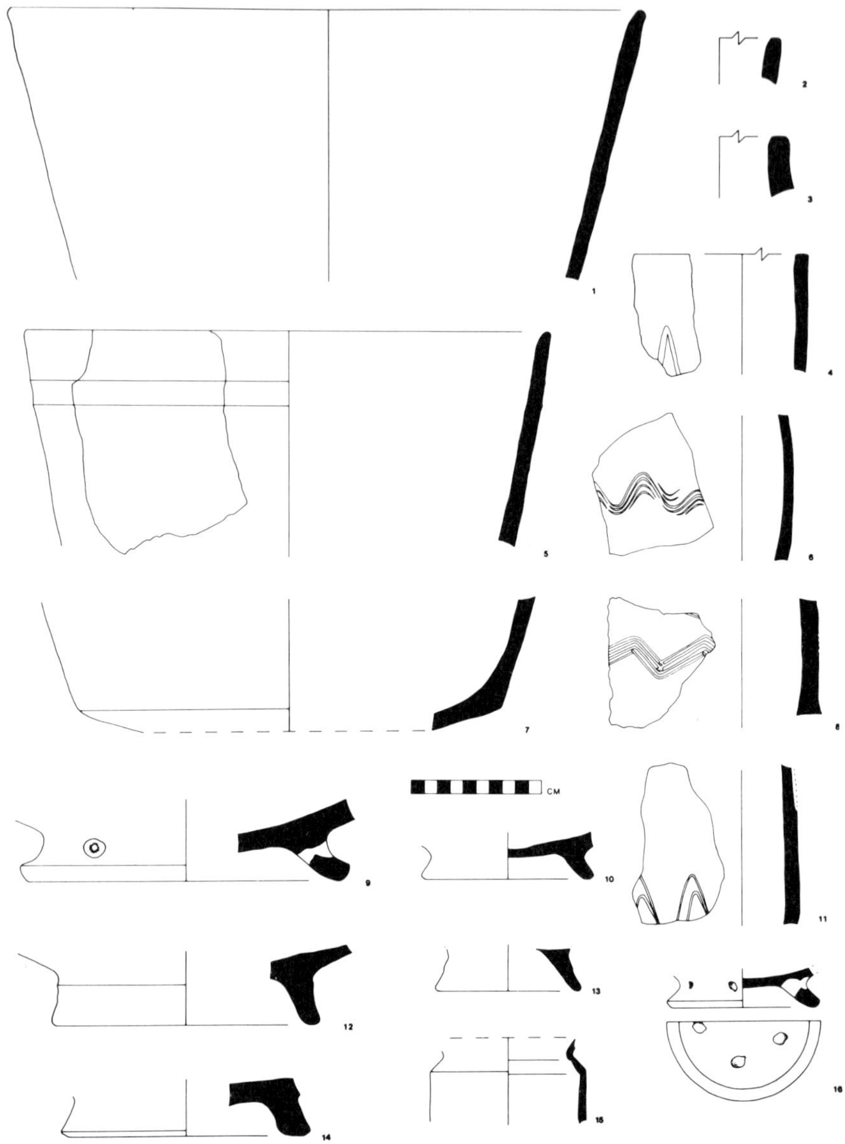

Fig. 9. Drawings of some potsherds collected from surface reconnaissance of HT 12; red-slipped wares, some with burnish, are present. From Blakely in Blakely, Sauer, and Toplyn, 1985, fig. 40.

one at Harib (ancient Haribat) and one in the Wadi al-Jubah (Hajar ar-Rayhani [HR3]), dependent upon a well-organized agricultural base. These cities were separated by a series of smaller walled sites. Haribat was probably one day's journey by caravan through the Mablaqah Pass from Timna, and the Wadi al-Jubah was probably one day beyond Haribat and one day from Marib (von Wissmann and Höfner, 1952, pp.41-42; Groom, 1976, pp.73-75).

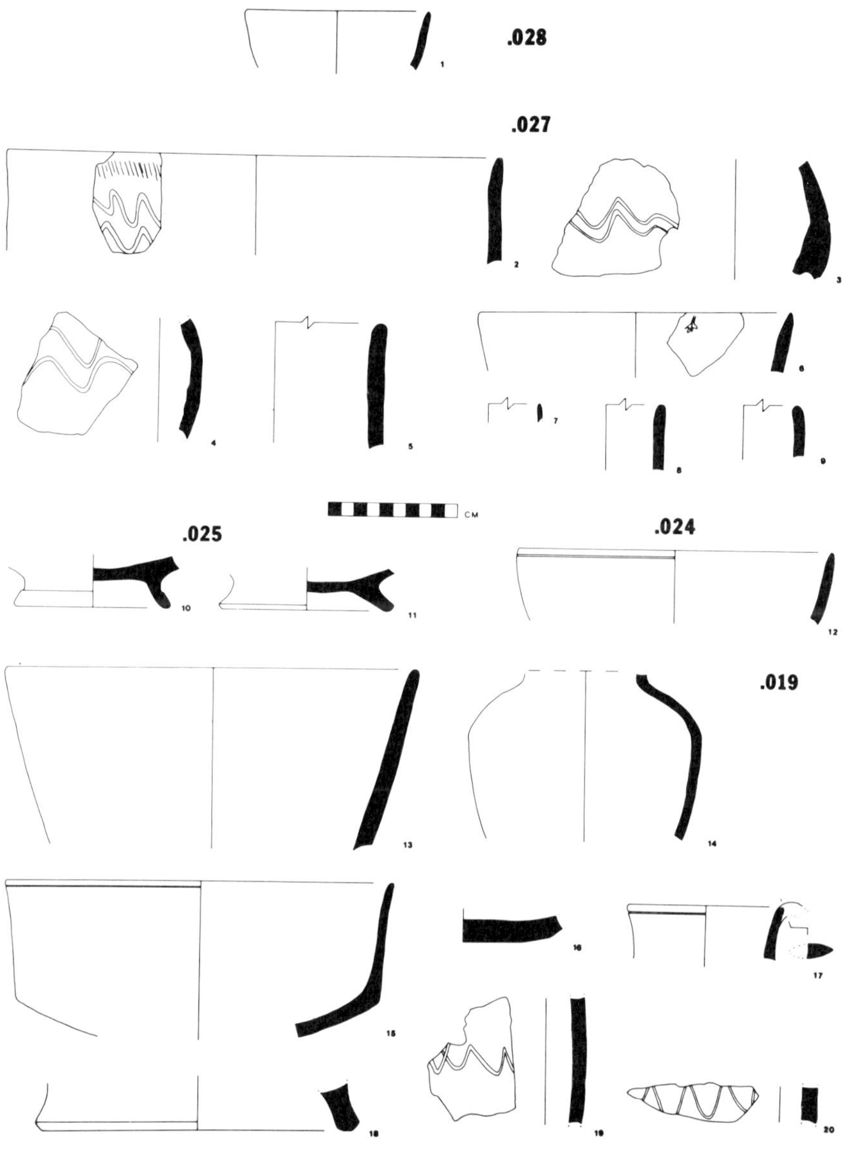

Fig. 10. Drawings of some stratified pottery from HT12. Red-slipped wares, some with burnish, predominate. From Blakely in Blakely, Sauer, and Toplyn, 1985, fig. 35.

The question of why these farming communities grew up along the spice route is a very important one. Which came first, the spice route or the agricultural community? In terms of absolute dates, it has been argued above that the caravan trade would not have been feasible prior to the domestication of the camel as a beast of burden, and this is thought to have occurred in the Late Bronze or Early Iron Age. At the bottom of the Hajar at-Tamrah probe, we obtained an uncalibrated date of 1330 ± 110 B.C. for carbonized/charred wood (see above) that was found in conjunction with Pre-Islamic pottery. This might suggest a Late Bronze or Early Iron Age date for the beginning of the site, and thus for agriculture in the wadi. This is, however, the earliest date published for such a context in South Arabia, although other excavated sites in Arabia may soon support it (e.g., Parr and Gazdar, 1980; Adams et al., 1977, p.29). Three radiocarbon dates obtained from the collapse of a roofed structure from the same site, nearly four meters above the former sample, and the ceramic evidence in the intervening layers, suggest that this site was abandoned about 400 B.C. (Blakely, 1983; see Blakely in Blakely, Sauer, and Toplyn, 1985, pp.87, 118; CRD dates of 880-620, 785-405, and 760-390 B.C.). Similar radiocarbon dates were obtained for unexcavated contexts at the sites of Hajar al-Husn (HJR45; see fig.3, site no.45) and Hajar ar-Rayhani (HR3) (Blakely, 1983): 530 ± 60 B.C. (CRD date of 810-420 B.C.) for HJR45; and 510 ± 200 B.C. and 410 ± 50 B.C. (CRD dates of 1015-170 B.C. and 755-275 B.C., respectively) for HR3. Could these data suggest that these agriculturally based sites were also abandoned around the same time?

Subsequent excavation at HR3, however, produced a coin datable within the mid-1st through mid-2nd centuries A.D., lying stratified well below the modern surface. The relative dating of the pottery recovered from those overlying layers is provided by parallels from Hajar Bin Humeid, spanning the 3rd century B.C. through the 5th century of this era. Furthermore, pottery and other artifacts recovered from Hajar al-Husn (HJR45) show that this site was contemporary with HR3. Thus neither of these sites seems to have been abandoned at the same time as Hajar at-Tamrah. Site abandonment, however, did and still does occur in the Wadi al-Jubah, but not all of the sites were necessarily abandoned at a single point in time. Thus the outer limits of the Sabaean/Qatabanian occupation in the wadi are Late Bronze/Early Iron Age to at least the first centuries of this era. The beginning seems to be contemporary with the domestication of the camel and the hypothetical beginning of camel caravans. Its end may coincide with the general abandonment of the overland caravan route in favor of the sea route. Can these correlations be mere coincidence?

In present-day Yemen, in the mountains immediately west of the Wadi al-Jubah, there is a large agricultural population farming in wadi beds that have been dammed up and have collected the aeolian silt in a manner resembling that seen in the wadi proper. This population is much larger than the current population of the wadi, and it has much better crop production due to more rainfall at the higher elevations and a cooler climate. In addition to wheat, barley, and lotus, fig and olive are cultivated. Also there is considerable land, suitable for expansion of agriculture, which appears never to have been used. These people claim to have been living there for many centuries, if not a few millennia, using the same techniques as their relatives in the main wadi (who claim settlement of the main wadi area only a few generations ago). Unless there is an outside stimulus, indigenous agriculture in the main wadi appears unlikely. Two outside stimuli might promote such occupation: a strong central authority that wished to see the area inhabited; or profit to be made via trade, or both. It is suggested that as trade along the spice route began, the local rulers seized upon the opportunity of gathering tolls by colonizing the habitable land along that route with agricultural communities that could support the military control of the area. The military communities offered protection to the caravans in exchange for tolls which would drop into the coffers of the local rulers, and later of the kings of Qataban and Saba.

The demise of the system is even more unclear. In the Wadi al-Jubah region at least one of the farmsteads seems to have disappeared about 400 B.C. Yet the major city (Hajar ar-Rayhani) seems to have lasted well into the first centuries of this era, on the basis of coin and ceramic evidence. If the underlying hypotheses are correct, did the caravan route collapse and obviate the need for such areas, or did the agriculture collapse and cease to support the caravans?

During our analysis of the pottery, soluble salts in high concentrations were found to have impregnated the vessels' clay after it had been fired, used, and subsequently buried in the soil. The fired color of the pottery from the upper layers of Hajar ar-Rayhani is predominantly yellowish, as opposed to the earlier red wares from the lower layers. Clay mixed with salt can produce a yellowed ware when fired. This could mean an increase in the saline content of the soils and clays due to centuries of intensive irrigation (for distant Mesopotamian evidence, see Jacobsen and Adams, 1958). Soils from various locales in the Wadi al-Jubah have been tested for soluble salt content, and their concentrations were found to be abnormally high (to be published in vol.4 of our preliminary report series). It is possible that the soil became saline and ceased to grow adequate crops, thus reducing the agricultural support for this part of the trade system. Alternatively, it is possible that the caravan route shifted, resulting in the wadi's abandonment by its inhabitants (Bowen in Bowen and Albright, 1958, pp.82-85), who perhaps moved up into the seemingly more productive mountains. Whatever the cause, it seems that no substantial sedentary life persisted in the wadi from that date until modern times.

What emerges, then, for the Qatabanian/Sabaean periods is an almost symbiotic relationship between trade and agriculture along the spice routes between Qataban and Saba. The geomorphological and agricultural settings of the Wadi al-Jubah could have provided natural defences and sustenance for the

Fig. 11. Photo of burial cairn F56C at al-Faraah, prior to partial excavation in 1985. View to north.

merchants who passed through. In exchange, tariffs could have been levied to bolster the agriculturally based economy.

Another activity taking place in the Wadi al-Jubah at that time appears to have been the production of tin-bronzes. In the lower layers reached in our unfinished probe at Hajar ar-Rayhani was the debris of a metal-production/working installation replete with furnace lining, possible crucible fragments, ash, and small pieces of vesicular, glassy slag. One piece of charcoal found in association with this debris yielded a date of 540 ± 60 B.C. (CRD date of 795-415 B.C.). So far no copper mines have been found in the Wadi al-Jubah.

Other questions arise about the Wadi al-Jubah region at this time, the foremost being who controlled it, Qataban or Saba. Both Qatabanian and Sabaean inscriptions are known from the wadi. For the period from the initial occupation of Hajar at-Tamrah to the abandonment of Hajar ar-Rayhani within the first few centuries of this era, the political alignment of the wadi must remain a matter of speculation until all of the inscriptions have been fully studied. Yet some of the sites around the wadi seem to be oriented against northern incursion. The northern route into the wadi would be well protected by them. The commanding position of Hajar ar-Rayhani within the wadi faced north to the exit toward Marib from the Wadi al-Jubah basin, and lay due west of an easily defensible pass leading toward Harib and Timna. About 7 km. north of sites F56A-H lies another walled site, Hajar Ramis, which commands the route between our wadi and Marib. One interpretation of this configuration could be that the border between Qataban and Saba ran just north of the Wadi al-Jubah basin, and that the walled sites within the wadi protected the northwest extent of Qataban; conversely, the large site between the Wadi al-Jubah and Marib seems to have been the southern outpost of Saba. Support for the latter site's having been in Saba is the nearby location of both the major Sabaean sanctuary at al-Masajid (Fakhry, 1951-52; Schmidt, 1982; pp.135-41) and the inscribed Sabaean kinglist at Jabal al-'Amud (Jamme, 1980).

At the eastern side of the Wadi al-Jubah are two high passes leading toward Harib and Timna. Neither is fortified; rather they are blocked in such a way as to direct traffic into specific areas, more like a toll post than an international barrier (see fig.1). Could this arrangement lend support to the idea of Qatabanian control?

At a later point in time the political control of the Wadi al-Jubah may have changed. Were the northern walled sites also abandoned then? It is known that the Sabaean kingdom was expanding at the expense of neighboring kingdoms. Could the abandoned sites be evidence for that expansion?

Fig. 12. Photo of possible barrier wall in a saddle north of the southeastern pass. View to north.

After the demise of the irrigation systems and the associated farmsteads, settlements, and fortified town, sendentary life seems to have ended in the Wadi al-Jubah until modern times. Scant remains do exist for this period, however, such as a burial tumulus (site F56C; see above and fig.12) with an uncalibrated radiocarbon date in the late 6th century A.D. Thousands of these tumuli exist, but again, we cannot yet say whether they might be 'Neolithic' or post-Sabaean. Other evidence is more fleeting. 'Modern' pottery (cf. Weir, 1975) is found on the surface of about one-third of the sites in the wadi. Unfortunately, ceramic studies do not yet allow much precision in the dating of this material. Both early and late varieties seem to be present, but there is no absolute control on them.

The hills to the west of the wadi present an entirely different picture. Well-cared-for terrace systems of many meters depth, and ruined structures containing apparently early and late 'Islamic/Modern' pottery, suggest a sedentary agrarian lifestyle in the hills for centuries, if not millennia. Thus far, however, evidence for major Islamic remains such as those known to the west and along the coast of Yemen (e.g., Schmidt, 1982, pp.197-275; Keall, 1983) has not been found in the Wadi al-Jubah.

The last century has seen the resettlement of the wadi by villagers and renewed commerce on the desert tracks between present-day South Yemen, Saudi Arabia, and North Yemen. Trucks roar over the sand, transporting commodities in all directions. Unfortunately, building stones are one such commodity, and many times those stones come from ancient structures; inscribed blocks are among the most highly prized. Robbing of stones from the sites was widespread until the past few years in the Wadi al-Jubah region. Even parts of Mahram Bilqis, excavated in 1951-52, can be seen incorporated in modern structures.

For us the immediate future holds in store one last season of probing at Hajar ar-Rayhani, the major site in the Wadi al-Jubah. This will be followed by a few years' analysis of the wealth of material we have collected. We hope to be able to answer more questions than we have raised.

Acknowledgments

The Wadi al-Jubah Archaeological Project is sponsored by the American Foundation for the Study of Man. It has three participating institutions: the American Schools of Oriental Research; the Peabody Museum, Harvard University; and the University Museum, University of Pennsylvania. The project has been carried out under a five-year agreement with Qadi Ismail al-Akwa, Chief of the Organization for Antiquities and Libraries in Sanaa. In Sanaa, the project has benefited from use of the facilities of the American Institute for Yemeni Studies.

Notes

1. The term 'spices' refers to such aromatics as frankincense and myrrh, stacte (myrrh oil), cinnamon bark, nard, etc. These luxury goods were in great demand for domestic and ritual uses in the ancient world (see Groom, 1981).

2. Agreement on the interpretations presented in this and the following sections is not unanimous among the WAJAP staff members. We hope that the results obtained from our next field season will enable us to resolve these differences of opinion.

3. All radiocarbon dates cited in this article are presented in the uncalibrated B.C. date citation format for the 'Libby' half-life of 5568 years, followed by the Calibrated Radiocarbon Date (CRD) citation format for the 2.00 sigma, or 95%, level of certainty based on the 5730 half-life. The CRD date is the most current, and statistically most reliable, format for citing radiocarbon dates. The unpublished 2.00 sigma values were provided by Dr. Henry Michael of MASCA (Museum Applied Science Center for Archaeology, University Museum).

Bibliography

Adams, R.M., Parr, P.J., Ibrahim, M. and al-Mughannum, 'A.S. (1977), 'Saudi Arabian Archaeological Reconnaissance 1976', *Atlal*, vol.1, pp.21-40.

Albright, F.P. (1952), 'The Excavation of the Temple of the Moon at Mârib (Yemen)', *Bulletin of the American Schools of Oriental Research*, no.128, pp.28-38.

Albright, F.P. (1982), *The American Archaeological Expedition in Dhofar, Oman, 1952-1953* (Publications of the American Foundation for the Study of Man, vol.6), Washington, DC, American Foundation for the Study of Man.

Albright, W.F., (1955), 'On the Early South-Arabic Inscription in Vertical Columns', *Bulletin of the American Schools of Oriental Research*, no.138, p.50.

al-Ansary, A.R. (1981), *Qaryat al-Fau: A Portrait of Pre-Islamic Civilisation in Saudi Arabia*, New York, St. Martin's Press.

[Arrian, see Robson]

Bawden, G. (1979), 'Khief El-Zahrah and the Nature of Dedanite Hegemony in the al-'Ula Oasis', *Atlal*, vol.3, pp.63-72.

Bawden, G. (1981), 'Recent Radiocarbon Dates from Tayma', *Atlal*, vol.5, pp.149-53.

Bawden, G. (1983), 'Painted Pottery of Tayma and Problems of Cultural Chronology in Northwest Arabia', in J.F.A. Sawyer and D.J.A. Clines (eds.), *Midian, Moab and Edom*, Sheffield, England, JSOT.

Bawden, G., Edens, C. and Miller, R. (1980), 'Preliminary Archaeological Investigations at Tayma', *Atlal*, vol.4, pp.69-106.

Bayle des Hermens, R. de (1976), 'Première mission de recherches préhistoriques en République arabe du Yémen', *L'Anthropologie*, vol.80, pp.5-38.

Bayle des Hermens, R. de (1984), 'L'Arabie du Sud avant l'histoire: état actuel des connaissances au Yémen du Nord', in J. Chelhod et al., *L'Arabie du Sud: histoire et civilisation*, tome 1, *Le Peuple yéménite et ses racines*, Paris, Editions G.-P. Maisonneuve et Larose.

Bayle des Hermens, R. de and Grebenart, D. (1980), 'Deuxième mission de recherches préhistoriques en République arabe du Yémen', *L'Anthropologie*, vol.84, pp.563-82.

Benardelli, G. and Parrinello, A.E. (1970), 'Note su alcune località archeologiche del Yemen', *Annali dell'Istituto Orientale di Napoli*, vol.30, pp.117-20.

Benardelli, G. and Parrinello, A.E. (1971), 'Note su alcune località archeologiche del Yemen--II', *Annali dell'Istituto Orientale di Napoli*, vol.31, pp.111-18.

Bibby, G. (1970), *Looking for Dilmun*, New York, Alfred A. Knopf.

Blakely, J.A. (1983), 'Wadi al-Jubah Archaeological Project', *American Schools of Oriental Reserarch Newsletter*, vol.35, no.2, p.7.

Blakely, J.A. and Sauer, J.A. (1985), 'The Road to Wadi al-Jubah: Archaeology on the Ancient Spice Route in Yemen', *Expedition*, vol.27, no.1, pp.2-9.

Blakely, J.A., Sauer, J.A. and Toplyn, M.R. (1985), *The Wadi al-Jubah Archaeological Project*, vol.2, *Site Reconnaissance in North Yemen, 1983*, Washington, DC, American Foundation for the Study of Man.

Bowen, R.L., Jr. and Albright, F.P. (1958), *Archaeological Discoveries in South Arabia* (Publications of the American Foundation for the Study of Man, vol.2), Baltimore, Johns Hopkins Press.

Breton, J.-F. (1980), 'Rapport sur une mission archéologique dans le wâdî Ḥaḍramawt (Yémen du Sud) en 1979', *Comptes rendus de l'Académie des Inscriptions et Belles-Lettres*, janv.-mars., pp.57-80.

Brice, W.C. (1984), 'The Classical Trade-Routes of Arabia, from the Evidence of Ptolemy, Strabo and Pliny', in A.R. al-Ansary (ed.), *Pre-Islamic Arabia*, Riyadh, King Saud University Press.

Brunner, U. (1983), *Die Erforschung der antiken Oase von Mārib mit Hilfe geomorphologischer Untersuchungsmethoden* (Archäologische Berichte aus dem Yemen, Bd.2), Mainz am Rhein, Verlag Phillip von Zabern.

Bullit, R.W. (1975), *The Camel and the Wheel*, Cambridge, Harvard University Press.

Burkholder, G. and Golding, M. (1971), 'Surface Survey of Al-'Ubaid Sites in the Eastern Province', in H. Field (comp.), *Contributions to the Anthropology of Saudi Arabia*, Miami, Field Research Projects.

Caton-Thompson, G. (1944), *The Tombs and Moon Temple of Hureidha (Hadhramaut)* (Reports of the Research Committee of the Society of Antiquaries of London, no.13), Oxford, Society of Antiquaries of London.

Caton-Thompson, G. and Gardner, E.W. (1939), 'Climate, Irrigation, and Early Man in the Hadhramaut', *Geographical Journal*, vol.93, pp.18-38.

Cleveland, R.L. (1960), 'The 1960 American Archaeological Expedition to Dhofar', *Bulletin of the American Schools of Oriental Research*, no.159, pp.14-26.

Cleveland, R.L. (1965), *An Ancient South Arabian Necropolis* (Publications of the American Foundation for the Study of Man, vol.4), Baltimore, Johns Hopkins Press.

Copeland, L. and Bergne, P. (1976), 'Flint Artifacts from the Buraimi Area, Eastern Arabia and Their Relations with the Near Eastern Post-Paleolithic', *Proceedings of the Seminar for Arabian Studies*, vol.9, pp.40-61.

Costa, P. (1973), 'Antiquities from Ẓafar (Yemen)', *Annali dell'Istituto Orientale di Napoli*, vol.33, pp.185-206.

Costa, P. (1976), 'Antiquities from Ẓafar (Yemen) --II', *Annali dell'Istituto Orientale di Napoli*, vol.36, pp.445-56.

Dayton, J.E. (1972), 'Midianite and Edomite Pottery', *Proceedings of the Seminar for Arabian Studies*, vol.5, pp.25-37.

Dayton, J.E. (1975), 'The Problem of Climatic Change in the Arabian Peninsula', *Proceedings of the Seminar for Arabian Studies*, vol.8, pp.33-60.

Dayton, J.E. (1979), 'A Discussion on the Hydrology of Marib', *Proceedings of the Seminar for Arabian Studies*, vol.12, pp.124-29.

de Cardi, B. (ed.) (1978), *Qatar Archaeological Report: Excavations 1973*, Oxford, Oxford University Press.

Doe, D.B. (1971), *Southern Arabia*, London, Thames and Hudson.

Doe, D.B. (1983), *Monuments of South Arabia*, Cambridge, Oleander Press.

During Caspers, E.C.L. (1980), *The Bahrain Tumuli: An Illustrated Catalogue of Two Important Collections*, Leiden, Nederlands Instituut voor het Nabije Oosten.

Fakhry, A. (1951-52), *An Archaeological Journey to Yemen (March-May, 1947)*, 3 vols., Cairo, Government Press.

Faris, N.A. (tr. and ed.) (1981), *The Antiquities of South Arabia*, by al-Hamdani, Westport, CT, Hyperion Press.

Field, H. (1958), 'Stone Implements from the Rub' al Khali, Southern Arabia', *Man*, vol.58, pp.93-94.

Field, H. (1960), 'Carbon-14 Date for a "Neolithic" Site in the Rub' al Khali', *Man*, vol.60, p.172.

Garbini, G. (1970), 'Antichità yemenite', *Annali dell'Istituto Orientale di Napoli*, vol.30, pp.400-04, 537-48.

Glaser, E. (1890), *Skizze der Geschichte und Geographie Arabiens*, Berlin, Weidmann.

Godley, A.D. (tr.) (1921-24), *Herodotus*, 4 vols., London, W. Heinemann.

Groom, N.St.J. (1976), 'The Northern Passes of Qataban', *Proceedings of the Seminar for Arabian Studies*, vol.9, pp.69-80.

Groom, N. (1981), *Frankincense and Myrrh*, London, Longman.

[al-Hamdani, H.I.A., see Faris]

Hamilton, R.A.B. (1942), 'Six Weeks in Shabwa', *Geographical Journal*, vol.100, pp.107-23.

Hannestad, L. (1983), *Ikaros--The Hellenistic Settlements*, vol.2, *The Hellenistic Pottery from Failaka*, Aarhus, Jysk Arkæologisk Selskab.

Hansen, T. (1974), *Arabia Felix: The Danish Expedition of 1761-1767*, tr. J. and K. McFarlane, New York, Harper and Row.

Harding, G.L. (1964), *Archaeology in the Aden Protectorates*, London, Department of Technical Cooperation.

Hastings, A., Humphries, J.H. and Meadow, R.H. (1975), 'Oman in the Third Millennium BCE', *Journal of Oman Studies*, vol.1, pp.9-55.

[Herodotus, see Godley]

Horowitz, A. (1979), *The Quaternary of Israel*, New York, Academic Press.

Hourani, G.F. (1952), 'Did Roman Commercial Competition Ruin South Arabia?', *Journal of Near Eastern Studies*, vol.11, pp.291-95.

Huntingford, G.W.B. (tr. and ed.) (1980), *The Periplus of the Erythraean Sea*, London, Hakluyt Society.

Huzayyin, S.A. (1937), 'Egyptian University Scientific Expedition to South-West Arabia', *Nature*, vol.140, pp.513-14.

Ibrahim, M. (1982), *Excavations of the Arab Expedition at Sar el-Jisr, Bahrain*, State of Bahrain, Ministry of Information.

Ingraham, M.L., Johnson, T.D., Rihani, B. and Shatla, I. (1981), 'Preliminary Report on a Reconnaissance Survey of the Northwestern Province (with a Note on a Brief Survey of the Northern Province)', *Atlal*, vol.5, pp.59-84.

Jacobsen, T. and Adams, R.M. (1958), 'Salt and Silt in Ancient Mesopotamian Agriculture', *Science*, vol.128, pp.1251-58.

Jado, A.R. and Zötl, J.G. (eds.) (1984), *Quaternary Period in Saudi Arabia*, vol.2, New York, Springer Verlag.

Jamme, A. (1962), *Sabaean Inscriptions from Maḥram Bilqîs (Mârib)* (Publications of the American Foundation for the Study of Man, vol.3), Baltimore, Johns Hopkins Press.

Jamme, A. (1976), *Carnegie Museum 1974-1975 Yemen Expedition*, Pittsburgh, Carnegie Museum.

Jamme, A. (1980), 'Sabaean Texts of J. 'Amûd al-'Ayraf, Yemen', in *Miscellanées d'ancient arabe*, vol.11, Washington, DC.

Jones, H.L. (tr.) (1967), *The Geography of Strabo*, 8 vols., Cambridge, Harvard University Press.

Keall, E.J. (1983), 'The Dynamics of Zabid and Its Hinterland: The Survey of a Town on the Tihamah Plain of North Yemen', *World Archaeology*, vol.14, no.3, pp.378-92.

Lambert, W.G. (1972), 'Nabonidus in Arabia', *Proceedings of the Seminar for Arabian Studies*, vol.5, pp.53-64.

Lombard, P. and Salles, J.-F. (1984), *La nécropole de Janussan (Bahrain)*, Lyon, Maison de l'Orient Méditeranéen.

Masry, A.H. (1974), *Prehistory in Northeastern Arabia: The Problem of Interregional Interaction*, Coconut Grove, Miami, FL, Field Research Projects.

[Masry, A.H. (ed.)] (1975), *An Introduction to Saudi Arabian Antiquities*, Riyadh, Department of Antiquities and Museums.

Masry, A.H. (1977), 'The Historic Legacy of Saudi Arabia', *Atlal*, vol.1, pp.9-19.

McClure, H.A. (1976), 'Radiocarbon Chronology of Late Quaternary Lakes in the Arabian Desert', *Nature*, vol.263, pp.755-56.

Montgomery, J.A. (1969), *Arabia and the Bible*, New York, Ktav.

Müller, W.W. (1984), 'Survey of the History of the Arabian Peninsula from the First Century A.D. to the Rise of Islam', in A.R. al-Ansary (ed.), *Pre-Islamic Arabia*, Riyadh, King Saud University Press.

Niebuhr, C. (1792), *Travels through Arabia and Other Countries in the East*, tr. R. Heron, Edinburgh, R. Morison.

Parr, P.J. (1982), 'Contacts between North West Arabia and Jordan in the Late Bronze and Iron Ages', in A. Hadidi (ed.), *Studies in the History and Archaeology of Jordan*, vol.1, Amman, Department of Antiquities of Jordan.

Parr, P.J. and Gazdar, M. (1980), 'A Report on the Soundings at Zubayda (al-'Amāra) in the al-Qasim Region: 1979', *Atlal*, vol.4, pp.107-17.

Parr, P.J., Harding, G.L. and Dayton, J.E. (1968-69), 'Preliminary Survey in N.W. Arabia, 1968', *Bulletin of the Institute of Archaeology, University of London*, vol.8-9, pp.193-242.

Parr, P.J., Zarins, J., Ibrahim, M., Waechter, J., Garrard, A., Clarke, C., Bidmead, M. and al-Badr, H. (1978), 'Preliminary Report on the Second Phase of the Northern Province Survey 1397/1977', *Atlal*, vol.2, pp.29-50.

[Periplus, see Huntingford]

Phillips, W. (1955), *Qataban and Sheba*, New York, Harcourt, Brace.

Pirenne, J. (1955), *La Grèce et Saba*, Paris, Académie des Inscriptions et Belles-Lettres.

Pirenne, J. (1956), *Paléographie des inscriptions sud-arabes; contribution à la chronologie et à l'histoire de l'Arabie du Sud antique*, vol.1, *Des origines jusgu'à l'époque himyarite*, Brussels, Académie Royale Flamande de Belgique.

Pirenne, J. (1961), *Le royaume sud-arabe de Qatabân et sa datation, d'après l'archéologie et les sources classiques jusqu'au Périple de la mer Erythrée*, Louvain, Publications Universitaires.

Pirenne, J. (1969), 'Notes d'archéologie sud-arabe, VI: Le péristyle du temple de Mârib d'après les fouilles de 1951-52', *Syria*, vol.46, pp.293-318.

Pirenne, J. (1974), 'Notes d'archéologie sud-arabe, IX: Hajar bin Ḥumeid', *Syria*, vol.51, pp.137-70.

Pirenne, J. (1975), 'Première mission archéologique française au Ḥadramout (Yémen du Sud)', *Comptes rendus de l'Académie des Inscriptions et Belles-Lettres*, janv.-mars, pp.261-79.

Pirenne, J. (1976), 'Deuxième mission archéologique française au Ḥadramout (Yémen du Sud), de décembre 1975 à février 1976', *Comptes rendus de l'Académie des Inscriptions et Belles-Lettres*, juil.-oct., pp.412-26.

Pirenne, J. (1978), 'Ce que trois campagnes de fouilles nous ont déjà appris sur Shabwa, capitale du Ḥadramout antique', *Raydān*, vol.1, pp.125-42.

[Pliny the Elder, see Rackham]

Potts, D., Mughannum, 'A.S., Frye, J. and Sanders, D. (1978), 'Preliminary Report on the Second Phase of the Eastern Province Survey 1397/1977', *Atlal*, vol.2, pp.7-27.

Pritchard, J.B. (ed.) (1969), *Ancient Near Eastern Texts Relating to the Old Testament*, 3rd ed., Princeton, Princeton University Press.

Pritchard, J.B. (ed.) (1974), *Solomon and Sheba*, London, Phaidon.

Rackham, H. (tr.) (1945), *Pliny's Natural History*, Cambridge, Harvard University Press.

Rathjens, C. and Wissmann, H. von (1932), *Vorislamische Altertümer*, Hamburg, Hamburgische Universität.

Rathjens, C. and Wissmann, H. von (1934), *Landeskundliche Ergebnisse*, Hamburg, Hamburgische Universität.

Ripinsky, M.M. (1975), 'The Camel in Ancient Arabia', *Antiquity*, vol.49, pp.295-98.

Roaf, M. (1976), 'Excavations at Al Markh, Bahrain', *Proceedings of the Seminar for Arabian Studies*, vol.9, pp.144-60.

Robin, C. (1976), 'Résultats épigraphiques et archéologiques de deux brefs séjours en République arabe du Yémen', *Semitica*, vol.26, pp.167-93.

Robin, C. (1979), 'Mission archéologique et épigraphique française au Yémen du Nord en Automne 1978', *Comptes rendus de l'Académie des Inscriptions et Belles-Lettres*, avr.-juin, pp.174-202.

Robin, C. (1981), 'Les inscriptions d'Al-Mi-'sâl et la chronologie de l'Arabie méridionale au IIIe siècle de l'ère chrétienne', *Comptes rendus de l'Académie des Inscriptions et Belles-Lettres*, avr.-juin, p.315-39.

Robin, C. (1982), *Les hautes-terres du Nord-Yémen avant l'Islam*, 2 vols., Istanbul, Nederlands Historisch-Archaeologisch Instituut.

Robin, C. and Breton, J.-F. (1982), 'Le sanctuaire préislamique du Ǧabal al-Lawḏ (Nord-Yémen)', *Comptes rendus de l'Académie des Inscriptions et Belles-Lettres*, juil.-oct., pp.590-629.

Robson, E.I. (tr.) (1929-33), *Arrian*, 2 vols., London, W. Heinemann.

Rothenberg, B. and Glass, J. (1983), 'The Midianite Pottery', in J.F.A. Sawyer and D.J.A. Clines (eds.), *Midian, Moab and Edom*, Sheffield, England, JSOT.

al-Sayari, S.S. and Zötl, J.G. (eds.) (1978), *Quaternary Period in Saudi Arabia*, vol.1, New York, Springer Verlag.

[Schmidt, J. (ed.)] (1982), *Archäologische Berichte aus dem Yemen*, Bd. 1, Mainz am Rhein, Verlag Philip von Zabern.

Smith, G.H. (1976), 'New Neolithic Sites in Oman', *Journal of Oman Studies*, vol.2, pp.189-98.

[Strabo, see Jones]

Tindel, R.D. (1984), 'Zafar: Archaeology in the Land of Frankincense and Myrrh', *Archaeology*, vol.37, no.2, pp.40-45.

Toplyn, M.R. (1984), *The Wadi al-Jubah Archaeological Project*, vol.1, *Site Reconnaissance in North Yemen, 1982*, Washington, DC, American Foundation for the Study of Man.

Van Beek, G.W. (1952), 'Recovering the Ancient Civilization of Arabia', *Biblical Archaeologist*, vol.15, pp.2-18.

Van Beek, G.W. (1956), 'A Radiocarbon Date for Early South Arabia', *Bulletin of the American Schools of Oriental Research*, no.143, pp.6-9.

Van Beek, G.W. (1960), 'Frankincense and Myrrh', *Biblical Archaeologist*, vol.23, pp.69-95.

Van Beek, G.W. (1969a), *Hajar Bin Ḥumeid: Investigations at a Pre-Islamic Site in South Arabia* (Publications of the American Foundation for the Study of Man, vol.5), Baltimore, Johns Hopkins Press.

Van Beek, G.W. (1969b), 'The Rise and Fall of Arabia Felix', *Scientific American*, vol.221, pp.36-46.

Wade, R. (1979), 'Cairn Structures on Jebel Balaq al-Junūbi and Jebel Balaq al-Awsat', *Journal of Yemen Centre for Studies and Research*, vol.3, pp.23-34.

Wapnish, P. (1981), 'Camel Caravans and Camel Pastoralists at Tell Jemmeh', *Journal of the Ancient Near Eastern Society*, vol.13, pp.101-21.

Weir, S. (1975), 'Some Observations on Pottery and Weaving in the Yemen Arab Republic', *Proceedings of the Seminar for Arabian Studies*, vol.8, pp.65-76.

Whalen, N., Killick, A., James, N., Morsi, G. and Kamal, M. (1981), 'Preliminary Report on the Western Province Survey', *Atlal*, vol.5, pp.43-58.

Wissmann, H. von (1964), *Zur Geschichte und Landeskunde von Alt-Südarabien*, Vienna, Österreichischen Akademie der Wissenschaften.

Wissmann, H. von (1968), *Zur Archäologie und antiken Geographie von Südarabien*, Istanbul, Nederlands Historisch-Archaeologisch Instituut.

Wissmann, H. von (1976), 'Die Geschichte des Sabäerreichs und der Feldzug des Aelius Gallus', in H. Temporini (ed.), *Aufstieg und Niedergang der Römischen Welt*, 2, *Principat*, vol.9, pt.1, pp.308-544.

Wissmann, H. von and Höfner, M. (1952), *Beiträge zur historischen Geographie des vorislamischen Südarabien*, Mainz, Akademie der Wissenschaften und Literatur.

Zarins, J. (1978), 'The Camel in Ancient Arabia: A Further Note', *Antiquity*, vol.52, pp.44-46.

Zarins, J., Ibrahim, M., Potts, D. and Edens, C. (1979), 'The Preliminary Report of the Third Phase of the Comprehensive Archaeological Survey Program -- The Central Province', *Atlal*, vol.3, pp.9-42.

Zarins, J., Murad, A.J. and al-Yish, K.S. (1981), 'The Second Preliminary Report on the Southwestern Province', *Atlal*, vol.5, pp.9-42.

Zarins, J., Whalen, N., Ibrahim, M., Mursi, A.J. and Khan, M. (1980), 'Preliminary Report on the Central and Southwestern Provinces Survey: 1979', *Atlal*, vol.4, pp.9-36.

Zeuner, F.E. (1954), '"Neolithic" Sites from the Rub-al-Khali, Southern Arabia', *Man*, vol.54, pp.133-36.

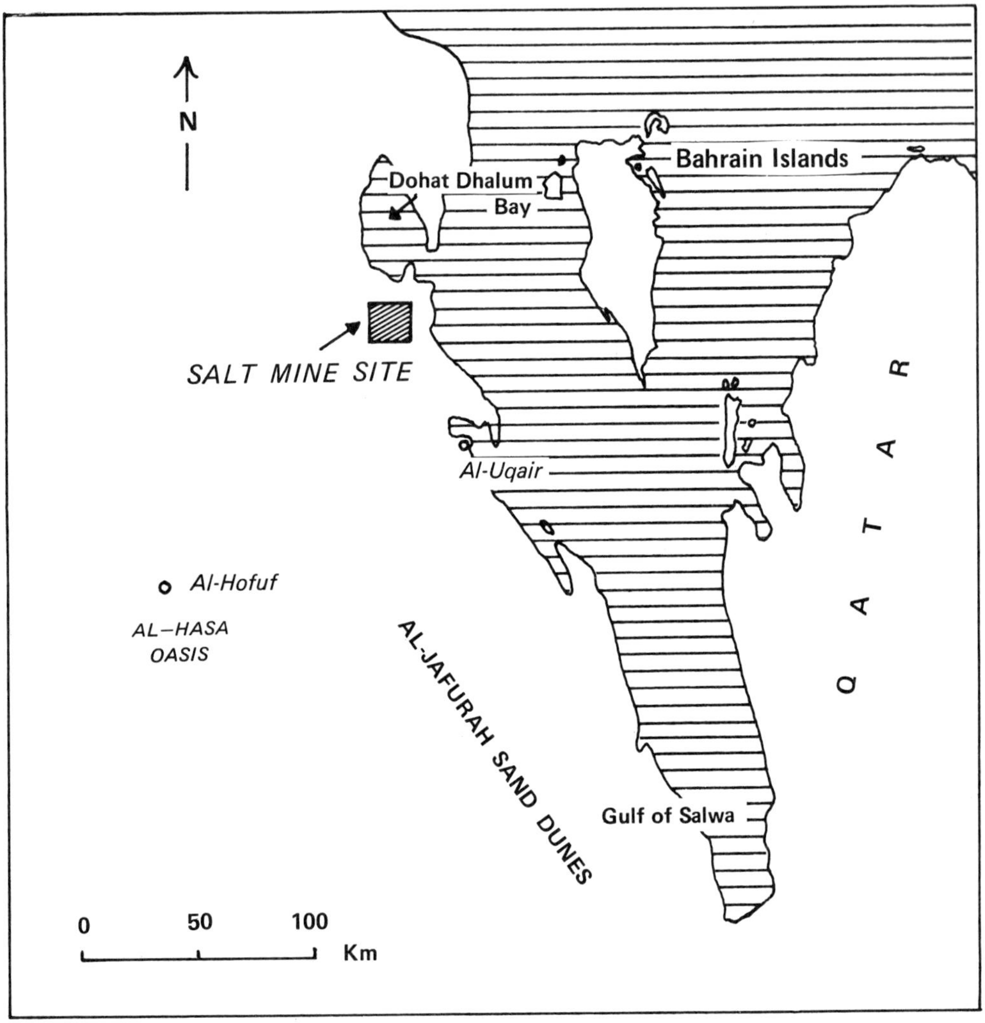

Fig. 1. The Salt Mine Site and its surroundings.

The Salt Mine Site and the 'Hasaean' Period in Northeastern Arabia

BY PIERRE LOMBARD

The Eastern Province of Saudi Arabia is still a somewhat neglected area, when compared to the rest of the Arabian side of the Gulf, where the recent development of archaeology has indeed been impressive. The region was first explored in the second half of the 19th and more so at the beginning of the 20th century by European travellers who provide us with the first mention or description of important sites such as Thaj and al-Hinna (Potts, 1984a, p. 85ff). Several systematic surveys were carried out in the footsteps of these explorers who were, in general, non-archaeologists (Cornwall, 1946; Bibby, 1964, 1965, 1973; Adams et al., 1977; Potts et al., 1978). The only recorded early excavation is the rescue operation carried out at the tomb of Ain Jawan (Bowen, 1950).

Undeniably, the subsequent development of archaeological research during the last few years was unexpected. Until 1986, very few excavations had actually followed up the first preliminary explorations. With the exception of the important work carried out at the Dhahran tumuli field in 1983 (Zarins et al., n.d.), recent archaeological activity has consisted mainly of limited but promising soundings (Bibby, 1973; Masry, 1974; Potts et al., 1978 and n.d.)[1].

In addition to these rare, official surveys and sondages, the activities of the ARAMCO (Arabian American Oil Company) community have been of particular importance. Over the years amateur investigators have surveyed and discovered a large number of archaeological sites belonging to various periods, mainly in the coastal area (Golding, 1974; n.d.; Burkholder, 1984). Their systematic surface-collecting has often been denounced by scholars, such as Adams et al. (1977, p. 26), who compare this activity to 'a giant vacuum cleaner' (sic). This humorous comment is perhaps excessive. We must not lose sight of the fact that many sites would not be known to the scientific community today were it not for the efforts of several ARAMCO members who never hesitated to welcome professional archaeologists, or to present and publish their finds, and even to return them to the local archaeological authorities and museums once these were established (cf. Burkholder, 1984, p. 182).

The present contribution deals in fact with one of the sites reported by ARAMCO members, the 'Salt Mine Site', recently examined in a comprehen-

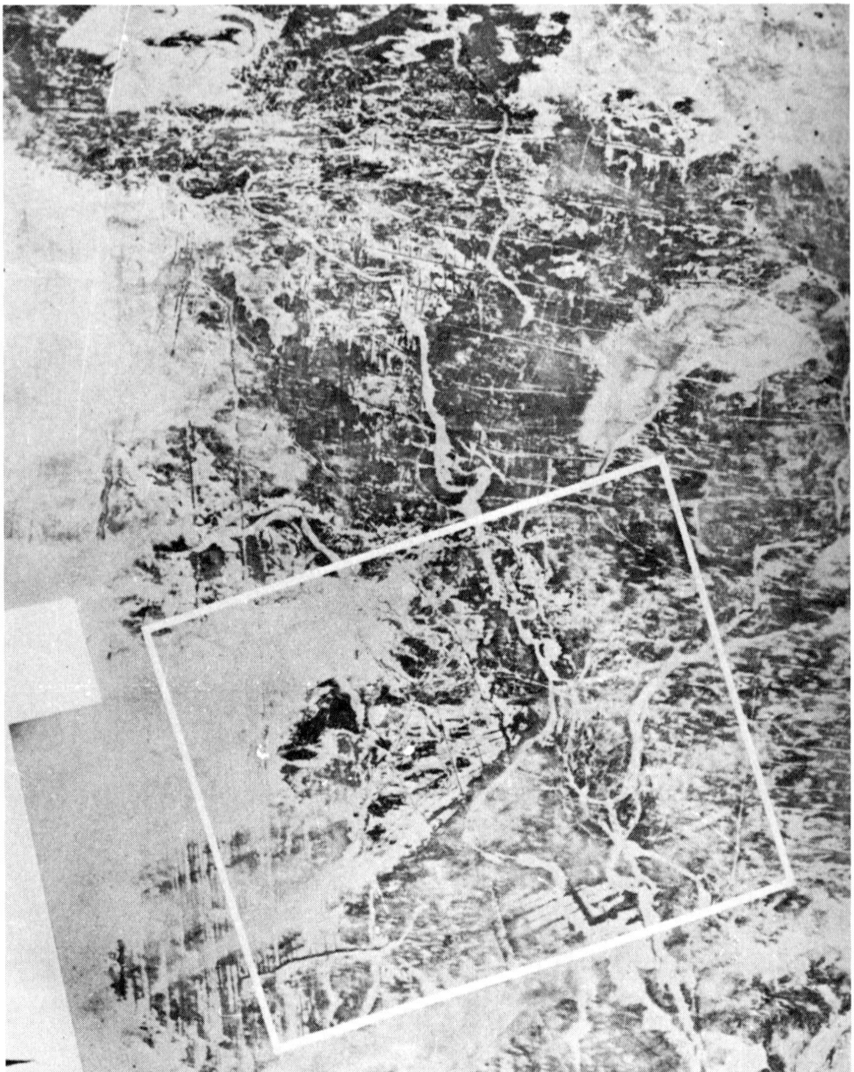

Fig. 2. Aerial photograph of the Salt Mine Site area (after *Natural History*, no. 70, 1961, p.24).

sive study I carried out on the Iron Age in eastern Arabia (Lombard, 1985) (2). My purpose here is, first, to assemble the relevant material, still quite sparse at the present time, and to focus on some unpublished finds, particularly the cylinder seals; then I shall try to situate the site's occupation within the chronological framework for northeastern Arabia recently suggested by Potts (1984a, p. 119). In conclusion, I shall briefly discuss, in light of the evidence reviewed here, the valildity of the equation often formulated: the Salt Mine Site = Gerrha (cf. James, 1969; Golding, 1984; Burkholder, 1984).

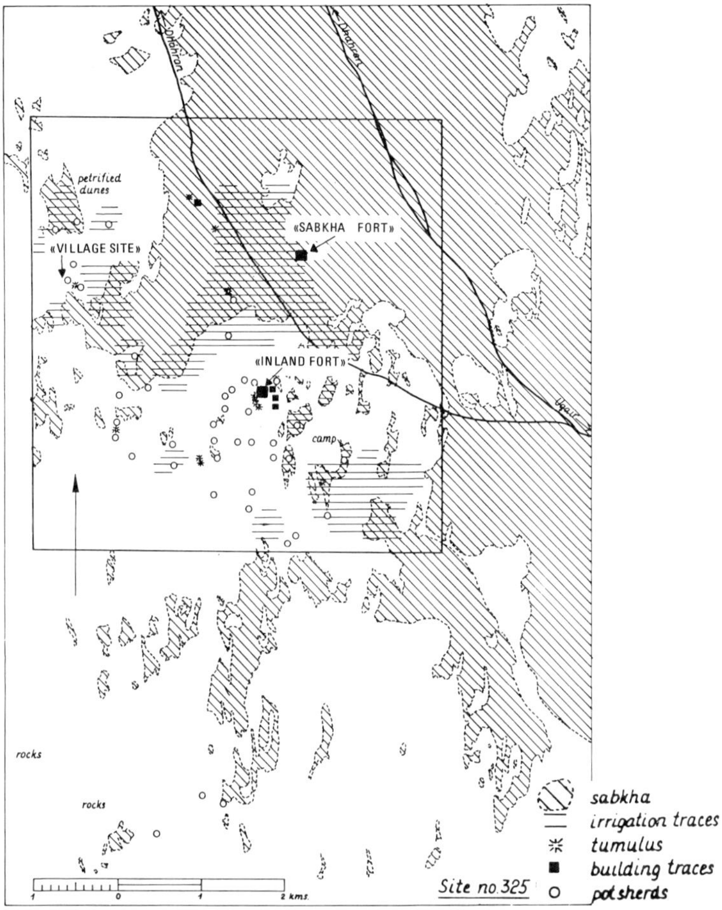

Fig. 3. The Salt Mine Site, ground plan of surface remains (after Bibby, 1973, fig. 37).

I. The Salt Mine Site: the archaeological remains

Situated ca. 25 km. northwest of al-Uqair (3), the Salt Mine Site is not a proper settlement, in the true sense of the word. Structures are scarce, but various traces of human activity can be seen spread over an exceptionally wide area (more than 10 sq. km.). The present environment of the site is rather unattractive and the area is one of the most desolate on the east Arabian littoral. To the east is an irregular belt of *sabkha*, several kilometers wide, which separates the archaeological area from the sea and, to the west are the al-Jafurah sands which threaten and probably already cover parts of the site. The area is named for the many salt flats nearby, some of which have been mined commercially for local consumption in recent years (Figs. 1 and 3).

Visible structures

The Ṣalt Mine Site was first recorded by P.B. Cornwall during his survey of al-Hasa. He reported '... a long, low, peat-like wall running from East to West..., pieces of crude pottery, polished stone implements and small chips of opal ... some beads, part of a copper object (perhaps a knife) and an oblong limestone trough...' (Cornwall, 1946, p. 33). Cornnwall dated the site to the 2nd or 3rd millennium B.C. His visit was probably as rapid as his conclusions. The material he collected was negligible and apparently atypical, and one may rightfully ask on what grounds he based his dating. We shall see that, since then, no further evidence has been brought to light to support his opinion. Moreover, Cornwall remained silent about the most impressive feature of the site. He never mentions seeing any traces of the fascinating irrigation network that the technicians of Aero Service Corporation (ASC) photographed some twenty years later (Linton, 1961, pp. 24-26).

The aerial photographic survey of the area, made by ASC as part of ARAMCO's search for oil, immediately catches the archaeologist's attention. Over a stretch of several square kilometers one can discern a broadly regular grid pattern which obviously recalls a modern irrigation or drainage system (Fig. 2). Indeed, nothing like this existed there at the time of the survey, and still does not, especially on such a scale. On the other hand, the aerial photographs clearly show part of the network disappearing to the west beneath the al-Jafurah sand dunes, which could bear witness to the relative antiquity of these features. Several visits to the site by ARAMCO geologists and by the Danish Archaeological Expedition have confirmed these observations. The traces are definitely those of old irrigation channels which show the common phenomenon of relief inversion: '...These channels had, during their use, accumulated a layer of clay and, after cultivation had been discontinued, the surface of the cultivation area had been denuded by wind erosion, leaving the channel beds, which were more resistant to erosion, standing at a higher level...' (Bibby, 1973, p. 40). This so-called 'relief' is all relative. G. Bibby reports that the earth banks do not exceed 5 to 10 cm. in height, reaching 30 cm. in one exceptional case. In fact, the photographs taken on the ground and published by the Danish expedition are rather disappointing when compared with the aerial shots of the site. Thus, one can well understand why these remains were not reported by Cornwall.

The structures visible on the ground, as well as the major occurrences of potsherds, were systematically mapped by the Danish expedition (Bibby, 1973, p. 42, figs. 37 and 40) (Fig. 3). With the exception of two fortified, quadrangular constructions, c. 1.5 km apart from each other, they do not appear very spectacular. The first one, known as the 'sabkha fort', is the easiest to see on the aerial photographs of the site [4], although the limited sounding carried out in 1965 demonstrated that nothing remains of it except for some traces of clay. These traces reveal a 50 x 50 m. square associated with a thick occupation layer containing charcoal and potsherds. The second, 'inland fort', is of a similar size (52 x 49 m.). A sounding on its western side identified a wall of small stones 1.4 m. wide, resting on a solid base of squared blocks. This fort seems to have burned down, as indicated by a thick, black destruction level [5]. In addition, G. Bibby reports a 'village site' 2 km. west of these buildings, but badly effected by wind erosion. Only the floors of the houses were actually preserved. Finally, several concentrations of tumuli were plotted in the area and one of these graves, situated close to the 'inland fort', was excavated without success by the Danish team (Bibby, 1973, pp. 46-47).

Archaeological material

Archaeological material is scarce due to the limited nature of the work carried out on the site. Only fragmentary vessels or sherds were discovered. These are comparable to types found in the Hellenistic levels at Thaj and in City V contexts on Bahrain (Bibby, 1973, p. 43). Most of the material currently known from the site actually comes from the surface collecting of ARAMCO amateurs. Precise locations are often unknown, which considerably limits the interest of some objects. This material, summarized in Fig. 4, is in many cases anomalous, and deserves careful study.

Pottery

Most of the material reported seems to be in the Hellenistic tradition (cf. *supra*, the parallels with Thaj and Bahrain). In this connection, one must note that the parallels drawn by Marny Golding to pottery found at Susa in the Persian-Achaemenian village (Golding, 1974, p. 29; n.d.) are not so convincing if one takes into consideration the paucity of reported types and the poor preservation of the Salt Mine Site material. On the other hand, a bowl with strong, carinated profile published by Burkholder (1984, fig. 35b) is likely to be earlier than the Hellenistic date that she assigns to it. (Fig. 5). Its shape and fabric ('olive-green paste') recall the commonest type represented in the 'snake-bowl' series from City IV at Qal'at al-Bahrain (Bibby, 1972, fig. p. 180; Lombard, 1986, fig. 67. 4-10). I have recently proposed a 6th century B.C. date for this material, based on both typological and stratigraphic considerations (Lombard, 1985, pp. 96-97).

CATEGORY	MATERIAL	DESCRIPTION
Pottery	–	Various types and shapes (handled jar, bowl, jug...)
Metal		
– arrow-heads	Copper/bronze « «	Tanged, leaf-shaped « «
Jewellery		
– beads	Carnelian, bone	–
	Gold	–
	Carnelian, agate, rock-crystal, shell, *«and other coloured stones»*	Various shapes
– earrings	Gold	–
Numismatic		
(1) – coin	Silver	Tetradrachm
(2) – coin	«	Tetradrachm ?
Glyptic		
(3) – stamp-seal	?	Roughly circular; scorpion and South-Arabian inscription: «KALBUM»
(4) – cylinder-seal	Frit	Geometric design
(5) – cylinder-seal	?	Winged quadrupeds (very worn)
(6) – cylinder-seal	?	Winged quadrupeds facing left; in the field: star
(7) – cylinder-seal	White chalcedony	A running winged monster (griffin?) pursues two gazelles
(8) – cylinder-seal	?	An archer on one knee aims at a standing griffin; in the field: star, spear-head, altar (?), bird
(9) – cylinder-seal	Carnelian	Two left-facing winged goats; in the field: globe, star, altar (?)
(10) – cylinder-seal	?	A full-face standing hero, wearing a short kilt, holds a spear-head and an unknown symbol; other character apparently facing right with a spear-head; in the field: dog (?), undetermined animal or symbol

Fig. 4. Summary of surface finds made at the Salt Mine Site.

MEAS.	LOCATION	REFERENCES	FIG. N° (This study)
–	«Sabkhah fort»	Bibby 1973, fig. 39, 42 Burkholder 1984, fig. 35b, 38a Golding, *forth.*, fig. 7-9	*Fig. 5*
max. L. 6 cm	«Sabkhah fort» ?	Bibby 1973: 43 Burkholder 1984, fig. 35c	– –
– – –	«Sabkhah fort» «Seal Flat» «Seal Flat» ?	Bibby 1973: 43 Golding, *forth.*, fig. 18-14 Burkholder 1984, fig. 42	– – –
–	–	Burkholder 1984: 33	–
w.: 13,15gr.	«	Altheim & Stiehl 1968: 96 Potts 1984b	*Fig. 6*
Ø : 1,5cm	«Seal Flat»	Golding, *forth.*, fig. 16-17	–
Ø : ca. 1cm	«Seal Flat»	Golding, *forth.*, fig. 15	–
H. ca. 1,75cm	9km NW of «Seal Flat»	*id. ibid.*, fig. 20	*Fig. 7*
?	«Seal Flat»	unpublished	–
H. 2,1cm; Ø : 0,64cm	«	Golding, *forth.*, fig. 13	–
H. 2,25cm Ø : 1,15cm	«	*id. ibid.*, fig. 11-12	*Fig. 8*
?	«	Lombard 1985, fig. 48: 138 Golding, *forth.* fig. 14	*Fig. 9*
H. 1,95cm Ø : 0,80 cm	«	*id. ibid.*, fig. 10	*Fig. 10*
?	«Seal Flat» ?	unpublished	*Fig. 11*

Fig. 5. Olive-green ware bowl from the Salt Mine Site (after Burkholder, 1984, fig. 35b).

Coins

The well-known 'Arados coin' (Fig. 4, no. 1) from the site, mentioned in passing by Altheim and Stiehl, has never been described. It is one of two archaic staters from the site showing the head of a male deity on the obverse, facing right, and a Phoenician galley on the reverse. It should probably be dated to the early 4th century B.C. (R. Morris, pers. comm. to D. Potts). In addition, a well-worn silver tetradrachm from the site, now in the Morris collection (Potts, 1984b, Fig. 6a,b), is probably a regular Alexander issue from Byblos (R. Morris, pers. comm. to D. Potts). We note that its weight of 13.15 gr. differs both from the official standard of 17.2 gr. introduced by Alexander for his tetradrachms, and from the average weight (c. 16.50 gr.) of the coins issued by the east Arabian kings of Hagar (Robin, 1974, pp. 85-92). A third coin (Fig. 4, no. 2) from the site is presently at Moesgaard (Denmark). We are not aware of its exact weight, but it is said to be another pseudo-Alexander tetradrachm. According to M. Golding (n.d.), it bears a legend written in Aramaic, which would suggest an issue of Abīʾēl, one of the supposed kings of Hagar (Robin, 1974, pp. 88-90; Potts, 1984b). The presence of an Aramaic legend probably accounts for the 3rd century B.C. date proposed by the late O. Mørkholm, who examined the coin. However, it should be recalled that the date of Abīʾēl is disputed, notably – and convincingly – by Robin, who places him around 150-140 B.C. (1974, p. 99).

Fig. 6a-b. Obverse and reverse of a Byblos tetradrachm from the Salt Mine Site (courtesy of D.T. Potts).

Glyptic

This is one of the most informative classes of surface finds. The stamp and cylinder-seals, often mentioned in descriptions of the site, remained essentially unknown until 1983 when M. Golding presented some of them at the 'Bahrain Through the Ages Conference' held in Manama (Golding, n.d., figs. 10-15). In fact, this material has never been properly studied, nor are matters helped by the poor quality of the photographs available. Nevertheless, I shall try here to shed some new light on these objects. Although almost all of the seals were found in one area, known as 'seal flat' (Golding, n.d.), they do not form a homogeneous series. Different stylistic traditions are represented, suggesting differences in both their origins and dates.

A unique inscribed stamp seal (Fig. 4, no. 3) will only be discussed briefly, as I do not have a satisfactory photograph of it. Its legend, written in South Arabian script, might be read 'KALBUM'. Based on this, A. Jamme has suggested a southern orgin for the seal (cited by Golding, n.d.). However, he notes that the central motif, a scorpion, 'must have been borrowed from some northern source'. In my opinion, the 9th-8th century B.C. date suggested by Jamme, which reflects an 'early' chronology for the Sabaean civilization, should be considered cautiously today.

Only one cylinder seal bears a geometric design (Fig. 4, no. 4 and Fig. 7). This has often been assigned to the end of the 4th millennium B.C.(e.g. Burk-

Fig. 7. Cylinder seal no. 4.

Fig. 8. Cylinder seal no. 7.

Fig. 9. Cylinder seal no. 8.

Fig. 10a-b. Cylinder seal no. 9.

holder, 1984, p. 32). According to Burkholder, this seal is the only one from the northern part of the Salt Mine Site where 'a few Jamdat Nasr rims can be seen'. I cannot evaluate this opinion, as none of the associated pottery has been published, but the dating of the seal to the Jamdat Nasr period seems unfounded. There is indeed no doubt that the central fishbone motif as well as the lateral horizontal lines recall some specimens from this period (cf. for instance Frankfort, 1955, pl. 17: 163-164). However, the seal is made of frit, and has a very small diameter, whereas seals of the Jamdat Nasr period are much more massive and are generally made of stronger material, such as glazed steatite. A comparison with the late 2nd millennium Elamite glyptic is more appropriate, in light of the features just mentioned (Porada, 1970, pl. XII: 144-145).

I shall not consider seals 5 and 6 (Fig. 4) here, as their state of preservation and poor iconography considerably hamper any analysis.

The winged griffin chasing two gazelles on cylinder 7 (Figs. 4, 8) shows a theme well-known in the 1st millennium B.C. glyptic of Mesopotamia. It appears on Neo-Assyrian seals carved in the so-called Linear Style (Porada, 1948, pp. 75-76). However, the vigorous but well-finished cutting of this specimen suggests rather that it belongs to the Late Cut Style, where the same theme is also common. This style is dated by Porada (1948, p. 49) and Teissier (1984, pp. 43, 180) to the 8th/7th centuries B.C. The posture of both the gazelles (looking back at the monster) and the griffin (the whole body leaning forward and its clawed paws reaching towards its prey) are particularly diagnostic and suggest a Babylonian origin (Porada, 1948, pl. CXI: 741-742; Von der Osten, 1934, pl. XXXIX: 436; Legrain, 1951, pl. 35: 594, pl. 36: 600). This attractive specimen is probably, therefore, an import.

This is obviously not the case with cylinder 8 (Figs. 4, 9), which shows another favorite theme of the Linear Style, an archer aiming at his prey. The coarseness of its manufacture suggests that this is a 'provincial' item. The archer's posture is unskillfully executed and the whole scene, ordinarily well-codified, deviates from the traditional schema (Porada, 1948, pl. LXXXVIII: 610-618; Buchanan, 1966, pl. 39: 574-577; Teissier, 1984, p. 151, nos. 144-154). The seal-cutter added the Marduk spear-head, which is unusual. Moreover, the traditional palm-leaf placed between the archer and the animal (which is supposed to represent the sacred tree defended by the armed hero) is replaced by a long-billed bird and a kind of altar (?). In fact, it is not very easy to attribute this object to a particular century within the 1st millennium B.C. E. Porada has suggested that such iconographical heterogeneity characterizes the earliest examples of the Linear Style (1948, p. 73). On the other hand, the strange headgear of the archer recalls a Persian crown (cf. Teissier, 1984, p. 183, nos. 289, 291). In this connection, it must be remembered that such unconven-

Fig. 11. Cylinder seal no. 10.

tional scenes are also found in the glyptic of the early Achaemenian period (Teissier, 1984, p. 183, no. 288), to which this seal could equally be assigned.

I am inclined to give a somewhat similar date (mid-6th century B.C.) to cylinder 9 (Figs. 4, 10a) which is, however, much better made. The unusual posture of the quadrupeds (one of the front paws is raised) is also attested on a cylinder seal dated to the Neo-Babylonian period from 'Ali East, on Bahrain (Roaf, 1976, fig. 2:1). P. Amiet, who kindly examined an impression of the seal, emphasizes the very atypical appearance of the animals' wings. These could recall some representations on Persepolitan glyptic (Amiet, pers. comm.). I should add to this remark that the shape of the seal, which is slightly tapered (cf. Fig. 10b), is similar to that of Achaemenian cylinder seals (Teissier, 1984, p. 183, no. 293).

The last seal (Figs. 4: 10, 11) is the most problematic. It is coarsely made, in spite of its rich if puzzling iconography. The strange, full-face character is unknown in the Neo-Assyrian/Neo-Babylonian glyptic répertoire, and its attributes are unclear. The dog (?) is surprising as well, especially as it is cut very differently from the other figures. The strange animal above the dog (a fantastic bird?) is even more confusing, as its spread wings and paws incongruously recall the oldest representations of the Uruk period (cf. Porada, 1948, pl. II: 4a). Only the decoration of the borders points to a 1st millennium B.C. date. It is clear that the circumstances of the seal's discovery have to be clarified. It is probably a forgery.

II. The Salt Mine Site and the Local Iron Age

The finds just reviewed suggest an occupation spanning approximately the last three quarters of the 1st millennium B.C. It is now advisable to consider how these finds fit into the current chronological schema for the later pre-Islamic cultures of northeastern Arabia (cf. Potts, 1984a, p. 120, table 9).

(a) – The 'Late Hasaean' phase (0-400 A.D.) is not attested in the material thus far recorded from the site. It must be remembered, however, that the various teams of the Saudi Arabian Comprehensive Survey did not visit the Salt Mine Site.

(b) – The soundings carried out by the Danish team seem to indicate that several of the structures can be assigned to the 'Middle Hasaean' phase (300-0 B.C.). This is notably so in the case of the two 'forts', where occupation layers yielded Hellenistic pottery. This phase is also represented by at least two of the silver coins found at the site. A 'Middle Hasaean' occupation at the Salt Mine Site is not so surprising if one takes into account that this period 'witnessed the greatest flourishing of the Eastern Province in the late pre-Islamic era' (Potts, 1984a, p. 119)

(c) – In contrast, the evidence for an 'Early Hasaean' occupation (800-300 B.C.) is particularly significant and merits some comment. As Potts recalls

Fig. 12. 'Pseudo-Barbar' ware jar from the Eastern Province (after Burkholder, 1984, fig. 36a).

Sources / Type of data	CHRONOLOGY	ENVIRONMENT	TOPOGRAPHY	Type of data / Interpretation
STRABO *Geography*, XVI,3,3			Gerrha situated: *«at a distance of 2400* stadia *from Teredon»*	+
			«on a deep gulf»	+
			«200 stadia *from the sea»*	–
		The soil of Gerrha *«contains salt and the people live in houses made of salt»*		+
	Gerrha inhabited by *«Chaldaeans, exiles from Babylon...»*			+ ?
PLINY *Natural History*, VI,32,7			Gerrha situated on *«Sinus Gerraicus»*, the second major bay from Ikaros	+
			Attene district (al-Hasa?) at 50 r. miles	+
			Tyros Island (Bahrain) at 50 r. miles	+
			Gerrha city is *«5 miles round»*	– ?
		Gerrha *«has towers made of squared blocks of salt»*		+
POLYBIUS *Histories*, XIII,9			Gerrha apparently situated at the South of Tylos	– ?
		The inhabitants of Gerrha cultivate Chattenia, *«a poor district... but villages and towers have been established for the convenience of the Gerrhaeans...»*.		+ ?
C. PTOLEMY acc. to James 1969, *abb.* 11 and Groom 1982, pl.99			Gerrha situated on the 5th bay from Spasinou Charax	+
This study	**Early Hasaean** evidence (pottery, seals...)			+
	Middle Hasaean evidence (pottery, coins...)			+
	No evidence for a **Late Hasaean** phase			+

Fig. 13. Critical table of sources for the location of Gerrha in light of the characteristics of the Salt Mine Site (+ = positive argument; - = negative argument).

(1984a, p. 119), this phase remains, in fact, poorly documented throughout the area. He only assigns to this period a 'proto-Arabic' inscription (Ja 1049) from al-Hofuf (comparatively dated to between the 9th and the 5th centuries B.C.) and a bathtub coffin cemetery south of Dhahran, which yielded pottery resembling that found in similar earthenware coffins on Bahrain in City IV contexts (Golding, 1974, p. 29; Potts, 1984, p. 110). Since Potts' review was written, some additional, isolated finds assignable to this phase have been published, such as a 6th century B.C. jar (Fig. 12) in 'pseudo-Barbar' ware [(6)], purchased in Qatif (Burkholder, 1984, fig. 36a). Above all, the 1983 excavations at the Dhahran tumuli field have greatly enriched the 'Early Hasaean' corpus with new 'pseudo-Barbar' pottery vessels and an interesting series of seals including stamps, cylinders, and scarabs (Zarins et al., n.d.). Several stamp seals, obviously of South Arabian origin (cf. *Atlal*, vol. 7, pl. 98b), can be compared with the Salt Mine Site specimen discussed above (Fig. 4, no. 3). The cylinder seals reported from Dhahran, judging by their descriptions, do not appear to be of purely Mesopotamian origin.

It can be seen that, although numerically few, the Iron Age finds from the Salt Mine Site represent an appreciable part of the presently known corpus of 'Early Hasaean' material. Nevertheless, the evidence is still very limited and must be interpreted with care. The presence of Mesopotamian-style cylinder seals certainly points to a relationship with this area. However, the earliest finds (assigned to the Linear Style) were probably in use over a long period of time in a marginal area like the Eastern Province. Moreover, most of the seals examined seem to belong to later periods, i.e. the Neo-Babylonian or Achaemenian eras. This could correspond to the situation on Bahrain at this time. I have recently suggested (Lombard, 1985, pp. 248-249) that the cultural influence as well as the overlordship of Mesopotamia was undoubtedly weak in Iron Age Dilmun up until the middle of the 7th century B.C. In contrast, the material culture of the island during the 6th/5th centuries B.C. shows strong ties to the Neo-Babylonian/Achaemenian tradition (pottery, glyptic, funerary customs, etc.). A similar pattern can be seen in the Mesopotamian historical texts which refer to this region (Lombard, 1985, pp. 34-35). Certainly, in our present state of knowledge, it would be unwise to attempt to assimilate the situation in the Eastern Province with the one on Bahrain too closely, since we do not know whether the concept of Great Dilmun (including the east Arabian coast) still obtained during the 1st millennium B.C. Moreover, the Iron Age cultures of the mainland apparently show a clear relationship to the South Arabian area (cf. Zarins et al., n.d.). At present, there is no real evidence of such a relationship with Bahrain.

Stratigraphic evidence of an 'Early Hasaean' level at the Salt Mine Site might be present in the Danish sounding carried out at the 'inland fort', where Bibby reported an occupation layer preceding the Hellenistic construction (Bibby, 1973, p. 45). A new campaign of excavation at the site is necessary in order to verify this hypothesis, however.

III. The Salt Mine Site: a candidate for Gerrha?

It is not my intention here to review the historico-geographical dispute over the location of Gerrha (cf. particularly Groom, 1982, and Potts, 1984c). Rather, and in concluding this paper, I wish to briefly examine to what extent the evidence supplied by the historical sources or suggested in this study can confirm the hypothesis which identified the 'chief emporium of the east side of Arabia' (Cornwall, 1946, p. 30) with the Salt Mine Site. It may be recalled that such a proposition has been formulated on several occasions, notably by James (1969, p. 55), Burkholder (1984, p. 31), and Golding (n.d.). In order to clarify this question, I have summarized and evaluated the various topographical, environmental, and chronological data concerning Gerrha in Fig. 13. This table, and the interpretations suggested here, require some comment.

Topography

The numerous geographical indications identified here as 'positive' support the candidature of the Salt Mine Site. However, it is advisable to temper this statement. For instance, the exact distance represented by the 2400 *stadia* said by Strabo to be the distance from Teredon to Gerrha is still debated. Depending on the value assigned to the classical *stadium* (Olympic, Eratosthenian, or Philetairian), measures of 240, 384, and 445 km., respectively, can be obtained (Potts, 1984c, p. 87). In fact, while the last figure reinforces the position of the Salt Mine Site, the 384 km. figure is favored by D. Potts, who proposes an identification of Gerrha with Thaj/al-Jubayl (Potts, 1984c, p. 89). In another connection, the list of successive Arabian Gulf bays which is provided by Ptolemy (Mesanites, Sacer, Leanites, Magorum, and Capeus) allows us to equate the fifth, Gerrha's bay, with the present bay of Dohat Dhalum on which the Salt Mine Site was presumably situated in antiquity. However, Pliny does not situate Gerrha on this *sinus* (in spite of James' assertion), but on the *sinus Gerraicus* which is supposed to be further south. If one adds that the location of Teredon, from which these various measurements are calculated, has yet to be established, one is inclined to agree with James that 'the classical authors had much to confuse and little to clarify' (James, 1969, p. 42).

Environment

The picture here is apparently more coherent. The salt blocks and saline mud reported by Strabo and Pliny in the construction of the Gerrha houses could have been obtained from the numerous salt flats all around the site. In any case, this building material recalls the 'slabs of a hard, apparently baked, salt-incrusted clay' mentioned by Bibby in the construction of the tumulus excavated by the Danish Expedition (Bibby, 1973, p. 46). Moreover, it is tempting to link Polybius' district of Chattenia (which was cultivated by the Gerrhaeans) with the ancient irrigation area discovered at the Salt Mine Site. It will be remembered that Polybius refers to this area as 'a poor district'. One must admit that this term is rather inadequate for characterizing the flourishing al-Hasa oasis which is regularly cited as the possible location of Chattenia. In contrast, the agricultural area which is possible to imagine at the Salt Mine Site probably never presented exceptional agricultural possibilities, even if significant climatic deterioration since the 1st millennium B.C. has skewed our impression of things. It is clear that the gradual silting up and salinization of the soil must account for the site's abandonment. Nevertheless, this raises one question: is such an agriculturally precarious region compatible with the image of the rich and flourishing city of Gerrha?

Chronology

The arguments cited in Fig. 13 appear quite positive. The Salt Mine Site shows an occupation which apparently squares with the various references to Gerrha in historical sources (roughly extending from 700 B.C. to the beginning of the Christian era) [7]. If the absence of Late Hasean material at the site were to be confirmed, this would appear to be particularly significant. Indeed, this argument *a silentio* is a short one. It needs to be strengthened appreciably by new surface sampling which could demonstrate the various links between Gerrha and its neighboring commercial partners. Unfortunately, the archaeology of the Salt Mine Site remains at present silent on this point.

However attractive the possibility may seem, it must still be admitted that the various points which can be advanced for considering the Salt Mine Site as a possible location of the legendary Gerrha are not really conclusive. The baffling, though rather seductive appearance of this site should not delude the observer. The archaeological area does not show any traces of an important city. There is no fortification wall; structures are scarce; and there is apparently no real settlement site here. Until such time as a future survey can come up with better evidence, the Salt Mine Site can only be considered one of the rare sites in the Eastern Province which bears witness to the local, pre-Hellenistic Iron Age. This point, however, is far from negligible and must henceforth be acknowledged in any reconstruction of northeastern Arabia's past.

Notes

1. It is not for me to analyze the reasons for this situation. The drastic changes in landscape that have occurred over the last twenty years must certainly be taken into consideration. Many sites have already been destroyed in this area due to industrial development, intensive agriculture, and growing urbanization.

2. Access to then unpublished material from eastern Saudi Arabia was greatly aided by the late Marny Golding.

3. The coordinates given by Burkholder (1984, p.31) are 25°50' N. Lat. and 50°02' E. Long.

4. The 'Sabkha fort' can easily be seen on several slides of the site given to me by M. Golding. No trace of the building, however, can be found on the aerial photographs originally published in *Natural History Magazine* (cf. Fig. 3 here).

5. In the northern part of the site, G. Burkholder reports a third fort, 'much more impressive than those in the southern section'. This rectangular building, c. 80×110 m., is apparently preserved to a height of 2 m. at its southwestern corner. It is not mentioned in any other descriptions of the site.

6. I recently proposed this name for a very peculiar class of pottery which seems to be widespread on Bahrain and in other parts of eastern Arabia during the 1st millennium B.C. (Lombard, 1985, p.86). Its paste (red ware, with 'exploding' white lime grits) obviously recalls Bronze Age Barbar pottery. In all likelihood, the superficial similarity to these earlier wares is due to the use of the same clay sources on Bahrain. The shapes known in 'pseudo-Barbar' ware, however, are quite original and easily identifiable.

7. Many historians date the earliest mention of Gerrha to the Neo-Assyrian period. This is based on H.G. Rawlinson's assertion that the 'Chaldaeans (were expelled) in 694 B.C. by Sennacherib (who) sent them to dwell in Gerrha' (Rawlinson, 1916, p.6). Nothing permits us to draw this conclusion from a reading of Strabo, who refers only to the presence of 'Chaldaeans, exiles from Babylon', at Gerrha.

Bibliography

Adams, R. McC., Parr, P.J., Ibrahim, M. and al-Mughannum, A.S. (1977). 'Preliminary Report on the First Phase of the Comprehensive Archaeological Survey Programm', *Atlal*, vol.1, pp.21-40.

Altheim, F. and R. Stiehl (1968), *Die Araber in der Alten Welt*, vol.V/1, Berlin, Walter de Gruyter.

Bibby, G. (1964), 'Arabian Gulf Archaeology', *Kuml*, 1964, pp.101-111.

Bibby, G. (1965), 'Arabian Gulf Archaeology', *Kuml*, 1965, pp.144-152.

Bibby, G. (1972), *Looking for Dilmun*, Harmondsworth, Pelican Books.

Bibby, G. (1973), *Preliminary Survey in East Arabia, 1968*, Reports of the Danish Archaeological Expedition to the Arabian Gulf II (=Jutland Arch. Soc. Publ. XII), Copenhagen, Gyldendal.

Bowen, R. le B. (1950), *The Early Arabian Necropolis of Ain Jawan*, BASOR Suppl. Studies, vol.7, 9.

Burkholder, G. (1984), *An Arabian Collection: artifacts from the Eastern Province*, Las Vegas, Graphics West.

Cornwall, P.B. (1946), 'Ancient Arabia: explorations in Hasa, 1940-1941', *Geographical Journal*, vol.107, pp.28-50.

Frankfort, H. (1955), *Stratified Cylinder Seals from the Diyala Region*, OIP LXXII, Chicago.

Golding, M. (1974), 'Evidence for pre-Seleucid occupation of Eastern Arabia', *Proc. of the Seminar for Arabian Studies*, vol.4, pp.19-32.

Golding, M. (n.d.), 'Artifacts from later pre-islamic occupation of Eastern Arabia', *Atlal*, in press.

Groom, N. (1982), 'Gerrha - a "lost" Arabian city', *Atlal*, vol.6, pp.97-108.

James, W.E. (1969), 'On the location of Gerrha', in Altheim and Stiehl, *Die Araber...*, vol.v/2, pp.36-57.

Legrain, L. (1951), *Ur Excavations, X. Seal Cylinders*, London.

Linton, D. (1961), 'Aerial Aid in Archaeology', *Natural History*, vol.70, pp.24-26.

Lombard, P. (1985), *L'Arabie orientale à l'Age du Fer*, Doct. Thesis, University of Paris I (Pantheon-Sorbonne), mimeo.

Lombard, P. (1986), 'Iron Age Dilmun. A Reconsideration of City IV at Qala'at al-Bahrain', in Shaikha Haya Ali al-Khalifa and M. Rice (eds.), *Bahrain through the ages: the Archaeology*, London, Kegan Paul Int., pp.225-232.

Porada, E. (1948), *The Collection of the Pierpont Morgan Library, Corpus of the Ancient Near Eastern Seals*, Washington, The Bollingen Series XIV, Bollingen Foundation.

Porada, E. (1970), *Tchoga Zanbil, IV. La glyptique*, Paris, MDAI XLII, Geuthner.

Potts, D.T. (1984a), 'Northeastern Arabia in the later pre-Islamic era', in R. Boucharlat and J.-F. Salles (eds.), *Arabie orientale, Mésopotamie et Iran méridional, de l'Age du Fer au début de la période islamique*, Paris, Editions Recherche sur la Civilisations, Mémoire n°37, A.D.P.F., pp.85-144.

Potts, D.T. (1984b), 'A preliminary report on coins of Seleucid date from Northeastern Arabia in the Morris Collection', paper delivered at the Seminar for Arabian Studies, Cambridge, July 17-19, 1984.

Potts, D.T. (1984c), 'Thaj and the location of Gerrha', *Proc. of the Seminar for Arabian Studies*, vol.14, pp.87-91.

Potts, D.T., Mughannum, A.S., Frye, J. and Sanders, D. (1978), 'Preliminary Report on the Second Phase of the Eastern Province Survey 1397/1977', *Atlal*, vol.2, pp.7-28.

Potts, D.T., Pedde, F. and Fanelli, J. (n.d.), 'Preliminary Report on the First Season of Excavations at Thaj, Winter 1983', *Atlal*, in press.

Rawlinson, H.G. (1916), *Intercourse between India and the Western World from the Earliest Times to the Fall of Rome*, Cambridge University Press, Cambridge.

Roaf, M. (1976), 'The work of the British Archaeological Expedition to Bahrain,' 1976, unpublished report.

Robin, C. (1974), 'Monnaies provenant de l'Arabie du Nord-Est', *Semitica*, vol. XXIV, pp.83-125.

Teissier, B. (1984), *Ancient Near Eastern Cylinder Seals in the Marcopoli Collection*, Berkeley, University of California Press.

Von der Osten, H.H. (1934), *Ancient oriental seals in the Collection of Mr. E.T. Newell*, Chicago, OIP XXII.

Zarins, J., Mughannum, A.S. and Kamal, M. (n.d.), 'Excavations at Dhahran South - The Tumuli Field (208-91), 1403 A.H./1983, A Preliminary Report', *Atlal*, in press.

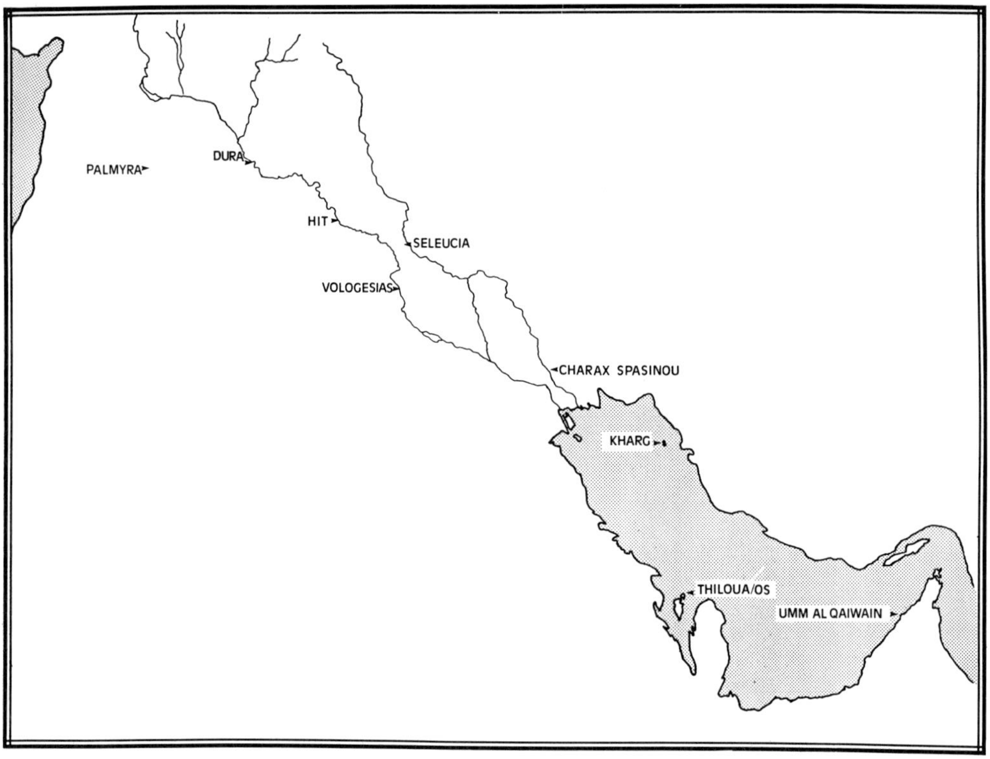

Fig. 1. Map of the region discussed in the text.

Arabia and the Kingdom of Characene

BY D. T. POTTS

'Arabia commences on the side of Babylonia with Mesene.'
– Strabo, *Geog.* 16,4,1 -

Introduction

During the Parthian and Sasanian periods the area in which the Euphrates, Tigris, and Karun rivers debouch into the Šatt al-Arab (Fig. 1) was known as Mesene/Maišān (1). Here, in the spring of 324 B.C., Alexander the Great founded a new city (2) 'on an artificial elevation between the Tigris on the right and the Eulaeus [Karun] on the left, at the point where these two rivers unite' [Pliny, *Nat. Hist.* VI, 31, 139].

Pliny, drawing on Juba, is our only source for the city's early history [*Nat. Hist.* VI, 31, 138]. He tells us, 'The original town was founded by Alexander the Great with settlers brought from the royal city of Durine, which was then destroyed, and with the invalid soldiers from his army who were left there. He had given orders that it was to be called Alexandria, and a borough which he had assigned especially to the Macedonians was to be named Pellaeum, after the place where he was born'. Later, the city became the capital of the 'satrapy of the Erythraean Sea', probably created by either Seleucus II (246-226/5 B.C.) or Seleucus III (226/5-223 B.C.)(3). After it 'was destroyed by rivers', Pliny says, Alexandria was 'restored by Antiochus, the fifth king of Syria, who gave it his own name'. It has long been recognized that this must refer to Antiochus IV (4), and the rebirth of the city as Antiochia almost certainly took place before 170 B.C., by which time it appears that Antiochus IV had established a new mint there (5).

According to Juba, Antiochus' satrap at Antiochia was one 'Spaosines, son of Sagdodonacus, king of the neighboring Arabs' [Pliny, *Nat. Hist.*, VI, 31, 138] (6). The demise of not only the satrapy of the Erythraean Sea, but of the entire eastern empire was not far off, however. In 139 B.C. Demetrius II was defeated and captured by Mithridates I. Several cuneiform texts from the reign of Demetrius' brother and successor, Anthiochus VII Sidetes, are extant. The earliest (7), dating to 130 B.C., calls him *Ian-ti-'u-uk-su*. A number of astronomical texts dating to 129 B.C. (8), the year in which Antiochus VII lost his life in battle with the Parthians near Ectabana, are also preserved. A scant two years later, in 127 B.C., a text from Babylon refers to Spaosines, the former satrap of the Erythraean Sea, as *šarru*, i.e. king [9]. As Pliny tells us, Spaosines restored Antiochia and, following in the tradition of both Alexander and Antiochus IV, named it after himself, whence it became known in Greek as *Charax S/Pasinou* or *Spasinou Charax* [10], i.e.'Charax of Hyspaosines' [11]. Thus was born the 'kingdom of Characene'.

Of all the states in antiquity to have exercised sway over some part of Babylonia, few have remained quite as obscure as the one founded by Hyspaosines. With varying degrees of success, the kings of Characene were able to remain independent of their Parthian neighbors for nearly 350 years. This is not to say that a single dynasty remained in power throughout the entire period of the state's existence, or that the Parthians did not occasionally attempt to and succeed in toppling the Charence monarch in order to install a more favorable one in his place. Yet it can be said that, in general, the kingdom of Characene prospered until finally succumbing to Ardašīr i Pāpakān, probably in 222 A.D. [12].

While the Greek and Latin sources concerning Charax and Characene have, of course, never been 'lost', the identification of any of its material remains was not achieved until the beginning of the last century. During the eighteenth century various coins in European collections were incorrectly attributed by numismatists [13] to Parthian, Armenian, or Bactrian monarchs [14]. By 1811, however, E.Q. Visconti had succeeded in correctly ascribing them to the kings of Characene, thereby giving substance for the first time to the various notices of classical authors concerning Charax [15]. Since then, the literary, epigraphic, and above all, numismatic sources relating to Characene have been periodically reappraised by a distinguished series of scholars.

In view of the fact that Pliny calls Hyspaosines 'king of the neighboring Arabs', and Strabo reckons Mesene to Arabia, it is hardly surprising that the relationship between Arabia and the kingdom of Characene was discussed at some length in the early years of Characene scholarship. In 1817 the classical sources concerning the distribution of Arab tribes in and around Characene were thoroughly treated by Saint-Martin [16]. In 1873, Blau distilled what could be found in early Arabic sources, principally Hamza al-Iṣfahānī, al-Bakrī, and Ṭabarī, pertaining to the movement of Arab tribes into Babylonia during the Parthian period, and tried to put this into the framework of Characene political history [17]. Since the nineteenth century, a small but significant body of material pertaining to the relationship between Characene and Arabia has accumulated. In view of this, it may be worthwhile re-examining the issue in light of some recent finds. The dated material available spans the period between c.

Fig.2. Characene coins from ed-Dur and A.de Longpérier's drawing of a tetradrachm of Meredat.

125 B.C. and 142 A.D. While every attempt has been made to make the following discussion complete, the rapid pace of excavation in the countries of the Arabian peninsula, coupled with the inevitable time lag between discovery and publication, may result in the omission of some new discoveries, in which case we apologize. We will treat the material below in chronological order.

A Bronze Coin of Hyspaosines from Failaka

In 1961 a bronze coin of Hyspaosines was found on the surface of Failaka by the Danish expedition [18]. Four other bronzes of this type are known from Susa and Dura Europus, two from each site. The dating of this material has been considered at length by Le Rider [19], but it remains uncertain. Hyspaosines began minting silver tetradrachms after he assumed the kingship of Characene, and these all date to between 124 and 120 B.C. [20]. It would seem most likely that his bronzes are of similar or slightly later date.

Ps.-Lucian preserves a fragment of the well-known writer Isidore of Charax in which Hyspaosines is called 'king of Charax and the neighboring countries of the Erythraean Sea' [*Macrobii*, 16] [21]. On the basis of this, Blau suggested more than a century ago that the realm of Hyspaosines comprised not only the territory of Mesene, but also the east Arabian littoral [22]. More recently, H.E. Mathiesen has proposed that, during the reign of Hyspaosines, Failaka 'was presumably part of Characene' [23]. Providing that Failaka was not immediately de-populated upon the collapse of the Seleucid empire in the east this could easily have been the case politically, but geographically speaking it is unlikely. Mesene was strictly a geographical term, whereas Characene was a political one. Cl. Ptolemy knew the northern Gulf as *Mesanites kolpos* [24], the 'Gulf of Mesene' [*Geog.* VI, 3, 3], but this usage does not carry the kind of political overtones that, for example, nineteenth century references to the Arabian Gulf as a 'British lake', clearly did [25]. Certainly none of the classical sources, which do contain a considerable amount of information on the territorial extent of both Mesene and the state of Characene, ever suggests that Ikaros/Failaka was considered part of either.

Miscellaneous Characene Coins from Failaka, 'Akāz, and Umm al-Namal

Excavations recently conducted by the Kuwait Dept. of Antiquities on the small island of Umm al-Namal and on the coral reef of 'Akāz are said to have yielded, in each case, a Characene coin. In addition, while studying some unpublished coins found on Failaka by the Danish expedition, O. Callot identified an additional coin of an Attambelos, which he will be publishing shortly [26].

A Characene Coin of Uncertain Attribution from ed-Dur, Umm al-Qaiwain

We turn now to a number of recent numismatic finds made on the surface of the site of ed-Dur, emirate of Umm al-Qaiwain, United Arab Emirates. The coins are at present in a private collection. The first to be discussed (Fig. 2:1-2) is a bronze coin weighing 9.71 gr. The obverse shows the diademed head of a bearded king, facing right. The reverse is badly corroded, and only the vaguest suggestion of the legs and throne of a seated Heracles can be made out. Thus, no attribution is possible.

A Tetradrachm of Attambelos III from ed-Dur, Umm al-Qaiwain

This bronze tetradrachm (Fig. 2:3-4), which weighs 15.34 gr., has a bearded and diademed head facing right on the obverse, along with an indistinct monogram. The reverse shows Heracles seated, and parts of the legend can be read: ATTA on the right, ωTH on the left. For the reading of the date TMΘ, i.e. 349 S.E. = 38/39 A.D., I would like to thank Martin Price, Dept. of Coins and Medals, The British Museum.

The coinage of Attambelos III was first identified by Le Rider in 1959 (27) on the basis of 6 tetradrachms in Paris, two of which are dated TMΘ, like the example here, and TNЄ, 355 S.E. = 44/45 A.D. In his now standard study of the kingdom of Characene, Nodelman completely misunderstood the distinctions between Attambelos III, IV, and V established by Le Rider, thereby introducing confusion into his list of Characene kings. Although aware of Le Rider's publication, he altogether omitted a king for the regnal years 38/39-44/45, i.e. precisely those years for which dated coinage is available. Moreover, he neglected the stylistic differences established by Le Rider between the coins of Attambelos IV, dating to between 54/55 and 64/65, and Attambelos V, datable to 73/74. Lumping the two series together, he assigned the entire period 54/55-73/74 to Attambelos III (28).

It should be noted that the monogram on the obverse of our coin, presumably that of the mint magistrate, differs from the one visible on the reverse of the Paris exemplars.

Two Tetradrachms of Attambelos IV from ed-Dur, Umm al-Qaiwain

These coins (Fig. 2:5-6, 7-8), which weigh 15.4 and 15.08 gr., respectively, show a bearded and diademed head facing right, and a border of dots, on the obverse. On the reverse we see a seated Heracles. In the case of Fig. 2:6 the monogram E, and part of the legend can be made out: A]TTAM[on the right, ωTHP[/ KA[I on the left. Once again, I wish to thank Martin Price for the reading of the date TO i.e. 370 S.E. = 58/59 A.D. The reverse of Fig. 2:8 is much more worn than its counterpart, and only traces of the title can be discerned. The date TO, difficult to see on the photograph, is again read courtesy of Martin Price.

The coinage of Attambelos IV is well-represented by an unbroken, dated series minted between 54/55 and 64/65 A.D. (29). Most of the examples in Paris come from a hoard discovered at Tello in 1878, and subsequently published by Babelon (30). Coins of the type illustrated here, i.e. those dating to 58/59 A.D., are the first to show the king bearded (31).

Two Tetradrachms of Attambelos VI from ed-Dur, Umm al-Qaiwain

In 1973-74, Iraqi archaeologists excavating at ed-Dur discovered a very worn Characene tetradrachm with no legible date on the surface of the site (32). This was later re-published by J.-F- Salles (33), who attributed it to Attambelos III. For Salles 'les critères de datation les plus sur sont le diadème à la mode parthe et l' *oméga* de la légende qui s'inscrit désormais en écriture minuscule et non plus majuscule' (34). In fact, neither trait is restricted to the issues of Attambelos III. The diadem is worn by most of the kings of Characene, and as Le Rider noted, the omega, which appeared as a small letter for the first time in the legends of Attambelos III, maintained that form from then on (35). Thus, Attambelos III can only represent a *terminus ad quem* for the ed-Dur coin.

The name Attambelos is clear enough in the legend, however, so that we can turn to an examination of the portrait in order to establish his exact identity. The king on the ed-Dur coin has a short beard, and his whole neck is exposed. In addition, his hair falls in seven long, slightly modelled but still rather flat locks. A comparison of the portrait on this coin with the ones on the dated coins of Attambelos III quickly reveals that both the locks of the hair and, above all, the beard, are completely different. Attambelos III is always shown wearing a long, full beard, entirely covering his neck, with many strands of hair indicated (36). Attamblos IV has a relatively short beard, but not as short as the one shown on the ed-Dur coin. A very similar portrait, however, with a short beard, exposed neck, and seven, flat locks of hair is found on the coinage of Attambelos VI from 416 S.E., i.e. 105/106 A.D. (37), and it is to this series that we assign the coin from ed-Dur.

Another, fortunately dated tetradrachm of Attambelos VI is also known from ed-Dur (Fig. 2:9-10). It is in the same collection as the Attambelos III and IV coins discussed above, and weighs 14.83 gr. In addition to the short bearded and diademed head facing right seen on the observe, there is also a monogram clearly visible in front of the mouth in the shape of a six-pointed star. The reverse again shows a seated Heracles, facing left, and fragments of the legend: ATTAM on the right, [ωTH[P / KAI E on the left. The date, YIE, i.e. 415 S.E. = 104/105 A.D., is again read courtesy of Martin Price.

The six-pointed star monogram found on the example here was already known from pieces in Paris [38] and London [39], similarly dated to 104/105 A.D. In 105/106 A.D., however, the star was replaced by a hollow triangle [40], perhaps indicating a change of mint magistrate. Unfortunately, either because of wear or the position of the die when it was struck, this cannot be seen in the published photographs of the ed-Dur coin, but the hairstyle is distinctive. Attambelos VI's hair is plaited in his portrait of 104/105, as the example published here shows, while the flat, smooth locks of the ed-Dur coin correspond to the hairstyle seen on the coinage of the following year.

Dio Cassius related that when Trajan invaded Babylonia in 116 A.D. the reigning Characene monarch, whom he calls Attambelos, submitted to Trajan and paid him tribute, and that for doing so his position as client of Rome was acknowledged [41]. It is unlikely that this was Attambelos VI for, although he was on the Characene throne a decade earlier, another king, Theonesos IV, struck coins in 111/112 and 112/113 A.D. [42]. The retreat of Trajan's army in 117, however, opened the way for a vigorous re-assertion by Parthia of its power in southern Babylonia. It is generally believed by historians that, after driving Rome's puppet, Parthamaspates, off the Parthian throne, Osroes I turned to settle other scores, including one with the kingdom of Characene. With Trajan's protection gone, the position of Attambelos was obviously endangered, and we hear no more of him after the Roman emperor's retreat.

The Career of Meredat, -131 to 151 A.D.

Following the brief intervention by Trajan in the political affairs of Characene, there is a gap in the Characene kinglist lasting until 131 A.D., when we hear for the first time of 'Meredat, king of Spasinou Charax', in a Greek inscription found during the 1939-1940 season of excavations at Palmyra. The text belongs to a well-known genre of inscriptions in which prominent Palmyrene citizens who had served abroad in cities such as Babylon, Vologesias, Forat, or Spasinou Charax, as caravan leaders (*synodiarchs*) or heads of mercantile groups (*archemporoi*), were honored for their services [43]. The extant inscriptions of this type in which Charax is mentioned span a period from 50/51 or 70/71 to 193 A.D. [44]. In view of the fact that, by this time, Charax was certainly the most important Babylonian *emporium* for luxury goods from the east, and considering that Palmyra was by far the most important commercial center in the Roman province of Syria, it is hardly surprising that Palmyrene merchants should have established a trading colony there for the purpose of acquiring the commodities so much in demand within the Roman empire.

The inscription in question was engraved upon the base of a statue erected at Palmyra in honor of Yarhai, a Palmyrene, by the merchants of Spasinou Charax in April, 131 A.D. [45] The most important point, however, is the fact that Yarhai is identified (1.3-5) as 'satrap of the Thilouanoi [*satrapes Thilouanôn*] for Meredat, king of Spasinou Charax'. As several scholars have recently pointed out, the ethnic *Thilouanôn* is derived from the toponym *Thiloua* or *Thilouos*, which is merely a variant of Tylos, the name by which the larger of the Bahrain islands was known in classical antiquity [46]. As already noted, Blau believed that the Gulf coast littoral formed part of the state established by Hyspaosines. This text provides us with the first unequivocal confirmation of Characene political domination in the region. When and how Thiloua/os came under Characene control we do not know. There are five more inscriptions from Palmyra in which the name Meredat (MHRDT) occurs [47], but nothing suggests that the person(s) named in them is the same Meredat, king of Characene.

A single issue of Meredat's coinage, of which c. 28 examples have been published to date, is known. Because of its important but problematic legend, this series has attracted the attention of numismatists for more than a century and a half. Until recently, however, a satisfactory reading was not possible. Because the legend relates directly to Meredat's involvement with Arabia, we shall pass rapidly over the history of research on it, before discussing the new reading and its implications for the history of Arabian-Characene relations.

In 1829 Domenico Sestini published a bronze coin of an 'Arsaces incerti' belonging to Count Wiczay of Hedewar, Austro-Hungary [48]. Although he attempted a transcription of the coin's 'epigraphe confusa', Sestini was unable to offer a reading of the Greek legend. In his 1835 commentary on Sestini's catalogue, Stanislas Baron de Chaudoir attributed the same coin to the Parthian king Vologases II [49], based on the coin's date which he read YNΔ, i.e. 454 S.E. or 142 A.D. A more legible example of the same type in the collection of John Robert Steuart [50] was published in 1837 by James Millingen[51]. In a letter to Millingen, much of which is reproduced in his catalogue, Steuart identified the names *Meredat* and *Uiphoba* in the coin's legend, suggesting that they were king and queen of Characene, and confirmed the date to be 454 S.E. Steuart also made some other important observations on the coin type, noting that 'many similar coins are found in the vicinity of Bussorah, and are not infrequently struck upon those of an Attambilus, king of Characene'. Moreover, it was Steuart who suggested that this was the Attambelos who reigned at the time of Trajan's invasion, and while it would be 'impossible to say whether he succeeded to the kingdom of Charax by inheritance or conquest. The circumstance of so many of his coins being struck on those of his predecessor, would lead to the supposition that his succession was hasty and perhaps transient'[52]. Steuart also noted that Meredat's coinage differed from those of his predecessors on the Characene throne in two important respects. First, he is shown wearing a diadem and tiara, symbols reserved for the kings of Parthia (see below), rather than the simple Characene diadem; and second, the reverse shows a female bust wearing a crown, instead of the traditional figure of Heracles seated.

By the middle of the last century, Meredat and U/Viphoba had become established in the growing body of literature on Characene numismatics. A.C.E. Von Werlhof's handbook of Greek numismatics, published in 1850, lists them in his section on Characene [53]. Three years later J. Lindsay briefly discussed and illustrated two examples of 'the coins of Meredates and Vippoba' in his influential study of Parthian coinage [54], which inspired a brief note by William H. Scott in 1856-57 [55]. Scott was the first scholar to attempt to decipher the difficult and hitherto ignored part of the legend which began 'OM..' He concluded that 'we cannot tell what it means, whether it is a title belonging to Meredates, or perhaps the name of his father, imperfectly written'. At the end of his study he wrote, 'I shall be glad if this note induces any numismatist to compare the coins of these unknown sovereigns, so as to confirm or reject my conjectures', and the following year W. S. W. Vaux published a small collection of Characene coins made by one Dr. Hyslop during his stay as a surgeon in Baghdad. Although Vaux accepted the reading of the names Meredates and Uiphoba, he wrote, 'concerning the attribution of the coins bearing these names, we have considerable doubt. They are not uncommon; and the [British] Museum possesses several specimens – there is nothing, however, certain to be made out from what remains of their legends'[56].

Adrien de Longpérier was the first scholar to make a serious attempt at offering a coherent decipherment of the legend on Meredat's coins, accounting for all of the visible letters[57]. This brilliant numismatist and antiquary is remembered by Orientalists largely for his 1847 identification of the name of Sargon II in the Khorsabad inscriptions which, as historians of Assyriology have noted, was 'the first royal Assyrian name that had yet been read' [58]. Yet his influence in numismatics was far greater. Percy Gardner, author of one of the most important works on Parthian coinage ever written, paid him the following tribute: 'The collection of Parthian coins in the British Museum was arranged by the late Count de Salis in accordance with the opinions of M. de Longpérier; and no doubt, if the truth were known, much of what is best in the following pages would be found to be due to the latter savant's ingenuity and experience'[59].

De Longpérier noted the existence of nine 'new' Meredat coins, including seven in the Bibliothèque Impériale (now Bibl. Nationale), three of which were struck over the coins of an Attambelos, and at least two in the collections of MM. Rollin and Feuardent. In comparison with those of his predecessors, however, at least one of the coins available to de Longpérier (Fig, 2:11-12) was extremely well-preserved. This enabled the French numismatist to offer the first accurate transcription of the coin's legend. De Longpérier rejected V/Uiphoba as a personal name, and suggested a radical new interpretation of the reverse legend. Beneath the letters VIΦO, as can be seen on the example illustrated here, are the letters OMΛN. Up until that time, however, this had never been so clear. Scott, for example, had noted that on the engravings of coins published by Millingen and Lindsay, OM was legible, but at least one of the coins at his disposal seemed to read OMΛK. On many of the examples which have since become known, only the top halves of the letters O and M can be seen. De Longpérier suggested these letters represented a word written in boustrophedon fashion, which he read OMANOΦIΛ, i.e. 'Omanophilos'. The title BACIΛЄYC engraved on the opposite side of the field, he suggested, was the first half of the ephithet, *basileus Omanophilos*, or the 'king, beloved of the Omani'.

De Longpérier was not, in 1863, able to provide a concrete historical explanation for this epithet, but he very naturally turned to the well-known passage in the sixth book of Pliny's *Natural History* [VI, 145] which we quote here.

> After Petra the country as far as Charax was inhabited by the Omani, with the once famous towns of Abaesamis and Soractia, founded by Samiramis; but now it is a desert. Then there is a town on the bank of the Pasitigris named Forat, subject to the king of the Characeni. This is resorted to by people from Petra, who make the journey from there to Charax, a distance of 12 miles by water, using the tide.

De Longpérier suggested that the Omani of Characene minted the coins in honor of their sovereign. Had Meredat merely been their ally, he argued, he might have styled himself *philomanos*, but this is not the case. De Longpérier did not believe that the Omani in question were to be linked with either the country of Oman or the port of Omana. Moreover, noting that most of Meredat's coins seemed to come from around Basra, the presumed location of the Characene city of Forat, and that some of them were struck over the coins of an Attambelos, he suggested that Meredat may have moved his capital away from the hostile 'Characene' city of Charax, the former capital of Attambelos, to the friendlier city of Forat where the Omani were. In favoring the Omani, he might have earned the gratitude which resulted in the monetary issue of

142 A.D. Moreover, he suggested that the female head on the reverse, which had already caught Steuart's attention, was Tyche, the genius of Forat [(60)].

Reaction to de Longpérier's thesis did not come immediately. W. H. Waddington's well-known study of 1866 does not include Meredat in the Characene kinglist [(61)]. In 1881 A. von Sallet published six 'new' coins of ' "Meredates" and "Yiphoba" ' in the Berlin museum [(62)]. Von Sallet readily admitted that OMΛN was clearly legible on de Longpériers' example, but this was not the case on any of his coins. In one case, the first three letters were legible, along with the left vertical bar of the final N. Otherwise, one example showed only OM, while another showed the O clearly, but only a fragment of the M. On the remaining three coins no trace of OMΛN could be seen at all. Von Sallet did not try to account for the presence of OMΛN on de Longpérier's examplar, but he rejected the reading *Omanophilos*, on the grounds that no parallel case could be adduced [(63)]. Instead, he suggested a return to the reading of a female name, *Yiphoba*, which he hesitantly connected with the Characene place-name Forat [(64)], followed by BACIΛ, which he considered an abbreviation of *basilissa*, or 'queen'. The female portrait, he proposed, was that of the queen as Tyche.

In 1888, the brilliant historian of Iran, Alfred von Gutschmid, took up the issue of Meredat in earnest [(65)]. His reading of the coin legend deviated from that of all his predecessors

BΛCIΛ MЄPЄΔΛT	'King Meredat'
VI ΦOBΛ	'son [uios] of Phoba(s)'
BΛCILЄΥC OMΛN	'king of the Omani'

Von Gutschmid began his analysis of the legend by citing the passage in Pliny's *Natural History*, quoted above, as evidence of the presence of the Omani in the desert around Charax. Unlike de Longpérier, however, who saw no connection between these Omani and the country of Oman, von Gutschmid interpreted Pliny's notice as a reflection of the northward migration of the Azd Oman, whose infiltration of eastern Arabia and southern Iraq is attested in later Arabic sources [(66)].

In 1890, E. Drouin proposed dissociating Meredat from the kingdom of Characene, attributing him to an undetermined neighboring vassal of the Parthians [(67)]. He considered the suggestions of both de Longpérier and von Gutschmid unacceptable. Five years later, however, von Gutschmid's reading was enshrined in F. Justi's long-standard study of Iranian personal names, where Meredat is listed as 'son of Phobas, king of the Omani' [(68)].

Two important works on Characene appeared in 1898. A numismatic and chronological survey by the well-known numismatist E. Babelon is completely silent on the subject of Meredat, referring cautiously to the indecisive nature of the numismatic sources for the period between Trajan's retreat and the rise of the Sasanians [(69)]. More surprising, however, is the fact that H. Winckler ignored Meredat entirely, even though he explicitly stated that a study published by de Longpérier in 1874-1877, in which Meredat is mentioned, was one of the two principal sources for the Characene kinglist which he compiled [(70)]. Nor does F.H. Weissbach's article on 'Charakene' in Pauly-Wissowa's *Realencyclopädie*, published in 1899, mention Meredat [(71)].

In 1911, however, Barclay Head proposed an entirely new classification of Meredat's coins. As we have seen, a number of scholars had been reluctant to assign Meredat to the kingdom of Characene, listing him instead as king of one of Parthia's vassal states. Head made a radical departure from the prevailing opinions of his time listing the coinage of the 'Omani' alongside that of Elymais and Characene as an independent issue within the greater Parthian sphere [(72)]. The basis for Head's classification was again the passage from Pliny quoted above. Meredat's was the only issue assigned to this category, and Head accepted both de Longpérier's reading of the Greek legend, and his interpretation of the female bust on the reverse as Tyche.

Head was assisted in the preparation of his work by G.F. Hill, later keeper of the Department of Coins and Medals at the British Museum. In 1922, Hill devoted considerable space to a discussion of Meredat's coinage, rejecting de Longpérier's interpretation. Hill restored the coinage of Meredat to the kingdom of Characene, but grouped it, together with that of Orabzes II, under the heading 'Sub-Characene'. The grounds for the creation of this sub-group were not fully explained, but among those characteristics cited which differentiated these coins from standard Characene issues were their fabric; the small size of the die used on the obverse and the wide margin surrounding it; and the scattered distribution of the legend [(73)]. Hill disputed the presence of the name Oman, and wrote, 'of the crucial part of the word only the M is certain; the letter before it may be O, that which follows may be Λ or A, and the next letter may be Λ or K or N'. Moreover, Pliny's reference to the Omani, he insisted, was anachronistic. Pliny says that the cities of the Omani, Abaesamis and Soractia, had already been abandoned by his time ['*Nunc sunt solitudines*'], and as he died sixty-three years before Meredat's coins were minted, Hill saw no grounds for supposing that the Omani still lived in Characene during Meredat's reign. He rejected the boustrophedon reading of Meredat's epithet and, initially unaware of von Gutschmid's work, read the legend as 'son of King Phoba'. As for the word OMΛN, Hill merely noted that, while there was 'nothing improbable in the theory' that this might have something to do with the migrations of the Azd-Oman, it was 'mere theory-spinning to base such an identification on apparent similarity in names'(74).

Both Hill's classification and interpretation were followed in their entirety by J. de Morgan in a pair of studies which appeared in 1933 and 1936 (75). Thereafter, the problem of Meredat and the Omani remained in abeyance for some time. In his article 'Omani', published in the eighteenth volume of Pauly-Wissowa's *Realencyclopädie* in 1942 (76), A. Grohmann takes no cognizance of the scholarly debate over Meredat which was by then already over a century old. In 1960, however, S.A. Nodeman published his well-known 'Preliminary History of Characene', in which Meredat was accorded considerable space (77). Following von Gutschmid's reading of the problematic coin legend, Nodelman inserted Phobas into the Characene kinglist during the undocumented period between Trajan's retreat and the first mention of Meredat at Palmyra in 131 A.D. He did not address the problem of OMΛN and the Omani, but he did attempt to provide an historical explanation for the peculiar qualities of Meredat's coins which both Steuart and de Longpérier had noted, and which had ultimately led Hill to call them 'Sub-Characene'. Like de Longpérier, Nodelman took the unusual fabric of Meredat's coins as a sign that they had not been minted at Spasinou Charax where, it is generally assumed, the mint established by Antiochus IV was used by the later kings of Characene. Because the majority of the coins seemed to come from the vicinity of Basra, he suggested that they had been minted at Forat, and that Meredat had made Forat his capital. Nodelman was apparently unaware that de Longpérier had already made this suggestion in 1863 (78).

With the exception of a brief discussion by Le Rider in 1965 (79), little was said of Meredat until 1983, when D. Sellwood published a new overview of Characene coinage (80). Here, Meredat's coins are briefly mentioned, and Hill is followed for the reading of the Greek legend. In his recent synthesis of early Iranian history, published in 1984, R.N. Frye includes Meredat in the Characene kinglist, but does not actually discuss him (81)

This, in brief, was the course of scholarship on Meredat up until 1984 when a discovery was made which revolutionizes our understanding of the entire topic. During the course of clandestine excavations at Seleucia-on-the-Tigris, an 85.5 cm. tall bronze statue of Heracles was found. The statue has a bilingual inscription in Greek and Parthian, written in a combination of syllabic and logographic Aramaic, engraved on its thighs. The *editio princeps* is soon to be published by F. Pennacchietti, who has kindly provided the following English translation (82).

Greek

In the year of the Greek 462 the king of kings Arsaces Vologases, son of the king Mithradates, conducted a military expedition in Mesene against the king Mithradates, son of Pacorus, who reigned previously, and, after expelling the king Mithradates from Mesene, becoming master of all Mesene and placed this statue of the god Heracles, which he transported from Mesene, in this sanctuary of the god Apollo who is on the guard of the bronze gate.

Parthian

(...Arsaces) Vologases, king of kings of king Mithradates fought the king Mithradates, son of Pacorus, king of kings, in all Mesene, expelled from there the king Mithradates, conquered all Mesene and, on the 17th day of Tir raised this statue of the god Verethraghna which he transported from Mesene, after having (it) incised

The Greek dedication is dated to 462 S.E., i.e. 150/151 A.D., while the Parthian version specifies that it was set up in the temple of Verethraghna/Apollo on the 17th of Tir, or July 5. This allows us to identify the victorious king of kings named with Vologases IV [(83)], king of Parthia from 148 to 191 A.D. The king of Mesene defeated by Vologases is Meredat, and this can hardly be anyone but the same Meredat, king of Spasinou Charax, mentioned at Palmyra in 131 A.D. Before considering the events described, however, let us examine the implications of the new inscriptions for the beginning of Meredat's career and the interpretation of the problematic legend on his coins.

According to the new texts, Meredat was the 'son of Pacorus, who reigned previously'. In the Parthian text he is called 'king of kings'. This can only be Pacorus II, the Parthian king whose reign spanned the years c. 78-105 A.D., and included a long and eventually successful power struggle with his rival Vologases II [(84)]. Pacorus II had a brother, Meherdotes, as well as either a brother [(85)] or brother-in-law [(86)], Osroes I. It was he who succeeded Pacorus II on the Parthian throne. As we know from Dio Cassius [lxviii, 17 and 19] and Arrian [*Parthica*, frags. 37f. and 40], Pacorus II had at least two other sons, Axidares/Exedates and Parthamasiris, in addition to Meredat, and it appears that, after the death of Pacorus II, Osroes I called upon the services of the latter's sons on several occasions. Around 110 A.D., Osroes I put Axidares on the throne of Armenia, later desposing him in favor of Parthamasiris [(87)]. Six years later, following Trajan's retreat, it was probably also Osroes I who, after driving Rome's puppet off the Parthian throne, toppled the pro-Roman Characene king Attambelos.

We can diagram this family as follows:

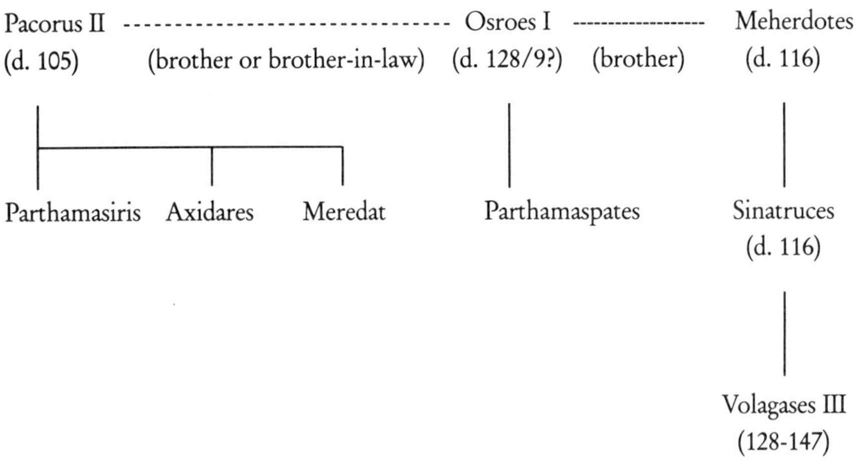

As both his name and family tree attest, Meredat was Iranian, a member of a prominent Parthian family, rather than Semitic or Arabian, as was the ruling house of Characene before his reign. It is logical to think that Osroes I installed his blood relative Meredat on the Characene throne after Trajan's withdrawal from Babylonia, all the more so since, as we have seen, the coins of Meredat from 142 A.D. include many which were struck over those of an Attambelos, and it is natural to assume that this was the Attambelos who reigned at the time of Trajan's invasion. On the other hand, it must be admitted that Meredat is not heard of as king until 131 A.D., and thus there is a gap of fully 15 years between the last mention of Attambelos and the first attestation of a new king in Characene.

This may, of course, be nothing but a gap in our sources. On the other hand, it could be that after the welcome given to Rome by the last Characene monarch, Parthia was loathe to grant the state any sort of autonomy whatsoever, lest it make more trouble. Following Trajan's retreat and the removal of Attambelos, Mesene may have been ruled directly as a Parthian fief. Eventually, after some years had passed, Meredat may have been installed by the Parthian king of kings as 'king' of Characene, which would explain the gap between 116 and 131 A.D. If this were done only shortly before Meredat is mentioned at Palmyra, then it could even have been his second cousin, Vologases III (128-147 A.D.), who put him on the Characene throne. In any case, the point is that Meredat was a member of a leading Parthian family. It thus becomes obvious that, during his reign, the kingdom of Characene cannot be considered 'independent' as it had been before. It was, rather, very much a satellite of Parthia. This is important to bear in mind when considering the achievements and events of Meredat's reign.

Surely one of the most important new pieces of information in the Seleucia texts is the name of Meredat's father, Pacorus. We can, therefore, discount all readings of the coin legend which interpret VIΦOBΛ as 'son of Phobas'. In his publication of the Seleucia texts, Pennacchietti suggests that VIΦO may have been an abbreviation of *ui(os) φo(korou)*, or 'son of *Phokoros', assuming the existence of *Phokoros as a variant of Pakoros/Pacorus [87]. The arguments of Hill and others against reading the word OMΛN in the legend turn on the fact that on most of the examples in the British Museum, the Bibliothèque Nationale and the Berlin museum, the die was struck off-center, leaving only fragments of the letters visible. On the example illustrated by de Longpérier, however, it is clear what the traces of letters on the others must stand for. Pennacchietti has suggested that the entire legend might be understood as follows:

ΜЄΡЄΔΛΤ	Meredat
VI[ΟΣ] ΦΟ [ΚΟΡΟV] ΒΛ[CIΛЄωC] ΒΛCIΛ[ЄωΝ]	son of *Phokoros, king of kings
ΒΛCIΛΕΥC ΟΜΑΝ[ΑIωΝ]	king of the Omanites
ΥΝΔ	454 (S.E. = 142 A.D.)

This reading [88] is far and away the most satisfactory to date, and we see no reason not to accept it. We turn now to the interpretation of the legend.

De Longpérier was the first scholar to point to the passage in Book VI of Pliny's *Natural History* in which the Omani, 'in the country as far as Charax', are mentioned. This is, to my knowledge, the earliest extant attestation of the Omani in southern Iraq and/or northern Arabia. It is well known that Pliny began to assemble the material for his *Natural History* in the early 50's, and the work was finally presented to Titus in 77 A.D. [89], almost forty years before the earliest possible arrival of Meredat in Mesene, if we place this sometime shortly after Trajan's campaign in 116 A.D.

Several scholars have contested Pliny's reference to the Omani. J. Neubauer considered it an error for 'Ammonites' [90], while Blau saw it as a confused transcription of *Humanija*, the name of a large town on the right bank of the Tigris mentioned in the Babylonian Talmud and in Yaqut's geographical dictionary [91]. Hill's objections as noted above, revolved around his belief that the cities of the Omani had long been deserted by Pliny's lifetime.

Yet, there may be another piece of evidence, datable to the reign of Meredat, which suggests the presence of an Omani element in the region. As noted above, the name of the northernmost part of the Arabian Gulf in Cl. Ptolemy's *Geography*, generally dated to c. 150 A.D., is *Sinus Mesanites*, or 'Gulf of Mesene'. The first toponym below this on the Arabian side of the Gulf is *Coromanis polis* [92]. S.B. Miles noted in 1878 that 'the prefix Cor in this and similar instances is equivalent to Khor, the Arabic word for a creek or inlet. Pliny ...mentioned the Omani as a tribe extending from Petra to Charax, and I take Coromanis therefore to be Khor Omani, the creek of the Omani'[(93)].

De Longpérier's reluctance to link Pliny's Omani with the country of Oman was not shared by von Gurschmid, who saw Pliny's notice as an early reflection of the northward migration of the Azd Oman. This tribe, whose south Arabian origins were described by Mas'ūdī [(94)], was the easternmost branch of a large group split into several sub-groups, including the Azd As-Sarāt, Azd Šanua, and Azd Oman. Their presence in eastern Arabia and around Basra is well attested in the early Islamic era [(95)]. The evidence for their probable presence in the north during the late third century A.D. is provided by a South Arabian inscription published in 1974 by W. W. Müller, which records the return of an embassy sent by Šammar Yuharʿiš, king of Saba' and D̲ū Raydān, to Seleucia and Ctesiphon, probably sometime prior to Diocletian's conquest of Mesopotamia in 297 [(96)]. As the text tells us, the caravan went first to Mālikum, son of Ka'bum, king of the Asd [(97)] before continuing on to the twin cities of the Sasanians[(98)].

Finally, a further indication of the presence of the Azd Oman in the north Arabian area may be provided by the well-known Nemara inscription, in which Imru al-Qays bears the title *mlk'l 'sdyn*, or 'king of the two Asds' i.e. the Azd as-Sarāt and Azd Oman [(99)].

The evidence just reviewed suggests that the Omani, perhaps ancestors of the Azd Oman later found in northeastern Arabia and southern Iraq, were present in lower Iraq by the first century A.D. The Palmyrene text, on the other hand, shows that Meredat's political control extended at least as far south as *Thiloua/os* (Bahrain), where he had a satrap. A fragment of Isidore preserved in Chapter XV of Ps. Lucian's *Macrobii* is also relevant: 'Goaesus, so says Isidore of Charax, who in his time was king of the Omani in the Incense Land, after he had lived one hundred and fifteen years, died of desease' [(100)]. Isidore of Charax has been variously dated to the time of Christ [(101)], the reign of Augustus, 27 B.C. - A.D. 14, [(102)] or the reigns of Augustus and Tiberius, 27 B.C. - 37 A.D. [(103)]. As M.-L. Chaumont has recently noted, although we know nothing of the Omani state to which Goaesus belonged, it was apparently familiar to the inhabitants of Characene by the beginning of the 1st century A.D. [(104)]. The presence of coins minted by Attambelos III, IV and VI at ed-Dur is further evidence of ties betwen the western shores of the Oman peninsula and Charax, during the first century A.D.

F. Pennacchietti has suggested that Meredat's title should perhaps be understood as 'king of all countries on the Arabian side of the Gulf and of their Arab populations (OMAN)' rather than as an allusion to the Omani in lower

Iraq [105]. This is an attractive hypothesis, and it may well be that, having extended his sphere of influence to *Thiloua/os* by 131 A.D., Meredat was able to reach even further south in the following decade, so that by 142 A.D. he had taken the title BACIΛЄΥC OMAN. There is, however, a related consideration which may indicate that the title implied something more specific.

In his description of the Arabian coast 'from Charax onward', Pliny describes the area south of Qatar [*Catharrei nomades*] as follows: 'According to Juba the voyage beyond on that side has not been explored [i.e. the Arabian side, whereas Nearchus had explored the Persian side], because of the rocks – Juba omits to mention Batrasavave, the town of the Omani, and the town of Omana which previous writers have made out to be a famous port of Carmania, and also Homna and Attana, towns said by our traders to be now the most frequented ports in the Persian Gulf' [*Nat. Hist.* VI, 32, 149]. Moreover, at around the same time or slightly later we have some relevant allusions in the *Periplus of the Erythraean Sea* [106]. In §36, we are told that upon passing through the Straits of Hormuz and sailing for six days, one comes to 'another mart of Persis, Ommana', and this is, in my opinion, a reference to the same town known to Juba as *Omana*[107].

The *testimonia* may be scattered and vague, but it is tempting to suggest a tentative reconstruction of the circumstances which lay behind the adoption of the title BACIΛЄΥC OMAN by Meredat in 142 A.D. As we have just seen, the Omani were probably present in the environs of Mesene by the time of Christ. Among the more important towns on the southern coast of the Gulf known to Juba at this time was one called Omana. Whether through the travels of the Omani to and fro between Oman and Babylonia, or from Characene merchants who had made the journey south, stories had reached Characene of some of the illustrious kings of the Omani, such as Goaesus. The circulation of Characene coins on the western coast of the Oman peninsula in the first century A.D. may also reflect the growth of commerce between the two regions at this time. By the time the *Periplus* was written, Parthian influence may have spread to the region, for Ommana is called 'a mart of Persis'. Since Parthia was the only major power in Persia at this time, it is unlikely that this allusion can mean anything else.

Meredat, as we have seen, was a member of an important Parthian royal family. Indeed, he was a prince whose father had been king of kings. When he assumed the Characene throne, he did so as a Parthian, imposed upon the local population. By 131 he had succeeded in bringing Bahrain under his control, and knowing the Parthian taste for pearls, this must have been a lucrative acquisition. It is interesting that he appointed a Palmyrene to serve him as satrap in *Thiloua/os*. The Palmyrenes had long been settled in Charax and, short of sending a Parthian, this was probably the best alternative. No doubt he would not have trusted a native of Mesene, for although he was himself king of Characene, one cannot imagine that there was any love lost between Parthia and Characene. One cannot, I think divorce the governance of *Thiloua/os* by the kingdom of Characene during the reign of Meredat from the more fundamental point that Meredat's government in Mesene was a Parthian government.

The Omani and the market of Ommana were, as we have seen, well-known at Charax. According to the *Periplus* (§36), both Apologos and Ommana exported textiles, purple dye, wine, dates, gold and slaves, to Barygaza[(108)] in India, and A. Herrmann has suggested that Ommana was the principal transit station for trade between Apologos and India [(109)]. It is easy to imagine that the port of Omana/Ommana – a wealthy town, an active center of international commerce – could have been a temptation to Meredat, whose rule had already reached Bahrain. If then, such were indeed the case, it may be that the coins of 142 A.D., on which he is called BACIΛЄΥC OMAN, commemorate his annexation or acquisition of Omana. Surely this would have made Meredat a kind of 'emperor' of the Arabian side of the Gulf. One can hardly resist the temptation to identify ed-Dur, the largest site of the period anywhere on the western coast of the Oman peninsula and the source of the coins published here, with Omana [(110)].

What prompted the expedition of Vologases IV, one of Parthia's strongest rulers in the late period and an influential figure in contemporary religious history [(111)], against Mesene in 152 A.D.? We can only speculate, yet there are some suggestive indications of potential strife between the two. To begin with, it will be remembered that Meredat and Vologases IV belonged to different Parthian royal families. Parthian history is replete with stories of internecine rivalry, and it is interesting to note that, in this particular case, conflict is attested. The father of Vologases IV, Mithradates IV, was an unsuccesful contender for the Parthian throne against Vologases III, a second cousin of Meredat who, we have suggested, may even have put Meredat on the Characene throne.

Next, it will be recalled that Ommana, which we suggest Meredat may have annexed, was a 'mart of Persis'. By taking possession of this rich town in 141 A.D., Meredat may have antagonized some factions in the Parthian ruling hierarchy. With most of the western Arabian Gulf in his possession, Meredat may have posed a serious threat to the succession to the Parthian throne when it became vacant five years later. The portrait of Meredat on his coins, moreover, is a good indication that such may have been the case. Whereas the kings of Characene had always been shown wearing the diadem, Meredat did not hesitate to have himself depicted on his coins wearing the tiara and diadem, symbols of highest authority normally reserved for the Parthian king of kings[112].

These and perhaps other facts of which we have no knowledge may have prompted Vologases IV to finally mount an expedition against Meredat in 152. Vologases does not say that he killed or captured Meredat, only that he expelled him. Thereafter, we hear nothing more of him and it could well be that with his fall from grace, the net of influence which he had cast over the western Arabian Gulf rapidly disintegrated.

Acknowledgements
My sincere thanks go to the late Nicholas Lowick and Martin Price, Dept. of Coins and Medals, British Museum, who in August, 1985, drew my attention to the Umm al-Qaiwain collection, of which only the Characene coins are published here, and subsequently provided me with photographs of it. I have also benefited enormously from the helpful comments and information provided by Prof. F.A. Pennacchietti, Istituto di Orientalistica dell'Università di Torino, who is editing the important new Greco-Parthian bilingual from Seleucia-on-the-Tigris which bears so heavily on the topic treated here.

Addendum. Nov. 27, 1987.
The original version of this manuscript was completed in the spring of 1986. Since that time, several studies of Meredat, the Seleucia inscription, and the Seleucia statue have been read at conferences and/or published. The Palmyrene inscription mentioning Meredat is treated briefly in my 'Dilmun's further relations: the Syro-Anatolian evidence from the third and second millennia B.C.', in Shaikha H.A. Al Khalifa and M. Rice, eds., *Bahrain through the ages: the Archaeology*, London, Kegan Paul International, 1986, p.397, while a condensed, popular version in Danish which concerns the material discussed here appeared as 'Palmyra, Charax og den Persiske Golf', in B. Alster and P.J. Frandsen, eds., *Dagligliv blandt guder og mennesker,* Copenhagen, Museum Tusculanums Forlag, 1986, pp. 195-201. While in Baghdad in November of 1986, I learned of J. Black's work on the inscription which subsequently appeared as 'The History of Parthia and Characene in the Second Century A.D.', *Sumer*, vol., 43 1984, pp. 230-234. In April, 1987, I discussed the main results of the present paper in a lecture entitled 'The Political Landscape of Eastern Arabia during the Seleucid and Parthian Periods' at the 197th meeting of the American Oriental Society, at which time I first learned of J.C. Green–

field's work on the Seleucia inscription. On June 15, 1987, A. Invernizzi read a paper on the Seleucia statue at a symposium on Arabian Gulf archaeology in Göttingen, while G.W. Bowersock's paper, 'Antonine Maišān', which deals with the historical implications of the Seleucia inscription, was read at a meeting on pre-Islamic Arabia in Strasbourg ten days later. Finally, in September, 1987, J.C. Greenfield discussed the Seleucia inscription at the meeting of Iranologists in Western Europe held in Torino. For various reasons, however, I have felt it best to ignore these various contributions, the texts of which were in any case largely unavailable to me, and revisions made in the manuscript of 1986 concern other matters entirely. Clearly, we shall be hearing much more about Meredat and his career as time passes.

A more important development concerns the site of ed-Dur at which the Characene coins published here were found. In October-November, 1986, a short survey and several sondages were carried out at the site. See, R. Boucharlat, E. Haerinck, C.S. Phillips, and D.T. Potts, 'Archaeological Reconnaissance at ed-Dur, Umm al-Qaiwain, U.A.E.', *Akkadica*, in press. Following the survey, the four authors of that report, representing the Universities of Lyon, Gent, Edinburgh, and Copenhagen, established the European Expedition to Umm al-Qaiwan with the primary purpose of excavating ed-Dur and investigating other sites of interest in the emirate. Excavations by the Danish, French, and British teams were conducted between February and May, and by the Belgian team in November and December, 1987. In January, 1988, a second season at the site was begun.

Abbreviations

AfO	Archiv für Orientforschung
AMI	Archäologische Mitteilungen aus Iran
AUAE	Archaeology in the United Arab Emirates
BSOAS	Bulletin of the School of Oriental and African Studies
IrAnt	Iranica Antiqua
JAOS	Journal of the American Oriental Society
JOS	Journal of Oman Studies
JRAS	Journal of the Royal Asiatic Society
JSS	Journal of Semitic Studies
KP	Der Kleine Pauly
NC	Numismatic Chronicle
NESE	Neue Ephemeris für Semitische Epigrafik
PSAS	Proceedings of the Seminar for Arabian Studies
RE	Pauly's Realencyclopädie der classischen Altertumswissenschaft
RN	Revue Numismatique
ZA	Zeitschrift für Assyriologie
ZDMG	Zeitschrift der Deutschen Morgenländischen Gesellschaft
ZfN	Zeitschrift für Numismatik

Notes

1. On the geographical limits of the designation Mesene/Maišān, cf. A.-J. Saint-Martin, *Recherches sur l'histoire et la géographie de la Mésène et de la Characène*, Paris, Imprimerie Royale, 1838, pp.5-28; J.T. Reinaud, *Mémoire sur le commencement et le fin du royaume de la Mésène et la Characène*, Paris, 1861; H. Graetz, 'Das Königreich Mesene und seine jüdische Bevölkerung', *Jahresbericht des Jüdisch-theologischen Seminars*

"Fraenckelscher Stiftung", 1879, pp.3-44; J. Marquart, 'Ērānšahr nach der Geographie des Ps. Moses Xorenac'i', *Abhandlungen der königlichen Gesellschaft der Wissenschaften zu Göttingen*, Phil.-Hist. Kl., N.F. vol. III, No. 2, Berlin, 1901, pp.40-42; E. Herzfeld, 'Untersuchungen über die historische Topographie der Landschaft am Tigris, kleinen Zâb und Ǧebel Ḥamrîn', *Memnon*, vol. 1, 1907, pp.138-140; H.H. Schaeder, 'Hasan al-Basri. Studien zur Frühgeschichte des Islam', *Der Islam*, vol. 14, 1925, pp.11-42; J. Obermeyer, *Die Landschaft Babyloniens im Zeitalter des Talmuds und des Gaonats*, Frankfurt, Kauffmann, 1929, pp.90-100; F.H. Weissbach, 'Mesene', RE, vol. XV/1, 1931, col.1082-1095; J.M. Fiey, *Assyrie Chrétienne III: Bét̲ Garmaî, Bét̲ Aramâyé et Maišân Nestoriens*, Beirut, Dar el-Machreq, 1968, pp.263-282.

2. F. Andreas, 'Alexandreia 13', RE, vol. I, 1894, col.1390, 1393.

3. G. Le Rider, 'Un Atelier Monétaire Séleucide dans la Province de la Mer Erythrée?', RN, 1965, p.38.

4. V. Tscherikower, *Die hellenistische Städtegründungen von Alexander dem Grossen bis auf die Römerzeit*, Leipzig, Dietrich'sche Verlagsbuchhandlung, 1927, p.95, 'die Bezeichnung quintus regum kann auf Antiochos IV. gut passen, wenn man berücksichtigt, dass der frühverstorbene Sohn Antiochos' III., ebenfalls Antiochos, offiziell im Herrscherkulte als König mitgezählt wurde'.

5. For the convincing arguments in support of the existence of a mint at Antiochia from the time of Antiochus IV (175-164 B.C.) until the Parthian conquest of Babylonia in 141 B.C., see O. Mørkholm, 'The Seleucid Mint at Antiochia on the Persian Gulf', *American Numismatic Society Museum Notes*, vol. 16, 1970, pp.42-44.

6. Although Pliny expressly says [*Nat. Hist.* VI, 31, 138] that Spaosines 'is wrongly stated by Juba to have been a satrap of Antiochus', it is now generally believed that just the opposite is true. Hyspaosines' success is much more easily explained if he launched himself as king from the already powerful position of satrap. Cf. Weissbach, 'Mesene', op.cit., col.1090. For the suggestion that Hyspaosines' father, Sagdodonacus, is the Adad-nadin-aḫe known from his inscribed bricks at Tello, see H. Winckler, 'Zur Geschichte des alten Arabien IV. Die Könige von Characene', *Altorientalische Forschungen*, 2nd ser., Vol. I, 1898, p.80, and cf. the disussion in A. Parrot, *Tello*, Paris, Albin Michel, 1948, p. 309-313. J. Oelsner, *Materialien zur babylonischen Gesellschaft und Kultur in hellenistischer Zeit*, Assyriologia VII, Budapest, 1986, p.99 and n. 333, following R. Bellinger, rejects Winckler's hypothesis.

7. G. Reisner, *Sumerisch-babylonische Hymnen nach Thontafeln griechischer Zeit*, Berlin, Spemann, 1896 [=Königliche Museen zu Berlin, Mittheilungen aus den orientalischen Sammlungen, Heft X], No.25, is dated to the 22nd of Aiaru, 182 S.E., i.e. June 1, 130 B.C. Cf. also Oelsner, *Materialien zur babylonischen Gesellschaft...* op. cit., p.276. Dates according to the Seleucid Era are restated in terms of the Julian calendar following R.A. Parker and W.H. Dubberstein, *Babylonian Chronology, 626 B.C. – A.D. 75*, Providence, Brown University Studies XIX, 1956, pp.37-47.

8. E.g. T.G. Pinches and J.N. Strassmaier, *Late Babylonian Astronomical and Related Texts*, prepared for publication by A.J. Sachs with the co-operation of J. Schaumberger, Providence, Brown University Press, 1955, Nos. 1045 and 1046 (normal-star almanacs); Nos. 1137 and 1138 (almanacs); No. 1274 (goal-year text); No. 1283 (Venus observation text); and No. 1288 (moon observation text), are all dated to 183 S.E., i.e. 129 B.C.

9. The text was first published by T.G. Pinches, 'A Babylonian Tablet Dated in the Reign of Aspasine', *Babylonian and Oriental Record*, vol. IV, (1890), pp.:131-135, and discussed again by him, with translation, in *The Old Testament in the Light of the Historical Records and Legends of Assyria and Babylonia*, London, Society for Promoting Christian Knowledge, 1903, pp.481-483. Cf. also later treatments in E. Unger, *Babylon, die heilige Stadt nach der Beschreibung der Babylonier*, Berlin und Leipzig, De Gruyter, 1931, pp.319-323; B. Landsberger's review of Unger, ZA, vol. 41, 1933, pp.298-299; J. Oelsner, 'Ein Beitrag zur keilschriftlichen Königstitulaturen in hellenistischer Zeit', ZA, vol. 56, 1964, p.271, and *Materialien zur* *babylonischen Gesellschaft...*, op. cit., p.276.

10. For the variants of the name see F.H. Weissbach, 'Charax 10', RE, vol. III/2, 1899, col.2122.

11. *Charax* itself is nothing but a Hellenized form of an Aramaic word, *karəkā* meaning 'city', cf. W. Eilers, 'Geographische Namengebung in und um Iran', *Bayerische Akademie der Wissenschaften, phil.-hist. Kl., Sitzungsberichte*, Heft 5, 1982, pp.36-37.

12. See, most recently. V.F. Piacentini, 'La presa di potere sassanide sul Golfo Persico fra leggenda e realtà', *Clio*, vol. XX, 1984, p.176.

13. See, for example, J. Foy-Vaillant, *Arsacidarum Imperium sive Regum Parthorum historia ad fidem numismatum accomodata*, Paris, 1725, pp.335-341; E. Corsini, *De Minnisari aliorumque Armeniae regum numis et Arsacidarum epocha*, Liburni, 1754, pp.1-2, 10-11, 13-29; E. Fröhlich, *Dubia de Minnisari aliorumque Armeniae regum numis et Arsacidarum epocha nuper vulgatis*, Vienna, 1754, p.6-16; and Eckhel, *Doctrina Numor. Veterum*, vol. III, Vindobonensis, 1792, pp.546-548, 559-562.

14. For details of the revised attributions, by Saint-Martin, *Recherches sur l'histoire...*, op.cit., pp.157ff.

15. E.Q. Visconti, *Iconographie Ancienne*, 1811; cf. the discussion of Characene's rediscovery in E. Drouin, 'Notice historique et géographique sur la Characène', *Le Muséon*, vol. IX, 1890, p.130.

16. Saint-Martin, *Recherches sur l'histoire...*, op.cit., p.35ff. Although posthumously published in 1838, the study was in fact finished in 1817.

17. O. Blau, 'Altarabische Sprachstudien, 2. Theil', ZDMG, vol. 27, 1873, pp.327-337. Blau suggested, p.331, that Hamza's account of the satraps who ruled over the Arabs for the Persians, in which *Sakht* and his son *Sindad*, the builder of numerous fortresses including *Khouarnac*, are mentioned, is a reminiscence of Sogdodonacus and his son Hyspaosines, who founded Charax. This explanation was later adopted by Drouin 'Notice historique et géographique...', op.cit., p.144. The orthography of *Khouarnac* seems to reflect a confusion with the well-known Laḫmid fortress of the same name south of al-Ḥīra.
For more on the migrations of the Arab tribes, see Blau, 'Die Wanderung der sabäischen Völkerstämme im 2. Jahrhundert n. Chr., nach arabischen Sagen und Ptolemäus', ZDMG, vol. 22, 1868, pp.654-673, and F. Wüstenfeld, 'Die Wohnsitze und Wanderungen der Arabischen Stämme, aus der Vorrede des Abu 'Obeid el-Bekrí zu seinem geographischen Wörterbuche', *Abhandlungen der Königlichen Gesellschaft der Wissenschaften zu Göttingen*, vol. 14, 1869, pp.93-172.

18. O. Mørkholm, 'Nye Møntfund fra Failaka (New Coin Finds from Failaka)', *Kuml*, 1981, Fig. 4, 9.

19. G. Le Rider, 'Monnaies de Characène', *Syria*, vol. XXXVI, 1959, pp.231-232.

20. The first coin of Hyspaosines known was a piece in the collection of Baron von Prokesch-Osten, later in the Berlin Museum. It is dated to 188 S.E., i.e. 124 B.C., and was published simultaneously in 1866 by W.H. Waddington, 'Numismatique et chronologie des Rois de la Characène', RN, vol. XI, 1866, pp.305-311, Pl. XI:2, and Baron B. von Köhne, 'Unedirte Münzen aus der Sammlung S.E. des K.K. Internuntius zu Konstantinopel Herrn Freiherrn von Prokesch-Osten', *Berliner Blätter für Munz-, Siegel- und Wappenkunde*, vol. III, 1866, pp.256-262, and Taf. XLIV:5. A second example was acquired in 1877 by the Cabinet de Médailles in Paris, see E. Babelon, 'Sur la numismatique et la Chronologie des Dynastes de la Characène', *Journal International d'Archéologie Numismatique*, vol. I, 1898, p.384, and Pl. IH':2.

21. Cf. the discussion in Drouin, 'Notice historique et géographique ..., op.cit., p.143.

22. Blau, 'Altarabische Sprachstudien', op.cit., pp.326-327, 'Hyspaosines...ward der Ahn einer Dynastie, die bis zum Sturz der Arsakiden die Landschaften Mesene und Bahrein unter ihrem Scepter vereinigte'.

23. H.E. Mathiesen, *The Terracotta Figurines*, Ikaros: The Hellenistic Settlements, vol. 1 [=Jutland Archaeological Society Publications, vol. XVI:1], Copenhagen, Nordisk Forlag, 1982, p.36. Cf. the discussion of this suggestion in R. Boucharlat and J.-F. Salles, 'L'Arabie orientale: d'un bilan à un autre', *Mesopotamia*, in press.

24. A. Sprenger, *Die alte Geographie Arabiens*, Bern, 1875, §200.

25. B.C. Busch, *Britain and the Persian Gulf, 1894-1914*, Berkeley and Los Angeles, Univ. of California Press, 1967, p.1.

26. For information on these unpublished finds, I would like to thank Jean-François Salles, Maison de L'Orient, Lyon, who is director of the French Archaeological Mission to Kuwait. For the smaller, lesser known islands of Umm al-Namal and 'Akāz, cf. H.R.P. Dickson, *Kuwait and her Neighbours*, London, Allen & Unwin, 1956, p.32.

27. Le Rider, 'Monnaies de Characène', op.cit., pp.238-239.

28. S.A. Nodelman, 'A Preliminary History of Characene', *Berytus*, vol. XIII, 1960, p.101 and Appendix II, 'Kings of Characene'.

29. Le Rider, 'Monnaies de Characène', op.cit., p.262, n.4.

30. Babelon, 'Sur la numismatique...', op.cit., p.392, cf. p.403 for a table with all of Attambelos IV's year dates. For the circumstances surrounding the discovery of the Tello hoard, cf. Parrot, *Tello*, op.cit., pp.310, 312.

31. Babelon, 'Sur la numismatique...' op.cit., p.392, 'La première partie du règne nous offre le portrait d'un adolescent imberbe, les cheveux calamistrés; puis, dans le courant de l'année TO (370 Sél.=58 de J.C.) la tête du meme prince parait avec une barbe courte; cette barbe grandit et devient plus touffue d'année en année jusqu'à la fin du règne'.

32. R. al-Qaisy, 'Archaeological Investigations and Excavations at the State of the United Arab Emerites (sic) – Arabian Gulf', *Sumer*, vol. XXXI, 1975, p.155 (in Arabic).

33. J.-F. Salles, 'Notes sur l'archéologie des périodes hellénistique et romaine dans les Emirats Arabes Unis', AUAE, vol. II-III, 1979, p.85; cf. 'Monnaies d'Arabie Orientale: éléments pour l'histoire des Emirats Arabes Unis à l'époque historique', PSAS, vol. 10, 1980, p.99.

34. Salles, 'Notes sur l'archéologie...', op.cit., p.77.

35. Le Rider, 'Monnaies de la Characène', op.cit., p.239.

36. Le Rider, 'Monnaies de la Characène', op.cit., Pl.XXI:31-36, for comparison.

37. Babelon, 'Sur la numismatique...', op.cit., PI. IΘ:5-6; cf. J. de Morgan, *Manuel de Numismatique Orientale*, vol. I, Paris, Geuthner, 1936, p.221, Fig.264.

38. Waddington, 'Numismatique et chronologie...', op.cit. Pl. XII:14; Babelon, 'Sur la numismatique...', op.cit., Pl. IΘ:6.

39. A. de Longpérier, 'Monnaies de la Characène, le roi Obodas', RN, vol. XV, 1874-77, p.310 and Pl. V:1, for an example in the British Museum.

40. Babelon, 'Sur la numismatique...', op.cit., Pl. IΘ:5; de Morgan, *Manuel de Numismatique...*, op.cit., p.221, Fig.264.

41. The available bibliography on Trajan's Parthian war is long. Among the many works which have dealt with it, see J. Guey, *Essai sur la guerre parthique de Trajan (114-117)*, Bucharest, Bibliothèque d'Istros 2, 1937; F.A. Lepper, *Trajan's Parthian War*, Oxford, 1948; A. Maricq, 'La Province d'"Assyrie" crée par Trajan: à propos de la guerre parthique de Trajan' [=Classica et Orientalia 6], *Syria*, vol. 36, 1959, pp.254-263; and K.-H. Ziegler, *Die Beziehungen zwischen Rom und dem Partherreich*, Wiesbaden, Steiner, 1964, pp.100-104. Here we cite only two of the many available discussions of Attambelos' capitulation to the Roman emperor: N.C. Debevoise, *A Political History of Parthia*, Univ. of Chicago, Chicago, 1938, p.234 and n.107; Nodelman, 'A Preliminary History...', op.cit., p.110.

42. For the coins of Theonesos IV, see Le Rider, 'Monnaies de Characène', op.cit., p.252.

43. Some of the most important discussions of these texts in general, and of the caravan trade between Palmyra and Charax in particular, include, R. Mouterde and A. Poidebard, 'La Voie Antique des Caravanes entre Palmyre et Hit au IIe Siècle ap.J.-C. d'après une inscription retrouvée au s.-e. de Palmyre (Mars 1930)', *Syria*, vol. XII, 1931, pp.101-115; M. Rostovtzeff, 'Les Inscriptions Caravanières de Palmyre', *Mélanges Gustave Glotz*, vol. II, Paris, Presses Universitaires de France, 1932, pp.793-811; *Caravan Cities*, Oxford, Clarendon Press, 1932, pp.143-146; E. Will, 'Marchands et Chefs de Caravanes à Palmyre', *Syria*, vol. XXXIV, 1957, pp.262-277; D. Schlumberger, 'Palmyre et la Mésène', *Syria*, vol. XXXVIII, 1961, pp.256-260; M. Gawlikowski, 'Palmyre et l'Euphrate', *Syria*, vol. LX, 1983, pp.53-68; and most recently, the excellent study of J. Teixidor, 'Un port Romain du désert: Plamyre et son commerce d'Auguste à Caracalla', *Semitica*, vol. XXXIV, 1984, pp.7-125.

44. See, especially, Rostovtzeff, 'Les Inscriptions...', op.cit., pp.798-803; and Gawlikowski, 'Palmyre et l'Euphrate', op.cit., pp.63-66.

45. For the Greek text, see H. Seyrig, 'Antiquités Syriennes 38. Inscriptions grecques de l'agora de Palmyre', *Syria*, vol. XXII, 1941, pp.254-55; cf. for the Aramaic, J. Starcky, *Inventaire des Inscriptions de Palmyre*, Fasc. X, Damascus, Direction Générale des Antiquités de Syrie, 1949, No. 38, p.25.

46. This was first recognized by E. Herzfeld, 'Tilmun, the Bahrain Islands in the Sargon Itinerary', *The Persian Empire*, ed. G. Walser, Wiesbaden, Steiner, 1968, p.62. Cf. R. Zadok, 'Iranian and Babylonian Notes IV. Thilouana', AfO, vol. XXVIII, 1981-82, p.139, who mistakes the genitive for a toponym *Thilouana*. This has been corrected now by G.W. Bowersock, 'Tylos and Tyre: Bahrain in the Graeco-Roman world', in Shaikha Haya Ali Al Khalifa and M. Rice, eds., *Bahrain through the ages: the Archaeology*, London, Kegan Paul International, 1986, p.405, n.9.

47. J.K. Stark, *Personal Names in Palmyrene Inscriptions*, Oxford, Claredon Press, 1971, pp.30, 93, s.v. 'MHRDT'. For the texts themselves, see J. Starcky, 'Trois inscriptions palmyréniennes', *Mélanges Univ. St. Joseph*, vol. 28, 1949-50, p.46 (471 S.E. = 159 A.D.); D. Schlumberger, *La Palmyrène du Nord-Ouest*, Paris, Geuthner, 1951, Nos. 55 (458 S.E. = 146 A.D.), 59; and H. Ingholt, H. Seyrig, and J. Starcky, *Recueil des Tessères de Palmyre*, Bibliothèque Archéologique et Historique, vol. LVIII, Paris, Geuthner, 1955, Nos. 36, 567.

48. D. Sestini, *Descrizione della Medaglie Antiche Greche del Museo Hedervariano*, Parte Terza, Firenze, Presso Guglielmo Piatti, 1829, p.139, and T.XXXII:15.

49. Stanislas B. de Chaudoir, *Corrections et additions*, Paris, 1835, p.100. I have been unable to find this.

50. I have not been able to find any information on Steuart in the standard dictionnaries of British biography. However, S.A. Pallis, *The Antiquity of Iraq*, Copenhagen, Munksgaard, 1956, p.83-84, notes that 'about 1827 Mr. Steuart (Stewart) and M. Vidal, the consular dragoman at Aleppo' copied Xerxes' Mt. Elwend inscription together. Some years later, when Vidal was French consul in Baghdad, he acquired four of the Meredat coins subsequently studied by de Longpérier (see below). I think it more than likely that the Steuart with whom Vidal worked was the John Robert Steuart in question. I have also seen a paper by Steuart entitled 'Two Plates of Coins presented to the Royal Asiatic Society', read Feb. 18, 1837.

51. J. Millingen, *Sylloge of Ancient Unedited Coins of Greek Cities and Kings, from various collections principally in Great Britain*, London, 1837, Pl. IV. No. 67, pp.85-86. This was later included as No. 460 in a catalogue published by Steuart of his own collection, which I have not been able to find. It is now in the British Museum, cf. G.F. Hill, *Catalogue of the Greek Coins of Arabia, Mesopotamia and Persia*, London, British Museum, 1922, Pl.XLVII:3.

52. Millingen, *Sylloge...*, op. cit., p.85.

53. A.C.E. von Werlhof, *Handbuch der griechischen Numismatik*, Hannover, Hahn, 1850, p.249, 'Meredates und Viphoba, dessen Gemahlin (Zeit und Land ungewiss,

muthmasslich Characene)'.

54. J. Lindsay, *A view of the History and Coinage of the Parthians, with Descriptive Catalogues and Tables...*, Cork, John Crowe, 1852, p.229, Pl. 10:13-14.

55. W.H. Scott, 'Note on the Coins of Meredates and Uiphoba', NC, vol. IX, 1856-57, pp.226-227.

56. W.S.W. Vaux, 'On Some Coins of Characene, brought from Baghdad, by Dr. Hyslop', NC, vol. X, 1857-58, p.38.

57. A. de Longpérier, 'Mérédate, roi des Omanes', RN, vol. VIII, 1863, pp.333-341, reprinted in G. Schlumberger, ed., *Oeuvres de A. de Longpérier*, vol. I, Paris, Leroux, 1883, pp.200-206.

58. Rev. A.H. Sayce, *The Archaeology of the Cuneiform Inscriptions*, London, Society for Promoting Christian Knowledge, 1908, p.19.

59. P. Gardner, *The Parthian Coinage*, London, 1877, p.1.

60. For Tyche or Nike as city goddesses on Parthian coins, see e.g. Gardner, *The Parthian Coinage*, op.cit., Pl. VI, No. 9-14 (Pacorus II), 16-19 (Osroes); Pl. VII, No. 3 (Vologases III), 9 (Vologases IV). De Longpérier's suggestion that the female bust on Meredat's coins represented the Tyche of Forat is followed by Hill, *Catalogue...*, op.cit., p.ccxii, and Nodelman, 'A. Preliminary History...' op.cit., p.113.

61. Waddington, 'Numismatique et chronologie...', op.cit.

62. A. von Sallet, 'Die Münzen der Könige von Characene', zfN, vol. 8, 1881, pp.218-219.

63. Von Sallet, 'Die Münzen...', op.cit., pp.218-219, 'die Lesung Longpériers ΟΜΑΝΟΦΙΛ und die Uebersetzung, "aimé des Omani" scheint mir völlig verfehlt, gänzlich beispiellos und auch nach der Umschrift unmöglich.... Das OMAI oder OMAN harrt freilich noch seiner Erklärung und es kann ja in diesem Wort allerdings eine Hindeutung auf die Omani liegen, von denen es heisst... "a Petra incoluere Omani ad Characenen usque etc."'

64. Von Sallet, 'Die Münzen...', op.cit., p.219, 'Plinius spricht an der angeführten Stelle von einer Stadt "oppidum quod Characenorum regi aret in Pasitigris ripa, Forath nomine"; ist hier etwa eine Verwandtschaft mit dem ΦΟΒΑ zu suchen?' Note, however, the orthography of the name Forat in Arrian's Parthica XVI, where we find *Oratha*.

65. A.v. Gutschmid, *Geschichte Irans und seiner Nachbarländer von Alexander dem Grossen bis zum Untergang der Arsaciden*, Tübingen, Laupp, 1888, p.161.

66. Von Gutschmidt, *Geschichte Irans...*, op.cit., p.161, 'Beachtung verdient, dass wenig früher, im Jahre 143, der Prägung der mesenischen Könige die eines Königs Meredates, Sohns des Phobas, Königs der Omaner, zur Seite tritt. Diese Omaner, die schon Plinius [(3). VI §.145] als Bewohner der Wüste im Westen von Charax kennt, können nur Auswanderer aus Oman sein und sind wahrscheinlich identisch mit dem Stamme el-Azd, der nach der arabischen Tradition [(4). Vgl. Caussin de Perceval, Essai sur l'histoire des Arabes avant l'Islamisme II p.5 ff.] theils als el-Azd von Oman dort zurückblieb, theils mit der grossen südarabischen Völkerwanderung über Bahrein nach Norden zog und sich endlich in Anbar und Hira niederliess. Es ist dies ein neues Anzeichen davon, dass die ersten Wellen dieser bedeutsamen Bewegung sich schon um die Mitte des 2. Jahrhunderts im Euphrat- und Tigrisgebiet fühlbar machten. Wenn arabische Historiker diese Nomaden durch die Schwäche der Theilkönige der Arsacidenzeit angelockt werden lassen, so ist das vielleicht blosse Combination; die Combination ist aber richtig'.

67. Drouin, 'Notice historique et géographique...', op.cit., p.147, n.2, 'M. de Longpérier... a cru devoir lire sur les monnaies de ce roi *basileus Omanophilos* "roi aimé des Omani"et enafait un roi des Omanes peuple dont parle Pline (VI, 32, 4) et qui aurait été voisin du Tigre. Mais la lecture *Omanophilos* est contestable; elle a été acceptée par M. de Gutschmid... qui considère ces Omanes comme étant les même que les Arabes Azdites venus d'Oman et d'autres parties de l'Arabie dans le courant du IIe siècle de notre ère. Il lit seulement la légende "Meredates fils de Phoba roi des Omanes". On sait que Lucien cite parmi ses exemples de longévité, un certain Goaesus roi des Omanes dans le pays des aromates; il est question vraisemblablement chez l'auteur grec, du vrai pays d'Oman en Arabie, et non pas des Omanes de Pline et de Meredates'.

68. F. Justi, *Iranisches Namenbuch*, Marburg, 1895, p.213, s.v. 'Miþradāta'.

69. Babelon, 'Sur la numismatique...', op.cit., pp.397-98, 'On sait qu'après la mort de Trajan, Hadrien dut abandonner toutes les conquêtes romaines de la Mésopotamie et de la vallée du Tigre. Il y eut dans ce pays des révolutions et des bouleversements au milieu desquels Attambélos IV, l'ami des Romains, perdit vraisemblablement sa couronne. C'est à l'époque contemporaine des premières années du règne d'Hadrien, vers l'an 118 environ, que le roi des Parthes, Chosroès, rétablit à son profit l'espèce de suzeraineté que ses ancêtres avaient excercée sur le petit royaume characènien. Mais à partir de ce moment de profondes ténèbres enveloppent les annales de la basse Chaldée et des régions adjacentes jusqu'à l'an 228, époque de la ruine du royaume des Parthes par le sassanide Ardeschir. C'est à l'aide de la numismatique seule jusqu'ici, qu'on a essayé de projeter quelque lueur, -- mais combien indécise, -- sur ce point de l'histoire de l'Orient. Nous sommes certains, par elle, que le royaume de Characène continua à subsister, mais singulièrement affaibli, si l'on en juge par la barbarie des monnaies qu'on continua à y frapper, les premières à légendes grecques, les dernières à légendes mandéennes.'

70. Winckler, 'Zur Geschichte des alten Arabien IV. Die Könige von Characene', op.cit., p.77, with reference to de Longpérier, 'Monnaies de la Characène...', op.cit., pp.136-143.

71. F.H. Weissbach, 'Charakene', RE, vol. III/2, 1899, col. 2116-2119.

72. B.V. Head, *Historia Numorum*, Oxford, Clarendon Press, 1911, pp.823-824.

73. Hill, *Catalogue...*, op.cit., pp.ccx-ccxi.

74. Hill, *Catalogue...*, op.cit., p.ccxiv.

75. J. de Morgan, *Numismatique de la Perse Antique*, Paris, Leroux, 1933, col.538, 540, and *Manuel de Numismatique*, op.cit., p.228.

76. A. Grohmann, 'Omani', RE, vol. XVIII/1, 1942, col. 344.

77. Nodelman, 'A Preliminary History...', op.cit., pp.111-114.

78. De Longpérier, 'Mérédate...', op.cit., is not cited in Nodelman's bibliography.

79. G. Le Rider, *Suse sous les Séleucides et les Parthes*, Mémoires de la Mission Archéologique en Iran XXXVIII, Paris, 1965, p.189 and Pl. XXXVII, No. 444, drew a comparison between an obviously different, late Characene coin on which BA can be made out on the obverse, and Meredat's coins. He suggested that this might represent part of the name Phobas, following von Gutschmid's reading of Meredat's legend as 'son of Phobas'. It is certain, however, that the example from Susa, which may date to 155/156 A.D., has no direct bearing on the coinage of Meredat. For an attempt to strike Le Rider's proposal, which also makes an ill-informed reference to Meredat's coinage, see M.R. Zamir-Dahncke, 'Phraates: ein bisher unbekannter Herrscher in der Charakene', AMI N.F. 10, 1977, pp.209-210. Speaking of Meredat, p.209, n.3a, all Zamir-Dahncke has to say is, 'Ich muss gestehen, dass mir ein solcher völlig unbekannt war, und da Le Rider es versäumt einen Hinweis zu geben, kann ich nach längerem Suchen nur annehmen, dass er sich auf die in J. de Morgan, Manuel de Numismatique Orientale... unter dem Abschnitt "Principauté de Subcharacène" abgebildete Münze bezieht'.

80. D. Sellwood, 'Minor States in Southern Iran', *Cambridge History of Iran*, vol. 3/1, Cambridge, 1983, p.313.

81. R.N. Frye, *The History of Ancient Iran*, Handbuch der Altertumswissenschaft, vol. III.7, Munich, Beck, 1984, p.277.

82. For a preliminary treatment, see F.A. Pennacchietti, 'Eracle in riposo' in *La Terra tra i Due Fiumi: Venti anni di archeologia italiana in Medio Oriente*, Torino, Il Quadrante Edizioni, 1985, pp.420-422; cf. 'The Greek-Parthian Bilingual Inscription on the

Bronze Statue of Heracles from Seleucia on Tigris (Iraq)', and W. Al-Salihi, 'Mesene's Bronze Statue of Weary Hercules', unpublished papers read at a conference entitled 'Common Ground and Regional Features in the Parthian and Sasanian World', Universita' di Torino, June 17-21, 1985. For the *editio princeps* of the new inscription, see Pennacchietti's 'L'Iscrizione Bilingue Greco-Partica dell'Eracle di Seleucia', *Mesopotamia*, in press.

83. The view was sometimes expressed in early studies of Parthian history that Vologases IV was probably the son of Vologases III, e.g. G. Rawlinson, *The Sixth Oriental Monarchy*, London, Longmans, Green & Co., 1873, p.323; Gardner, *The Parthian Coinage,* op.cit., p.16. The new inscriptions tell us explicitly, however, that Vologases IV was the son of a king named Mithridates. Both Al-Salihi and Pennacchietti suggest that this was the shadowy figure known as Mithradates IV, a pretender to the Parthian throne known only from the coins he minted in Iran, cf. Gardner, *The Parthian Coinage,* op.cit., p.55; W. Wroth, *Catalogue of the Coins of Parthia*, London, British Museum, 1903,pp.lix-lx; A. von Petrowicz, *Arsaciden-Münzen*, Vienna, 1904, pp.154-157; Debevoise, *A Political History...*, op.cit., p.244; D. Sellwood, *An Introduction to the Coinage of Parthia*, London, Spink & Son Ltd., 1971, pp.262-264; 'Parthian Coins', *Cambridge History of Iran*, vol. 3/1, Cambridge, 1983, p.297; and K. Schippmann, *Grundzüge der Parthischen Geschichte*, Darmstadt, Wissenschaftliche Buchgesellschaft, 1980, pp.64-65. Unfortunately, none of Mithridates IV's coins are dated, but he has traditionally been slotted between Vologases III and IV, c. 130-147 A.D.

Several scholars have made the error of confusing Meredat and Mithridates IV. In this connection, it must be stressed that a statement by Nodelman concerning Meredat has twice been misquoted and taken as a reference to Mithridates IV. In 1960, Nodelman wrote, 'A Preliminary History...', op.cit., p.113, 'Meredates [Meredat] may have found it advisable to move from Charax, the traditional capital... to Forat'. J. Hansman, 'Charax and the Karkheh', *IrAnt*, vol. VII, 1967, p.25, however, writes, 'Nodelman suggests that Mithradates IV (A.D. 128-147) further moved the capital from Charax to Forat'. The same mistake is made by M.G. Raschke, 'New Studies in Roman Commerce with the East', in H. Temporini and W. Haase, ed., *Aufstieg und Niedergang der Römischen Welt*, vol. II.9.2, Berlin, de Gruyter, 1978, p.987, n.1361, who cites Nodelman, but repeats Hansman almost *verbatim*: 'cf. S.A. Nodelman... who suggests that Mithridates IV (A.D. 128-147?) moved the capital of the kingdom to Forat'. Mithridates IV was a rebellious pretender to the Parthian crown who, so far as we know, never had anything to do with Characene, as both Hansman and Raschke could have seen if they had looked at the Nodelman kinglist. As the Seleucia texts show, however, it was the son of Mithridates IV, Vologases IV, who drove Meredat off the Characene throne.

84. Justi, *Iranisches Namenbuch*, op.cit., p.239, suggested that Pacorus II was identical with the Afquršah, son of Balaš (Volagases) mentioned by Ṭabarī 710, 6 und al-Bīrūnī 113, 2. The Balaš in question is, of course, Vologases I (51/52-78/79), the founder of Vologesias, on which cf. T. Nöldeke, 'Zur orientalischen Geographie 1. Vologesias', ZDMG, vol. 28, 1874, pp.93-98; A. Maricq, 'Vologésias, l'emporium de Ctésiphon', *Syria*, vol. 36, 1959, pp.264-276; and J.M. Fiey, 'Topography of Al-Madā'in', *Sumer*, vol. 23, 1967, pp.12-13. There are no other extant sources which suggest that Vologases I was the father of Pacorus II, but Justi's thesis is the most likely. Pacorus I (d. 38) can be eliminated as a possibility for he was the son of Orodes II. Pacorus of Atropatene Media can probably also be eliminated, if we accept the testimony of Tacitus itus [*Ann.* XII,14,7] who says that Pacorus' brother, Vologases I, was the son of Vonones II, Debevoise, *A Political History...*, op.cit., p.174. If, therefore, Justi's thesis is accepted, it solves the problem of the Parthian succession following Vologases' death. Pacorus has often been seen as a pretender, e.g. by Debevoise, *A Political History...*, op.cit., p.213, and the fact that both he and Vologases struck coins at Seleucia during the latter's last year of rule has been interpreted as evidence of a power struggle. If, however, Pacorus was the son of Vologases, then 78/79 may represent a brief co-regency. Cf. E. Yarshater, 'Iranian National History', *Cambridge History of Iran*, vol. 3/1, Cambridge, 1983, p.475, who writes, 'Tha'ālibi depicts them [Arsacid kings] generally as just and valiant. Interestingly, he says of Afqur Shah (Pakores) (6. In the text, Aqfur) that he recovered the Kaviyan banner and took good care of it'. It seems most likely that Tha'ālibi is referring to the same individual known to Ṭabarī and al-Bīrūnī. When, therefore, Justi, *Iranisches Namenbuch*, op.cit., p.412, proposes a hypothetical 'Pakoros (Afqur)?' as son of the late Parthian king Vologases V (208-227), apparently because of the variant orthography (Afqur vs. Aqfur), one cannot consider it likely since Tha'ālibi's description hardly fits the image of the last years of Parthian rule. For Moslem sources on the Parthians in general, see F. Spiegel, 'Die muhammedanischen Berichte über das Reich der Arsakiden' in his *Eranische Altertumskunde*, vol. III, Leipzig, Engelman, 1878, pp.191-198.

85. The opinion of Wroth, *Catalogue...*, op.cit., p.lvii.

86. The opinion of Debevoise, *A Political History...*, op.cit., p.216.

87. Pennacchietti, 'L'Iscrizione Bilingue...', op.cit., p.13.

88. Personal communication, letter of Jan.29, 1986. I do not want to dwell here on all of the merits of this reading over previous readings, comparing them point for point. It may suffice to simply recall several of the most important features. We have already noted that a personal name *Phobas* is out of the question, since Pacorus was the name of Meredat's father. Pacorus is called 'king of kings' in the Seleucia inscriptions, and it is therefore apposite to interpret ΒΛΒΛCIΛ as an abbreviation of this title in its Greek form, *basileus basileon*, as originally suggested by de Longpérier, albeit with reference to Meredat himself. J. Neusner has tabulated the occurrence of this title on Parthian coinage, based on Wroth's catalogue. This reveals that 'the title "king of kings", which was hardly used before 100 b.c.e. was almost always used after 38 b.c.e., and that in the first half of the last century b.c.e., this title became important to the Arsacid monarchs, and remained significant thereafter'; see, 'Parthian Political Ideology', *IrAnt*, vol.3, 1963, pp.46-47. Cf., for more on the use of this title, R.N. Frye, 'The Charisma of Kingship in Ancient Iran', *IrAnt*, vol.4. 1964, pp.36-40, 44.

While the shortening of 'son of Pacorus, king of kings' into VIΦΟΒΛΒΛCIΛ may strike us as extreme, F. Pennacchietti has pointed out to me a Roman example of such drastic reduction in the coinage of Severus. A coin found at Dura Europus reads: IMP.CÆ.L.SEP.SEV.PART.AUG.II.

89. K. Sallmann, 'Plinius', KP, vol. 4, 1979, col. 932.

90. A. Neubauer, *La Géographie du Talmud*, Paris, Michel Lévy, 1868, p.367.

91. Blau, 'Altarabische Sprachstudien', op.cit., p.325. For Humanija, cf. Nöldeke, 'Zur orientalischen Geographie', op.cit., p.94, n.1; M. Streck, *Die alte Landschaft Babylonien nach den arabischen Geographen*, Leiden, Brill, 1900, p.294; and Obermeyer, *Die Landschaft Babyloniens...*, op.cit., pp. 192-194.

92. For a reproduction of a 1478 version of Ptolemy's map of Arabia, showing the *sinus Mesanites* and *Coromanis polis*, see G.R. Tibbetts, *Arabia in Early Maps*, Cambridge, Falcon-Oleander, 1978, Pl. 2 opposite p.35.

93. Maj.-Gen.SB. Miles, 'Note on Pliny's Geography of the East Coast of Arabia', JRAS, vol. 10, 1878, p.160. Cf. Sprenger, *Die alte Geographie Arabiens*, op.cit., §199, who saw a connection with the Arabic toponym *Qarn*.

94. See, *inter alia*, O. Blau, 'Die Wanderung der sabäischen Völkerstämme...', op.cit., pp.666-667, and F. Wüstenfeld, 'Die Wohnsitze und Wanderungen der Arabischen Stämme...', op.cit., pp.93-172. On the spread of the Azd Oman from southern Arabia to Oman, see more recently J. Wilkinson, *Water and Tribal Settlement in South-East Arabia*, Oxford, Clarendon Press, 1977, p.126ff. Note expecially the South Arabian inscription from Mleiha in Sharjah, p.135, n.6, which A.F.L. Beeston dates approximately to the fifth century B.C. or slightly later, calling it 'the first authentic proof of South Arabian penetration to the east coast'.

95. O. Blau, 'Arabien im sechsten Jahrhundert: eine ethnographische Skizze', ZDMG, vol. 23, 1869, p.392; J. Hell, 'Al-Farazdaḳ's Lieder auf die Muhallabiten', ZDMG, vol. 59, 1905, p.595; and Ch. Pellat, *Le Milieu Bas-*

rien et la Formation de Ǧāḥiẓ, Paris, Librairie d'Amérique et d'Orient, 1953, p.24.

96. W.W. Müller, 'Eine sabäische Gesandtschaft in Ktesiphon und Seleukeia', NESE, vol. 2, 1974, pp.155-165. Although the text is not dated, Prof. Müller has suggested privately to me that the events described probably preceded Diocletian's conquest.

97. The writing Asd instead of Azd is the original and, according to early Arab grammarians, more correct form. Cf. Müller, 'Eine sabäische Gesandschaft...', op.cit., p.159.

98. As Müller, 'Eine sabäische Gesandtschaft...', op.cit., p.159, wrote, 'Von den Asd bzw. Azd, die sich in die Azd as-Sarāt und die Azd 'Omān gliedern, können in unserer Inschrift natürlich nur die letzteren gemeint sein'.

99. Müller, 'Eine sabäische Gesandtschaft..', op.cit., p.161. Müller's treatment of this long problematic portion of the Nemāra inscription was apparently unknown to I. Shahid when he suggested the same interpretation in his 'Philological Observations on the Namāra Inscription', JSS, vol. 24, 1979, p.37. Cf. A.F.L. Beeston, 'Nemara and Faw', BSOAS, vol. LXII, 1979, p.3, who states that the reading 'can be taken as certain'. Note, however, that Shahid has recently proposed identifying the two Asds with tribes in the western, Byzantine sphere, rather than with the northeast Arabian region. See his *Byzantium and the Arabs in the Fourth Century*, Washington, Dumbarton Oaks, 1984, pp.37-38. Shahid's argument seems forced to me, however. J.A. Bellamy, 'A New Reading of the Namārah Inscription', JAOS, vol. 105, 1985, pp.36-37, retains the old reading of 'al-Asadayn', meaning the two Asads, instead of the two Asds. The historical arguments against this adduced by Müller, Beeston, and Shahid seem convincing.

100. Cited after W.H. Schoff, *Parthian Stations by Isidore of Charax*, London, 1914, p.15.

101. Schoff, *Parthian Stations...*, op.cit., p.17.

102. W. Spoerri, 'Isidoros 5', KP, vol. II, 1979, col. 1461.

103. M.-L. Chaumont, 'Etudes d'histoire Parthe V. La route royale des Parthes de Zeugma à Séleucie du Tigre d'après l'itinéraire d'Isidore de Charax', *Syria*, vol. LXI, 1984, p.65.

104. Chamont, 'Etudes d'histoire Parthe...', op.cit., p.64. Cf. E. Herzfeld, 'Sakastan, geschichtliche Untersuchungen zu den Ausgrabungen am Kuh i Khwadja', AMI, vol. IV, 1932, p.7, who, in discussing the same passage more than fifty years earlier, wrote, 'Der andere König, der aus Isidor zitiert wird, Goaisos von 'Omān ist uns naturgemäss völlig unbekannt'.

105. Personal communication, letter of Feb. 12, 1986.

106. W.H. Schoff, *The Periplus of the Erythraean Sea*, New York, Longmans, Green & Co., 1912, p.36. Cf. the discussion of this passage in E. Kornemann, 'Die historischen Nachrichten des Periplus maris Erythraei über Arabien', *Janus*, vol. I [=Festschrift zu C.F. Lehmann-Haupts sechzigstem Geburtstage], 1921, pp.66-67.

107. Contra A. Herrmann, 'Omana', RE, vol. 18/1, 1942, col.343, and Salles, 'Monnaies d'Arabie orientale...', op.cit., p.104. I do not want to rehearse all of the arguments here for a location on the Arabian vs. the Persian side of the Gulf. For a short survey of opinion concerning the location of Omana, see my 'From Qadê to Mazûn: four notes on Oman, c. 700 B.C. to 700 A.D.', JOS, vol. 8, 1985, p.86. Cf. the review of G.W.B. Huntingford's edition of the *Periplus*, by A.F.L. Beeston, BSOAS, vol. 44, 1981, p.357.

108. E. Glaser, *Skizze der Geschichte und Geographie Arabiens*, Berlin, Weidmann, 1890, p.80, for a discussion of this paragraph.

109. Herrmann, 'Omana', op.cit., col.344.

110. Salles' objection that the six day journey from the entrance of the Gulf to Omana rules out ed-Dur is invalid. In 1904 H. Burchardt sailed from Basra to Muscat in a traditional *būm*, and under rough sailing conditions, took 8 days to sail from Dubai to Kumzar, the northernmost point on the Oman peninsula. See, 'Ost-Arabien von

Basra bis Maskat auf Grund eigener Reisen', *Zeitschrift der Gesellschaft für Erdkunde zu Berlin,* 1906, pp.319-320.

111. For the political history, cf. Debevoise, *A Political History...,* op.cit., p.244-255. Aside from his campaigns, however, there are interesting religious questions pertaining to Vologases IV. The first concerns Christianity in the Parthian period, while the second concerns the compilation of the *Denkard.*

In the Syriac *History of Karka of Bét Slōḫ,* i.e. Kirkuk, specific mention is made of a ninety year period of peace in the community which lasted from the reign of Balaš/Vologases to the twentieth year of Šapur I. Cf. A. Christensen, *L'Iran sous les Sassanides,* Paris, Geuthner, 1936, p.35; J.M. Fiey, 'Vers la Réhabilitation de l'*Histoire de Karka d'Bét Slōḫ*', *Analecta Bollandiana,* vol. 82, 1964, p.196, and *Jalons pour une Histoire de l'Église en Iraq,* Corpus Scriptorum Christianorum Orientalium Subsidia, vol. 36, Louvain, 1970, p.49. Calculating backwards ninety years from Šapur I's twentieth year on the throne, 261, as Christensen and Fiey have done, brings us to the year 171, which falls almost exactly in the middle of the reign of Vologases IV (148-191). In 1964, Fiey, 'Vers la Réhabilitation...', op.cit., p.196, asked the obvious question raised by this passage: 'Mais pourquoi l'auteur choisit-il cette année 171 comme point de départ de ses années de paix? Cette date marque-t-elle la fin d'une période ou la communauté eut à souffrir d'autres troubles que de la "zizanie", par example de persécution? L'écrivain ne le dit pas.' Regardless of whether or not the reasons behind the chronicler's statement are no longer clear, the fact remains that a period of peace in the lives of the Christians of Babylonia, and perhaps also by implication one of offical tolerance, is explicitly indicated as having begun under the reign of Vologases IV.

The question also arises as to whether or not 'Valakhsh, the Arsacid', to whom the *Denkard* (IV.24) ascribes an order commanding the collection of all fragments of the Avesta scattered throughout his realm, may have been Vologases IV. A long line of scholars have attributed this deed to Vologases I, including Von Gutschmid, *Geschichte Irans...,* op.cit., p.137; Herzfeld, 'Sakastan..', op.cit., p.88; Debevoise, *A Political History...,* op.cit., p.196; O. Klima, 'Awesta, die altpersischen Inschriften, das mittelpersische Schrifttum', in J. Rypka, ed., *Iranische Literaturgeschichte,* Leipzig, Harrassowitz, 1959, p.27; E. Yarshater, 'Were the Sasanians Heirs to the Achaemenids?', *La Persia nel Medioevo,* Rome, Accademia Nazionale dei Lincei, 1971, p.528; R.N. Frye, *The Heritage of Persia,* London, Weidenfeld and Nicolson, 1962, 1962, p.201, repeated in 'Methodology in Iranian History', in Frye, ed., *Neue Methodologie in der Iranistik,* Wiesbaden, Harrassowitz, 1974, p.65; and M. Boyce, 'Iconoclasm among the Zoroastrians', in J. Neusner, ed., *Christianity, Judaism and other Greco-Roman Cults, Studies for Morton Smith at Sixty,* Pt. IV, Leiden, Brill, 1975, p.103. As K. Geldner stressed in 1906, however, there is no internal indication of which Vologases is meant in the *Denkard.* See 'Die altpersische Literatur', *Die orientalischen Literaturen,* Berlin and Leipzig, Teubner, p.223. More recently Gh. Gnoli, *Zoroaster's Time and Homeland,* Naples, Istituto Universitario Orientale Series Minor VII, 1980, pp.221-222 and n.118, has also expressed a word of caution concerning the traditional attribution to Vologases I. Virtually alone amongst Iranianists H.S. Nyberg, 'Die Religionen des alten Iran', *Mitteilungen der Vorderasiatisch-Aegyptischen Gesellschaft,* vol. 43, 1938, pp.408, 417, suggested that it was Vologases IV [III] who ordered the compilation of the Avestan fragments. In view of his long reign and many achievements, this possibility should perhaps be given more credence than has generally been the case.

112. B.J. Overlaet, 'Contribution to Sasanian Armament in Connection with a Decorated Helmet', *IrAnt,* vol. XVII, 1982, p.191, writes of Parthian royal headgear as follows, 'From Mithridates II onwards (c. 123-88 B.C.) the king often wears his diadem tied around a tiara'. P. Calmeyer, 'Zur Genese altiranischer Motive IV. "persönliche Krone" und Diadem', AMI, N.F., Bd. 9, 1976, writes, 'das eigentliche Hoheitszeichen der Arsakidenzeit war das Diadem... Ein gutes Beispiel für die Geltung von Diadem und Tiara nebeneinander in mittelparthischer Zeit liefert Josephus (37): die "Krönung" sowol des Königs von Adiabene als auch die Anerkennung des Grosskönigs erfolgt durch das Diadem; die aufrechte Tiara gehört zu den Vorrechten des Partherkönigs und wird als besondere Auszeichnung dem Adiabener verliehen'.

Two Inscriptions from Qaryat al-Fâw Mentioning Women

BY CHRISTIAN ROBIN

Qaryat al-Fâw is located c. 280 km. north-northeast of Najrân, along an ancient route leading from this ancient city to the Arabo-Persian Gulf. Today it is well-known, but such was not the case at the beginning of this century. H.St.J.B. Philby seems to have heard of it for the first time in May, 1918, while he was visiting As Sulayyil (Philby 1920, p.178). He later mentions being told by some bedouin of important archaeological remains there (Philby, 1939, pp.430-431). It was not until February, 1948, however, that Philby was finally able to visit the site (Philby, 1949, p.90). The inscriptions discovered at that time, together with those found by several Americans working for Aramco who had been there the previous year (notably Messrs. Geare and Owens), were turned over to Gonzague Ryckmans for publication (Ryckmans, 1949, pp.87-102, 113 and Pls. III, V, and VIII: texts numbered Ry 405-429; 1951, pp.111, 116: Ry 455).

In 1952, the Philby-Ryckmans-Lippens expedition returned to Qaryat al-Fâw with the intention of completing the epigraphic and archaeological exploration of the site and its environs (Lippens, 1956, pp.160-166, photograph no. IV and 28-29 between pp.170-71 and 178-179), but the results of their work remain only partially published (Ryckmans, 1957, p.558 ff.; Grohmann, 1962, pp.160-162 and Pl. XXI). In the meantime, Albert Jamme has published a large number of texts from the site:

- Ja 2099-2105 (Jamme, 1966a)
- Ja 2122 and 2126-2127 (Jamme, 1967, pp.181-183, 185, 186-187, and Pl. XLVII/1)
- Ja 2135, 2138 and 2142 (Jamme, 1970, pp.119, 120, 122 and 137; for the provenance of these texts, see Ryckmans, 1984, p.75)
- Ja 2524-2814 (Jamme, 1973, pp.1-182, and Pl. 1-25 (This is not to mention the photographs and copies reproduced in various works; see the list in Jamme, 1973, p.3)

The exceptional richness of Qaryat al-Fâw has been confirmed by the excavations undertaken there by the University of Riyâḍ (recently renamed 'King Sa'ûd University') since 1970 (al-Anṣârî, 1979, 1982, 1984; Ghoneim, 1980). The preliminary reports published on this work attest to the presence of a well-developed architectural tradition; a previously unknown, local coinage; and a rich and varied material culture, as illustrated by the variety and quality of the objects found. In addition, 33 new inscriptions (or panels of graffiti) have been published or simply illustrated, among which are many of great importance (see, notably al-Anṣârî, 1979, and the remarks in Beeston, 1979, pp.1-2; Bâfaqîh et al., 1985, pp.342-343, No. 122; Robin, 1985).

None of the inscriptions from Qaryat al-Fâw gives us the ancient name of the site, but one finds it in several Sabaean texts from the beginning of the 3rd century A.D. (such as Ja 634/4-5; 635/25-26, 28, 36; 641/5) as *Qryt*^{m} *ḏt Khl*^{m} (Qarya of *Khl*^{m}) or simply *Qryt*^{m} (Jamme, 1962, p.136ff). The addition of a qualifier, *ḏt Khl*^{m} (a reference to the principal deity of the oasis) in antiquity, and al-Fâw (the name of the nearby pass through the Ṭuwayq escarpment) in our own day, can be explained by the banality of the name *Qryt*^{m}/Qarya, which simply means 'town'.

The inhabitants of Qaryat al-Fâw exclusively employed South Arabian writing in their inscriptions. Although one frequently finds graffiti in the area written in what is called the 'Thamudic' script (Ryckmans, 1984, p.75), it would seem most probable that these were the work of persons simply passing through the region. The question of the language of the Qaryat al-Fâw inscriptions is a complex one. The inhabitants certainly spoke a dialect of Arabic (characterised notably by the absence of the sibilant s^{3}; the article *'l-*; or the preformative '– in verbs in the factitive form), but they always retained South Arabian (cf. the use of the article –^{n}; the preformative *h-/s*^{1} –, etc.) as a model. As a result, the inscriptions show a blend, in varying degrees, of South Arabian terminology, grammar, and orthography, with a local language. The funerary inscription of the king Mu'âwiya, in which we find the article –^{n} in *qḥṭny*^{n} (al-Anṣârî, 1979, pp.7, 8-9 and Pl. 2), is closest to the South Arabian model, whereas that of 'Ijl (al-Anṣârî, 1979, pp.6-8 and Pl. 1) is furthest from it, both linguistically and palaeographically.

This linguistic situation accords well with the little we know of the history of Qaryat al-Fâw. The oasis was the capital of Qaḥṭân before becoming, around the beginning of the 3rd century A.D. or perhaps slightly earlier, the capital of Kinda. It was integrated into the Himyarite empire near the end of the 3rd or beginning of the 4th century (Robin, 1985, pp.304-305).

The two short texts in the collection of Mr. Sam Roach which we publish here, thanks to the kindness of their owner to whom we gratefully acknowledge our debt, nicely complement the extant documentation on Qaryat al-Fâw and its inhabitants.

Robin-al-Fâw 1 (Fig.1) (=Roach 1)

A flat stone engraved with a short, two line inscription; the text is complete, although the side of the stone was re-cut after the inscription had been engraved, thus damaging the first letter of each line. It is possible that the side of the stone was trimmed in antiquity when it was mounted, no doubt in a funerary monument.

1	*'lht bnt ʿd*	*'lht* daughter of *ʿd*
2	*ʿbd bn 'ftḥ*	client of the banû *'ftḥ*

'lht: a proper name previously unattested for a woman. It was already known from two rock inscriptions in the area of Qaryat al-Fâw, where it occurs as a patronymic: see Ja 2621/2 (*Rzb² 'lht*) and 2643/2 (*Zby² 'lht*). It is known as a personal name, more likely male than female, in two graffiti copied by Philby in the area of Najrân: see Ph 166 w 1 and 177 f (Branden, 1956, pp.83, 117 and facsimiles at the end of the volume). *'lht* is also attested in 'Thamudic' and, very frequently, in Safaitic inscriptions: see Ja 2621/2, commentary, and Harding, 1971, p.71. One can recognize in it the Arabic name Alîha: see Caskel, 1966 I, Tables 220 and 263; II, p.153, where the name appears in the genealogies of two Qaḥṭânite tribes, 'Akk and Maḏḥij.

ʿd: the name of the father (less likely of the lineage) of *'lht*. One can compare it with the name of the Minaean lineage ḏ-ʿd (RES 3512/2). *ʿd* is attested as a personal name in two rock graffiti in the Qaryat al-Fâw area: see Ja 2773 and 2784 j. It is also known at Najrân (see Ja 1011c in Jamme, 1966b, pp.16-17 and, at the back of the volume, Fig. 5 and Pl. 1), as well as in Safaitic and in 'Thamudic' inscriptions (Harding, 1971, pp.408-409). At first sight, one might be tempted to identify *ʿd* with Arabic 'Âd, the name of that celebrated, mythical tribe of the Jâhiliyya (*EI²*, s.v. "Âd') to whom the ancient monuments of Southern Arabia are often attributed. There are, however, two objections to this hypothesis. First, there is the fundamental difference in nature between a tribal name and the name of a person or lineage. Second, 'Âd is never attested in the onomasticon of ancient Arabia, at least not in the form in which it has been transmitted to us by the genealogists of the Islamic period (see notably Caskel, 1966). According to Jamme, *ʿd* should be vocalized as "Awd'. In fact, the proper name *ʿwd* is attested epigraphically on several occasions: see Ja 2776 aq from Qaryat al-Fâw, etc. But 'Awd never occurs in the works of the Arab genealogists. We would prefer to vocalize the name as 'Adî (Caskel, 1966 II, pp.137-141), 'Awdâ (Caskel, 1966 II, p.206), 'Idâ, 'Idd or 'Iddâ (Caskel, 1966 II, p.352), while noting that dipthongs and long final vowels are only found occasionally in the Qaryat al-Fâw texts.

Fig. 1. Robin-al-Fâw 1

'bd: this word was already attested at Qaryat al-Fâw in line 3 of the funerary inscription of king Mu'âwiya; in the short, fragmentary text Ry 426/1; and in two graffiti, Ja 2102 g (where Jamme believes he has identified a verb: 'to be a servant') and Ja 2760 b/2. In South Arabian texts, as A.F.L. Beeston has shown, *'bd* occurs only in the singular and in the dual; in order to express the same notion in the plural, the word *'dm* or one of its variants was used (see most recently *DS*, p.11, root 'BD). During a special meeting held in conjunction with the Seminar for Arabian Studies in 1985, Beeston also demonstrated that *'bd* by no means signified 'slave', but rather 'a person bound in service or under some sort of obligation to someone of superior rank'. *'bd* can apply to persons of modest social position, but it can also refer to persons of high rank. The antonym of *'bd* is *ḥr*, pl. *'ḥrr*, which one could translate as 'noble'. A good illustration of this distinction is found in RES 3945; on three occasions (l.6, 9, and 12) the author, in order to emphasize that he is referring to all the members of a tribe, employs the expression *ḥr-hw w-'bd-hw*, 'nobles and clients'. This fundamental distinction in South Arabian society appears to obtain at Qaryat al-Fâw as well. The tomb of king Mu'âwiya was built by *'bd-hw Hf'm bn Br*ⁿ *ḏ*-⟨'1⟩ *'1*[?]⟨ , 'his client *Hf'm* son of *Br*ⁿ, of ⟨the lineage of⟩ *'1*[?]⟨'. It is difficult to imagine that a royal tomb was the work of a 'slave'; *Hf'm* was most probably an important person attached to the sovereign. As for the nobles, we find a direct mention of them in the text of 'Ijl; only women belonging to this social class (*ḥryr* = *ḥarâ'ir/ḥarâyir*) could be buried in a family tomb.

In our text, one must ask whether *'bd* is singular or plural. If it is singular, then *'d* is a personal name; if not, it is the name of a lineage. Provisionally we prefer the first alternative, based on South Arabian usage.

bn: defective writing of *banî*.
'fth: the name of a lineage. This is the first occurrence of this name at Qaryat al-Fâw. The name is also found in 'Thamudic' inscriptions (Harding, 1971, p.58).

The engraving in this text is closely comparable to that in the inscription of 'Ijl, particularly in the irregular placement of the letters; the broken, upper bar of *bâ'*; the upward extension of the *alif*; the upper part of the *hâ'* and *ḥâ'* which is larger than the stem; and the accentuated grooves of the ends of all the letters. Thus, both texts should be approximately contemporary. It is difficult to suggest an exact date for them, however, since this style of engraving is not found in Southern Arabia. The forms of some letters, such as the *râ'* and the *mîm*, suggest a relatively early date, in any case prior to the inscription of king Mu'âwiya. One might propose the 1st century B.C. or 1st century A.D., allowing for a considerable margin of error.

Robin-al-Fâw 2 (Figs.2-3) (=Roach 2)

A monolithic incense burner consisting of a cube, the top of which has been slightly chiselled, on a socle, trimmed on three sides. The face of the cube bearing the inscription is decorated by a row of small, upright triangles, resembling a battlement, made by cutting along the top edge of the stone (cf. al-Anṣârî, 1982, p.147, Fig. 2). One side of the incense burner probably rested against a wall, no doubt in a temple or domestic sanctuary where it served to remind the deity of the merits of its donor.

1	*Ddh bn=*	*Ddh* daughter
2	*t Dd'l*	of *Dd'l*

Ddh: female name, attested for the first time at Qaryat al-Fâw, but known in Safaitic and 'Thamudic' inscriptions (Harding, 1971, p.237). It can be analysed as a theophoric name, *Dd-h*, where the pronoun suffix *-h* refers to an unnamed deity, masculine (cf. the masculine singular pronoun suffix *-h* in the inscriptions of 'Ijl and king Mu'âwiya) or feminine. Another, less likely, possibility would be to consider *Ddh* as a local spelling of Sabaean *Ddt* (see RES 4536/1 and Fa 121), anticipating the Arabic orthography of the ending *-ah/-at*$^{u(n)}$. One should note, however, that personal names at Qaryat al-Fâw, such as *'lht* (text 1, here), *M'wyt* or *Rb't* (see the text of king Mu'âwiya) are always written with a final *-t*, in the Sabaean manner. A spelling with final *-h* seems to appear late, and then only sporadically (e.g. notably *'wdh* in CIH 541/37, from the 6th century A.D.).
Dd'l: this could be the name of a man, woman, or lineage. The first possibility is provisionally adopted here, in view of the fact that, at present, *Dd'l* is only

Figs. 2 and 3. Robin-al-Fâw 2

attested as a male personal name in the various ancient languages of Arabia (Harding, 1971, p.236). We find a Dadûl in the genealogies of Ibn al-Kalbî. This name, the reading of which is not completely certain, could derive from *Dd'l* (Caskel, 1966 I, Table 229, and II, p.230).

The engraving of this text reflects the canons of South Arabian writing more closely than that of text 1. Notable features include the proper alignment of the letters; the rectilinearity of the upper bar of the *bâ'*; and a *hâ'* and an *alif* composed of segments of equal proportions. The date of this text is difficult to establish on palaeographic grounds alone, however, due to its brevity and lack of diagnostic characteristics. We note only that the rigidity of the letters and the pronounced engraving of their ends suggest a date not too far removed from that of text 1.

As indicated above, text 1 is probably a funerary stela. It is not rare in Arabia to find a woman mentioned in a text of this sort. A similar example is already known from Qaryat al-Fâw (al-Anṣârî, 1982, p.147, Fig.5). In the case of another inscription from the site authored by a woman (al-Anṣârî, 1982, p.144, Fig.3), the funerary character of the text is less certain. The region of the Arabo-Persian Gulf is however, by far the richest in funerary stelae commemorating women. Out of eighteen funerary inscriptions of any length from northeastern Arabia, no less than twelve come from the graves of women (see the forthcoming study of this topic by Daniel Potts).

Nor is the situation any different when we turn to Southern Arabia. The tombs of several women are known (see RES 4536, or DJE 10 in Müller, 1972, pp.81-84 and Fig.34). Moreover, a large number of funerary plaques mentioning women are attested at the necropolis of Timna' (see Ja 127, 138, 160, 161, 167 etc., in Jamme, 1952, p.32ff). Finally, we should not forget an important literary source from the 10th century. In his chapter on ancient tombs, the Yemeni *savant* al-Ḥasan al-Hamdânî, renowned for his encyclopaedic knowledge, mentions a whole series of tombs belonging to women (al-Hamdânî/Fâris, 1940, p.124ff). Even if his descriptions show a marked degree of embellishment, the fact remains that the Yemenis of his day recognized that, in the ancient past, a woman might be honored by a magnificent grave, something so exceptional in medieval Yemen that it prompted comment.

Text 2, obviously stemming from the dedication of an incense burner by a woman, offers supplementary evidence of the relatively important social role played by women at Qaryat al-Fâw in antiquity. The donation of such an object, and the engraving of the accompanying text, however brief, represent a not inconsiderable expense, which implies that its female donor enjoyed a certain level of comfort and financial autonomy.

The position of women in Southern Arabia has recently been the subject of a study published by Beeston (Beeston, 1983). Thanks to these two small pieces in the collection of Mr. Sam Roach, we are beginning to better appreciate the role of women in an important oasis town in *Arabia deserta*.

Abbreviations

CIH *Corpus inscriptionum semiticarum*, Pars quarta: Inscriptiones ḥimyariticas et sabæas continens, 3 vol., Parisiis, E Reipublicæ Typographeo, 1889-1932.

DS A.F.L. BEESTON, M.A. GHUL, W.W. MÜLLER, J. RYCKMANS, *Sabaic Dictionary/Dictionnaire sabéen/al-Muʿjam as-saba'î* (English-French-Arabic) (Publication of the University of Sanaa, YAR), Louvain-la-Neuve, Editions Peeters, - Beyrouth, Librairie du Liban, 1982.

EI² *Encyclopédie de l'Islam*, nouvelle édition, Leiden, Brill, - Paris, Editions G.-P. Maisonneuve et Larose, since 1960.

FA Ahmed FAKHRY, *An Archaeological Journey to Yemen (March-May, 1947)*, Part II: *Epigraphical Texts*, by G. RYCKMANS, Cairo, Service des Antiquités de l'Egypte, 1952.

RES *Répertoire d'épigraphie sémitique*, publié par la Commission du *Corpus inscriptionum semiticarum*, Académie des Inscriptions et Belles-Lettres, I-VIII, Paris, Imprimerie nationale, 1900-1968.

Bibliography

al-Anṣârî, ʿAbd ar-Raḥmân aṭ-Ṭayyib (1399/1979), 'Aḍwâ' jadîda ʿalà dawlat Kinda min ḫilâl âṯâr Qaryat al-Fâw wanuqûši-hâ,' in A.M. Abdalla, S. Al-Sakkar, R.T. Mortel (eds.), supervision by A.T. Al-Ansary, *Sources for the History of Arabia* (= *Studies in the History of Arabia*, Vol.1), University of Riyadh Press, Part 1, pp.3-11, pl.1-3 and 1 map, in the Arabic section.

al-Anṣârî, A.R. (1982), *Qaryat al-Fau. A Portrait of Pre-Islamic Civilisation in Saudi Arabia*, Riyadh, University of Riyadh 1957-1982.

al-Anṣârî, A.R. (1404/1984), 'al-Mawsim ar-râbiʿ li-ḥafriyyât Qaryat (al-Fâw): taqrîr muḫtaṣar', in A.M. Abdalla, S. Al-Sakkar, R. Mortel (eds.), supervision by A.T. al-Ansary, *Pre-Islamic Arabia* (= *Studies in the History of Arabia*, Vol.II), King Saud University Press, pp.11-24 in the Arabic section.

Bâfaqîh, Muḥammad ᶜAbd al-Qâdir, Beeston, A.F.L., Robin, C. and al-Ġûl, M., (1985) *Muḫtârât min an-nuqûš al-yamaniyya al-qadîma*, Tûnis, al-Munaẓẓama al-ᶜarabiyya li-t-tarbiya wa-ât-ṯaqâfa wa-âl-ᶜulûm.

Beeston, A.F.L. (1979), 'Nemara and Faw', *Bulletin of the School of Oriental and African Studies*, vol.XLII, pp.1-6.

Beeston, A.F.L. (1983), 'Women in Saba', in R.L. Bidwell and G.R. Smith (eds.), *Arabian and Islamic Studies*, Articles presented to R.B. Serjeant on the occasion of his retirement from the Sir Thomas Adams's Chair of Arabic at the University of Cambridge, London and New York, Longman, pp.7-13.

Branden, A. van den (1956), *Les textes thamoudéens de Philby*, Vol.I: Inscriptions du sud (Bibliothèque du *Muséon*, vol.39 ⟨corrected in 40⟩), Louvain, Publications universitaires/Institut orientaliste.

Caskel, W. (1966), *Ǧamharat an-nasab. Das genealogische Werk des Hišām ibn Muḥammad al-Kalbī*, 2 vol., Leiden, Brill.

Ghoneim, W. (1980), 'Saudi-Arabien', *Archiv für Orientforschung*, vol.XXVII, pp.317-324.

Grohmann, A. (1962), *Arabic Inscriptions* (Expédition Philby-Ryckmans-Lippens en Arabie, IIᵉ Partie: Textes épigraphiques, Tome 1 = Bibliothèque du *Muséon*, vol.50), Louvain, Publications universitaires/Institut orientaliste.

al-Hamdânî/Fâris, N.A. (1940), *al-Iklîl (al-juz' aṯ-ṯâmin)* by al-Ḥasan ibn Aḥmad al-Hamdânî, edited ... by ... (Princeton Oriental Texts, vol.VII), Princeton.

Harding, G.L. (1971), *An Index and Concordance of Pre-Islamic Arabian Names and Inscriptions* (Near and Middle East Series, 8), Toronto, University of Toronto Press.

Jamme, A. (1952), *Pièces épigraphiques de Ḥeid bin ᶜAqîl, la nécropole de Timnaᶜ (Hagr Koḥlân)* (Bibliothèque du *Muséon*, vol.30), Louvain, Publications universitaires/Institut orientaliste.

Jamme, A. (1962), *Sabaean Inscriptions from Maḥram Bilqîs (Mârib)*, with foreword by Wendell Philips (Publications of the American Foundation for the Study of Man, vol.III), Baltimore, The Johns Hopkins Press.

Jamme, A. (1966a), 'Inscriptions Photographed at Qaryat al-Fa'w by Ambassador Parker T. Hart (Documentation sud-arabe IV)', *Rivista degli Studi orientali*, vol.XLI, pp.289-301 and Pl.I-II.

Jamme, A. (1966b), *Sabaean and Ḥasaean Inscriptions from Saudi Arabia* (Studi semitici, vol.23), Roma, Istituto di Studi del Vicino Oriente, Università di Roma.

Jamme, A. (1967), 'New Ḥasaean and Sabaean Inscriptions from Saudi Arabia', *Oriens antiquus*, vol.6, pp.181-187 and Pl.XLVII-XLIX.

Jamme, A. (1970), 'The Pre-Islamic Inscriptions of the Riyādh Museum', *Oriens antiquus*, vol.9, pp.115-139.

Jamme, A. (1973), *Miscellanées d'ancient* (sic!) *arabe*, IV, Washington (without name of publishing house).

Lippens, P. (1956), *Expédition en Arabie centrale*, Paris, Librairie d'Amérique et d'Orient Adrien-Maisonneuve.

Müller, W.W. (1972), 'Epigraphische Nachlese aus Ḥāz', in R. Degen, W.W. Müller, and W. Röllig (eds.), *Neue Ephemeris für Semitische Epigraphik*, vol.1, pp.75-85 and Fig.26-33, Pl.IX-XI.

Philby, H.St.J.B. (1920), 'Southern Najd', *The Geographical Journal*, vol.LV, pp.161-191.

Philby, H.St.J.B. (1939), *Sheba's Daughters*, being a Record of Travel in Southern Arabia, with an Appendix on the Rock Inscriptions by A.F.L. Beeston, London, Methuen.

Philby, H.St.J.B. (1949), 'Two Notes from Central Arabia', *The Geographical Journal*, vol.CXIII, pp.86-93.

Robin, C. (1985), 'Bulletin critique', [review of al-Anṣârî 1982], *Annales islamologiques*, vol.XXI, pp.303-305.

Ryckmans, G. (1949), 'Inscriptions sud-arabes. *Huitième série*', *Le Muséon*, vol.LXII, pp.55-124 and Pl.I-VIII.

Ryckmans, G. (1951), 'Inscriptions sud-arabes. *Neuvième série*', *Le Muséon*, vol. LXIV, pp.93-126 and Pl.IV.

Ryckmans, G. (1957), 'Graffites sabéens relevés en Arabie saᶜudite', *Rivista degli Studi orientali = Scritti in onore di Giuseppe Furlani*, vol.XXXII, pp.557-563.

Ryckmans, J. (1984), 'Alphabets, Scripts and Languages in Pre-Islamic Arabian Epigraphical Evidence', *Pre-Islamic Arabia (op.cit.)*, pp.73-86.

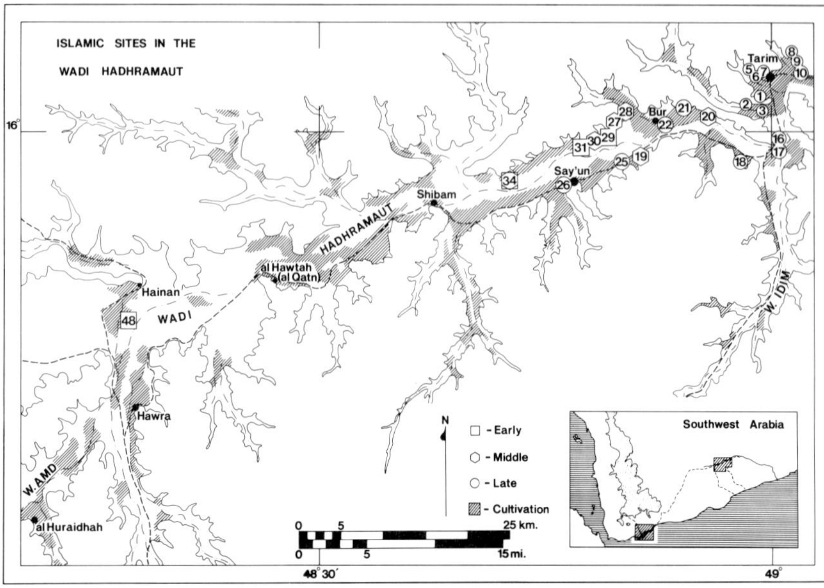

Map 1. Islamic Sites in the Wadi Hadhramaut

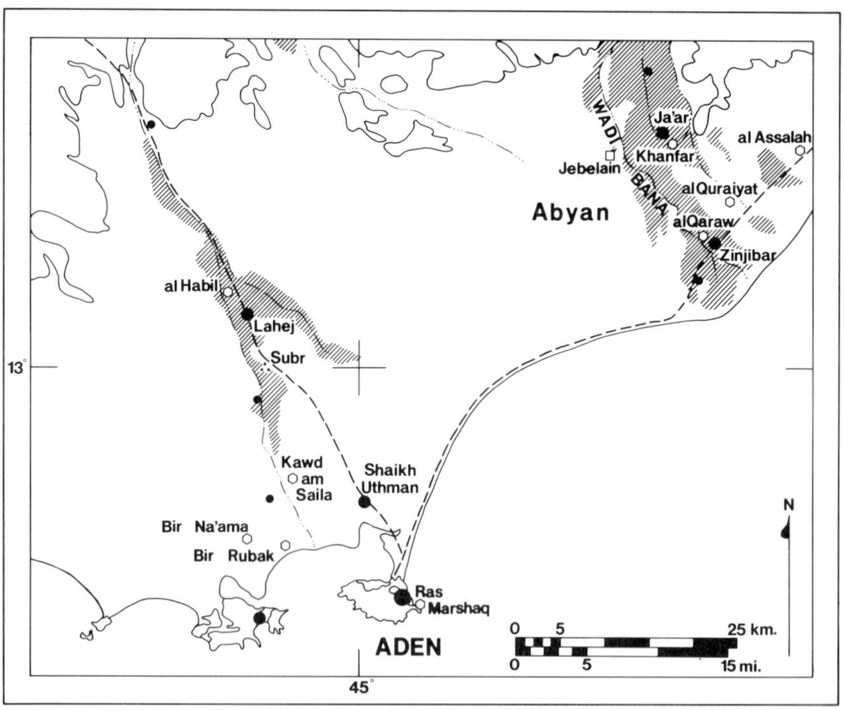

Map 2. Islamic Sites in the Vicinity of Aden

Islamic Archaeology in Aden and the Hadhramaut

BY DONALD S. WHITCOMB

'And for archaeologists in particular the Indian Ocean offers probably more bread and butter than almost any part of the world except for the Mediterranean and the Middle East. Bread and butter, but not much jam: that is to say, there is a great volume of potsherds and many ruins dotted about but much less has survived whole, or nearly whole, than in the sands of Egypt or Mesopotamia or the gentle climate of the Mediterranean.' (Allen, 1969, p.27)

Introduction

This study pairs two distinct areas -- Aden and its immediate littoral with the Wadi Hadhramaut. 'Hadhramaut' in this paper is taken to mean the main wadi and its tributaries (see map 1). The main wadi itself is over 200 km. long running parallel to the south Arabian coast; the wadi bed averages five km. in width in the most populous section between Hainan and Tarim. The wadi cuts through a high plateau (the *jōl*), some 300 m. above the wadi, with precipitous cliffs and talus slopes marking the transition. With less than 200 mm. of rainfall yearly, agriculture is dependant on flood-water (*sail*) irrigation; wells in the main wadi reach the water table at 15 to 20 m. depth (Van Beek et al., 1963, p.522; see map 1). Population in the Hadhramaut is concentrated in three cities, Shibam, Say'un, and Tarim (each 10-20,000) and a number of towns (about 2,000 each) for an estimated population of over 100,000 (Bujra estimates over 300,000 including tribal groups; 1971, p.3).

The port of Aden is situated on a peninsula, volcanic in origin, connected to the littoral plain, some 30-50 km. wide, backed by the mountains of the Yemeni massif. The sites under consideration here are located along the two wadi systems which water this plain (see map 2), the Wadi Kabir with Lahej as its chief settlement (Maktari, 1971) and the Wadi Bana and its tributaries. This latter system forms the oasis region of Abyan with a number of towns, the largest of which are Zinjibar and Ja'ar.

Ingrams has stressed that the Hadhramaut is not the hinterland for Aden, nor complementary, but that each area has a separate history and geography, as reflected in the Eastern and Western protectorates of his day (1966, p.67). While the relationship between these two areas can not be taken as a simple port-hinterland model, a comparison of the archaeological history is not unreasonable, especially in the absence of evidence from highland Yemen and the ports opposite the Hadhramaut (Shihir, Mukalla).

Ingrams quotes a certain Saiyid 'Abdul Qadir as saying, 'The people of the interior attribute everything old to 'Ad (a mythological tribe to which Hud was a pre-Muslim prophet) and those of the coast to the Portuguese. Neither are right.' (1936, p.18, n. 3) This misconception is hardly due to a lack of knowledge of regional history, especially in the Hadhramaut which is noted for its centers of scholarship. The failure is a lack of recognition of the information available in traces of material culture, in this case very humble sherds, which failure is by no means peculiar to this region of the world. The history of the period between 'Ad and the Portuguese is susceptible to study with both documentary and archaeological evidence, available in unsuspected richness. If it may be said, as many do generalize, that Egypt, Greece, and Rome paid for the temples at Shabwa, then Java and Singapore may be said to have paid for the palaces at Tarim and Say'un. This is one way of saying that the economy (and influence) of the Hadhramaut has been tied closely with a wide and well-travelled world. No such case needs to be argued for Aden, where the Portuguese arrival provided only a late chapter to its commercial history. It has been said that 'the Hadhramaut of today would perish just as the one of old did if the country could not get money from abroad' (Ingrams, 1966, p.47). It is patterns hopefully more developed than this simplification which will become apparent from research in this region.

A survey of the archaeological sites within the Wadi Hadhramaut was undertaken in 1961-62 under the direction of Dr. G. W. Van Beek on behalf of the Smithsonian Institution (1963, pp.521-43; the Islamic sites are briefly described on pp. 540-41).[1] At the same time a small comparative collection from archaeological sites in the vicinity of Aden was obtained through the assistance of D. B. Doe, then director of the Department of Antiquities, Aden. The aim of the Hadhramaut survey was the elucidation of the great gap in archaeological knowledge of southern Arabia for the prehistoric and early historic periods. There was, and remains, the strong likelihood that the role of southern Arabia may be of fundamental importance in the range of questions posed by Van Beek, 'the diffusion of cultural traits, the development of trade, the migration of man, and the interchange of cultivated plants and domestic animals between Africa and Asia' (1963, p.522). These are subjects of research which remain vital for the 'prehistoric' and 'pre-Islamic' periods and indeed for the more recent 'Islamic' period.

Islamic materials were well beyond the focus of the survey and the very brief treatment in the 1963 reports reflects not only parenthetical concern but the state of knowledge of Islamic archaeology at that time. It is to the great credit of this survey that extensive effort was expended to collect the remains of the Islamic period in a time when such archaeology was still often ignored. Van Beek felt compelled to justify this study and his reasons are worth examination.

'It was hoped that an investigation [of Islamic remains] would
1. provide the later material necessary to complete the development of a ceramic sequence for Hadhramaut,
2. determine whether a number of sites described in the literature and marked on maps as 'ancient' and 'pre-Islamic' are as represented or are Islamic and of comparatively recent date,
3. yield evidence that could be used to distinguish pre-Islamic from Islamic irrigation installations' (1963, p.540).

The first aim of the survey falls within the traditional methods of field research in that the ceramics obtained from surface collection allow development bf a chronological sequence marking the continuity of human settlement. Such a sequence does not suddenly end or lose its usefulness in the full historic, and here Islamic, period. To limit investigation to the chronologically more ancient is to seriously hamper research into questions of environmental and cultural continuity since patterns often find their clearest manifestation in comparatively recent remains. The romance of archaeology is difficult to attain when dealing with materials only a few hundred years old; but these 'fresh' depositions may offer analogies and evidence for interpretations of the far more ancient.

The broad 'dating' which early travelers (and archaeologists) used and placed on maps hides complex and interesting histories. As many investigators and historians have sensed, this remote corner of Arabia partook of a long and involved history which is only slowly finding systematic study. It is a world unto itself where the simple criterion of absence or presence of glazed sherds, the standard criterion for Islamic date, cannot guarantee antiquity or deem a monument uninteresting. Surface collection in the absence of excavation is too often an imprecise operation, but with careful observation and extensive fieldwork a surprising amount of information can be achieved.

The third aim approaches wider utilization of such investigations. The history of irrigation techniques is fundamental to any understanding of human adaptation in marginal and often hostile environments such as the Wadi Hadhramaut. Again the study of irrigation makes little sense without concern with the recent Islamic period as a source of information on long-established patterns and processes. Such investigations deserve specialized, hypothesis-based fieldwork; this survey provides only a preliminary corpus of archaeological evidence for broader cultural and environmental research. The following study of this survey data presents a chronological sequence of sites for which a generalized seriation of the ceramics has been attempted (this technique is discussed in Whitcomb, 1978, pp.96-98). The essay in cultural contexts of the archaeological materials is necessarily provisional and, hopefully, will provoke further field research.

The Early Islamic Period (800-1150 A.D.)

A definition of the early Islamic period in terms of archaeological materials is difficult. Part of the problem is due to the relatively scant attention paid to the archaeology of the latest pre-Islamic period in southwest Arabia. Thus we are faced with the paradoxical but often recurring situation of increasingly reliable historical documentation while the record of the material culture remains unclear. This latest pre-Islamic period was one of extreme importance in which the second Himyarite kingdom, the kingdom of Saba and Dhu Raydan, held all of southwestern Arabia and confronted Abyssinian occupations. This is also the period of the introduction of so-called 'confessional' religions and adoption of Christianity or Judaism by royal houses, which led, in turn, to involvement by the 'super-powers,' the Sasanian and Byzantine empires, in this corner of Arabia during the sixth century. (This fascinating history is concisely set out in S. Smith, 1954; see also I. Shahid, 1971.)

One might then argue for a late Himyarite period beginning in the fourth or fifth century concurrent with this Himyarite kingdom and continuing until the early Islamic. Southwest Arabia received a governor during the lifetime of the Prophet and was thus Moslem from 630, at least nominally (but see Beeston, 1952). There seems a consensus among epigraphers of South Arabian that writing in this script suddenly ceases at this time. The effective cause is usually assumed to have been the heavy emigration by both soldiers and urbanized administrators from southwestern Arabia during the Conquest. Such depopulation, combined with the changes of a new religio-political entity, suggests a decisive break with late Himyaritic culture although this cannot yet be identified in the archaeological record. A succession of caliphal and Umayyad governors suggests some attention to this region, but clearly the Hadhramaut was 'merely an eddy in the main current of events' (Serjeant, 1962b, p.239). Periodic conflicts and revolts are reported which seem to have intensified during the Abbasid period. The revolt of Ibn Ziyad in 818 seems to have ended the effective power of the Abbasid governors.

Ibn Ziyad, having been sent to Yemen as vizier, founded Zabid on the Tihamah coast and then, according to Omarah 'became master of Hadhramaut, of Diyar Kindah, of Shihir, of Mirbat, of Lahej, of Aden...' (Kay, 1892, p.5). One sees then, in the beginning of the ninth century, a unification of the Hadhramaut and the coast including Aden under Ziyadid rule. The material remains from this period illustrate both an Abbasid cultural influence and the emergence of a regional identity. The first identifiably Islamic tradition in southern Arabian archaeology thus begins about 800 A.D., and that date, rather than a more traditional 630 or even a compromise date of 700, as used by Doe, is here considered the beginning of the early Islamic period.

The character of this early Islamic period may be illustrated first from the site of Jebelain. Jebelain (also Jebel 'Ain, Doe, 1963, p.158) is situated in the region of Abyan about 50 km. east of Aden (see map 2). The Abyan has been identified with Ptolemy's Bana and with the Himyarite kingdom of Tafid (Doe, 1971, p.142). Jebelain lies west of the Wadi Bana, 7 km. west of Ja'ar; the site appears to have been a camp site around a well near a rock outcrop since there is no evidence of buildings (Doe, 1962, p.10; 1971, p.146; Harding, 1964, p.18-19). The ceramics from Jebelain are primarily in a red or red-brown ware with wavy-band comb decoration; both the ware and the decoration (e.g., Fig. 2e and 3e) recall earlier ceramic traditions in southern Arabia. The vessel forms are quite distinctive. Bowls usually have a pronounced or overhanging rim, often with incised or combed wavy line decoration; jars, which are usually incurving with a short flaring neck and rim, are similarly decorated (Fig. 1, 2).

Glazed wares found at Jebelain are well-known types found throughout Iraq (e.g., the type-site of Samarra; for important revisions in the chronology of Samarra based on the excavations at Siraf, see Whitehouse, 1979), and throughout the Persian Gulf (e.g., Siraf, Oman; Whitcomb, 1975; fig. 5, 7) on sites datable to the ninth and tenth centuries. These ceramics, made of cream ware, include two main types: blue-green glazed wares, usually large storage jars (Fig. 1m-s), and bowls with a white glaze, or white splashed with green (Fig. 1j-l). Cobalt decoration is not found in the present collections, but lustre wares are found in the Hadhramaut (see below). The occurrence of these Abbasid wares was first reported in Aden by Lane and Serjeant (1948); Keall has recently found the same wares on the Tihamah coast (1983, fig. 4:3, 5). These distinctive glazed wares provide one of the connective links for dating early Islamic occupations in the Wadi Hadhramaut. Blue-green wares are found at sites 48, 34.2, 27, 20, while lustre and splashed glazes occur at sites 34.2 and 29 (see map 1 for the location of numbered sites).

This link is confirmed by the unglazed wares, where bowls and jars with the same range of forms and incised and combed decoration recur (e.g., site 48).

However, they are made of a cream or buff ware, rather than the red ware of the coast. Close comparisons with Mesopotamian and Persian Gulf sites are not found, in contrast to the glazed wares. The sites in the Wadi Hadhramaut with the strongest unglazed pottery comparisons with Jebelain have been assigned to the early Islamic period (sites 48, 34.2, 29, 31). Note that, with the exception of 48, all these sites are located near the city of Say'un, in the eastern part of the wadi. This unglazed ceramic assemblage, clearly connected with the region of Aden, marks the beginning of a new ceramic tradition in comparison with pre-Islamic ceramics known from both areas.

With the increased reporting of Islamic remains within the Arabian peninsula, ceramic evidence for development during the early Islamic period is becoming better known. The unglazed wares from the site of Ma'abiyat in northwestern Arabia (Parr, Harding, and Dayton, 1968-69) bear striking similarities to Jebelain and sites in the Hadhramaut. This site was provisionally dated by Parr to the Umayyad period. Layla and sites in the Jawf also show similar combed wares (Zarins et al., 1979) and the remains along the Darb el-Zubeidah have blue-green glazed wares and other wares similar to those in the Hadhramaut (al-Rashid, 1980). This pilgrimage route illustrates a connection between Baghdad and settlements in central Arabia.

The Hadhrami connection with Abbasid materials from Baghdad depends not only on the formal administrative apparatus of the Abbasid Empire but on the Indian Ocean–Persian Gulf trade in which Siraf and Sohar figured prominently. Another intriguing possibility is some continuation of the pre-Islamic pattern of annual fairs in which 'merchants travelled by sea down the Persian Gulf, and the local Arabs assembled at Hud by land.' Qabr Hud is the locality in the eastern Hadhramaut for the fair of Shihir, which followed the fairs of Dumah, Hajar, Sohar, and Daba in a regular yearly cycle (Serjeant, 1954, p.126; Krenkow, 1947). The yearly pilgrimage (and fair) is still extant at this shrine.

A pilgrimage route more pertinent to the present discussion is that developed by the Ziyadid vizier Husain ibn Salamah (ca. 983-1011), who constructed a road for the Hajj with mosques and minarets (and no doubt rest-stations) at each stage (Kay, 1892, p.9). The pilgrimage road began at Tarim at the far eastern end of the Wadi Hadhramaut (see map 1), possibly passing site 48 as one station, and continued through the mountains down to Aden. Jebelain could have served as the station in the Abyan just before reaching Aden. (After Aden two routes led northward into the Hijaz.) Another site probably on the pilgrimage road is reported by Stark, who noted the occurrence of sherds of lustre ware and green glaze, as well as fragments of green glass and Chinese ceramics, at Andar near Hureidhah (see map 1, southwest corner) (1936, p.253).

Subsequent research at Hureidhah by Caton Thompson encountered similar sherds (1944, p.15). The presence of sites near Hureidhah suggests that a medieval road from Aden may have passed through the Wadi Amd to Hainan, just north of site 48, by-passing Shabwa further to the west, just as did van der Meulen's route from Aden to the Hadhramaut in 1939 (1947, map after xvi). It may be noted that the pre-Islamic cycle of yearly fairs often included a trip to Aden after the fair at Shihir, again suggesting possible antecedents for this medieval road.

That the early Islamic sites discovered during the survey, except site 48 near Hainan, are all concentrated around Say'un to the east of Hainan is rather unexpected given the fragments of information available from the medieval geographers. Foremost among these is Hamdani, who mentions Hainan as a great town with a market and castle (Müller, 1884, p.85). But the most important town appears to have been Shibam, where Hamdani found 30 mosques, half in ruins; this city may be identified with Bekri's Jarima, surrounded by gardens and called the most prosperous city of the Hadhramaut (*ibid*, p. 86; Sprenger, 1864, p.140). The 'city Hadhramaut' mentioned in other accounts may also have been Shibam. Lack of archaeological materials recorded from this area may be due to avoidance of this still intensively inhabited city. Tarim, at the eastern end of the Wadi Hadhramaut (Ibn Khordadhbeh reports a distance between Shibam and Tarim of seven *farsakhs),* is also known from Hamdani as a large city; it is more surprising that the survey failed to pick up any early Islamic material in its vicinity (see below).

The early Islamic sites which were discovered (sites 48, 34.2, 29, 31) are all low mounds within the wadi plain which had been accidentally uncovered by farmers digging for humus. When this fertile soil dug from old habitation areas is spread on the nearby fields, the sherds included in the soil mixture are also spread on the fields. Such sherds remain visible and are available for the modern archaeologist conducting a survey. Sherds may also make their way into the fields as part of contemporary urban compost (animal manure mixed with trash) used as fertilizer. This latter pattern of field fertilization, and the related pottery distribution, have been discussed recently by Wilkinson (1982).

Since humus fertilization results in sherds of an early date appearing in fields of a later date while in compost fertilization the sherds appear in contemporary fields, it is important to ascertain which of these patterns is applicable in south Arabia if one is to date fields and irrigation works by the sherds present.

Such humus collecting is common throughout the Middle East and is probably the single most common cause of the destruction of archaeological ruins. In Egypt the term *sebakh* (soil, fertilizer) is used to refer to organically rich soil taken from ancient sites. Note also that the word *damn* (manure, fertilizer) has a derived form *dimna*, defined by Wehr as 'vestiges or remnants of a dwelling, ruins.' Within the south Arabian context it is important to note that the flood (*sail*) irrigation of these valleys provides a silt covering which is usually 'the sole fertilizer' (Maktari, 1971, p.54). Serjeant notes that at Hureidhah silt is used instead of manure: 'Dung is not used in Hureidha because of its heat except in places frequently watered' (1964, p.44, n. 37).

The fields and dikes around site 48 (which may be identical with Harding's site 37 'Near Ajlaniah' [1964, p.40]) were covered with early Islamic sherds. Although these sherds could have been deposited contemporaneously with the early Islamic occupation, it must be remembered that these early Islamic sites were uncovered accidentally in the course of humus digging. For this reason it seems more likely that the distribution of the sherd-rich soil on the fields surrounding site 48 took place at the time of the humus digging, probably in the 16th or 17th century when Hainan was again an important center (Beckingham and Serjeant, 1950, p.198, n. 1; Harding's ceramics from Hainan all appear to derive from this late Islamic occupation [1964, pl. XXVIII-XXIX, 25-44; site 24, compared with the late Islamic materials discussed later in this paper].).

If the early Islamic inhabitants of southern Arabia used humus to fertilize their fields, they would presumably have mined extant Himyaritic sites and their fields would include Himyaritic, rather than early Islamic, sherds. Such a supposition would account for Caton Thompson's observation that in the area around Hureidhah,

> 'From the sixteenth century back to early Islamic times, the amount of foreign wares imported into the Hadhramaut seems to have been large. No abandoned village we visited failed to supply plentiful examples of them [note: ...complete jars were bought at Hureidha]; Chinese export porcelain and earthenware (mainly of the fifteenth century), Persian blue-and-white, besides glazed wares of many sorts, largely undatable because probably local, but including ninth- or tenth-century fragments. On the irrigated plain, amongst the numberless wind-worn sherds examined, not a single example was found.' (1944, p.15)

The wares she describes in addition to the ninth and tenth century materials are readily identifiable as typical middle and late Islamic ceramics by comparison with the finds at Khanfar and Kawd am-Saila near Aden (and are typically Rasulid; see below). The non-use of urban compost fertilizer would account for this apparent discrepancy between town and field.

The accidental discovery of the early Islamic sites during humus digging indicates that more early Islamic sites (and indeed older sites) may remain covered over with silt and unrecognizable in a surface survey. All such problems must be borne in mind when comparing the archaeological evidence with the evidence of the medieval geographers and historians.

The Middle Islamic Period (1150-1500 A.D.)

By the beginning of the 11th century the political situation in Yemen had degenerated into struggles among the last of the Ziyadids, the Ya'furids, the Najahids, and Fatimid influenced groups; the period of 1014-1056 saw wide-spread desolation and disorder. The Hadhramaut was on the periphery but no doubt was affected by this anarchy. Power in Yemen was consolidated by the Sulayhids; their vassals in Aden, the Zuray'ids (Banu Ma'n), incorporated the Hadhramaut within their realm. This dynasty was Fatimid in its orientation and marks a beginning of an Egyptian or Red Sea influence, rather than Abbasid. A crucial point in the history of Yemen was the Ayyubid conquest under Turanshah in 1173; though the Ayyubids attacked the Hadhramaut, they did not hold it; rather, a certain prosperity was achieved under Abdullah b. Rashid b. Abi Qahtan al-Himyari (d. 1216) (Stookey, 1978, pp.104-5).

In the aftermath of the Ayyubids a new dynasty, the Rasulids, ruled from the 13th to the 15th centuries. The Rasulids modeled their court on the Mamluks of Egypt and trade was strongly oriented toward the Red Sea, especially after the fall of Baghdad in 1258. The shift of political allegiance and trade away from the Persian Gulf may be reflected in the audacious enterprise of the King of Kish (the island of Qais in the Persian Gulf) in his desperation(?) attack on Aden in the 12th century (Goitein, 1954a).

The ceramics of the middle Islamic period in the Hadhramaut present, as suggested above, a continuation of the early Islamic tradition of cream wares. The forms of vessels are characterized by over-hanging rims with an internal lip (e.g., Fig. 4d, 5d, e), small triangular lug handles (Fig. 6n, 7k) and pierced lug handles (Fig. 5e, 7p) on round jars and bowls. Comb and incised wavy-line decoration continue as does the use of chain ridges. Parallels for this entire ceramic corpus are not easily found and thus indicate an independent tradition although individual connections with Oman (Ras al-Hadd [Whitcomb, 1975], Wadi al-Batha and am-Dhurra [de Cardi, 1977]; note the 'nail-head' rims at these sites) indicate some continuation of the trade connections with the Persian Gulf.

The Hadhramaut sites of this period begin to show parallels with the Red Sea and east African coast. Distinctive rim forms and the use of common chaff temper in certain categories of ceramics at the 13th-14th century site of Quseir al-Qadim, on the Egyptian Red Sea coast (Whitcomb and Johnson, 1978, 1980 [n.b.: references to this site are to excavation seasons 1978, 1980, published in 1979, 1982]) seem to indicate the importation to that site of south Arabian ceramics. Numerous similarities with the Hadhrami materials occur at Aidhab (El-Hakim and Elisseeff, 1980), another port on the Egyptian coast of the Red Sea, as well as on the Tihamah on the Yemeni coast (Keall, 1983). Comparisons on the east African coast, which experienced the rapid development of Swahili culture during this period, occur at Hafun (Chittick, n.d.), Kilwa (Chittick, 1974, although very few), and Gedi (Kirkman, 1954, 1963). The Abdu'l Mawahib dynasty at Kilwa is thought to have come from the Hadhramaut in the 14th century (Chittick, 1975; travel between Aden and Kilwa and other African ports is described by Ibn Mujawir for the same period; see Trimingham, 1975). One may also note the later rise of towns on the Somali coast in addition to the important port of Zaila in the 15th and 16th centuries (Curle, 1937). Rather surprising, though not completely unexpected, are the parallels with the ceramics from the site of Zimbabwe; the rather distinctive Hadhrami rectangular panelled large jars (Fig. 6p, 7j) have parallels only with Zimbabwe (Caton Thompson, 1931, pl.XIX:1-3, 6; other parallels may also be suggested: 7c, g = XXXI:1, LXX:53; this may also occur in Oman, de Cardi, pers. com.). Explanation of these isolated comparisons between south and eastern Africa and the Hadhramaut is obviously premature; nevertheless a tempting interpretation would be an early emigration of Hadhramis on the pattern of more recent times (see below).

A major problem in the interpretation of the middle Islamic materials in the Hadhramaut is the general lack of corresponding materials around Aden. Part of the problem is the size of collections from the coast and lack of collections from the ports of Shihir, Mukalla, and Mirbat, which are the more natural outlets for the Hadhramaut. In the vicinity of Aden, Lane and Serjeant report medieval remains from the site of Habil, north of Lahej (1948, p.108), where they found blue-green and lustre glazed wares mixed with Chinese porcelains and a Mamluk coin. An examination of the ceramics from this site in the Victoria and Albert Museum shows close parallels with Jebelain for the early Islamic (Fig. 1h, n, q; 2m, o, p), with al-Qaraw for the middle Islamic (Fig. 9a, k, m, n, o, q), and with the Hadhramaut in both periods (Fig. 4i, j; 5e; 7p; 8j; the incised wares are described as 'presumably local and impossible to date', p.121). They report one piece of sgraffiato from Habil, a ware which is completely absent from the survey collections (1948, p.122). This absence of sgraffiato wares, especially Style III, strongly confirms the reorientation away from the Persian Gulf in the 11th through 13th centuries (see Whitehouse, 1979).

The site of al-Qaraw in the Abyan would appear to have replaced Jebelain in this middle Islamic period and to date from the late 12th through 13th century. The site is also known as Zinjibar, a name suggesting African connections; it measures 600 m. across and seems to have been destroyed by burning (Harding, 1964, p.17 [site 5]; Doe, 1962, p.8, fig. 7; 1963, p.156; Lane and Serjeant, 1948, p. 108). The ceramics from al-Qaraw show affinities with the middle Islamic unglazed wares of the Hadhramaut. Perhaps more impressive are the comparisons with Quseir al-Qadim, graphically illustrating the Ayyubid-early Mamluk connection between Egypt and Aden (Whitcomb and Johnson, 1980; pl.9a=43b; 9c=43l; 9g=50i; 9h=40r; 9o=37; 9p=51d; 9q=34n; 9r=38y). The glazed wares are particularly close parallels and, in the absence of distinctively Egyptian wares at Aden, seem to indicate an export of Yemeni wares to the Egyptian coast. The brown and/or green painted yellow glazed ware (Whitcomb and Johnson, 1980, pl. 37) also occurs on east African sites and has usually been thought to have come from Yemeni kilns. Quseir, it may be noted, is described by Yaqut as a 'port of the Yemeni ships.'

The trade under consideration was not simply between Aden and the Egyptian coast but part of the long-distance trade with the Far East, the so-called spice trade. This was the commercial network involving India which is documented by Geniza texts (Goitein, 1954b; 1980) and is reflected in the visits to the city of Aden by Marco Polo in 1295 and by Ibn Battuta 35 years later. The involvement of Aden with this China trade is well documented by Lane and Serjeant from the 10th through the 14th century, quoting, for instance, Idrisi (ca. 1154), who cites Aden as the point of departure for ships destined for Sind, India, and China (1948, p. 113ff.). Wheatley, writing on Sung maritime trade, gives possible identifications of place-names known in Chinese sources–Shih-ho as Shihir, Ma-lo-pa as Murbat, and Nu-fa as Dhofar (Zufar). Curiously no name is brought forth for Aden; rather ports are named which would probably have been known to the Chinese as commodity sources, or as transshipment points mistaken for production centers (1959). Among the commodities discussed by Wheatley is frankincense (*Ju hsiang*), which the Chinese appear to have imported in immense quantities from the above ports (1959, p. 47-49). It is tempting to attribute at least part of the prosperity of the Hadhramaut during the middle Islamic period to the revival of this ancient trade, albeit to the East rather than the West. Serjeant, citing one of many medieval sources, mentions the occurrence of incense as a trade commodity for Aden in 1412 while cautioning against the 'romanticism' prevalent in discussions of ancient 'incense routes' (1960, p.584). Another commodity collected on the south Arabian and east African coasts and shipped to China was ambergris.

However important frankincense may have been for the Hadhramaut and for Shihir and other ports, this product was only one of a wide range of trade goods handled by the merchants of Aden. Among the aromatics and drugs, textiles and metals passing through this port (see Goitein, 1954b, 1980, for detailed lists), the trade in Far Eastern ceramics is particularly pertinent to archaeological discussion. The occurrence of celadons and porcelains on sites in the vicinity of Aden is the focus of the study of Lane and Serjeant, a study which may now be amplified with the excavated materials published from sites in east Africa (Kilwa, Gedi, etc.), from Aidhab, and from Quseir al-Qadim. The earliest Chinese ceramics found in the present survey come from al-Qaraw, followed by Khanfar and Kawd am-Saila; this sequence confirms the findings of Lane and Serjeant (1948; except for the last-named site; see below).

The two sites of Khanfar and Kawd am-Saila in the vicinity of Aden appear to have begun in the middle Islamic period. The first site, Khanfar, is located north of Zinjibar near the modern town of Ja'ar. At the foot of a large hillock are the remains of a large town with considerable deposition (at least two meters according to Harding, 1964, p.18, pl. IX:4) and evidence of burning which Doe attributes to 16th century wars (1962, p.8; 1963, p.156). The pottery collections (comparing pl. 9 with pl. 10 and the additional collection from Khanfar illustrated by Harding, 1964, pl. IV, V:3-12) suggests that Khanfar overlapped with the 13th century occupation at al-Qaraw.

Kawd am-Saila, on the other hand, is located northwest of Aden itself. It has been the object of several examinations. Doe made plans of the site and one of the building complexes (1962, pp.13-14, fig. 9; 1963, pp.161-62; 1971, pp.137-39, fig. 9, 10). He located numerous kilns on the site, probably associated with the manufacture of glass bracelets, for which there is abundant evidence. This industry was first reported by Reveil (1883) and is discussed by Lane and Serjeant (1948). Most recently, sondages were conducted at this site by a French expedition (J.-Fr. Breton, pers. comm.).

The ceramics from Khanfar and Kawd am-Saila present very similar ranges of types and will be treated here together. Lane and Serjeant described a collection from Kawd am-Saila in a type series, for which Lane had very few parallels. With the recent work on the Tihamah, there is now evidence for Rasulid ceramics and, indeed, Lane and Serjeant note among medieval lists of prized vessels 'also Zabid pottery (*fakhkhar*) evidently a local ware' (1948, p.115). The ceramics from Quseir al-Qadim (13th and 14th centuries) and a collection from Mocha (probably 16th century and later) provide some assistance in identifying earlier and later phases of this corpus. The glazed ceramics may be provisionally separated into the following categories:

a. A yellow-glazed red ware with painted decoration in brown and/or green, as described for al-Qaraw (above) and compared to 'mustard wares' at Quseir al-Qadim (Whitcomb and Johnson, 1980, pl. 37), is identical with Keall's 'Tihamah green-yellow' (1983). This ware occurs at Khanfar with brown paint (Harding, 1964: pl. IV, V:10) and at Kawd am-Saila (Fig. 12k, q) with green paint. (Lane hazarded a guess of the 15th century or later [1948, p.122, type f].) The Quseir al-Qadim examples confirm a 13th-14th century date; there is some evidence that the use of green paint is somewhat later, 14th rather than 13th century (as suggested above for al-Qaraw). The ware is absent from the Mocha collection.

b. A second painted ware has white glaze with blue decoration (green is sometimes added to or substituted for the blue). The fabric is usually red, although cream examples are found; in this latter instance the glaze is usually clear. Examples from Khanfar are Fig. 10b, e, f, g, j, q; those from Kawd am-Saila are Fig. 12a-g, j, m, n. This is apparently Lane's type h and i, for which he adduces a Chinese influence (14th-15th century) or, more vaguely, a similarity with 'Athlit' ware of Syria (13th century; 1948, pp.122-23). This ware occurs frequently on the Tihamah and is common at Mocha; on the other hand, it is completely absent from Quseir al-Qadim. This blue and white ware may thus date from the 15th through the 16th centuries and seems to replace the yellow and green painted style (a).

c. A red ware with blue or green glaze and a slip-painted design. This ware utilizes a white slip painted on the vessel before the glaze is applied, producing a light blue or green design against the darker areas without the reflective slip. This ware occurs at Khanfar (Fig. 10c, d; Harding, 1964, pl. V:11) and at Kawd am-Saila (Fig. 12p, r). Lane and Serjeant note it at Kawd am-Saila (1948, p.122, type g) and Keall takes this ware, his 'Blue Tihamah,' as a Rasulid type-indicator (13th-15th century) due to its ubiquitous occurrence on the Tihamah. The 'Blue slip painted' ware occurs also at Mocha and therefore may range from the 14th into the 16th century. While Keall looks to Syria for parallels, more useful comparisons may be made with Quseir al-Qadim, where such pottery occurs only in 14th century contexts and associated with a full range of Mamluk slip-painted wares, usually with yellow glaze. (These slip-painted wares are in turn closely paralleled by Mamluk sgraffiato wares, which do not occur in Aden or the Tihamah; see Whitcomb and Johnson, 1980, pl. 35, 36.) Thus there is technical precedent for slip-painting in Mamluk wares, though apparently no actual export of these ceramics into southwestern Arabia.

d. Red wares with glaze, often green, but also blue or white. These may be related to the 'glazed red wares' at Quseir al-Qadim (Whitcomb and Johnson, 1980, pl. 34), though the vessel forms are usually quite different. Lane describes this ware as imitative of Chinese celadons (1948, p.122, type e). The vessel forms parallel those used for blue and white wares (b) and blue slip-painted wares (c), for example, Khanfar Fig. 10a, b and Kawd am-Saila Fig. 12o, p. The glazed red wares would seem to date from the 14th through the 16th centuries from the present examples.

e. Two unusual sherds may form a separate type, being a red ware with a yellowish clear glaze with brown and turquoise-green paint (Khanfar, Fig. 10h; Kawd am-Saila Fig. 12h). While somewhat similar wares are found at Quseir al-Qadim (Whitcomb and Johnson, 1980, 38c) and Mocha, a close parallel exists at Adilabad (Delhi, India) in a Timurid context (ca. 1325; Waddington, 1946). It is likely that one should look to an Indian or Kermani origin for this style of ceramic. (Another sherd from Kawd am-Saila which is probably from Kerman is Fig. 12l, a blue and white with a 'tassel' mark, dated by Lane to the 17th century [1957, p.115, no. 29.])

f. The last and perhaps most interesting of the glazed ceramics from Khanfar and Kawd am-Saila is the Hays ware. Hays ware is characterized by small cups with a glossy green and/or yellow glaze. Decoration is added by fine incised lines or punctates, especially a line circling the inside of the cup at the base. The finest wares are hard, cream-buff fabric; other examples have a coarse red ware. This ware is commonly found on archaeological sites throughout southwestern Arabia (e.g., at Timna, where it was mistaken for Hellenistic lead glaze; Comfort, 1958, Pl. 142, 143). Harding publishes a selection from al-Assalah (1964, Pl. V) and examples are known from Mocha, both of which suggest a late date. The town of Hays marks the southern boundary of the Tihamah survey (Keall, 1983); the contemporary ceramic industry at Hays is described by Tufnell (1961, p.28) and by Weir (1974, p.67). These modern wares are 'dreadful coarse types' according to Keall, but seem to be related to this medieval ceramic ware. While one might see vaguely similar Mamluk prototypes, as in the collection of incised glazed wares at Quseir al-Qadim, the ubiquity of Hays ware on late Islamic sites suggests a range of 15th through 17th century. Examples of Hays ware from Khanfar (Fig. 10o, p, r-x) and Kawd am-Saila (Fig. 12w-ee) give a large range of forms and styles of decoration.

The unglazed ceramics from Khanfar and Kawd am-Saila are problematic. Some of these forms are related to those from al-Qaraw, as might be expected (Fig. 9e=10ff; 9g=11j; 9b=11g), and continue the red ware tradition in distinction to the middle Islamic cream-ware ceramics from the Hadhramaut. A number of parallels may be cited with Quseir al-Qadim (Whitcomb and Johnson, 1980; Fig. 10l=42a; 10bb=39k, l, m; 10gg=49a; 11a=42b; 11g=43i;

11h=42l; 11j=44o; 11p=41f; 11q=39r), though most of the ceramics at this site belong to an Egyptian tradition. A distinctive feature of these unglazed ceramics is the use of various decorative techniques. The incised decoration found at both sites (Fig. 10bb and 11q) is described by Keall as common in Rasulid contexts on the Tihamah (1983, fig. 5: 9, 12), where the incising is made through a lighter cream-pink slip. A second technique, stamped or molded decoration, is likewise found on the Tihamah (*ibid.*: fig. 5: 14) and at Khanfar (Harding, 1964, pl. V). Neither technique appears at Mocha, confirming a 13th through 15th century dating for such techniques. The remaining unglazed ceramics would seem to belong to the late Islamic period and may be better considered after an examination of materials from this period in the Hadhramaut.

The physical character of the archaeological sites in the vicinity of Aden has not been adequately described. The only planned site is Kawd am-Saila (Doe, 1971, fig. 9, 10), located on the lower reaches of the Wadi al-Kabir. As with the sites in the Abyan region, one might expect settlements to have been on slightly higher ground in the midst of or on the edges of the wadi irrigation systems. Such irrigation systems have been investigated for Lahej, north of Aden (near al-Habil), by Maktari (1971). (This study forms an interesting comparison with Serjeant's study of irrigation systems in the Hadhramaut and with pre-Islamic evidence [1964], see Bowen and Albright, 1958, and a review by Serjeant, 1960.) The earliest site, Jebelain, is described by Harding as a 'camping site' (1964, pp.18-19), but these low-lying remains covered with silt, and not without stratification, may in fact correspond to the early Islamic sites in the Hadhramaut. The mounding at Khanfar may correspond to that of Kawd am-Saila as a town site with visible perimeters where careful investigation might yield settlement plan and structures. (The more recent remains at al-Assalah would present a convenient beginning point for such studies; see Harding, 1964, Pl. IX:2.) The plans of Kawd am-Saila made by Doe emphasize the distribution of kilns on the site, giving the impression of a specialized industrial settlement. The plan of a single building and courtyard is reminiscent of the probably contemporary structures excavated at Siraf (Site E; Whitehouse, 1969, fig. 6) and provides a vivid impression of the information possible on such a site. It is unfortunate that sites near Kawd am-Saila such as Bir Na'ama and Bir Rubak are not more fully reported (Doe, 1962, p.13) and that Aden itself, its confined space now fully built up, has not been the subject of thorough investigations (for instance, at Ras Marshaq early remains were discovered by chance [*ibid.*]). Comparison of settlement patterns on the coastal littoral with those of the Hadhramaut are thus temporarily frustrated.

Within the Wadi Hadhramaut, the sites of the middle and late Islamic period are most frequently situated on outliers or mountain spurs; that is, the houses are on rocky slopes above the cultivable land and the reach of flood waters.

The town of Hureidhah, though not in the Wadi Hadhramaut itself (see map 1), may be studied as typical for the structure of such a small town. Bujra has outlined the social structure of Hureidhah in terms of the physical organization of the town (1971, fig. 2). The dwellings of the Sayyids (Attas) occupy one side of the slope of the hillside while the Mashaikh (Basahil) dwell on the other side. In the center is an open market square or suq, above which live the Masakin (Hirthan) who are the farmers, laborers and servants and are acknowledged as the original inhabitants of the place (cf. Serjeant, 1949b, 1957, on the class structure in the Hadhramaut). The town is surrounded by a number of small tribal settlements. The quarter of the Sayyids is known as al-Bilad, but the entire settlement is described by Bujra as an *hawtah*. The *hawtah* or 'sacred enclave' has been studied by Serjeant as a system for facilitating the interaction of tribal and sedentary groups (1962a); larger towns such as Tarim may be divided into a number of quarters and *hawtahs* (Serjeant, 1949b, 1950) with the Sayyids functioning as the mediators.

Van Beek, following other commentators, has adduced from the settlement location that the middle Islamic period was one of chronic insecurity which necessitated fortified settlements. One might also suggest that the strong government and increase in trade introduced by the Rasulids had produced an era of prosperity and increased population which mitigated against settlement on any irrigable land within the wadi. At this point it would be useful to have some evidence for settlement size and distribution. The present survey data is a beginning but confronts the problem of 'finding the ancient sites' discussed recently by Orchard (1982). Van Beek, commenting on the lack of ancient sites within the main wadi, considers that they '...were destroyed within the last thousand years or so by (1) the construction of irrigation installations, and (2) the erosion of the valley floor' (1963, p.538). These two seemingly contradictory processes are both explained by the flood-water irrigation system. These techniques, evidently perfected in pre-Islamic times, attempt to harness the sudden violent waters which rush through the wadis after the periodic rains, which occur either in Saif (April-June) or in Kharif (July- September) (Serjeant, 1964, p.55). In the main wadi the force of the floods was broken by a succession of barrages, which spread the waters over the surrounding fields so that 'as legend has it, one could walk most of the way under the shade of palm trees from Huraidah to Hud' (*ibid.*, p.51). The slowing of the flood also allows the deposition of silt on the fields, as noted above. In the absence of such barrages, the floods carve deep channels into the wadi bed. Serjeant notes an extreme example: 'At the famous *Nuqrah* below Inat the flood-waters have carved a small canyon, perhaps 50-60 feet deep, in the alluvial clay bottom of the Wadi Hadhramaut' (1964, p.51). Thus ancient sites constructed within the wadi might have been cut up and obliterated by the erosion, or levelled for fields in subsequent periods, or covered with silt. It is important to note that all of these processes are extremely localized events, the particular histories of which are likely to be extremely complicated. Measurement of silt accumulations, especially given the irregular nature of the floods, would not seem useful as a chronological technique.

The distribution of Islamic sites discovered during the survey shows an interesting pattern: The early Islamic sites are situated to the west (site 48) and around Say'un; the middle Islamic sites are found in the area between Say'un and Bur; and the late Islamic sites cluster around Tarim (see map 1). Several hypotheses may account for this seeming progression of settlement from west to east: 1) As the survey began at Tarim, less attention may have been paid to the ubiquitous (and less interesting) very recent Islamic sites in later stages of the survey; it should be remembered that from Shibam to Hainan only specific sites were investigated, rather than attempting a total archaeological recording. 2) Occupation may have, in a sense, progressed down the valley; as fields covered with silt became too high for flood-waters to reach, lower fields downstream became more optimal for irrigation. Medieval sources and modern commentators often suggest just such a deterioration of the agricultural potential of the wadi (Serjeant, 1962b, p.258). 3) Finally, as Tarim and Shibam are known place-names from at least the early Islamic period, it is possible that early sites have indeed been buried in the build-up of silt, as suggested above. Concerning more ancient sites, and the lack thereof, Van Beek would have it both ways,

> '...a gradual grading of the western two-thirds of the valley floor may have destroyed all evidence of pre-Islamic towns in that area, while deposition of this graded material together with silt from Wadi 'Idim has buried pre- Islamic towns below the surface in the eastern part of the main wadi.' (1963, p.539).

The point which seems to have been forgotten in this assessment is that these should not be considered entirely natural processes; one is dealing with processes altered by human action, in this case, the historical occupations from the early Islamic to the present. The patterns of occupation and agricultural practices cannot be deduced from the present survey evidence, nor can any one of the above hypotheses be proven. In addition to further archaeological field research, a search must be made for the indications which certainly lie buried in medieval manuscripts. Serjeant, who has compiled many of these resources (1949a, 1962b), presents a very interesting list of rains and floods for the period from 1260 to 1914 (1964, pp.67-72). In this account there are famines in 1538-39, 1541-42, and 1560-61, which Serjeant takes as evidence of a failure of rains. These famines might also imply a failure of political authority, excessive taxation and lack of investment (i.e., barrage maintenance) or an imbalance from the prosperity of the previous period (over-population, etc.). Such potential causes should be found in historical documents and the study of such manuscripts should lead to possible explanations for the archaeological evidence for the Islamic and even more remote periods and might 'actually be of some use even today in reviving the irrigation system' (Serjeant, 1962b, p.258)

The Late Islamic Period (1500-1850 A.D.)

In the latter part of the 15th century, two important events took place: the replacement of the Rasulids by the Tahirids and the immigration of the Kathiris from Dhofar (Zafar) into the Hadhramaut. The reign of the great Kathiri sultan Badr Bu Tuwairik began in 1516, the year after the Portuguese attack on Jeddah and the year before the fall of Mamluk Egypt to the Ottomans. The 16th century thus saw momentous changes in the Indian Ocean and, by extension, the culture of southwest Arabia. During the first half of the 16th century the Ottomans consolidated their presence in the Red Sea and, after 1538, secured Aden as the key to this area. During the same period, the Portuguese established their presence in India and in the Persian Gulf (at Muscat, Hormoz and Bahrain). Ottoman occupation of Basra and Lahsa (al-Hasa) and Portuguese raids into the Red Sea made both of these areas regions of conflict (Özbaran, 1972), while the coast of southern Arabia became the scene of naval engagements and raids. Nevertheless, by the second half of the 16th century, there was a revival of trade with India and Indonesia (Boxer, 1969) in spite of 'the increasing harassment of the piratical sallies of small numbers of Portuguese vessels' (Serjeant, 1974).

With the beginning of the 17th century the Dutch and English arrived in the Indian Ocean, setting the stage for a 'confrontation between older and newer entrepreneurial forms,' that is, between the caravan or 'peddling' trade and the organization of European 'companies' (Steensgaard, 1973). The tolerance of the Kathiri sultans coupled with the experience of Hadhramis in these newly colonized lands led to modernization attempts, culminating in the cooperation with the British after the occupation of Aden in 1839. In the latter part of the 17th and early 18th century occurred what Toussaint calls 'the Arab reconquest' (1966, pp.140ff.), by which he refers to the rise of Oman as a naval power and its conquest of the east African coast, especially Zanzibar. With Oman's conquests one sees an instance of inhabitants of the Arabian hinterland emigrating to foreign lands comparable to that of the Hadhramis.

The emigration of the Hadhramis during this late Islamic period was on a very large scale, both to east Africa and to India and Indonesia, where they went as traders (usually middlemen), mercenaries, and scholars (Serjeant, 1974, p.25; van den Berg dates this influence in Indonesia from the 15th century, 1886,p. 104). The port of embarkation was Shihir (hence Hadhramis in east Africa are referred to as Shihiris), an important trade port and port for the pilgrimage to Qabr Hud. Serjeant notes the presence of a ruin-field with, 'in great profusion, potsherds of the types described already in the Aden area [Kawd am-Saila], celadon, Persian pottery of many varieties, and other Near and Far Eastern wares, mostly of the later Medieval period' (1974, p.27). The port was a residence for the Kathiri sultans, who also had a residence in the Hadhramaut. The two Jesuits who were taken as prisoners to the Wadi Hadhramaut (in 1590) found the sultan living in Hainan (Beckingham and Serjeant, 1950, p.198, n. 1). These observers also noted that west of Tarim were 'many ruined forts along the mountain ridges' (*ibid.*, p.197).

Occupation in the Wadi Hadhramaut during this period, like that in the middle Islamic period, seems to have been based mainly on outliers on the edges of the wadi. Some of the late Islamic sites in the Wadi Hadhramaut are extremely well preserved.

> 'The very numerous ruins marked on von Wissmann's map are all of recently deserted villages, a curious phenomenon which seems to be peculiar to the Hadhramaut; some of these give interesting glimpses of a ruined site in the making, but it is difficult to see why they were abandoned.' (Harding, 1964, p.40)

A careful survey of these remains would offer an opportunity to examine their physical structure and artifactual distribution and to hypothesize on the class structure of the settlement. Such patterns might then shed light on the interpretation of earlier Islamic settlements and patterns for the pre-Islamic. Such investigations were obviously beyond the means of the present preliminary survey, though consideration of the archaeology of Islamic sites should bear in mind these important possibilities for future research.

A new architectural form, the fortified house, square in plan with round towers on the four corners, appears for the first time. This type of structure is depicted by van den Berg (1886, Pl. III) and is identified by Serjeant, in discussion of examples on Socotra and at Shihir, as a Yafi'i type of fort (1974, pp.26-27, Pl. 11). The need for fortification must have been dramatically increased in the wadi after the introduction of firearms; the earliest use of guns in warfare was under Badr Bu Tuwairik (Serjeant, 1974, p.29). The introduction of firearms must also have presented noticeable impediments to the conduct of farming. Sites of the late Islamic period often have well-preserved walls and were considered by Van Beek to date within the last 100 years.

The ceramics of the late Islamic period in the Hadhramaut are characterized, first of all, by a very soft, chaff tempered ware with buff-orange surfaces and a black core. Surfaces are often covered with a red or white-cream slip, the former sometimes burnished. Most distinctive is the painted decoration (discussed below). The vessel forms show some connection with the wares of the middle Islamic period, suggesting an indigenous development in the region. The more diagnostic forms and attributes are:

a. **Large vessels** (either jars or bowls) with heavy rims, such as Fig. 13a-d or 17c, j. Decoration consists of bands of wavy incised lines and 'rope' ridges (e.g., Fig. 13b, q); both of these attributes may be traced well into the pre-Islamic period and testify to the danger of simplified chronological assumptions.

b. **Simple bowls** with straight, flaring sides and slightly rounded bases are represented on Fig. 13e-f and 18g. These bowls, especially the smaller forms, are often painted and have a variety of additional attributes. Handles may be triangular lugs set on the rim or side (Fig. 13k), triangular projections (Fig. 14n, 15c), horizontal loop handles (Fig. 15b), so-called frying pan handles (Fig. 16i, 18j), or vertical loop handles (Fig. 18n).

c. **Smaller bowls** occasionally have a rounded side and flaring rim (Fig. 14b, these are usually undecorated except for a red or brown slip.

d. **Jars** with a rounded body and slightly flaring rim are very common, either with incised decoration (Fig. 14i) or, more frequently, with painted decoration (Fig. 14r). Handles and horizontal ridges are also found on these jars (Fig. 17f, g, n). Spouts also occur on this and some bowl forms (Fig. 17e, 16l, 14m).

e. **Deep bowls** or pots are found with triangualar lugs, notched and connected to a ridge; unpainted examples are of a burnished grey ware (Fig. 13j, l-n).

f. **Small jars,** often called ablution vases, have a high narrow neck, handle and occasionally a bridged spout; these vases are usually painted (Fig. 13p, r, 15h, 16o, p).

g. **Chalices** are known from unfortunately incomplete examples, characterized by a high ring base, slight carination, incurving rim and painted decoration (Fig. 16f, 17i).

h. **Small cups** are a common form, always decorated with a burnished red slip (Fig. 14q).

This list of forms is not meant to be exhaustive but to outline the most common characteristics of the ceramics of this period. The assemblage is fascinating in the adoption of many attributes of far earlier pre-Islamic ceramics within this region, among which are the soft, chaff tempered ware, the notched triangular lugs, the spouts, and the rim forms. While the possibility remains that specific pieces may in fact be prehistoric sherds mixed with this corpus, a comparison of the style within these assemblages leads to the conclusion that this is a consistent industry, albeit with definite 'archaizing' tendencies. The importance of definition of this 'late period' ceramic style will be obvious for the clarification of further surveys within this region.

This style of ceramics is not without parallels outside of southern Arabia. Connections with ceramics of the 16th and 17th centuries found in the region of the Persian Gulf may be discerned from the surveys of de Cardi and the seriations attempted by the author. Numerous attributes are shared with the ceramics from Julfar and Kashm Nadir, both coastal sites in northwestern Oman (de Cardi, 1971, fig. 13-15, as well as other sites). One finds in this area similar jar forms, ablution vases, and painted decoration. Likewise, ceramics from sites on Qatar have numerous parallels (Garlake, 1978).

A comparison of the seriation attempts of materials from Aden and the Hadhramaut with a similar range from al-Hasa oasis in eastern Arabia (Whitcomb, 1978) is shown in Table A. The comparisons during the early Islamic period (Fig. 1-4) are a predictable result of the Abbasid rule in both areas and the intensity of Persian Gulf trade. The interruption during the middle Islamic (Fig. 5-12) is surprising and illustrates, especially for Aden (Fig. 9-12), a reorientation of southern Arabia toward the Red Sea. Finally during the late Islamic period (Fig. 13-18) the Hadhramaut again shows contacts with eastern Arabia, though whether this is through the medium of trade or population movement under the Portuguese or the Ottomans is unclear. This correlation suggests that either the Hadhramaut late Islamic should be lowered to begin in the 14th century or the al-Hasa late Islamic I should be raised to begin in the 16th century (some time lag is of course possible).

The seriation of archaeological materials from Oman (Whitcomb, 1975) gives another sequence of ceramics for comparison with that of Aden and the Hadhramaut. (see Table B). As in the case with al-Hasa oasis, the early Islamic occupation in Oman reveals the same sphere of interaction as in Aden and the Hadhramaut (Fig. 1-4). The coastal site of Ras al-Hadd shows a number of similarities with both Aden and the Hadhramaut in the middle Islamic (Fig 5-12), as does the inland site of BB15 (both of these sites also show early Islamic

		al-Hasa			
Aden and Hadhramaut		early Islamic	middle Islamic	late Islamic I	late Islamic II
	Fig. 18				k
	17			b,e	j
late	16			j,o,r	d
Islamic	15				j,l
	14			c,i,r	l,q
	13			j,n	
	12				b
	11				
middle	10				
Islamic	9				
	8				
	7				
	6				
	5	c	a		
	4	b,h,u			
early	3				
Islamic	2	q			
	1	d,f,j, l,m,o q	c		

Table A: Seriation comparison of Aden and Hadhramaut sites with Al-Hasa

materials). The similarities of Wadi Qant with late Islamic sites in the Hadhramaut (Fig. 13-18) suggests that, like the situation in al-Hasa, the beginning date for this period may need to be lowered to at least the 14th century. This is made even more likely by the absence of connections with the late Islamic in Oman, other than the presence in the Hadhramaut of a few pieces of Bahla wares exported from Oman. This is in marked contrast to the connections with al-Hasa during this period.

The painted wares of the late Islamic period present a somewhat surprising innovation in the ceramic repertoire. The forms are usually either large open bowls or jars, although including beakers and bottles and a large chalice(?) as well. The painted decoration, usually red-brown on a cream surface, features 'dripped' hatching, dots, hanging triangles or semi-circles, and cross-hatched lozenges. Decorated areas are often organized into horizontal fields subdivided by multiple vertical lines (metopes).

Aden and Hadhramaut		Oman: early Islamic	middle Islamic: Ras al-Hadd	BB15	Wadi Qant	late Islamic
	Fig. 18					
	17					
late	16			m		
Islamic	15	l			e,l	l
	14	o	a		b,g,o	o
	13					
	12					
	11		i			n
middle	10		m			
Islamic	9		f			
	8		k			
	7	g,i	i			
	6	l	l,m,q	n,j		
	5			a,b,g		
	4	a,g,h i,j,k, s,t,u	p			
early	3	e				
Islamic	2	h,q	a			
	1	b,c,j k,l,m, o,s	l,j,o	b,c		

Table B: Seriation comparison of Aden and Hadhramaut sites with Oman

This style of decoration does not appear to have a precedent in south-western Arabia and may be suggested to have come from India. The medieval site of Banbhore near Karachi has, mixed with Islamic wares, an unglazed painted ware, a descendant of earlier painted ceramic traditions in India. This Islamic ceramic features painted dots, metope organization, and cross-hatched lozenges; the forms seem to be generally a jar form with wide, out-turned rim. This form may be reflected in Hadhramaut jars such as Fig. 14r; a rim on this same plate (14a) is probably an actual Indian import, though unpainted. Though Banbhore was destroyed in the 13th century, this tradition carried on in India (Khan, 1963, pp.37-38). The connection between south Arabia and India during the 16th-18th centuries is well attested, not only in terms of trade, but the emigration of Hadhramis to India and beyond (especially Indonesia;

van den Berg, 1886). These Hadhramis customarily would return to the Hadhramaut bearing their capital gains, Javanese and Indian fashions, and often foreign wives.

The glazed ceramics from the Wadi Hadhramaut present a rather anomalous picture in that the fine Rasulid glazed wares which characterize Khanfar and Kawd am-Saila are completely absent. (Some of these, rather attractive, wares may have been retained by the Yemeni authorities during the division.) The glazed ceramics which are present fall into two categories. The first is Bahla ware (Fig. 14o, 15l), a brown or green glazed ware which was produced in quantities in Oman during this period (Whitcomb, 1975, fig. 12). This ceramic is imitative of Martaban wares and is widely distributed throughout the Persian Gulf, where it is also known as Kung ware. The second glazed ware is Hays ware (Fig. 13s, 14d), the presence of which tends to confirm that this ware continued into the post-Rasulid period.

Along with the connection to Aden indicated by this Hays ware one might consider the unglazed wares from Khanfar and Kawd am-Saila, the forms of which show some similarities with those of the Hadhramaut but remain basically distinctive. Painted wares are absent in Aden with the exception of one ablution vase (Fig. 11n). This suggests that, in so far as occuption around Aden in the 16th and 17th centuries may be represented in the collections being discussed, the contacts with the Wadi Hadhramaut must have been minimal. It is tempting to see the Kathiri development of Shihir as a partial answer to this anomaly.

As a final note on south Arabian ceramics, one should mention the incense burners found on many sites. The examples illustrated in this collection show two main types. The first has four legs and a shallow pan for the incense; this was found on an early Islamic site (Fig. 4m) and would seem to represent a continuation of an earlier Himyaritic type (Bowen and Albright, 1958, pl. 96). The decoration on the sides, in the form of opposing rows of triangular cuts, is the same as that on a glazed incense burner from Kawd am-Saila (Fig. 11r). This burner and one from a late Islamic site (Fig. 17h) form a second type, characterized by a deep pan and four legs connected by clay at the base. An example of such an incense burner was found at Quseir al-Qadim in a 14th century context (Whitcomb and Johnson, 1980, Pl. 72c).

The sequence of Islamic ceramics may be amplified with consideration of other categories of artifacts-the stone vessels, glass, and Far Eastern ceramics. The stone vessels are mainly carved from steatite (chlorite) and are most common in the middle Islamic period. Stone vessels are mentioned among lists of trade goods as a product of southern Arabia (this industry is mentioned for the area behind Mukalla in Little, 1925 p.53). While one should not expect to find close similarities in form with ceramics, small lugs are present in both media (Fig. 19c, e = 4s, 6n, 7k) as are lids (Fig. 19d, t = 7q, 8n, 13t). Vessel carination is present in stone and ceramic at Khanfar (Fig. 10dd and 19h). Comparisons may be drawn from Quseir al-Qadim, where similar stone vessels were excavated (Whitcomb and Johnson, 1978, Pl. 72h, k; 1980, Pl. 68q); these show the same vertical cutting marks and have a ridge which may be related to the lug handles. The stone vessels from al-Qaraw closely parallel the forms of wooden bowls at Quseir al-Qadim (*ibid.*, 1978, Pl. 71m, n; 1980, Pl. 68m). A distinctive form carved in steatite is a small triangular vessel which Serjeant calls a 'fish-oil lamp' (1954, p.174, fig. 4, found at Shihir with medieval sherds). An example from Khanfar with a handle is published by Harding (1964, Pl. IV: 5); such a handle was also found at Quseir al-Qadim (Whitcomb and Johnson, 1980, Pl. 68o).

The glass vessels from the region of Aden offer a disappointing range of styles and forms, especially in light of the kilns at Kawd am-Saila and elsewhere reported by Lane and Serjeant (1948). Medieval glass from Quseir al-Qadim has recently been studied with reference to the Egyptian and Mediterranean glass industry and to trade connections between that Red Sea port and the Indian Ocean (Whitcomb, 1983). This minor port revealed a full range of 13th-14th century glass of the Syro-Egyptian Mamluk industry including enameled glass, marvered glass, moulded glass, glass with cut decorations, and glass with colored trailed decorations (Whitcomb and Johnson, 1980, Pl. 58). The glass collections from al-Qaraw (Fig. 20l-t) and Kawd am-Saila (Fig. 20u-ee) have the same general range of forms, with beaker rims (Fig. 20l = 58c), bulge-necked bottles (Fig. 20m, z = 58z, aa) and bases, but the amount of variation within forms is much less. In addition, the only decorated pieces involve the use of a mould (Fig. 20e, h, at Jebelain and site 34.2), which technique is found also at Quseir al-Qadim and in a collection from Malaya (Lamb, 1965, p.4). Lane and Serjeant report a cut blue vial (1948, p.129) possibly similar to examples from Quseir al-Qadim; the example from site 6 (Fig. 20hh) would appear to be much later in date.

The glass industry around Aden seems rather to have specialized in the production of glass bracelets. Indeed the collections in the Victoria and Albert Museum gathered by Lane and Serjeant include wasters and elements of this complicated production (wasters were also recovered by Van Beek at Kawd am-Saila; this industry was first reported by Reveil, 1883). The glass bracelets from Kawd am-Saila have recently been studied by Monod, who attempts a preliminary typology (1978). The bracelets may be described as additive in complexity, with a usually triangular or sub-triangular section. (Twisted bracelets do not occur in the collection under study here though they are present in the Victoria and Albert collections.) Bands of color are added to the core, while the more complicated add twisted bands (Fig. 21g, h), marvered glass (Fig. 21j, s, t), and prunts (Fig. 21e, f, m, n, y). As discussed in the context of the Quseir al-Qadim bracelets, these techniques seem derived from those used for decorating glass vessels (Whitcomb and Johnson, 1980, Pl. 59o-z; Whitcomb, 1983). The seriation of sites in this collection strongly suggests that the latest bracelets (from Kawd am-Saila and sites 25, 10 and 7) tend to have a thin, flattened section and spots of added color. These might be placed in the 16th century, when the Aden production centers seem to have ended and the production of glass bracelets was taken over by Indian centers.

Far Eastern ceramics present a very specialized field of study; their representation in these collections may be commented upon here only briefly to note similar pieces discovered in excavations and surveys. While these fine porcelains and celadons may often be more precisely dated than unglazed local wares, too often they seem to be far more recent than other sherds and may rather be the product of chance additions by recent visitors. Such would seem to be the case at site 29, where a 19th century blue and white porcelain occurs on a middle Islamic site (Fig. 22b).

The site of al-Qaraw, on the other hand, contains a consistent assemblage of Far Eastern wares datable to the 13th and 14th centuries. This collection most closely reflects the range of ceramics discussed in Lane and Serjeant (1948, pp.123-29). Among the wares which Lane recognized seem to be Yüeh celadon (a; Fig. 22d) and Lung Ch'üan celadon (b; Fig. 22h, l), brown-glazed stoneware (d, from Siam; Fig. 22g), Ying-ching porcelain (g; Fig. 22k), white porcelain (h; Fig. 22i) and blue-and-white porcelain (i; Fig. 22e, f). As Lane noted, the same Far Eastern ceramics seem to have reached the African coast about the same time; these have been reported from the excavations at Gedi (Kirkman, 1954, p.108-25) and at Kilwa (Chittick, 1974, 130d = 22d; 138c = 22f; 92b = 22h; all dating to the 14th century). These fine ceramics were traded to Egypt where the excavations at Fustat (old Cairo) have uncovered thousands of examples (Gyllensvärd, 1973, 1975; Mikami, 1982). Being a port on the Egyptian coast, Quseir al-Qadim closely parallels this assemblage of ceramic imports (Whitcomb and Johnson, 1980, Pls. 52q = 22d; 52b = 22f; 44t = 22g; 52y = 22h, i; 1978, Pls. 51s = 22d; 51b = 22e, f; 51y = 22i; 51x = 22j; see also Hobson, 1926-27, for Chinese wares at Aidhab).

The remainder of the Far Eastern ceramics present a very different assemblage, one of the 17th through the 19th centuries. One of the most useful excavations for the comparison and dating of these late Chinese exports is that of Fort Jesus at Mombasa (Kirkman, 1974); during the late 17th and 18th century this fort was ruled by Omanis and it is therefore not surprising to find close

Aden and Hadhramaut		Fort Jesus	Julfar	Maldives	al-Assalah
Fig.22	n		45:10		
	o	29:12			
	p			66a:384	
	q		45:6		
Fig.23	a	37:3	46:9	66b:396	V
	b	37:5			
	c	35:6	45:4	67a:487	
	e	29:3			V
	g			64c:285	
	m	37:6		66a:384	V
	q		45:2		
	t			64b:273	
	u			67a:490	V
	v	36:7			V
	x	25:7	45:11		V

Table C: Far Eastern ceramics on Aden and Hadhramaut sites and other sites

connections with the survey materials reported from Julfar (de Cardi, 1971). In addition to the porcelains, one may see an Omani influence in attributes such as bowl lugs, a bridged spout, red painted wares, and Bahla glazed wares (Kirkman, 1974, fig. 32: 21-22; 62:1; 33; 72). The Chinese wares, which Kirkman describes as K'ang Hsi, may also be compared with sherds recovered from a survey in the Maldives (Carswell, 1978), to name but one well-published example of the wide dispersal of these artifacts. These comparisons may be most conveniently presented in tabular form; see Table C. The absence in the collections being published here of earlier Far Eastern ceramics on the site of Kawd am-Saila, as found and described by Lane and Serjeant, is curious and may be an accident of collection. The comparisons with al-Assalah (Harding, 1964, Pl. V) confirm the late dating of al-Assalah. Two other wares should be noted: a European salt glazed ceramic (Fig. 23i) and very recent tea-cups (Fig. 23l, r, y-aa). In summary, the Far Eastern ceramics confirm the dating of the late Islamic sites and reflect the participation of the inhabitants of the Wadi Hadhramaut in this late trade.

Conclusion

In summary one may distinguish the following archaeological periods during the Islamic period in Aden and the Hadhramaut: an early Islamic period, beginning as a distinctively identifiable corpus perhaps as late as the beginning of the 9th century and continuing until the middle of the 12th century; this period encompasses the Ziyadid and Sulayhid dynasties in terms of Yemeni political history and shows a predominance of Abbasid influences. The middle Islamic period may be seen as Rasulid in character with Red Sea or Mamluk influences predominating, though the strong, separate ceramic tradition in the Hadhramaut suggests a complexity which must await further work in Yemen for clarification. The late Islamic period begins with the disruptions and changes of the 16th century, where again the archaeological remains of Aden are overshadowed by the materials from the Hadhramaut and a proper perspective must be sought in further archaeological work at Shihir, Mukalla, and other port sites. The survey materials studied in the present collection, while the most extensive and well-documented available, allow only a vague abstraction of the development of southern Arabia during the 1000 years under consideration. The Islamic archaeology of this region needs much further field work before a comprehensive picture will emerge; this picture will, however, shed important light on the cultural development of southern Arabia, including necessary connections with the pre-Islamic past, and will make important additions to an understanding of the history of the Indian Ocean and the rich interconnections among all the regions peripheral to it.

This study of Aden and the Hadhramaut is, then, an examination, over a period of 1000 years of history, of the cultural ties binding coastal settlements and agricultural highlands. On the one hand, there is the culture of the wadi, an urbanized setting inherited from more remote, Himyaritic times, based on the irrigation of this large wadi system. This is the story of farmers, scholars and shrines, and tribesmen. The tribesmen are in a sense peripheral and yet a fundamental element in the economic and political equation involving the towns and their connections with the coastal region. It should be remembered that the tribesmen are the carriers, the caravaneers, who supply the means to cross the *jōl*.

The culture of the coast is likewise an urbanized culture, one of merchants, carriers and fishermen in Ibn Battuta's words. While areas like the Abyan have a limited amount of irrigation agriculture, the impetus for settlement in this region is derived from an entrepreneurial spirit, of profits from distant lands, again an inheritance from more remote historical periods. Between the two areas there is an essential symbiosis, more fundamentally complex than the

Site	Ceramic	Stone Fig. 19	Glass Fig. 20, 21	Far Eastern Fig. 22, 23
Jabelain	Fig. 1, 2			
48	Fig. 3		1 example	
34.2	Fig. 4			
29				1 example
31	---			
30	Fig. 5		1 example	
27	Fig. 6			1 example
28				
20	Fig. 7	stone		
19		vessels		
34.1	Fig. 8			
Qaraw	Fig. 9		bracelets	
Khanfar	Fig. 10			
Kawd am-Saila	Fig. 11, 12			
25	Fig. 13			
18	Fig. 14		1 example	
17				
7	Fig. 15		1 example	
6				
5	Fig. 16			
10	Fig. 17		3 examples	
9				
3				
2	Fig. 18			
1				

Table D: Aden and the Hadhramaut: Site Sequence

usual port-hinterland relationship. Though dynasties were periodically established at Aden, political power of the Wadi Hadhramaut and its ports was normally centered on the wadi, which was always the religious and ethnic heart of southern Arabia. However one might wish to define this 'heartland,' its cultural history must be studied in terms of contact across the sand (to Yemen) or salt seas. The relations between Hadhramis and the outside world is akin to relations between Omanis and the east African coast, to the relation between inhabitants of the oasis of Mzab in Algeria to the Mediterranean coast, and others. Collected sherds provide a beginning toward an understanding of these relationships over time. Not that one will ever recover particular tribal structures, for example, from study of ceramics, but one may establish patterns of material culture-continuations, innovations, external instrusions-artifactual testaments to more non-material history. In southern Arabia one sees an example of a region with a rich and complex history, temporarily lost and waiting to be recovered; this is a situation where an archaeological approach in coordination with historical documentation may make a definite contribution.

Fig. 1

Jebelain

a dark red ware, grey core; common medium sand and medium chaff; diameter ca. 42 cm.
b red ware, black core; cream slip; moderate medium sand and medium chaff; diameter 40 cm.
c dark red ware; moderate medium sand and medium chaff; diameter 36 cm.
d red ware, grey core; tan surfaces; moderate medium sand and common chaff; diameter 46 cm.
e red ware; brown surfaces; common medium sand and medium chaff; diameter 27 cm.
f brown ware, grey core; moderate medium sand and common chaff; diameter 20 cm.
g red ware; moderate medium sand and medium chaff; diameter 22 cm.
h brown ware; cream surfaces, slightly blackened on exterior; moderate medium sand and common chaff; diameter 22 cm.
i brown ware; greenish cream surfaces; common medium sand and moderate chaff; diameter 20 cm. (rim not certain)
j cream ware; thick white glaze in interior and exterior; fine; diameter 20 cm.
k cream ware; green and white glaze on interior and exterior; fine; diameter 16 cm.
l cream ware; white glaze on interior and exterior and base; common medium sand; diameter 24 cm. (surfaces greyish)
m cream ware; blue-green glaze on interior and exterior; moderate medium sand; diameter 10 cm.
n cream ware; blue-green glaze on exterior, grey-white glaze on interior; moderate medium sand
o cream ware; blue-green glaze on exterior, black glaze on interior; moderate medium sand
p cream ware; blue-green glaze on interior and exterior; fine; diameter 12 cm.
q cream ware; blue-green glaze on interior and exterior; moderate medium sand; diameter 16 cm.
r cream ware; light blue-green glaze on exterior, black glaze on interior; moderate medium sand
s cream ware; blue-green glaze on exterior; moderate medium sand; diameter unknown

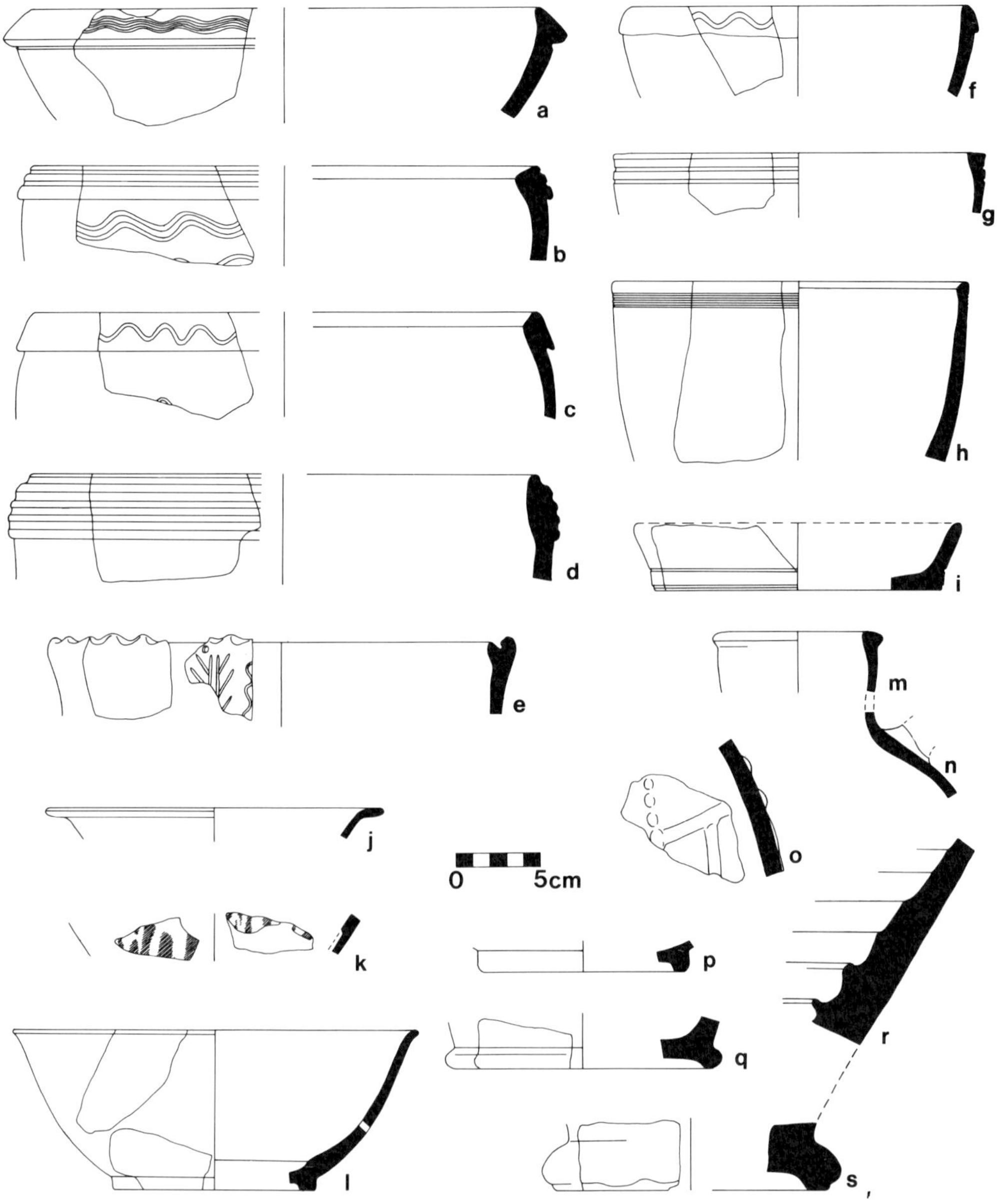

Fig. 1. Jebelain

Fig. 2

Jebelain

- **a** brown ware; abundant medium sand and common chaff; diameter 14 cm.
- **b** orange-red ware, grey core; cream surfaces; moderate medium sand and common chaff; diameter 10 cm.
- **c** cream-tan ware; moderate medium sand; diameter 8 cm.
- **d** red ware; common coarse sand; diameter 16 cm.
- **e** red ware; cream surface on exterior; moderate medium sand and moderate chaff; diameter 16 cm.
- **f** red ware; cream surfaces; moderate medium sand and common chaff; diameter 12 cm.
- **g** red ware, black core; traces of red slip on exterior; moderate medium sand and common chaff; diameter 16 cm.
- **h** red ware; cream surface on exterior; moderate medium sand and moderate chaff; diameter 16 cm.
- **i** red-brown ware; moderate medium sand and moderate chaff; diameter 16 cm.
- **j** red ware; cream surface on exterior; moderate medium sand and abundant chaff.
- **k** brown ware; cream surface on exterior; moderate medium sand and moderate chaff; diameter 11 cm.
- **l** dark red ware; moderate coarse sand and common chaff
- **m** red-brown ware; greenish-cream surfaces; moderate medium sand and common chaff
- **n** red-brown ware; abundant medium sand
- **o** orange-red ware; brown surface on interior; moderate medium sand
- **p** red ware, grey core; moderate medium sand
- **q** red ware, black core; common medium sand and moderate chaff
- **r** red ware; cream surfaces; moderate medium sand and abundant chaff; diameter 28 cm.

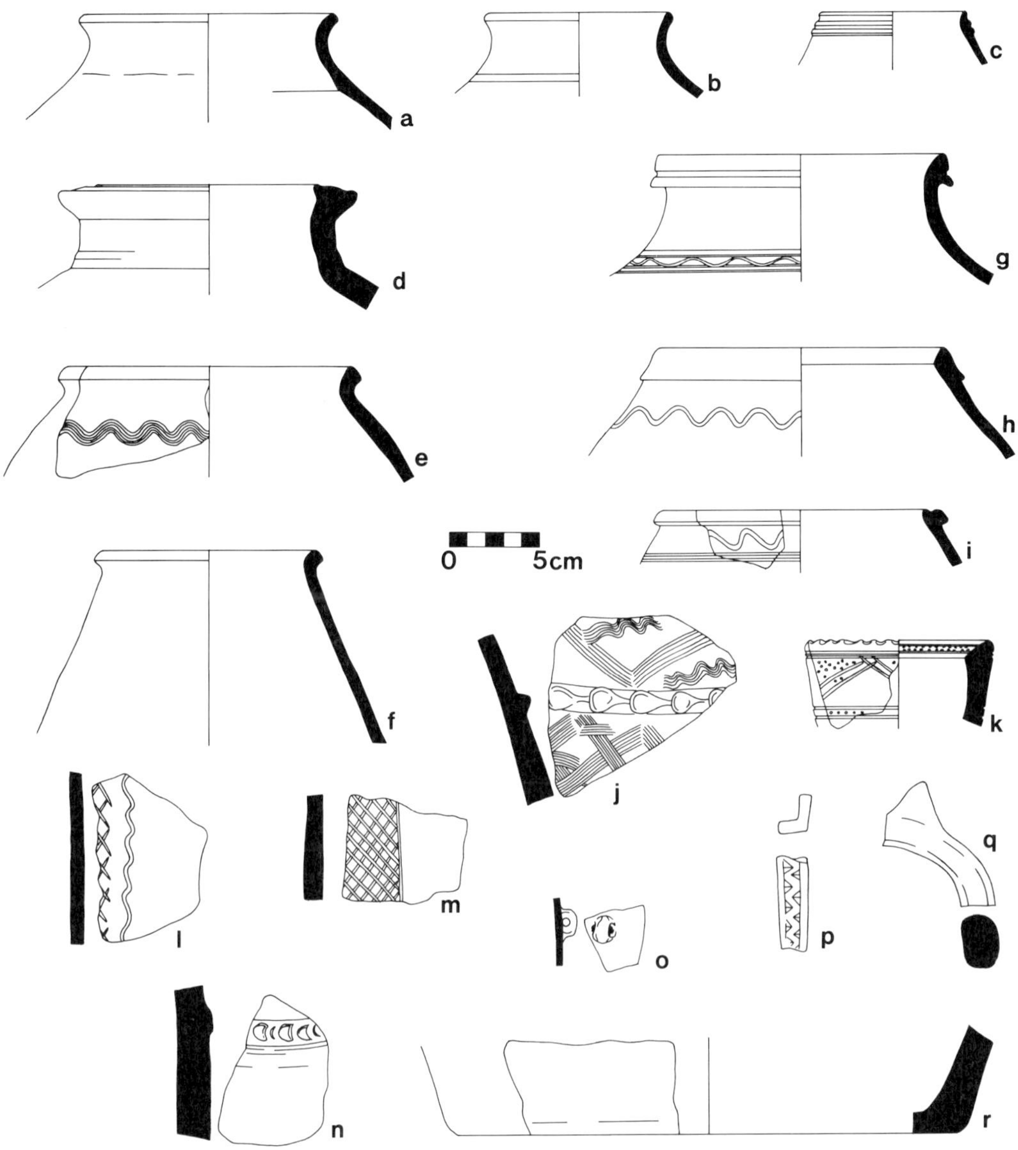

Fig. 2. Jebelain

Fig. 3

HDR 48

a buff ware; common very coarse sand and common chaff; diameter 50 cm.
b greenish-cream ware; common chaff; diameter unknown
c cream ware; moderate medium sand and common chaff; diameter 22 cm.
d orange-buff ware; moderate coarse sand and moderate chaff; diameter 15 cm.
e cream-buff ware; common very coarse sand; diameter unknown
f buff-orange ware, grey core; dark brown slip on exterior; common chaff; diameter 24 cm.
g cream ware; common chaff; diameter unknown
h greenish-cream ware; brown slip on exterior; moderate medium sand and common chaff; diameter 12 cm.
i black ware; orange surface on exterior; moderate coarse sand and abundant chaff; diameter 13 cm.
j buff-orange ware, grey core; moderate medium sand and common chaff; diameter 10 cm.
k cream ware; blue-green glaze on exterior, grey glaze on interior; moderate medium sand; diameter unknown
l black ware; brown surfaces; moderate medium sand and common chaff; diameter 18 cm.
m orange ware; cream surface on exterior; common coarse sand and common chaff; diameter 25 cm.
n buff ware; greenish-cream surface on exterior; moderate medium sand
o cream ware; green and yellow glaze on interior and exterior (spur mark on base); fine; diameter 6 cm.
p greenish-cream ware; moderate coarse sand and moderate chaff; diameter 20 cm.

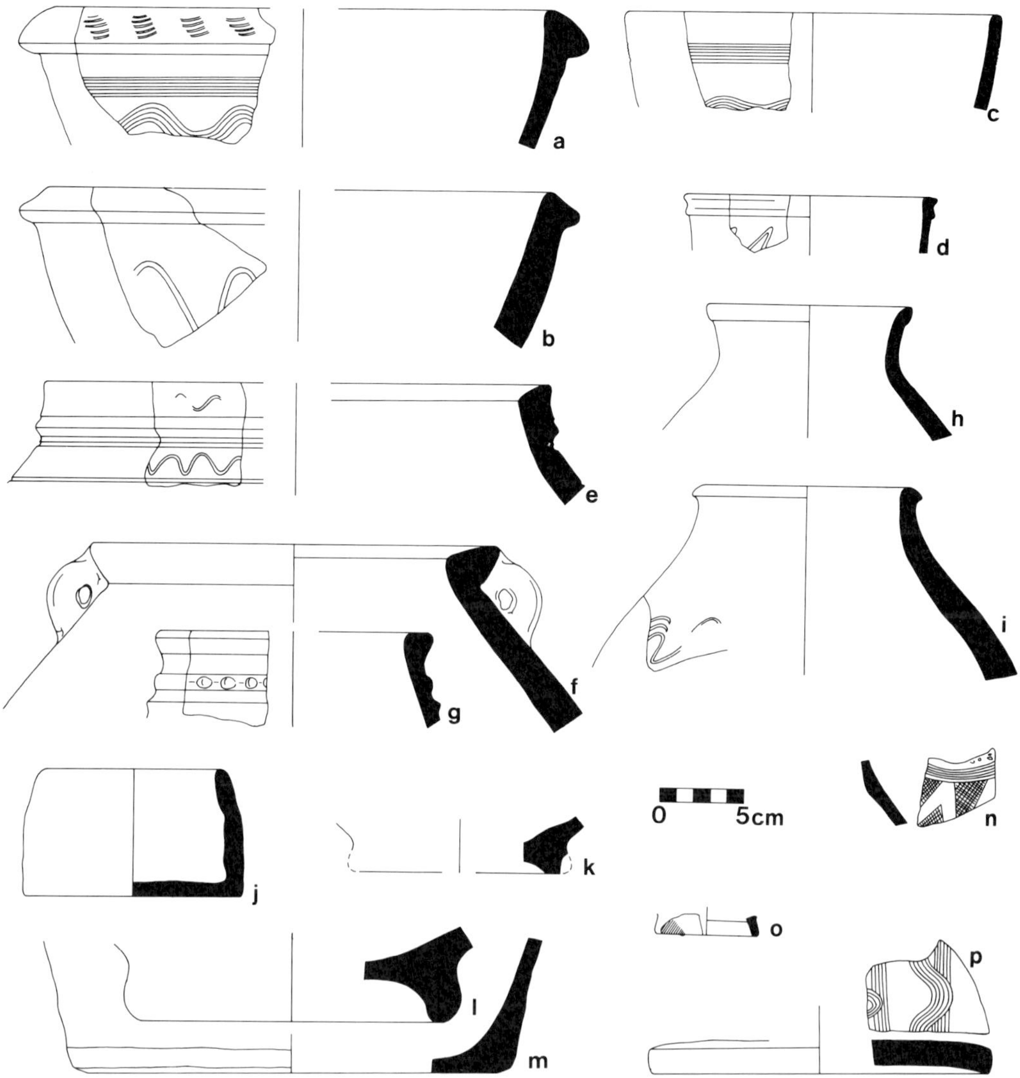

Fig. 3. HDR 48

Fig. 4

HDR 34.2

a buff ware; cream slip; moderate medium sand and coarse red sand and common chaff; diameter 30 cm.
b greenish-cream ware; moderate medium sand and moderate chaff; diameter 40 cm.
c cream-buff ware; moderate medium sand and moderate chaff; diameter 27 cm.
d buff ware; cream slip on interior and exterior; moderate medium sand and moderate chaff; diameter 20 cm.
e green-grey ware (vitrified); abundant coarse sand; diameter 14 cm.
f greenish cream ware; moderate chaff; diameter unknown
g dark orange ware; abundant coarse red sand; diameter unknown
h cream ware; blue-green glaze on interior and exterior; moderate medium sand; diameter unknown
i cream ware; gold lustre, white glaze on interior and exterior; fine; diameter unknown
j cream ware; green and white glaze on interior and exterior; moderate medium sand; diameter unknown
k cream ware; white glaze on interior and exterior; moderate medium sand; diameter 18 cm.
l cream ware; common medium and coarse black sand; diameter 8 cm.
m cream-buff ware; burned black interior; abundant chaff (badly eroded)
n cream ware; moderate medium sand
o greenish-cream ware; common medium sand and moderate chaff

HDR 29

p orange ware, buff core; traces of dark orange slip on exterior; abundant chaff; diameter 32 cm.
q orange-tan ware, red-grey core; common chaff; diameter unknown
r greenish-cream ware; traces of brown slip on exterior; abundant chaff; diameter unknown
s light grey ware; cream-buff surfaces; common medium sand and common chaff; diameter 32 cm.
t cream ware; green and white glaze on interior and exterior; fine; diameter unknown
u black ware; orange-buff surfaces; moderate coarse sand and common chaff; diameter 15 cm.
v buff ware; cream slip on interior and exterior; abundant very coarse sand; diameter 20 cm.

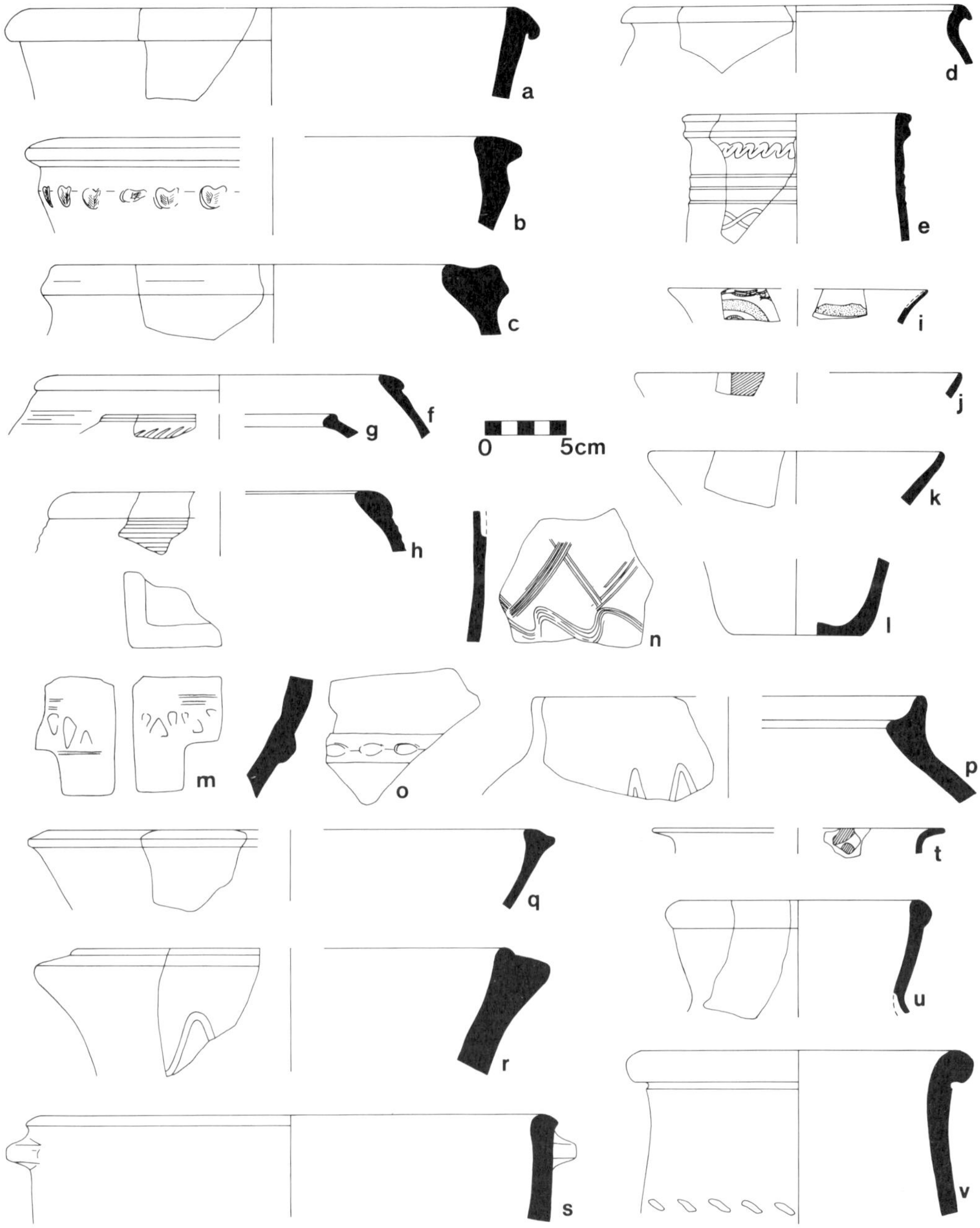

Fig. 4. HDR 34.2; HDR 29

Fig. 5

HDR 30

a greenish-cream ware; moderate medium sand and common chaff; diameter 30 cm.
b cream ware; moderate medium sand and moderate chaff; diameter 44 cm.
c orange ware, light grey core; cream slip on interior and exterior; abundant chaff; diameter 46 cm.
d cream ware, black-pink core; traces of orange slip on interior and exterior; moderate medium sand and common chaff; diameter 16 cm.
e cream-buff ware; common chaff; diameter 17 cm.
f grey-cream ware; smooth black slip or residue on interior; abundant chaff; diameter 9 cm.
g orange ware; grey surface on interior, cream slip on exterior, burned black at rim; abundant coarse sand and common chaff; diameter 32 cm.
h black ware; orange surfaces, brown slip, dark red paint; abundant chaff; diameter 22 cm.
i cream-buff ware; common coarse sand and common chaff; diameter 22 cm.
j black ware; orange surfaces, red slip on interior (and exterior?); abundant coarse sand and moderate chaff; diameter 27 cm.
k grey ware; common coarse sand and moderate chaff; diameter 16 cm.
l grey ware; abundant coarse sand and moderate chaff; diameter 11 cm.
m orange ware; brown surface on interior, cream surface on exterior; moderate coarse sand and abundant chaff; diameter unknown
n orange ware; cream slip on exterior; common medium sand and moderate chaff; diameter 42 cm.
o buff ware; grey surface on interior, brown paint; common coarse sand
p black ware; orange-brown surfaces, dark red paint; abundant chaff
q cream ware; grey surface on interior, brown paint; common coarse sand
r yellow-cream ware; black residue on exterior; moderate coarse sand and moderate chaff
s cream ware, buff core; moderate medium sand
t buff ware; cream surfaces; moderate medium sand and moderate chaff; diameter 13 cm.
u buff-orange ware, grey core; burned black on interior; abundant chaff; diameter 19 cm.

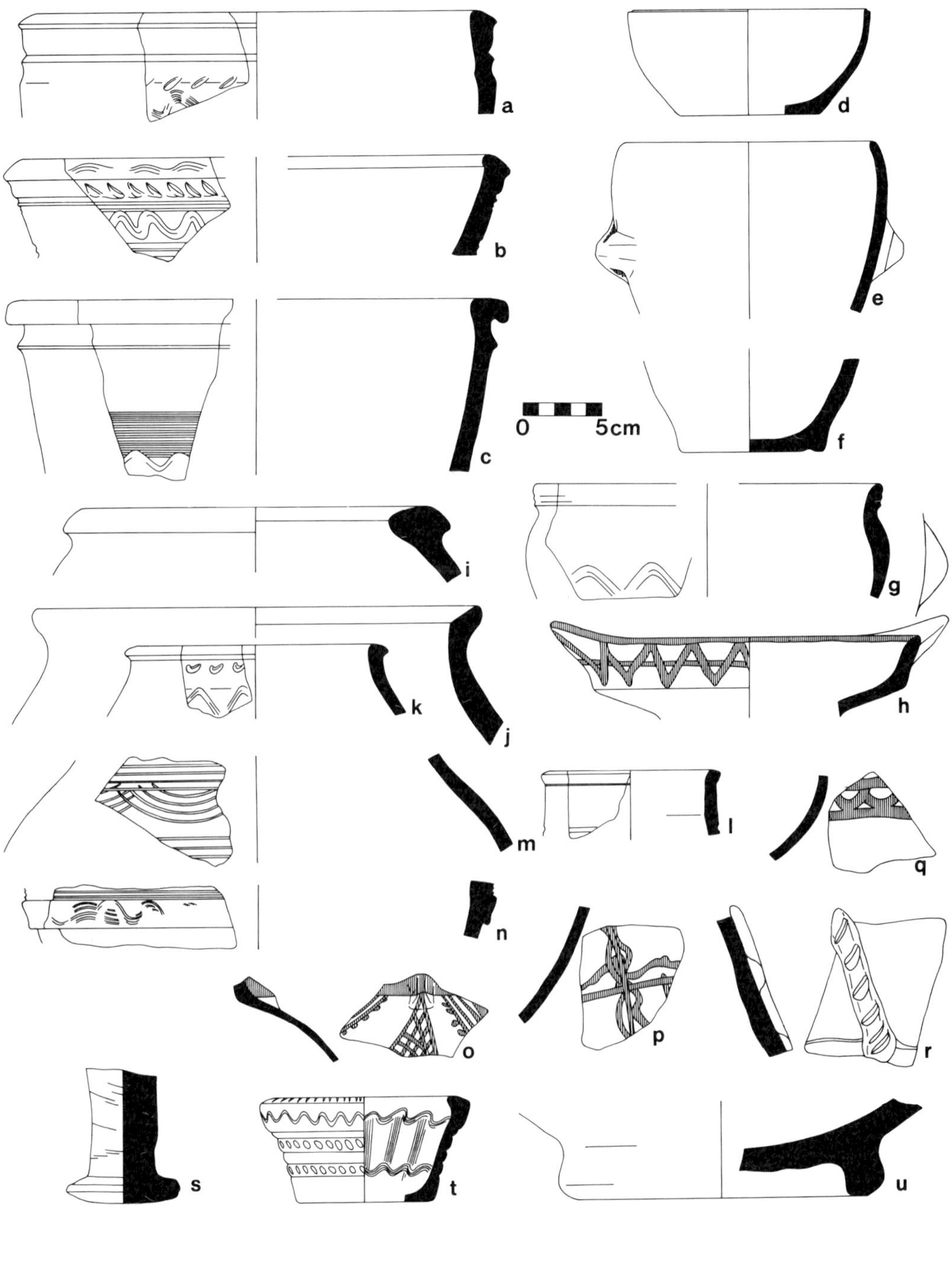

Fig. 5. HDR 30

Fig. 6

HDR 27

a cream ware; moderate medium sand and common chaff; diameter 38 cm.
b greenish-cream ware; moderate medium sand and common chaff; diameter 36 cm.
c cream ware; moderate medium sand and common chaff; diameter 30 cm.
d cream ware; moderate medium sand and common chaff; diameter 26 cm.
e cream ware; moderate medium sand and common chaff; diameter 26 cm.
f greenish-cream ware; moderate coarse sand and moderate chaff; diameter 12 cm.
g cream ware; moderate medium sand and common chaff; diameter 9 cm.
h greenish-cream ware; moderate medium sand and common chaff; diameter 18 cm.
i cream ware; moderate medium sand and common chaff; diameter 11 cm.
j grey ware; brown surface on exterior; common chaff; diameter 18 cm.
k cream ware; moderate medium sand and common chaff; diameter 22 cm.
l cream ware; blue-green glaze on exterior; moderate medium sand

HDR 28

m brown ware; greenish-cream surfaces; moderate chaff; diameter 22 cm.
n grey ware; red-brown surface on interior, cream slip on exterior; moderate chaff; diameter 17 cm.
o black ware; orange surface on exterior, red slip, purple and white paint; common chaff
p greenish-cream ware; common coarse sand and moderate chaff
q red-brown ware; cream surfaces; moderate coarse sand and common chaff; diameter 28 cm.
r grey-brown ware; moderate chaff; diameter 8 cm.
s buff ware; cream surfaces and slip; common chaff; diameter 20 cm.
t greenish-cream ware; common chaff; diameter 26 cm.

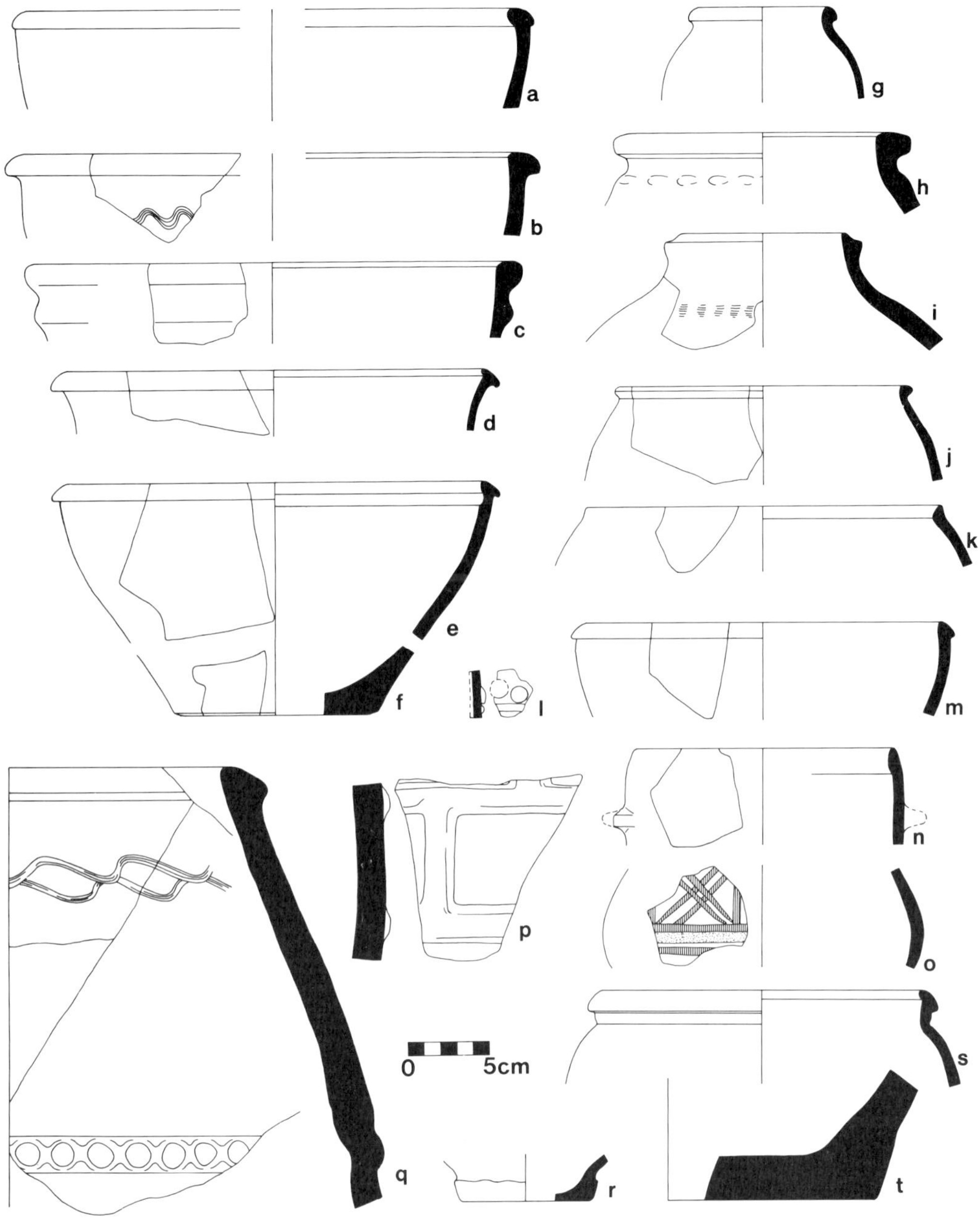

Fig. 6. HDR 27; HDR 28

Fig. 7

HDR 20

- **a** cream ware; moderate coarse red sand and abundant chaff; diameter 38 cm.
- **b** buff-orange ware, light grey core; dark red slip on interior and exterior; moderate medium sand and abundant chaff; diameter 30 cm.
- **c** buff-orange ware; cream surface on exterior; moderate medium sand and common chaff; diameter 24 cm.
- **d** light cream ware; moderate medium sand and common chaff; diameter 14 cm.
- **e** brown ware; cream slip on interior and exterior; moderate medium sand and moderate chaff; diameter 14 cm.
- **f** cream ware; common medium sand and moderate chaff; diameter 14 cm.
- **g** cream-grey ware; abundant chaff; diameter 12 cm.
- **h** orange ware, buff core; dark orange slip on exterior; abundant chaff
- **i** cream ware; blue-green glaze on exterior, greenish-white glaze on interior; fine
- **j** buff-grey ware; black slip on exterior; abundant chaff
- **k** buff ware; thick smear of white slip on exterior; moderate medium sand and common chaff; diameter 9 cm.
- **l** orange ware, buff-grey core; moderate coarse red sand and common chaff; diameter 12 cm.

HDR 19

- **m** orange ware; common chaff; diameter 17 cm.
- **n** orange ware; common chaff; diameter 17 cm.
- **o** buff-orange ware, grey core; white slip on exterior and interior; common chaff
- **p** black ware; orange surfaces, white slip on exterior; common chaff; diameter 12 cm.
- **q** buff ware, orange core; cream slip; common chaff; diameter 30 cm.

Fig. 7. HDR 20; HDR 19

Fig. 8

HDR 34.1

- **a** greenish-cream ware; orange slip on interior and exterior; common very coarse sand and moderate chaff; diameter 30 cm.
- **b** greenish-cream ware; orange slip on interior and exterior, brownish at rim; common medium sand and moderate chaff; diameter 24 cm.
- **c** cream-tan ware; moderate medium sand and moderate chaff; diameter 30 cm.
- **d** buff ware; orange-brown surfaces; moderate coarse sand and abundant chaff; diameter 46 cm.
- **e** greenish-cream ware; dark brown slip on interior and exterior; moderate coarse sand and abundant chaff; diameter 16 cm.
- **f** buff ware; moderate medium sand and moderate chaff; diameter 14 cm.
- **g** buff ware, grey core; cream slip, light brown slip on exterior; moderate coarse sand and common chaff; diameter 36 cm.
- **h** buff-cream ware, black core; brown-orange slip on interior and exterior; moderate medium sand and abundant chaff; diameter 30 cm.
- **i** red-brown ware, black core; cream surfaces, orange slip on interior, red-brown slip on exterior; moderate coarse sand and common chaff; diameter 36 cm.
- **j** buf-tan ware; moderate medium sand and moderate chaff; diameter 24 cm.
- **k** buff ware; greenish-cream surfaces; common coarse sand and common chaff; diameter 20 cm.
- **l** brown ware; dark red surface on interior; greenish-cream surface on exterior; common chaff; diameter 9 cm.
- **m** yellow-cream ware; moderate medium sand and common chaff
- **n** grey-cream ware; greenish-cream surfaces; common coarse sand and moderate chaff; diameter 30 cm.

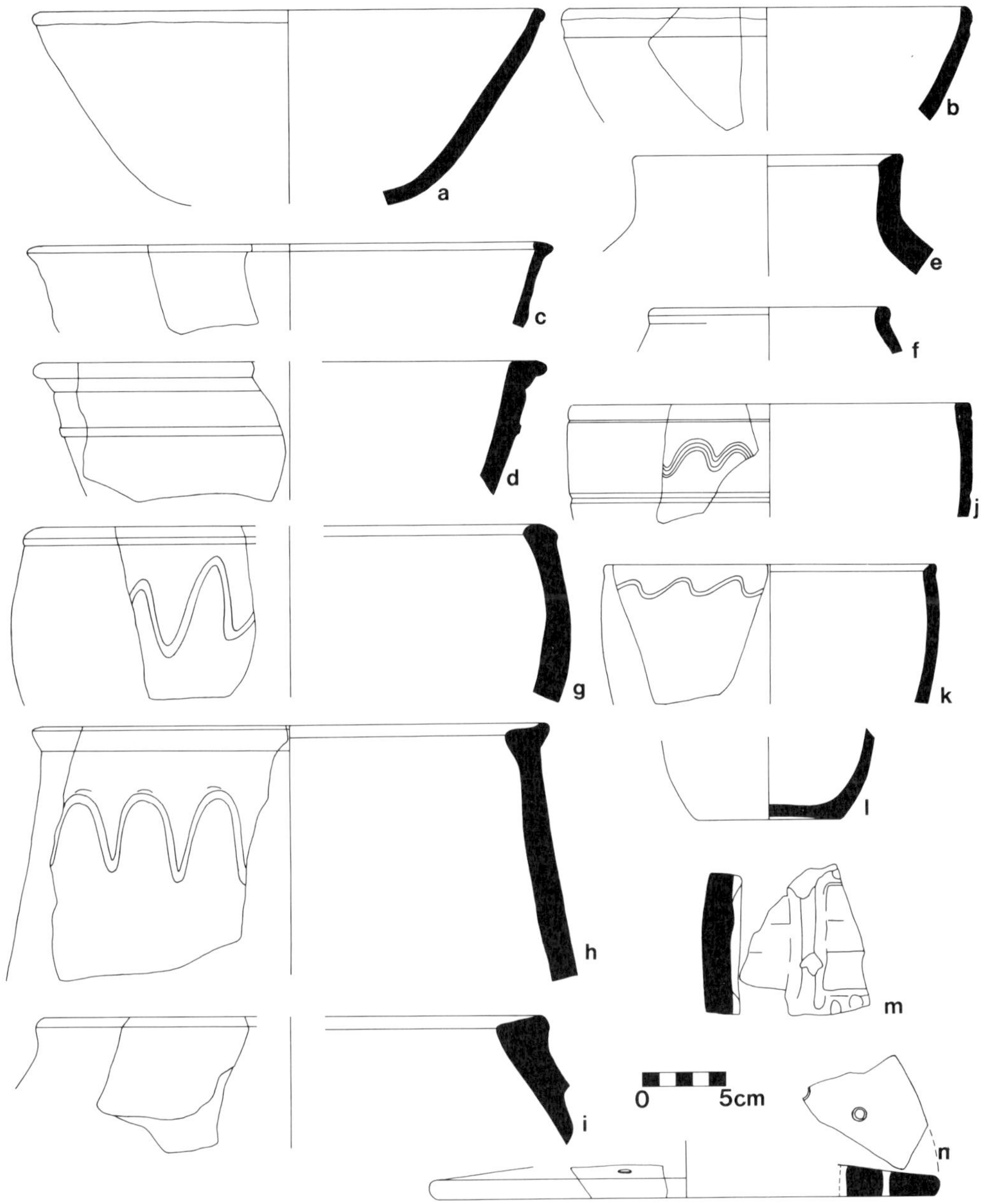

Fig. 8. HDR 34.1

Fig. 9

Qaraw

a brown ware; greenish cream surface on exterior; common medium sand and moderate chaff; diameter 33 cm.
b red ware; cream surfaces; abundant medium sand; diameter 46 cm.
c brown ware, black core at rim; common medium sand and moderate chaff; diameter 25 cm.
d red-brown ware; common medium sand; diameter 19 cm.
e greenish-cream ware; abundant medium sand; diameter 11 cm.
f brown ware; common medium sand and moderate chaff; diameter 11 cm.
g brown ware; cream surface on exterior; abundant medium sand and moderate chaff; diameter 19 cm.
h cream-tan ware; grey burned interior; abundant chaff; diameter 9 cm.
i red-orange ware; cream surfaces, moderate medium sand; diameter 4 cm.
j buff-orange ware; moderate medium sand and abundant chaff; diameter 18 cm.
k buff ware; cream surfaces; common medium sand and moderate chaff
l brown ware; cream slip on exterior; common medium sand; diameter 11 cm.
m greenish-cream ware; common medium sand and moderate chaff; diameter 8 cm.
n dark red ware; glossy olive green glaze; moderate medium sand; diameter 27 cm.
o red-brown ware; yellow glaze on interior, brown paint; common medium sand; diameter 27 cm.
p grey-green ware (vitrified); traces of yellow glaze; common medium sand; diameter 28 cm.
q red-ware; grey-green glaze on interior and rim; common medium sand; diameter 21 cm.
r red-orange ware; red glaze on interior, stripe of grey glaze on interior; common medium sand; diameter 15 cm.

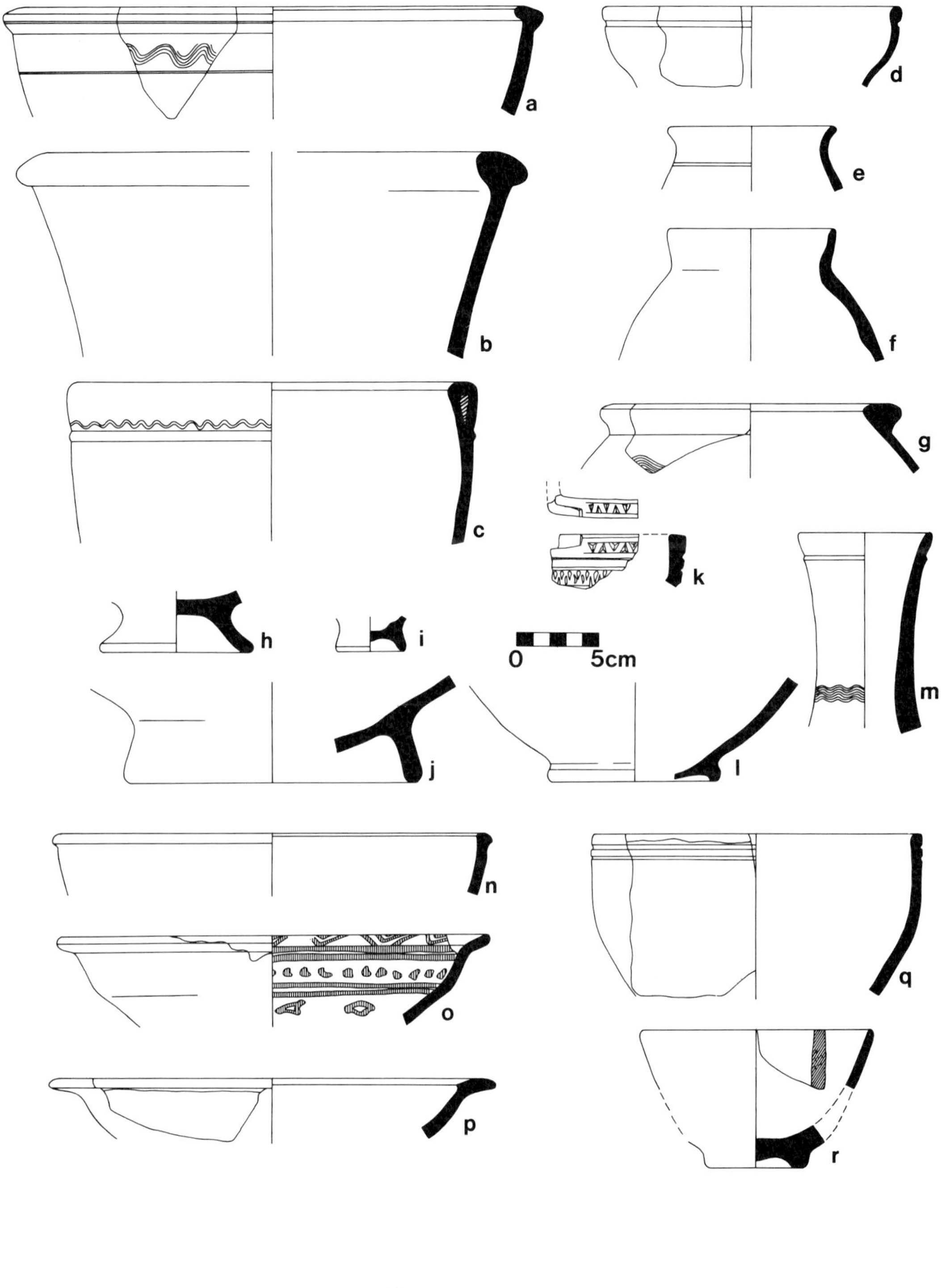

Fig. 9. Qaraw

Fig. 10

Khanfar

a red-buff ware; grey-green glaze on interior; moderate medium sand; diameter 26 cm.
b red ware; light blue and white glaze; common medium sand; diameter unknown
c red ware; turquoise blue glaze on interior and exterior, slip painted; moderate medium sand; diameter unknown
d red ware; turquoise blue glaze on interior and exterior, slip painted; moderate medium sand
e white ware; blue paint under clear glaze; grit; diameter 8 cm.
f red ware; blue and white glaze; moderate medium sand; diameter unknown
g red ware; blue, green and white glaze; fine; diameter unknown
h red ware; yellowish-white, brown, turquoise under clear glaze; common medium sand
i red ware; white slip, red paint, turquoise and clear glaze; common medium sand
j red ware; blue and white glaze; moderate coarse sand
k red ware; white glaze on interior; common medium sand; diameter 13 cm.
l red ware; dark red slip, burnished on exterior; common coarse sand and common chaff; diameter unknown
m orange ware; red slip; moderate medium sand and moderate chaff; diameter unknown
n red ware; cream slip on interior and exterior, turquoise blue glaze on interior common medium sand; diameter 8 cm.
o cream ware; glossy yellow glaze on interior and exterior, incised decoration; fine
p cream ware; glossy yellow glaze on interior, green glaze on exterior (not base); fine; diameter 4 cm.
q cream ware; blue and white glaze; fine; diameter 5 cm.
r cream ware; glossy yellow glaze on interior and exterior; fine
s buff ware; turquoise glaze on interior and exterior; fine; diameter 8 cm.
t buff ware; green glaze on interior and exterior, incised; moderate medium sand; diameter 9 cm.
u cream-buff ware; glossy green glaze on interior and exterior, incised; fine; diameter 10 cm.
v buff-orange ware; yellow glaze on interior; fine; diameter 4 cm.
w cream ware; green glaze on exterior, yellow glaze on interior; fine; diameter 4 cm.
x buff-cream ware; greenish-white glaze on interior and exterior; fine; diameter 4 cm.
y dark red ware; moderate medium sand and common chaff; diameter unknown
z orange-red ware; moderate medium sand and moderate chaff; diameter 7 cm.
aa buff-tan ware; moderate medium mica and moderate chaff; diameter 5 cm.
bb orange-brown ware; greenish-cream slip on exterior; moderate medium sand and moderate chaff
cc orange-red ware; common chaff
dd brown-black ware; common coarse sand; diameter 15 cm.
ee brown ware, black core; abundant medium sand with mica; diameter 19 cm.
ff red ware; dark red slip on exterior; common chaff; diameter 13 cm.
gg red ware; moderate medium sand with mica and moderate chaff; diameter 10 cm.

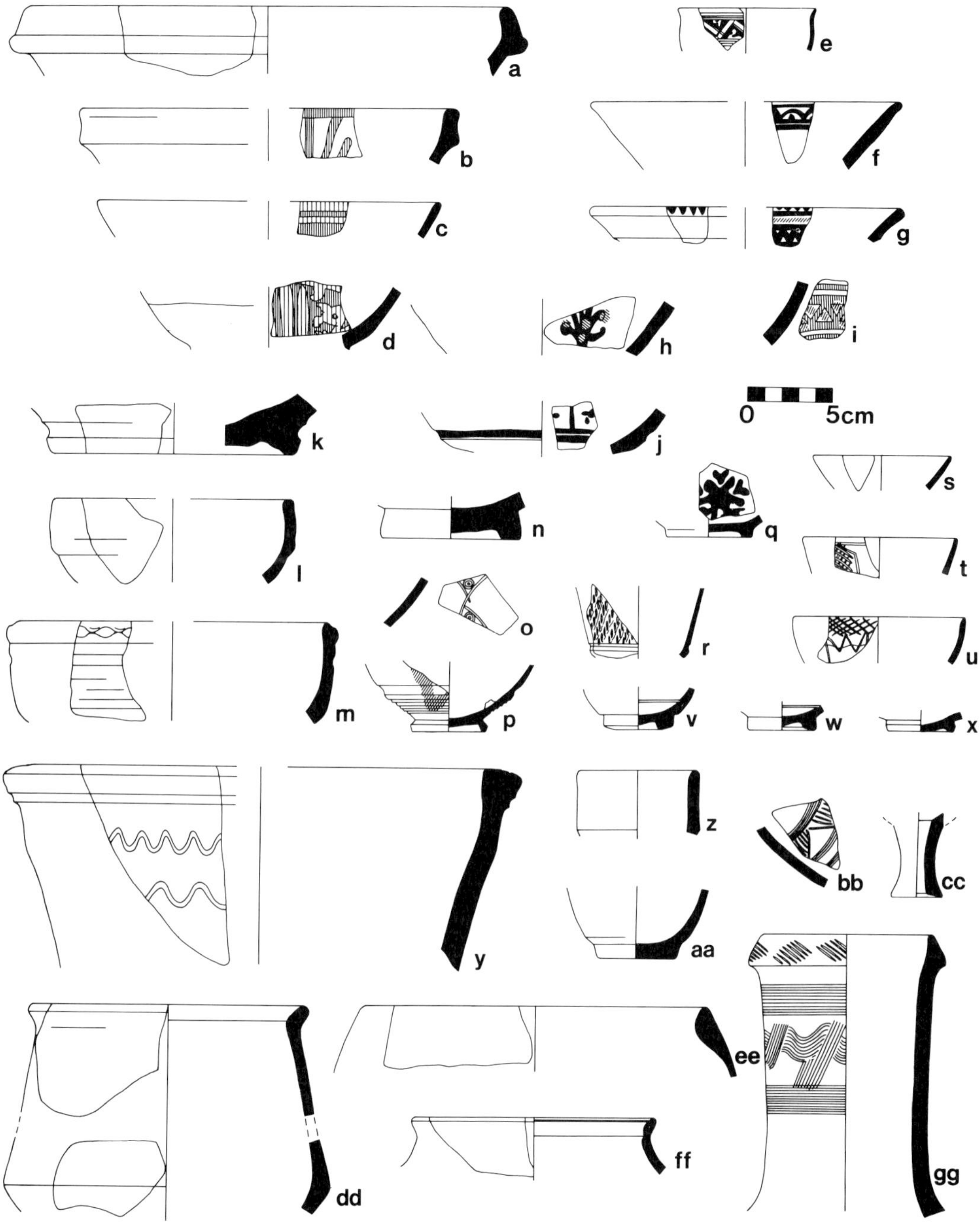

Fig. 10. Khanfar

Fig. 11

Kawd am-Saila

a orange-red ware; moderate coarse sand and moderate chaff; diameter 22 cm.

b red ware; brown surfaces; common medium sand and moderate chaff; diameter 24 cm.

c orange-tan ware; common medium sand; diameter 16 cm.

d brown ware; abundant medium sand with mica; diameter 27 cm.

e red ware; orange surfaces, scraped base; common medium sand with mica and moderate chaff; diameter 16 cm.

f red ware; moderate medium mica and common chaff; diameter 21 cm. (badly eroded)

g red-brown ware; moderate coarse sand and abundant chaff; diameter 46 cm.

h red ware; moderate coarse sand and abundant chaff; diameter 24 cm.

i brown ware, grey core; abundant coarse sand; diameter 23 cm.

j red ware; orange surfaces; common coarse black sand; diameter unknown

k buff-orange ware, grey core; traces of red slip; moderate medium sand; diameter 14 cm.

l brown ware; moderate coarse sand; diameter 15 cm.

m buff-brown ware; abundant coarse sand; diameter 6 cm.

n red ware; purple-brown paint; common very coarse sand

o buff-orange ware, grey core; burnished red slip on exterior, black paint on exterior; moderate medium sand

p cream-tan ware; paddle stamp; common medium sand

q brown ware; incised; moderate medium sand

r orange-tan ware; abundant medium sand

s dark red ware; clear glaze on interior, exterior and broken surfaces; abundant medium sand and moderate chaff; diameter 12 cm.

t brown ware; abundant medium sand

u orange ware; moderate medium sand and moderate chaff

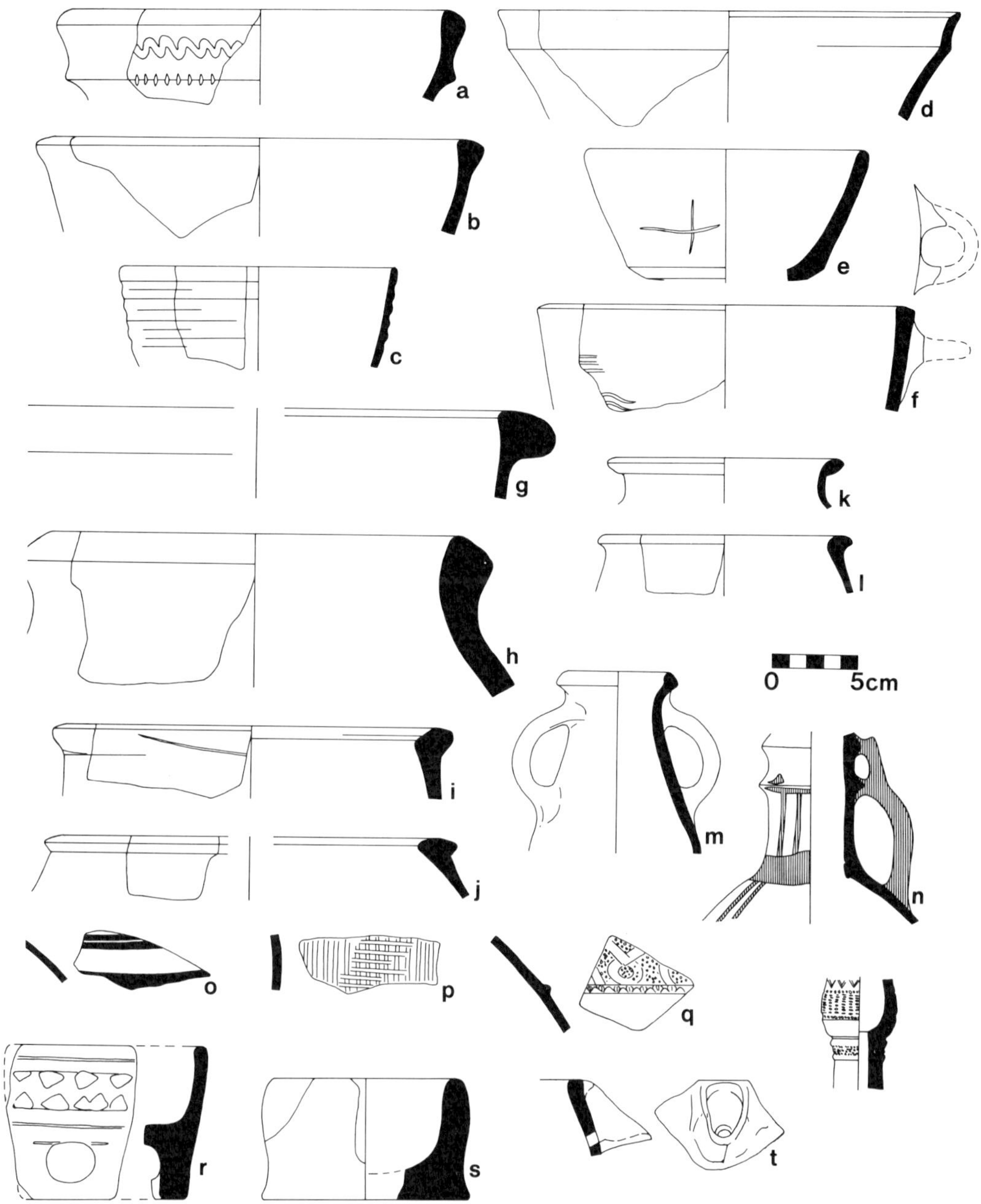

Fig. 11. Kawd am-Saila

Fig. 12

Kawd am-Saila

a red ware; blue and white glaze on interior and exterior; common medium sand; diameter 24 cm.
b red ware; blue and white glaze on interior and exterior; common medium sand; diameter 18 cm.
c red ware; blue and white glaze on interior and exterior; common medium sand; diameter 22 cm.
d red ware; blue and white glaze on interior and exterior; abundant medium sand; diameter 12 cm.
e red ware; blue and white glaze on interior and exterior; common medium sand; diameter 23 cm.
f red ware; white slip, blue and clear glaze on interior, white glaze on exterior; common medium sand; diameter 10 cm.
g red ware; blue and white glaze on interior, white glaze on exterior; common coarse sand; diameter 25 cm.
h red ware; black, turquoise and clear glaze; common medium sand; diameter unknown
i red ware; greyish-white glaze on interior; moderate medium sand; diameter 8 cm.
j cream ware; blue and clear glaze; moderate medium sand; diameter 13 cm.
k red ware; yellow and green glaze; abundant medium sand
l cream ware; blue and white glaze; fine; diameter 4 cm.
m cream ware; blue and clear glaze; fine; diameter 19 cm.
n cream ware; blue and clear glaze; fine; diameter 7 cm.
o red ware; brown surface on exterior, green glaze on interior and rim; common medium sand; diameter 23 cm.
p red ware; light blue glaze, slip painted; common medium sand; diameter 14 cm.
q red ware; yellow and green glaze on interior and rim; common medium sand; diameter 17 cm.
r red ware; green glaze, slip painted; common medium sand; diameter 12 cm.
s red ware; white slip on interior and over rim, yellow glaze on interior; moderate coarse sand; diameter 11 cm.
t red ware; light blue-green glaze; common medium sand; diameter 12 cm.
u red ware; green glaze, slip painted; moderate coarse sand; diameter 20 cm.
v red ware; green and clear glaze; common medium sand; diameter 10 cm.
w cream-buff ware; green glaze on interior and exterior; fine; diameter 8 cm.
x cream-buff ware; green glaze on interior and exterior; fine; diameter 8 cm.
y red ware; greenish-yellow glaze on interior and exterior; moderate medium sand; diameter 6 cm.
z pink-buff ware; yellow glaze on interior, mottled green glaze on exterior; fine; diameter 10 cm.
aa red ware; green glaze on interior and exterior; moderate medium sand; diameter 4 cm.
bb cream ware; yellow glaze (brown where thick); fine; diameter 4 cm.
cc red ware; green glaze on interior and exterior; moderate medium sand; diameter 7 cm.
dd cream-buff ware; olive green glaze on interior and exterior; moderate medium sand; diameter 5 cm.
ee buff ware; dark green glaze on interior and exterior; common medium sand; diameter 4 cm.

Fig. 12. Kawd am-Saila

Fig. 13

HDR 25

- **a** black ware; orange-brown surfaces, red slip on interior and exterior; moderate coarse sand and abundant chaff; diameter 36 cm.
- **b** cream ware; moderate medium sand and moderate chaff; diameter 38 cm.
- **c** orange-brown ware; cream surface and brown slip on exterior, red slip on interior; moderate coarse sand and common chaff (partially vitrified); diameter 20 cm.
- **d** cream ware; grey-brown slip; moderate medium sand and moderate chaff; diameter 19 cm.
- **e** black ware; cream-buff surfaces, red-brown paint; common chaff; diameter 17 cm.
- **f** red ware; cream slip on interior, red slip on exterior, red paint; abundant chaff; diameter 15 cm.
- **g** orange-brown ware; traces of red slip; moderate coarse sand and abundant chaff; diameter 14 cm.
- **h** buff-orange ware, black core; brown paint; common chaff; diameter 6 cm.
- **i** cream ware; black slip on interior and exterior; common chaff; diameter 10 cm.
- **j** grey ware, black core; black burnish on exterior; common coarse sand; diameter 14 cm.
- **k** cream ware; red-brown slip; common chaff; diameter 20 cm.
- **l** black ware; orange surfaces, cream slip, red paint; common coarse sand and common chaff; diameter 21 cm.
- **m** black ware; blackened exterior; common coarse sand; diameter 19 cm.
- **n** grey-black ware; burnished dark grey slip on interior and exterior; common coarse sand
- **o** black ware; brown surfaces, cream slip on interior and exterior, brown paint; common chaff; diameter 14 cm.
- **p** buff-orange ware, black core; dark orange slip on interior and exterior, black paint; moderate coarse sand and moderate chaff; diameter 4 cm.
- **q** buff-cream ware; abundant chaff
- **r** brown-grey ware; cream surface on exterior, brown paint; common medium and moderate coarse sand and moderate chaff
- **s** cream ware; yellow glaze on exterior, light green glaze on interior; fine
- **t** buff-grey ware; orange surfaces; moderate coarse sand and moderate chaff; diameter 20 cm.

Fig. 13. HDR 25

Fig. 14

HDR 18

- **a** grey ware; burnished grey slip; moderate medium sand; diameter 20 cm.
- **b** black-buff ware; brown slip on exterior; moderate medium sand and moderate chaff; diameter 22 cm.
- **c** greenish-cream ware; black slip on interior and exterior; moderate medium sand and common chaff; diameter 20 cm.
- **d** buff ware; green glaze on exterior, yellow clear glaze on interior; moderate medium sand; diameter 10 cm.
- **e** cream ware; dark brown paint; common chaff; diameter 12 cm.
- **f** grey ware; burnished interior; common medium sand
- **g** buff ware, grey core; burnished orange-buff surfaces; common coarse sand; diameter 15 cm.
- **h** black ware; red-orange surfaces, traces of red slip on exterior; common chaff; diameter 8 cm.
- **i** greenish-cream ware; black slip on interior and exterior; common very coarse sand; diameter 22 cm.
- **j** black ware; orange surfaces, cream slip, black paint; moderate medium sand and common chaff

HDR 17

- **k** black ware; orange surfaces, cream slip, red-brown paint; common chaff; diameter 40 cm.
- **l** red-orange ware; red slip on interior and exterior; moderate coarse sand and common chaff; diameter unknown
- **m** black ware; orange surfaces, cream slip, brown paint; common chaff
- **n** buff-orange ware; burnished red slip; common chaff
- **o** buff ware; brownish-green glaze on interior and exterior; moderate medium sand; diameter 14 cm.
- **p** orange ware; burnished red slip on interior and exterior; common chaff; diameter 8 cm.
- **q** cream-grey ware; burnished dark red-brown slip on interior and exterior; common chaff; diameter 6 cm.
- **r** black ware; orange surface on exterior, cream slip on interior and exterior, red paint on exterior and black paint on interior; common chaff; diameter 13 cm.
- **s** grey ware; orange surface on exterior, burnished and red paint; common medium sand
- **t** black ware; orange surfaces, cream slip, brown paint; common chaff; diameter 8 cm.

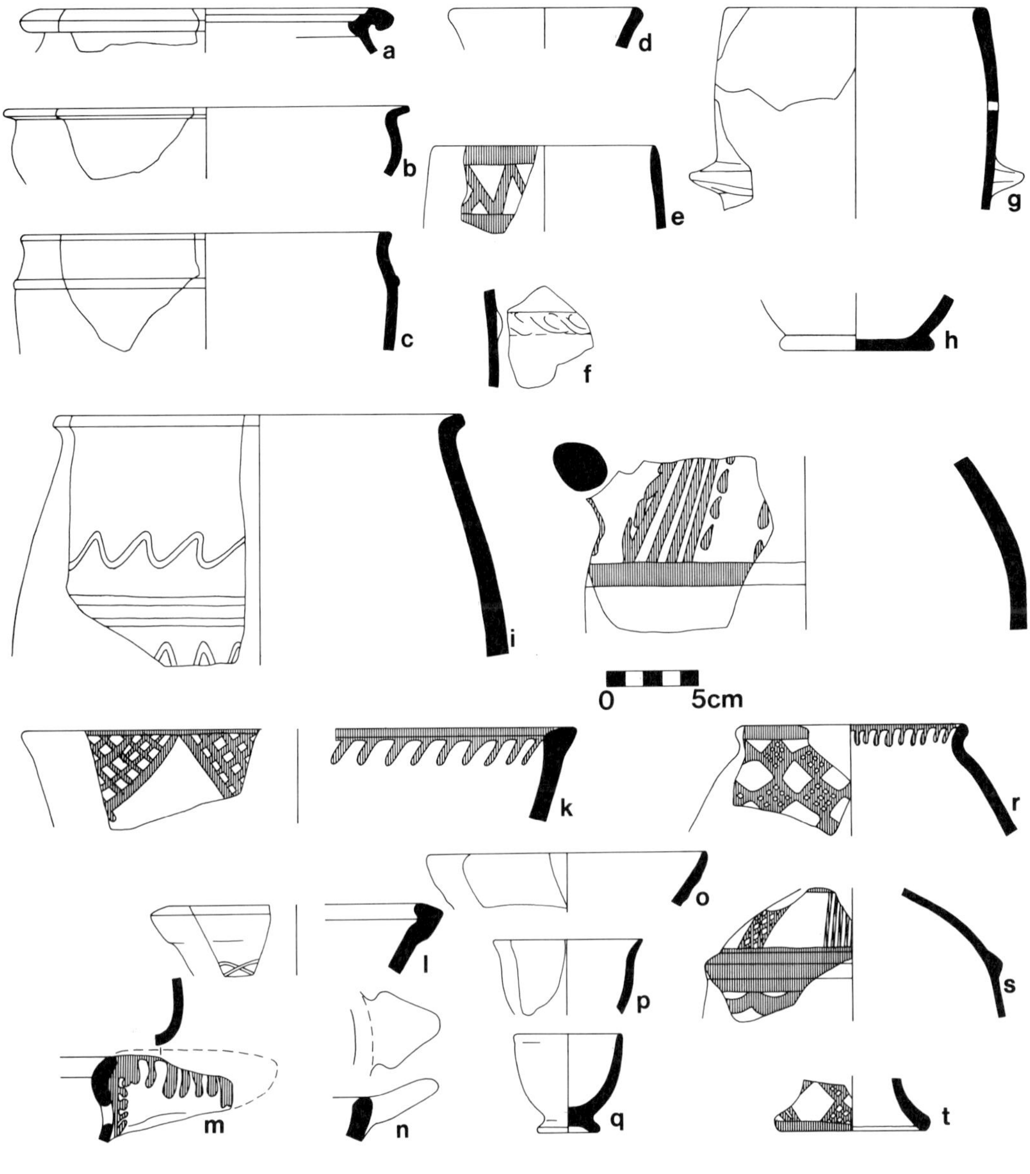

Fig. 14. HDR 18; HDR 17

Fig. 15

HDR 6

- **a** buff ware; red slip on interior and exterior; abundant chaff; diameter 36 cm.
- **b** cream-buff ware; burnished red slip on interior and exterior; common chaff; diameter 14 cm.
- **c** brown-grey ware; burnished grey-brown slip on interior and exterior; common coarse sand; diameter 16 cm.
- **d** buff-cream ware; burnished red-brown slip on interior and exterior; common chaff; diameter 8 cm.
- **e** black ware; orange-brown surfaces, cream slip on interior and exterior; abundant chaff; diameter 40 cm.
- **f** black ware; orange surfaces, cream slip on interior and exterior, red-brown paint; common chaff; diameter 14 cm.
- **g** cream ware; brown slip on interior and exterior; moderate chaff; diameter 24 cm.
- **h** black ware; orange surfaces on exterior, red slip on exterior, purple paint; common chaff

HDR 7

- **i** buff-cream ware; red paint; abundant chaff; diameter 16 cm.
- **j** orange ware; buff surfaces; moderate chaff; diameter 16 cm.
- **k** cream ware; red slip on interior and exterior; moderate medium sand and common chaff; diameter 26 cm.
- **l** orange-buff ware; mottled brown glaze on interior and exterior; fine; diameter 12 cm.
- **m** greenish-cream ware; black paint; moderate chaff; diameter 8 cm.
- **n** greenish-cream ware; red-brown paint; moderate chaff; diameter 6 cm.
- **o** greenish-cream ware; moderate very coarse sand and common chaff; diameter 20 cm.
- **p** black ware; buff-orange surface on exterior, orange-red slip on exterior, grey slip on interior; moderate very coarse sand and abundant chaff; diameter 50 cm.
- **q** cream ware; red slip on interior and exterior; moderate chaff; diameter unknown (handle?)
- **r** orange-buff ware, grey core; cream slip on exterior, brown paint; common chaff; diameter 14 cm.

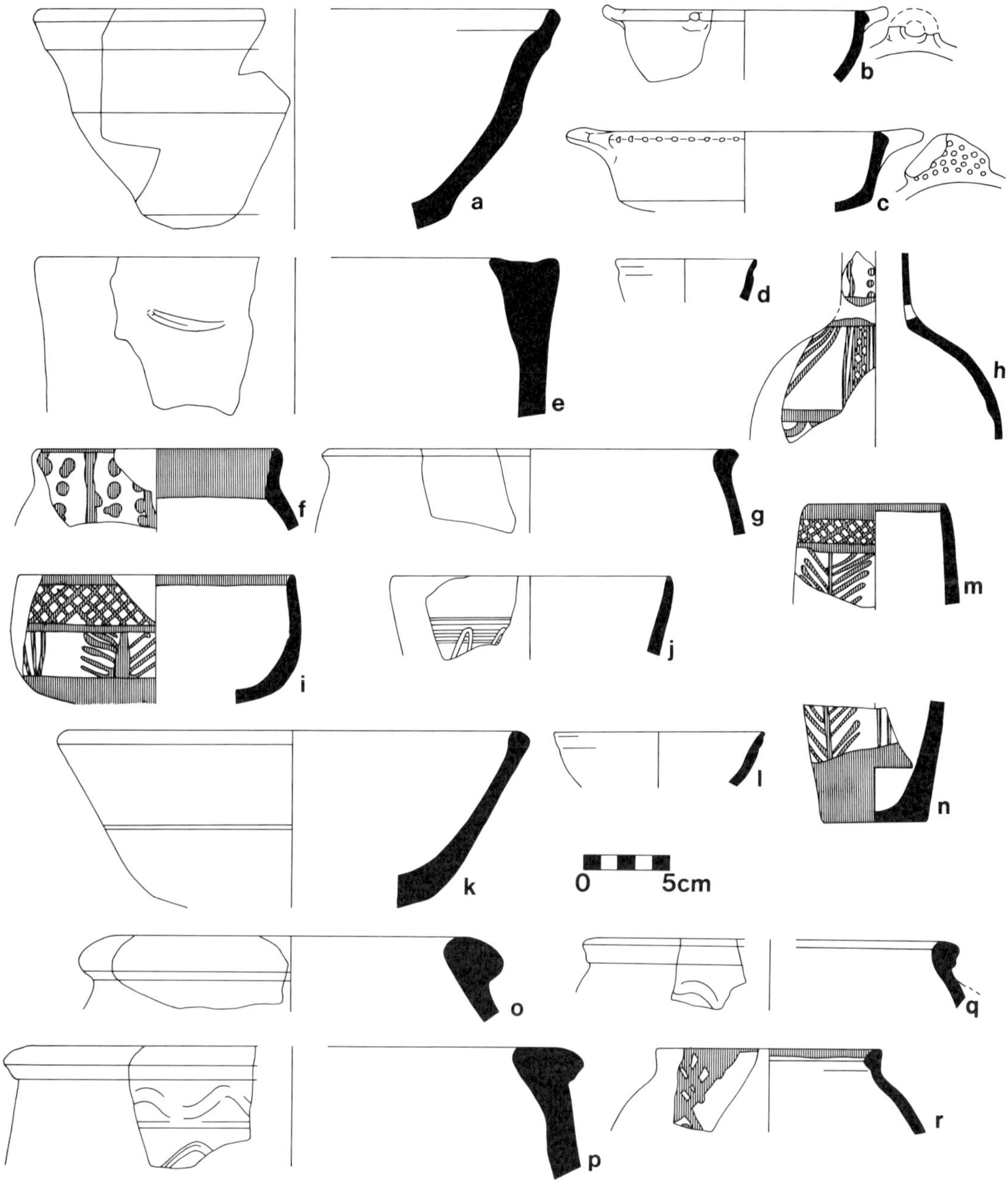

Fig. 15. HDR 6; HDR 7

Fig. 16

HDR 5

a greenish-cream ware; moderate coarse sand and common chaff; diameter 36 cm.
b black ware; orange-red surfaces, cream slip, brown paint; abundant chaff; diameter unknown
c orange ware; cream surfaces, orange slip on exterior, yellow-orange slip on interior, red paint; common chaff; diameter 22 cm.
d cream-buff ware; dark red-brown slip on interior and exterior; common coarse sand and moderate chaff; diameter 26 cm.
e orange ware, black core; red slip on interior and exterior; common chaff; diameter 7 cm.
f black ware; orange surfaces, cream slip, brown paint; common chaff
g orange-red ware, black core; burnished red slip on interior and exterior; common caff; diameter 12 cm.
h dark red ware, black core; red surfaces; abundant chaff
i grey-black ware; orange surfaces, red slip; common coarse sand and common chaff
j black ware; orange surfaces, cream slip on exterior; common chaff; diameter 18 cm.
k buff-tan ware; red slip on interior and exterior; moderate chaff; diameter 19 cm.
l grey-brown ware; abundant coarse sand; diameter 23 cm.
m black ware; burnished exterior; abundant coarse sand; diameter 23 cm.
n grey ware; burnished exterior; abundant very coarse sand
o black ware; buff surface on interior, dark orange surface on exterior, purple paint; common very coarse sand and moderate chaff; diameter 5 cm.
p black ware; orange surfaces, red slip, purple paint; common chaff; diameter 5 cm.
q greenish-cream ware; moderate medium sand and moderate chaff; diameter 8 cm.
r red ware, black core; cream slip on interior and exterior; abundant chaff; diameter 14 cm.
s red ware; orange surfaces; common coarse red sand and common chaff (finger marks); diameter 21 cm.

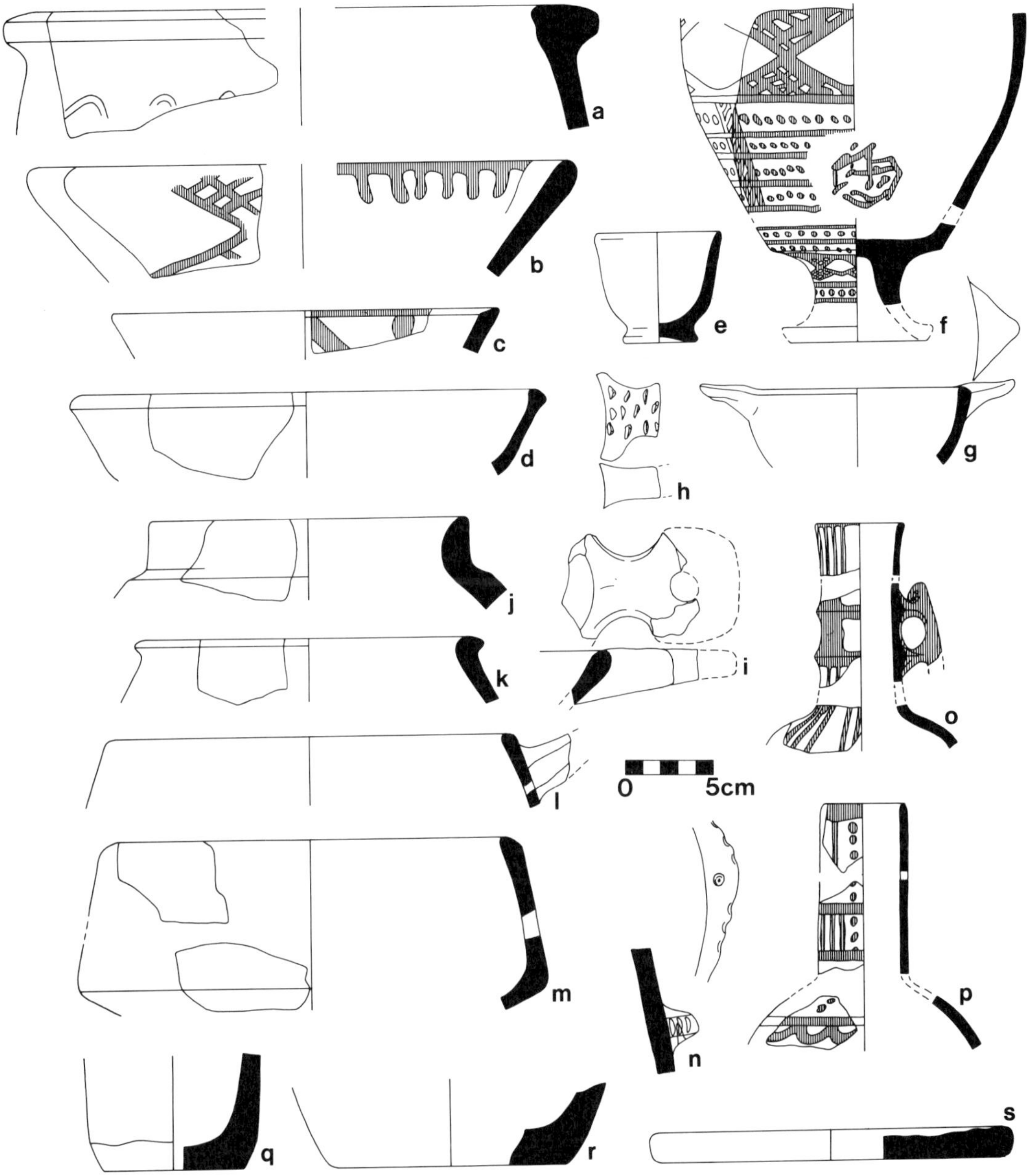

Fig. 16. HDR 5

Fig. 17

HDR 9

- **a** black ware; orange surfaces; cream slip, brown paint; common chaff; diameter 36 cm.
- **b** orange ware; red slip on interior and exterior; moderate coarse sand and common chaff; diameter 31 cm.
- **c** buff-orange ware, grey core; trace of cream slip on exterior; moderate coarse sand and common chaff; diameter 36 cm.
- **d** brown ware; orange surfaces, cream slip on interior and exterior, red paint; common chaff; diameter 17 cm.
- **e** black ware; orange surfaces, cream slip on interior and exterior, red-brown paint; common chaff; diameter 6 cm.
- **f** black ware; orange surfaces, cream slip on exterior, traces of brown paint; common chaff; diameter 8 cm.
- **g** black ware; orange surface on exterior, cream slip on exterior, brown paint; common chaff; diameter 13 cm.
- **h** black ware; orange surfaces, traces of cream slip; abundant chaff
- **i** black ware; orange surfaces, cream slip, brown paint; common chaff; diameter 16 cm.

HDR 10

- **j** black ware; cream-orange surfaces, dark brown slip on interior and exterior; abundant chaff; diameter unknown
- **k** orange ware; abundant medium sand; diameter 19 cm.
- **l** cream ware; red slip on interior and exterior; common chaff; diameter 19 cm.
- **m** buff-cream ware; red slip on interior and exterior; common very coarse sand and abundant chaff; diameter 23 cm.
- **n** greenish-cream ware; black slip on exterior; abundant chaff; diameter 20 cm.
- **o** orange-buff ware; orange-red slip on interior, blackened slip on exterior, black paint; common chaff; diameter 10 cm.
- **p** black ware; orange surfaces, cream slip on top; common very coarse sand and abundant chaff; diameter 31 cm.
- **q** orange ware, grey core; red slip on interior and exterior; abundant chaff; diameter 10 cm.

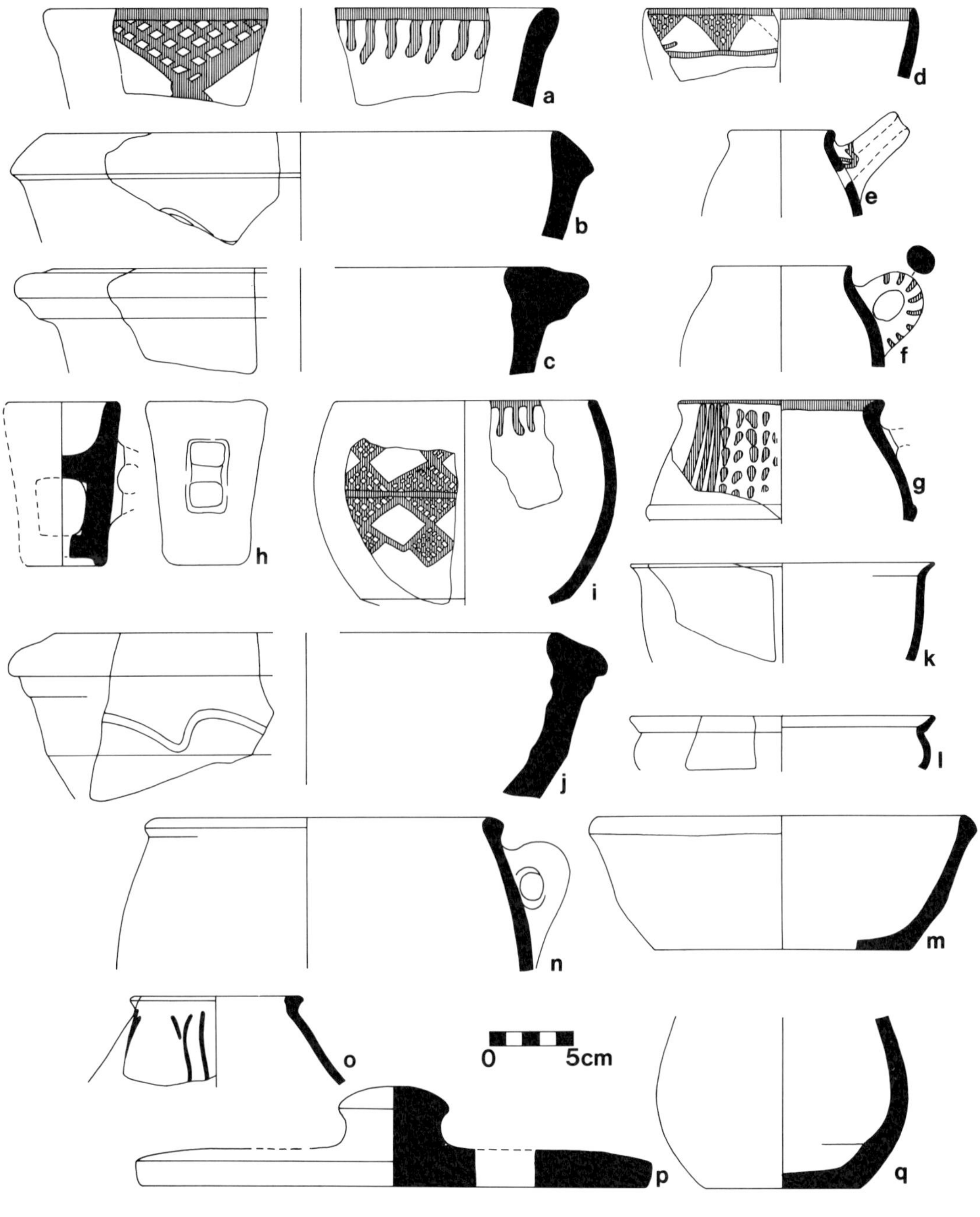

Fig. 17. HDR 9; HDR 10

Fig. 18

HDR 3

- **a** grey-rown ware; grey slip on interior and exterior, burnished on exterior; common very coarse sand; diameter unknown
- **b** buff-grey ware; burnished on interior and exterior; common coarse sand; diameter 17 cm.
- c red ware; orange-brown slip; abundant very coarse sand; diameter unknown
- **d** buff ware grey core; cream slip on interior and exterior, brown paint; moderate chaff; diameter 16 cm.
- **e** brown ware, grey core; cream slip on exterior, trace of brown paint; common chaff; diameter 10 cm. (drawing inverted)
- **f** brown ware, grey core; cream slip on interior and exterior, brown paint; common chaff; diameter 12 cm.

HDR 2

- **g** black ware; brown-orange surfaces, burnished on interior; common coarse sand and abundant chaff; diameter 32 cm.
- **h** dark grey ware; orange surfaces, burnished red-brown slip on interior and exterior; common chaff; diameter 13 cm.
- **i** buff ware; burnished dark red slip on interior and exterior; common chaff; diameter 8 cm.
- **j** black ware; orange-buff surfaces, red slip; common chaff

HDR 1

- **k** cream ware; black slip on interior and exterior; moderate medium sand and common chaff; diameter 27 cm.
- **l** black ware; buff surfaces, orange-red slip on interior and exterior; common chaff; diameter 17 cm.
- **m** cream ware; orange-cream slip on exterior, red paint; moderate chaff; diameter 4 cm.
- **n** black ware; orange surfaces, cream slip on interior and exterior, brown paint: common chaff; diameter 20 cm. (angle uncertain)
- **o** black ware; orange surfaces, burnished red slip on interior and exterior; common chaff; diameter 3 cm.
- **p** black ware; orange surfaces, cream slip, brown paint; common chaff; diameter 7 cm.
- **q** black ware; orange surfaces, burnished red slip; common chaff; diameter 9 cm.

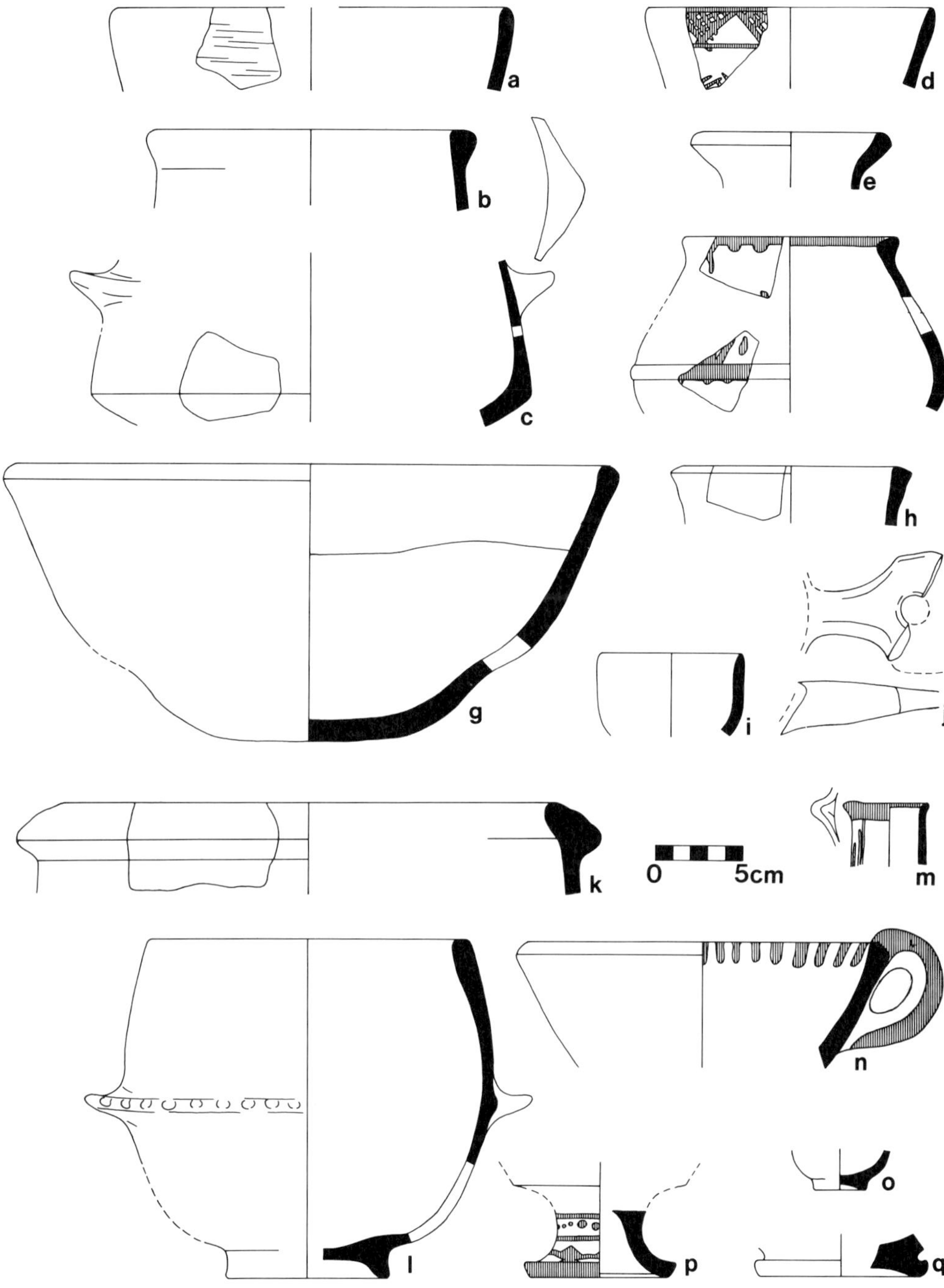

Fig. 18. HDR 3; HDR 2; HDR 1

Fig. 19

Stone Vessels

a	HDR 27	plaster
b	HDR 19	steatite (iron in the holes)
c	HDR 20	steatite; diameter 15 cm.
d	HDR 29	steatite, blackened exterior; diameter 22 cm.
e	HDR 34.1	steatite
f	Qaraw	steatite; diameter 15 cm.
g	Qaraw	red and white varigated travertine; diameter 14 m.
h	Khanfar	steatite
i	HDR 25	steatite (iron in repair holes); diameter 15 cm.
j	Jebelain	steatite; diameter 22 cm.
k	Jebelsin	steatite; diameter 22 cm.
l	Kawd am-Saila	steatite, burned black exterior
m	Kawd am-Saila	steatite; diameter 27 cm.

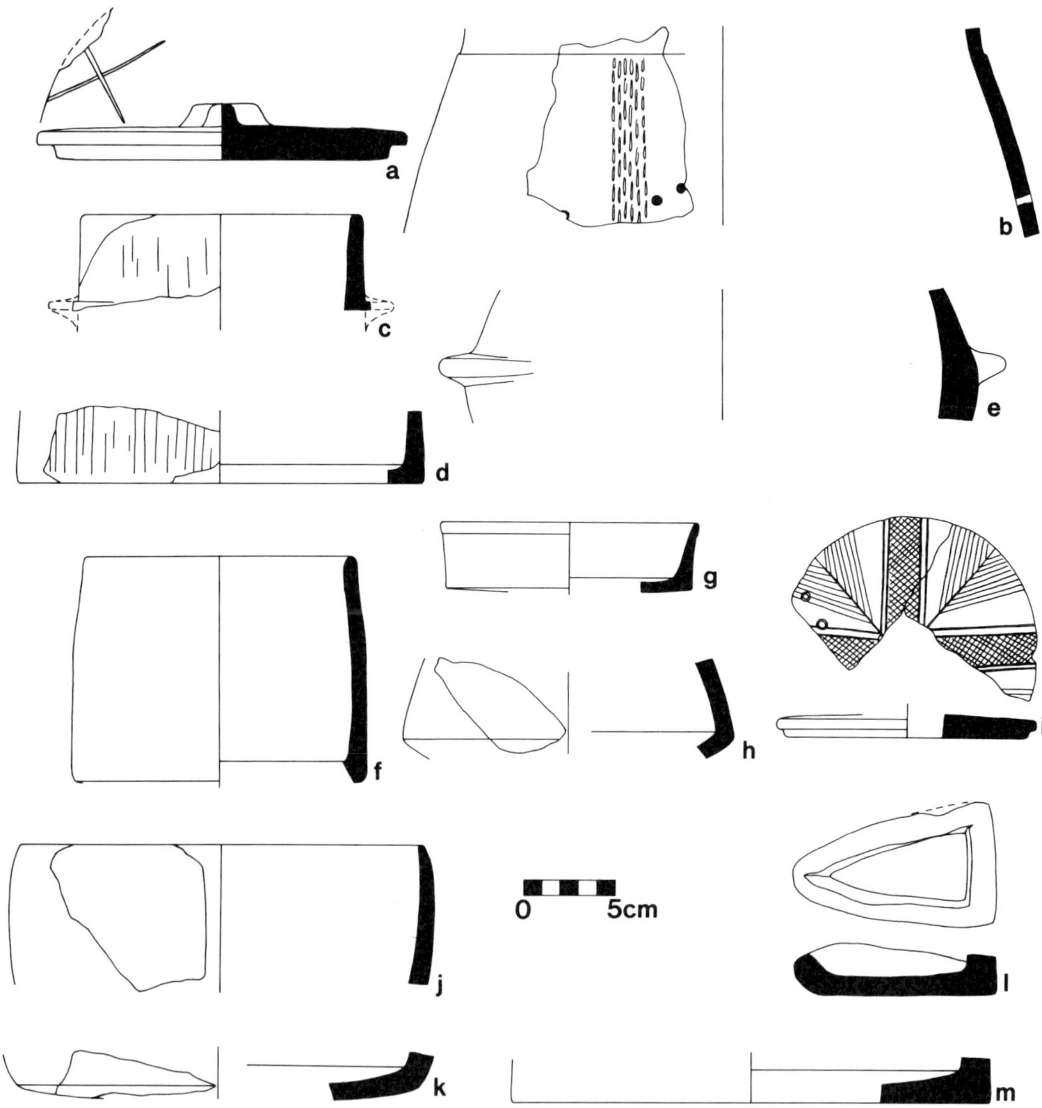

Fig. 19. Stone Vessels

Fig. 20

Glass Vessels

a	HDR 30	green
b	HDR 48	light green; diameter 8 cm.
c	HDR 48	light green; diameter 4 cm.
d	HDR 30	light green; diameter 2 cm.
e	Jebelain	yellowish clear; moulded; diameter 4 cm.
f	Jebelain	greenish clear; diameter 3 cm.
g	HDR 28	amber; diameter 3 cm.
h	HDR 34.2	light green; moulded
i	HDR 20	dark green
j	HDR 20	dark green
k	HDR 27	light green
l	Qaraw	green; vertical bubble; diameter 6 cm.
m	Qaraw	dark green; diameter 2.5 cm.
n	Qaraw	greenish-clear; diameter 3 cm.
o	Qaraw	blue; diameter 4 cm.
p	Qaraw	dark green; diameter 3.5 cm.
q	Qaraw	jellow; diameter 6 cm.
r	Qaraw	amber; diameter 4 cm.
s	Qaraw	dark green
t	Qaraw	green
u	Kawd am-Saila	yellowish-green; diameter 4 cm.
v	Kawd am-Saila	yellowish-green; diameter 5 cm.
w	Kawd am-Saila	green; diameter 3 cm.
x	Kawd am-Saila	green; diameter 4.5 cm.
y	Kawd am-Saila	yellowish-green; diameter 4 cm.
z	Kawd am-Saila	green; diameter 3 cm.
aa	Kawd am-Saila	green
bb	Kawd am-Saila	green
cc	Kawd am-Saila	green
dd	Kawd am-Saila	black
ee	Kawd am-Saila	green; diameter 3 cm.
ff	HDR 25	light green; diameter 4 cm.
gg	HDR 10	light green; diameter 4 cm.
hh	HDR 6	bluish-clear; cut decoration

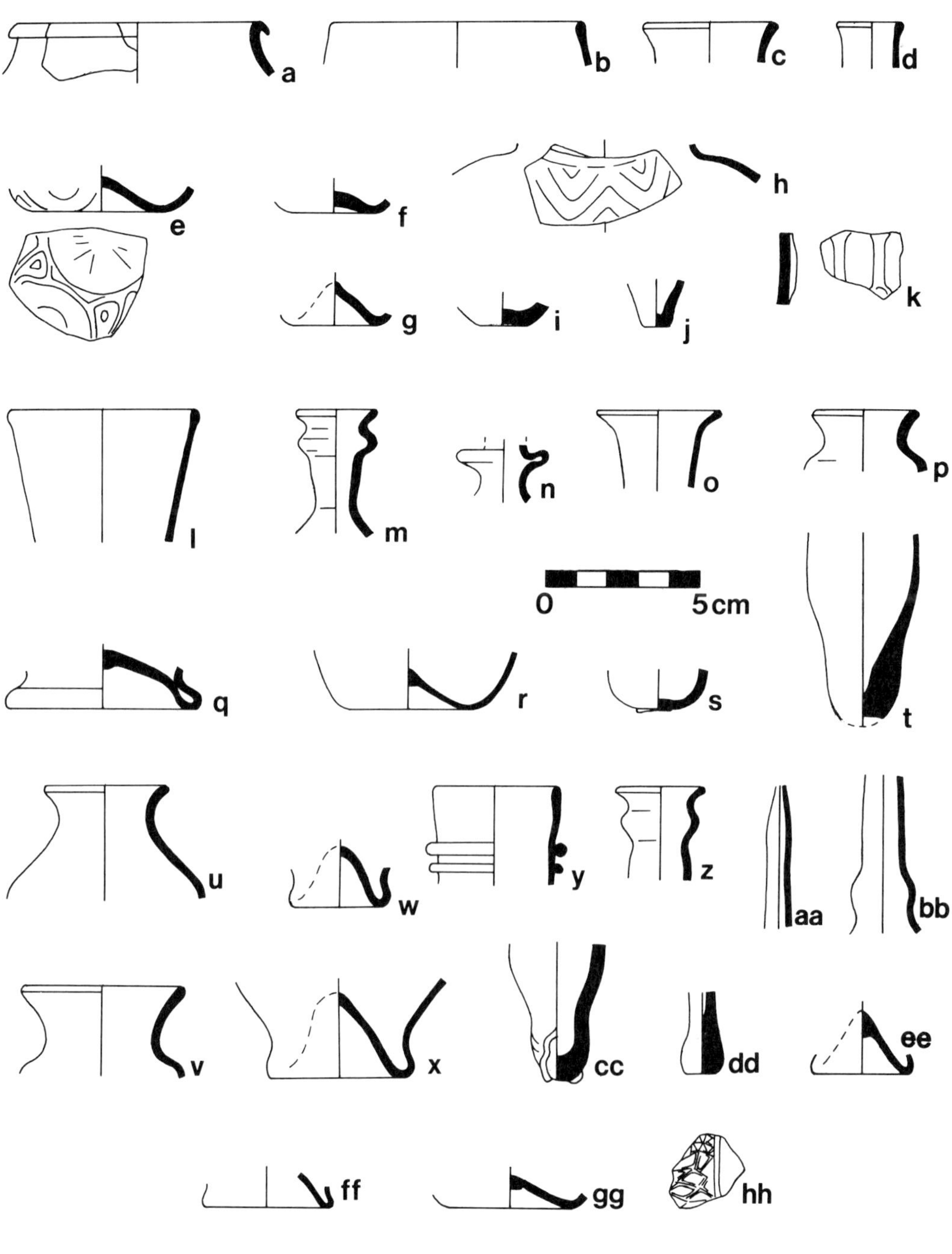

Fig. 20. Glass Vessels

Fig. 21

Glass Bracelets

a	HDR 48	black; diameter 6 cm.
b	HDR 19	blue; diameter 5 cm.
c	HDR 20	dark green; light green surface; diameter 5.5 cm.
d	HDR 20	black; diameter 6 cm.
e	HDR 20	black; red, white bands and prunts; diameter 5.5 cm.
f	HDR 20	black; light blue bands, yellow, red, white prunts; diameter 5 cm.
g	HDR 20	green; yellow, red bands, black, white twisted band; diameter 5 cm.
h	HDR 20	black; red, black, white twisted band; diameter 5 cm.
i	HDR 30	dark green; yellow, white, red bands, yellow prunts; diameter 6 cm.
j	HDR 20	black; white, red, yellow marvering; diameter 6 cm.
k	Khanfar	dark green; yellow, light green bands; diameter 6 cm.
l	Khanfar	blue; diameter 5 cm.
m	Khanfar	dark green; yellow, red bands, yellow prunts; diameter 5.5 cm.
n	Khanfar	dark green; red bands, yellow prunts; diameter 6 cm.
o	Qaraw	blue; diameter 5.5 cm.
p	Qaraw	amber; diameter 5.5 cm.
q	Qaraw	blue; diameter 5 cm.
r	Qaraw	black; diameter 5 cm.
s	Qaraw	dark green; red, light green marvering; diameter 4 cm.
t	Qaraw	black; red, yellow marvering; diameter 5 cm.
u	Kawd am-Saila	dark green; yellow, light green bands; diameter 5 cm.
v	Kawd am-Saila	light green; red band; diameter 4.5 cm.
w	Kawd am-Saila	dark green; yellow band; diameter 4 cm.
x	Kawd am-Saila	dark green; light green, red bands; diameter 6 cm.
y	Kawd am-Saila	amber; red bands, yellow prunts; diameter 6 cm.
z	Kawd am-Saila	dark green; yellow, red band, red, yellow spots; diameter 5 cm.
aa	HDR 25	blue; diameter 5.5 cm.
bb	HDR 25	black; white band, red, white prunts; diameter 6 cm.
cc	HDR 25	black; yellow, red, white bands, yellow prunts; diameter 5 cm.
dd	HDR 25	light green; yellow bands, black, white twisted band; diameter 5 cm.
ee	HDR 18	green; turquoise surface, red base; diameter 5 cm.
ff	HDR 10	black; yellow prunts; diameter 5.5 cm.
gg	HDR 10	black; yellow, red, light green bands, prunts; diameter 6 cm.
hh	HDR 7	dark green; light green bands; diameter 6 cm.

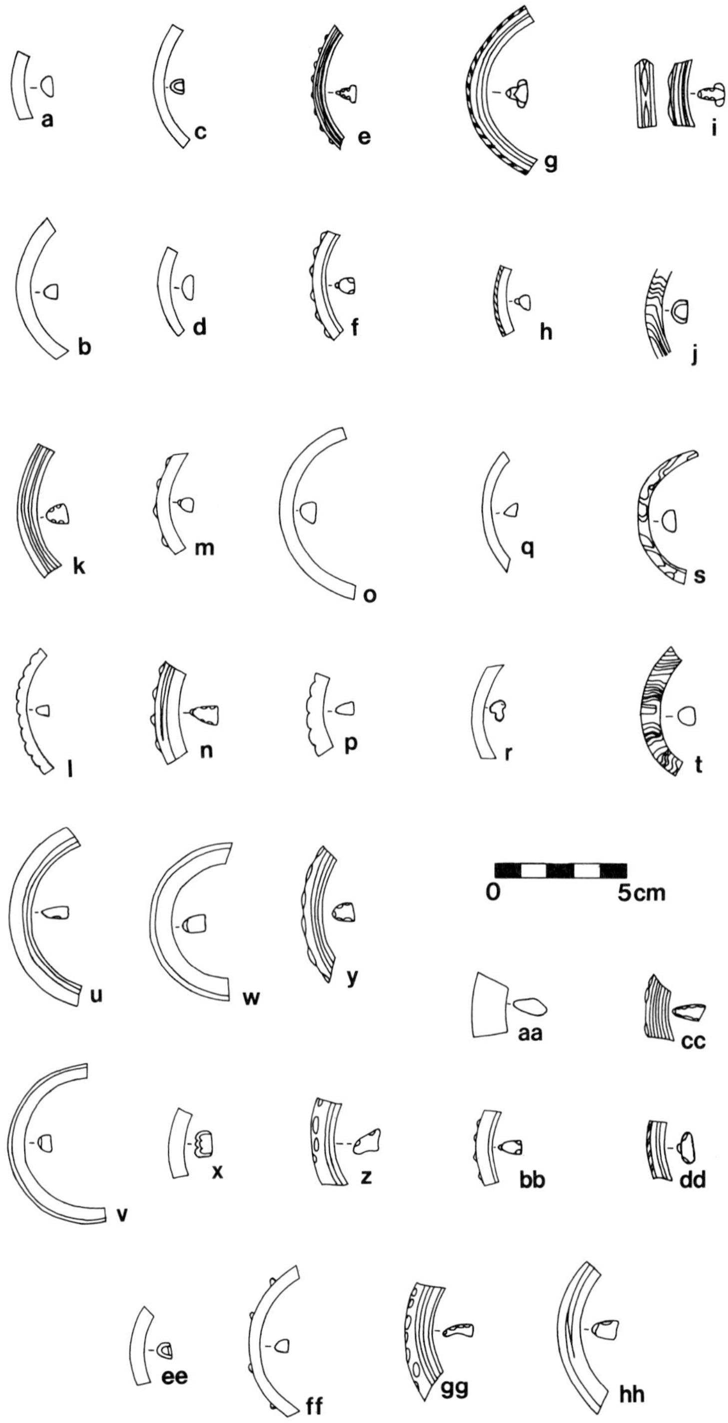

Fig. 21. Glass Bracelets

Fig. 22

Far Eastern Wares

a	HDR 27	celadon, yellowish green; diameter unknown
b	HDR 29	blue and white porcelain; diameter 10 cm.
c	HDR 20	blue and white porcelain
d	Qaraw	celadon (dark grey ware), lightly incised
e	Qaraw	greyish-blue and white porcelain; diameter 18 cm.
f	Qaraw	blue and white porcelain
g	Qaraw	grey ware; dark brown glaze on interior and exterior; moderate coarse white sand; diameter 11 cm.
h	Qaraw	celadon (light grey ware); diameter 12 cm.
i	Qaraw	stoneware (light grey ware); clear glaze, foot and ring on interior unglazed; diameter 10 cm.
j	Qaraw	grey-green celadon (light grey ware); diameter 8 cm.
k	Qaraw	bluish-white porcelain; glaze not on foot or base; diameter 5 cm.
l	Qaraw	celadon (light grey ware); broad crackle, red stain at foot; diameter unknown
m	Qaraw	celadon (light grey ware), glaze not on foot; diameter 4 cm.
n	HDR 25	blue and white porcelain; rim stained brown; diameter 26 cm.
o	HDR 25	blue and white porcelain; base blackened (repair holes); diameter 4 cm.
p	HDR 25	blue and white porcelain; base not glazed; diameter 3 cm.
q	HDR 25	blue and white porcelian; foot not glazed; diameter unknown
r	HDR 25	greyish-white porcelain; base not glazed; diameter 8 cm.

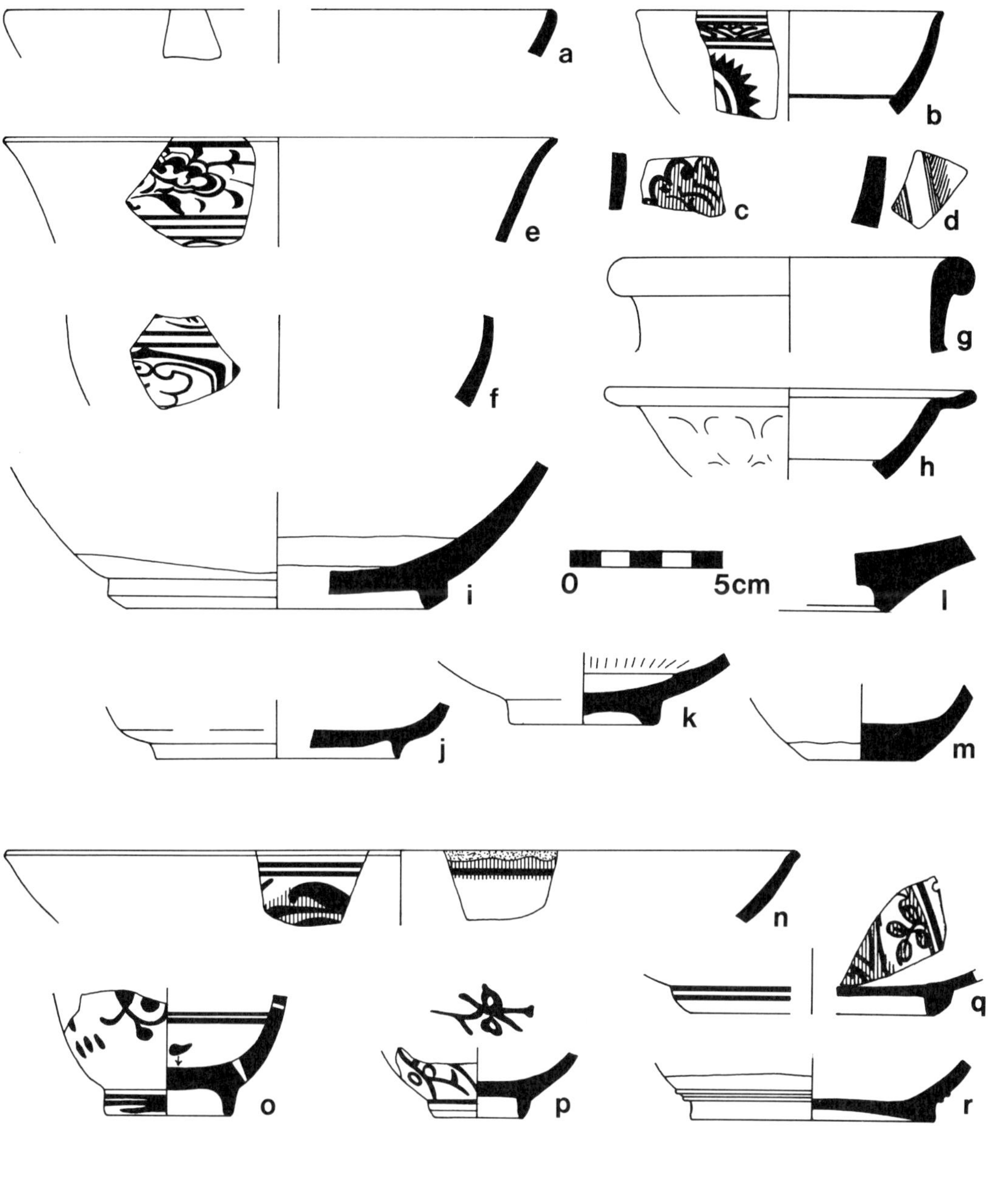

Fig. 22. Far Eastern Wares

Fig. 23

Far Eastern Wares

a	Kawd am-Saila	blue and white porcelain; diameter 16 cm.
b	Kawd am-Saila	black and white porcelain; diameter 8 cm.
c	Kawd am-Saila	blue and white porcelain; diameter 7 cm.
d	Kawd am-Saila	blue and white porcelain; brown stain on rim; diameter 26 cm.
e	Kawd am-Saila	blue and white porcelain; diameter 6 cm.
f	Kawd am-Saila	stoneware; blue on grey glaze; diameter 5 cm.
g	Kawd am-Saila	blue and white porcelain; diameter 3 cm.
h	Khanfar	blue and white porcelian
i	HDR 17	green, grey and white salt glaze ware
j	HDR 18	blue and white porcelain; diameter 14 cm.
k	HDR 18	very smokey blue and white porcelain; diameter 8 cm.
l	HDR 17	porcelain; red decoration; diameter 8.5 cm.
m	HDR 9	blue and white porcelain; diameter 8 cm.
n	HDR 10	stoneware (cream-grey ware): olive green glaze on exterior
o	HDR 10	blue and white porcelain; diameter 3 cm.
p	HDR 17	blue and white porcelain
q	HDR 7	blue and white porcelain
r	HDR 7	porcelain; blue decoration
s	HDR 3	blue and white porcelain
t	HDR 5	black and white porcelain; diameter 8 cm.
u	HDR 5	smokey blue-black and white porcelain; diameter 8 cm.
v	HDR 5	black and white porcelain; diameter 8 cm.
w	HDR 2	light blue and white porcelain; diameter 8 cm.
x	HDR 6	blue and white porcelain; diameter 3 cm.
y	HDR 5	porcelain; green decoration; diameter 8 cm.
z	HDR 5	porcelain; blue decoration; diameter 8 cm.
aa	HDR 2	porcelain; green decoration; diameter unknown

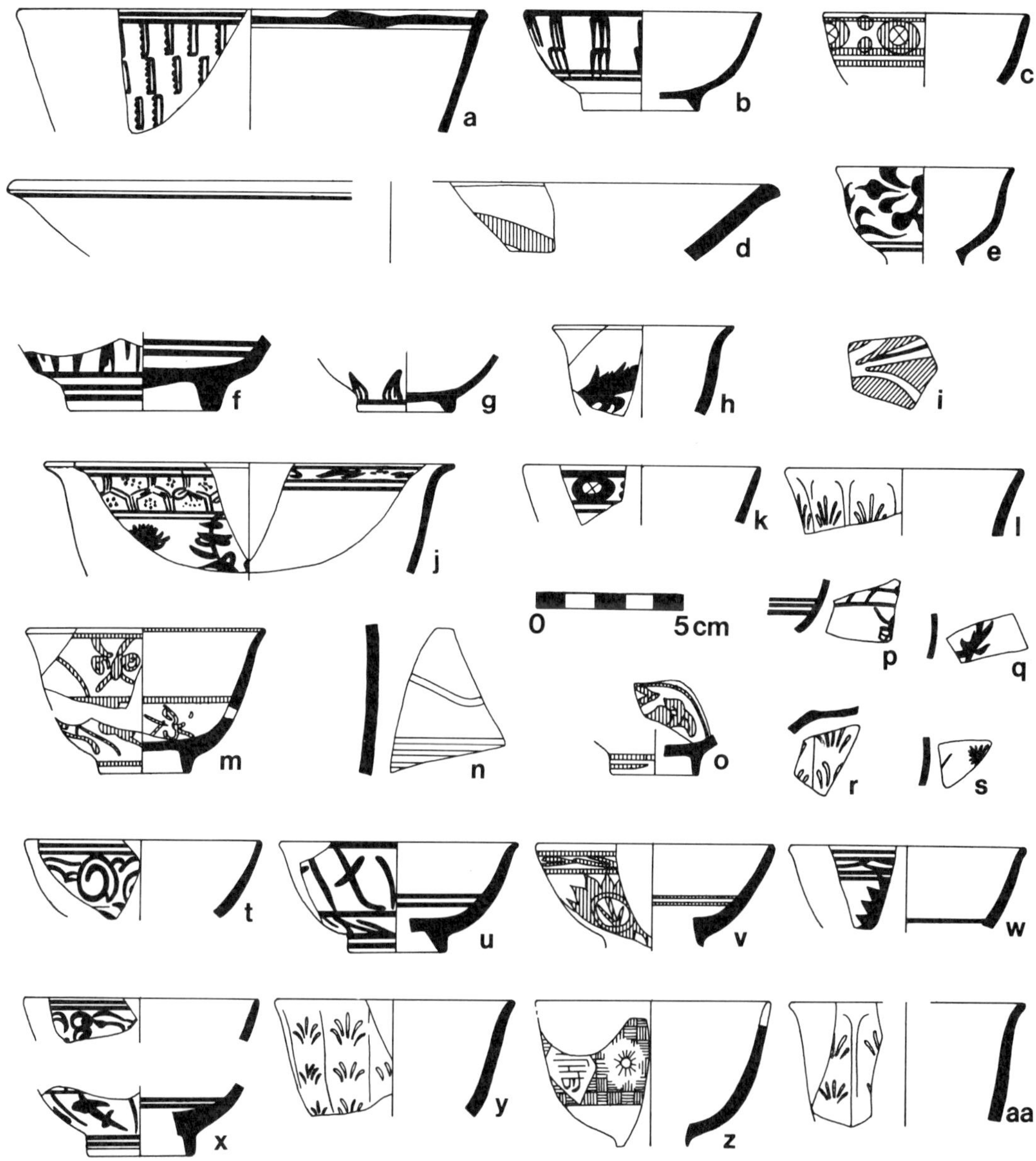

Fig. 23. Far Eastern Wares

Fig. 24. Site 25 (Maryama), looking east (above); Site 8 (in the Wadi Daman) (below)

Fig. 25. Site 48 ('Adiyah), looking south (above); Site 29 (west of Salilih), looking west (below)

Gazeteer [(2)]

Site 1. Two areas of sherds, widely scattered, on the northwest talus of Jebel Jayi bi-'Aydir, overlooking the Wadi Katabah. Both are perhaps associated with the remains of a small mud-brick house, apparently recent (twigs are still stuck in the mud) which probably functioned as an outpost guarding the former Kathiri road over the Jebel Jayi bi-'Aydir (circumventing Quaiti territory between Tarim and Seiyum). The road was built ca. 1925.
Coll.: 1 sm. bag of sherds, porcelain and glass

Site 2. Khalif el-Burrga. A small stone building on a natural outcroppng on the east side of the Wadi Thibi. The structure is built of rough dry-laid rubble masonry. The oval mounding of stones obscures the original wall-lines of what may have been a guard-post.
Coll.: 1 bag pottery

Site 3. An abandoned well on the east side of the Wadi Thibi constructed of dry- laid masonry, approximately 2.10 m. in diameter and silted up to within 1.83 m. of the uppermost preserved stone course. All masonry is missing from the northwest side. Surface slopes away from the well; the well-mouth is about 3 m. above the eroded silt into which it is cut.
Coll.: 1 bag of pottery from outer surface of slopes

Site 5. A pottery scatter, approximately 40×77 m., located on the slope within a sheltered bay of the mountain northwest of the village of Aydid. Immediately above the site on the east and north sides are shelters in the mountain face used as bedouin camp sites. There is no indication that pottery has eroded from a higher area, nor are there any indications of walls in this area or higher up the slope. Among the sherds, partially buried in the scree of the slope, were a quantity of rusted tin cans. There was some sherd scatter further to the east of the main concentration.
Coll.: 2 bags of pottery and glass

Site 6. An outcrop (actually part of the slope cut away from the talus) approximately 50 m. east of site 5, on the north slope of the mountain. The main sherd concentration is 35 m. square, probably an encampment as there is no evidence of buildings. A thin scatter of sherds links sites 5 and 6.
Coll.: 1 bag of pottery

Site 7. Qar et-Tas. This is a conical hill near the north side of Tarim, on the top of which is a modern *husn* defense tower, one of several overlooking Tarim

and probably dating from the Kathiri and Quaiti troubles in the 1930's. The hill is an eroded outcrop which is now separate from the mountain. The tower is built of mud-brick (some sherds are inside and protruding from the mud-brick). There is a heavy concentration of pottery around the tower and on the lower south slope (the lower slope is being used still as a dump).
Coll.: 1 bag of pottery

Site 8. A fallen mud-brick house on the talus slope on the northeast side of the Wadi Damun. Two rooms are clear; the remainder are filled with mud-brick. The building is square with round buttresses at each corner; the doorway is on the east wall.
Coll.: 1 bag of pottery (location unknown)
Photos: Fig. 24 (below)

Site 9. Husn el-'Ughetha (or Ghrama). Located northeast of Tarim and east of Damun is a standing mud-brick house with stone foundations. Many of the rooms are still clear while others are filled with mud-brick. This is a comparatively recent structure, probably no more than 100 years old.
Coll.: 1 bag of pottery

Site 10. A series of four low (ca. 1 m. high) mounds, approximately 40 m. apart, on the floor of the Wadi Hadhr. These were probably houses of a small settlement, now eroded almost to the level of the wadi bed and very difficult to distinguish from the surrounding silt. It is possible that earlier villages in the Tarim area suffered a similar fate and lie buried beneath the silt.
Coll.: 1 bag of pottery (from all four mounds)

Site 15. Qant (or Husn) el-Gahabah. Located near the entrance of the Wadi Idim, this site is a high conical mound crowned with a modern fort. Beneath the fort are indications of several periods of pre-Islamic occupation. The fort is made of mud-brick and connected with a modern fortification extending south and east forming a square enclosure.
Coll.: 2 bags of pottery

Site 16. Bel-Habban. This is a mud-brick house or probably fortress on the side of the mountain overlooking the junction of the Wadi Thibi and Wadi Idim. Similar structures are found on ridges to the northwest (Umbarrik bin Omar) and to the southeast, each with identical ceramics and construction; in the case of Umbarrik bin Omar there are five courses of stone retaining wall preserved.
Coll.: 1 bag of pottery

Site 17. Husn Muttahar. This is a large, well-preserved fortress made of mud-brick on the slope of the mountain just above the modern Kathiri customs post and police station on the road from Ghuraj to Tarim. The plan is square with round corner towers. Extending southeast from the southeast corner is a construction leading down to a deep well (with water still in it).
Coll.: 1 sm. bag of pottery

Site 18. el-Qarra. A well-preserved village ruin on the south side of the Wadi Hadhramaut situated on the top of an outcrop or slope isolated by erosion. The ruins consist of about 100 mud-brick buildings, including one mosque, all constructed on several courses of rubble masonry foundations.
Coll.: 1 bag of pottery
Photos: Van Beek, 1963, Pl.8: 2

Site 19. Qarat Hawtah as-Sultanah. A fortress located 800-1300 m. north of the modern village is, according to local tradition, a Christian site named Qarat al-'Urr. On the east and northwest sides of the site are stretches of masonry consisting of roughly squared blocks and mortar. There is standing and fallen mud-brick construction on the top and around the perimeter, though possibly not contemporary with the masonry.
Coll.: 1 bag of pottery
Photos: Van Beek, 1963, Fig.8: 1

Site 20. Qarat el-Harargeh Bor. This large building complex, possibly a single house, occupies a bench now connected to the wadi escarpment by only a saddle, the remainder having eroded away. The rocky contour of the site is levelled and the fill held by dry-laid rubble masonry. The construction is of mud- brick, badly eroded but preserved to several courses in some places. The site is ca. 150 × 50 m.
Coll.: 1 bag of pottery

Site 21. Qarat Ali Bin Hassan. This site occupies a long level bench projecting from the north side of the wadi. The buildings consist of mud-brick construction on stone rubble foundations and seem recently abandoned. Two of the buildings are square in plan with round towers at each of the four corners.
Coll.: none (= site 17)

Site 22.: Qarat Berrai. This modern ruin is built on a silt mound east-southeast of the village of Bor and adjoining it. Sands have encroached on the south

and east sides of the site. The silt seems to be water-lain rather than occupational debris.
Coll.: none (= site 17)

Site 25. Maryamah. The ruins of this mud-brick village lie north of and adjoin the village of Maryamah and consist of two areas. The upper area lies on a rock outcrop once part of the talis southeast of the site. The buildings are constructed of mud-brick on rubble masonry foundations (or on the rock). There is little depth of debris though the site is an excellent defensive position. One building has a square plan with round towers at each corner. Near the east side is a deep well without water. The lower site stretches east from the base of the outcrop and consists of more than 50 buildings including two mosques, one at the east end and the other at the west end of the site. The west mosque is covered by twelve domes, over half of which are preserved. These buildings are likewise of mud-brick on stone foundations built on the slope forming the south wall of the wadi bed. This site is probably not to be identified with Ptolemy's Marimatha (see von Wissmann and Höfner, 1952, p.352).
Coll.: 2 bags of pottery
Photos: Fig. 24 (above)

Site 26. Qarat Sheikh Ali. This site is a series of mud-brick buildings lying on an outlier west of Seiyun at the east side of the mouth of the Wadi Shehuh on an eroded portion of a bench.
Coll.: none

Site 27. Qarat Salilih el-Qadim. This site is located on an outlier west of the mouth of the Wadi Madar and consists of several rectangular rubble masonry structures. Superstructures were probably mud-brick but are nowhere preserved. There is a considerable amount of ash in various parts of the site.
Coll.: 1 bag of pottery (cf. site 19)

Site 28. Qarat Salilih el-'Adi. Situated on a small outlier ca. 300 m. north of site 27, this site has a series of dry laid rubble masonry walls forming rectangular structures; mud-brick superstructures have tumbled down the slope. One room is plastered and may have been a cistern. There is a thick layer of ash in some of the rooms and some of the stone walls show the effects of fire.
Coll.: 1 bag of pottery (= site 27)

Site 29. Low mound west of the village of Salilih at the juncture of the silt with a gravel plain extending south from the north wadi wall. This low mound was

exposed and is being dug by farmers for humus; it is 100×30 m., and perhaps larger. All exposed buildings are rectangular mud-brick constructions on dry laid rubble foundations. Some later pottery (e.g., porcelains) come from the northern end of the site and around a tamarisk tree. This mound is no more than two meters high at the highest point and may be typical of other buried sites waiting to be discovered.
Coll.: 1 bag of pottery
Photos: Fig. 25 (below)

Site 30. Qarat el-Habuthi. The top and more gentle slopes of an outlier are covered with remains of mud-brick structures (twigs from the roofs are still preserved in the debris). The site continues north of the outlier across the road from Seiyun to Bor, as well as northeast of the outlier.
Coll.: 1 bag of pottery

Site 31. Sheblilih. This site, located east-southeast of the village of Ard es-Saghir, has been accidentally exposed by humus digging, as was site 29. It consists of a series of low mounds (a maximum of one meter in height) at the juncture of the silt and the gravel from the slopes of the north side of the wadi wall. The area of the site is ca. 300 × 100 m., but this estimate is tentative due to the low height and the gravel covering.
Coll.: 1 bag of pottery

Site 34. Matargah. This is a large site consisting of constructions on two outliers (area 1) and on a lower level around the base, the most important of which is immediately west of the western outlier (area 2). There are few remains between the two outliers. Area 2 has been badly disturbed by humus digging; all buildings are rectangular, constructed of mud-brick on stone foundations. The western outlier, area 1, held square buildings with round towers at each corner, constructed of mud-brick on stone foundations. The entire site covers an area of c. 900 m. along the base of the north wadi wall.
Coll.: 2 bags of pottery (34.1 = area 1 and 34.2 = area 2)

Site 48. 'Adiyah. This is a low mound (ca. 1 m. high) in the midst of a system of irrigation dykes (*söm*) the middle of the Wadi Hadhramaut south of Hainan. No traces of architecture are visible; a scatter of sherds is oriented north-south (80×35 m.). This site was combined with site 49, a small mound (30×30 m.) with traces of mud-brick walls visible. The site has a South Arabian dedicatory stone which should be much earlier than the ceramics would suggest; this stone may have been introduced from some other site or may indicate a

destroyed or buried site beneath the present mound (see von Wissmann and Höfner, 1952,p.350). The ceramics in the *söms* are identical with those of the site, suggesting that the irrigation system post-dates the site and is probably relatively recent.
Coll.: 1 bag of pottery
Photos: Fig.25 (above)

Notes

1. I wish to express my appreciation to Dr. Van Beek for his generosity in making his survey notes and collections available for this study. This research was made possible by a fellowship from the Smithsonian Institution, Department of Anthropology. Dr. O. Watson of the Ceramics Department, Victoria and Albert Museum, very kindly made it possible for me to examine Lande and Serjeant's collections from sites near Aden; this was especially valuable for the dating of Habil, which was not visited during the Van Beek survey. I would also like to extend my appreciation to Mr. P. Parr for allowing me to study his surface collections from Mocha, which are in the Institute of Archaeology, University of London.

2. Based on Dr. G.W. Van Beek's field notes.

Bibliography

Allen, J. de V. (1969), 'A Proposal for Indian Ocean Studies', *Mawazo*, vol.2, pp.23-32.

Beckingham, C.F. and Serjeant, R.B. (1950), 'A Journey by two Jesuits from Dhufar to San'a in 1590', *Geographical Journal*, vol.115, pp.194-207.

Beeston, A.F.L. (1952), 'The so-called Harlots of Hadramaut', *Oriens*, vol.1, pp.16-22.

Bowen, R. LeBaron, Jr. and Albright, F.P. (1958), *Archaeological Discoveries in South Arabia*, Baltimore, Johns Hopkins.

Boxer, C.R. (1969), 'A Note on Portuguese Reactions to the Revival of the Red Sea Spice Trade and the Rise of Acheh, 1540-1600', *Journal of Southeast Asian History*, vol.10, pp.415-428.

Bujra, A.S. (1971), *The Politics of Stratification: A Study of Political Change in a South Arabian Town*, Oxford, Clarendon.

Carswell, J. (1978), 'China and Islam in the Maldive Islands', *Transactions of the Oriental Ceramics Society 1975-1977*, pp.121-198.

Caton Thompson, G. (1931), *The Zimbabwe Culture*, Oxford, Clarendon.

Caton Thompson, G. (1944), *The Tombs and Moon Temple of Hureidha (Hadhramaut)*, Oxford, Society of Antiquaries.

Chittick, H.N. (1974), *Kilwa: An Islamic Trading City on the East African Coast*, 2 vols., Nairobi, British Institute in East Africa.

Chittick, H.N. (1975), 'The Peopling of the East African Coast', in H.N. Chittick and R.I. Rotberg (eds.), *East Africa and the Orient: Cultural Syntheses in Pre-colonial Times*, New York, Africana, pp.16-43.

Comfort, H. (1958), 'Imported Pottery and Glass from Timna', in R. LeBaron Bowen, Jr. and F.P. Albright, *Archaeological Discoveries in South Arabia*, Baltimore, Johns Hopkins, pp.199-207.

Curle, A.T. (1937), 'The Ruined Towns of Somaliland', *Antiquity*, vol.11, pp.315-327.

de Cardi, B. (1971), 'Archaeological Survey

in the Northern Trucial States', *East and West*, vol.21, pp.225-288.

de Cardi, B. (1975), 'Archaeological Survey in Northern Oman, 1972', *East and West*, vol.25, pp.9-75.

de Cardi, B. (1977), 'Surface Collections from the Oman Survey, 1976', *Journal of Oman Studies*, vol.3/1, pp.59-70.

de Cardi, B., Collier, S. and Doe, D.B. (1976), 'Survey and Excavation in Oman, 1974-1975', *Journal of Oman Studies*, vol.2, pp.101-187.

Doe, D.B. (1962), *Notes on Pottery found in the Vicinity of Aden*, Aden, Department of Antiquities.

Doe, D.B. (1963), 'Pottery Sites Near Aden', *Journal of the Royal Asiatic Society 1963*, pp.150-162.

Doe, D.B. (1971), *Southern Arabia*, London, Thames and Hudson.

Garlake, P.S. (1978), 'An Encampment of the Seventeenth to Nineteenth Centuries on Ras Abaruk, Site 5', in B. de Cardi (ed.), *Qatar Archaeological Report, Excavations 1973*, Oxford, Oxford University Press, pp.164-171.

Goitein, S.D. (1954a), 'Two Eye-witness Reports on the Expedition of the King of Kish (Qais) against Aden', *Bulletin of the School of Oriental and African Studies*, vol.16, 1954, pp.247-257.

Goitein, S.D. (1954b), 'From the Mediterranean to India: Documents on the Trade to India, South Arabia, and East Africa, from the Eleventh and Twelfth Centuries', *Speculum*, vol.29, pp.181-197.

Goitein, S.D. (1980), 'From Aden to India, Specimens of the Correspondence of India Traders of the Twelfth Century', *Journal of the Economic and social History of the Orient*, vol.23, pp.43-66.

Gyllensvärd, B. (1973), 'Recent Finds of Chinese Ceramics at Fustat', *Bulletin of the Museum of Far Eastern Antiquities (Stockholm)*, vol.45, pp.99-119.

Gyllensvärd, B. (1975), 'Recent Finds of Chinese Ceramics at Fustat', *Bulletin of the Museum of Far Eastern Antiquities (Stockholm)*, vol.47, pp.93-117.

El-Hakim, A.A. and Elisseef, N. (1980), *Mission de recherche soudano-française dans la province de la Mer Rouge: Rapport préliminaire de la campagne 1980*, Lyon, Maison de l'Orient Méditeranéen.

Harding, G.L. (1964), *Archaeology in the Aden Protectorates*, London, H.M. Stationery Office.

Hobson, R.L. (1928), 'Chinese Porcelain Fragments from Aidhab, and some Bashpa Inscriptions', *Transactions of the Oriental Ceramics Society 1926-1927*, pp.19-22.

Ingrams, W.H. (1936), *A Report on the Social, Economic and Political Condition of the Hadhramaut*, London, H.M. Stationery Office.

Ingrams, W.H. (1966), *Arabia and the Isles*, New York, Praeger.

Kay, H.C. (1892), *Yaman, its Early Medieval History*, London, E. Arnold.

Keall, E.J. (1983), 'The Dynamics of Zabid and its Hinterland - The Survey of a Town on the Tihamah Plain of North Yemen', *World Archaeology*, vol.14, pp.378-392.

Khan, F.A. (1963), *Banbhore, a Preliminary Report on the Recent Archaeological Excavations at Banbhore*, Karachi, Department of Archaeology and Museums.

Kirkman, J.S. (1954), *The Arab City of Gedi: Excavations at the Great Mosque, Architecture and Finds*, Oxford, Oxford University Press.

Kirkman, J.S. (1963), *Gedi, The Palace*, The Hague, Mouton,

Kirkman, J.S. (1974), *Fort Jesus: A Portuguese Fortress on the East African Coast*, Oxford, Clarendon.

Krenkow, F. (1947), 'The Annual Fairs of the Pagan Arabs', *Islamic Culture*, vol.21, pp.111-113.

Lamb, A. (1965), 'A Note on Glass Fragments from Pengkalan Bulang, Malaya', *Journal of Glass Studies*, vol.7, pp.35-40.

Lane, A. (1957), *Later Islamic Pottery: Persia, Syria, Egypt, Turkey*, London, Faber and Faber.

Lane, A. and Serjeant, R.B. (1948), 'Pottery and Glass Fragments from the Aden Littoral, with Historical Notes', *Journal of the Royal Asiatic Society*, pp.108-133.

Little, O.H. (1925), *The Geography and Geology of Makalla*, Cairo, Geological Survey of Egypt.

Maktari, A.M.A. (1971), *Water Rights and Irrigation Practices in Lahj*, Cambridge, Cambridge University.

Mikami, T. (1982), 'China and Egypt: Fustat', *Transactions of the Oriental Ceramics Society 1980-1981*, pp.67-89.

Monod, T. (1978), 'Sur un site à bracelets de verre des environs d'Aden', *Raydan*, vol.1, pp.111-124.

Müller, D.H. (1894/1891), *Geographie der*

arabischen Halbinsel, al-Hamdani, 2 vols., Leiden, Brill.

Orchard, J. (1982), 'Finding the Ancient Sites in Southern Yemen', *Journal of Near Eastern Studies*, vol.41, pp.1-21.

Özbaran, S. (1972), 'The Ottoman Turks and the Portuguese in the Persian Gulf, 1534-1581', *Journal of Asian History*, vol.6, pp.45-71.

Parr, P.J., Harding, G.L., and Dayton, J.E. (1970), 'Preliminary Survey in N.W. Arabia, 1968', *Bulletin of the Institute of Archaeology, University of London*, vol.8-9, pp.193-242.

Parr, P.J., Harding, G.L., and Dayton, J.E. (1972), 'Preliminary Survey in N.W. Arabia, 1968', *Bulletin of the Institute of Archaeology, University of London*, vol.10, pp.23-61.

al-Rashid, S.A. (1980), *Darb Zubaydah, The Pilgrim Road from Kufa to Mecca*, Riyadh, Riyadh University Press.

Reveil, G. (1883), 'Fours et ateliers d'émailleurs antiques à Cheikh Othman près d'Aden', *Revue d'Ethnographie (Paris)*, vol.2.

Serjeant, R.B. (1949a), 'Materials for South Arabian History', *Bulletin of the School of Oriental and African Studies*, vol.13, pp.281-307, 581-601.

Serjeant, R.B. (1949b), 'The Cemeteries of Tarim'. *Le Muséon*, vol.62, pp.151-160.

Serjeant, R.B. (1950), 'The Quarters of Tarim and their Tansurahs', *Le Muséon*, vol.67, pp.277-284.

Serjeant, R.B. (1954), 'Hud and other Pre-Islamic Prophets of Hadramaut', *Le Muséon*, vol.67, pp.121-179.

Serjeant, R.B. (1957), *The Saiyids of Hadramaut*, London, School of Oriental and African Studies.

Serjeant, R.B. (1960), review of Bowen and Albright, Archaeological Discoveries in South Arabia, *Bulletin of the School of Oriental and African Studies*, vol.23, pp.582-585.

Serjeant, R.B. (1962a), 'Haram and Hawtah, the Sacred Enclave in Arabia', in A.R. Badawi (ed.), *Mélanges Taha Husein*, Cairo, Dar al-Maraf, pp.41-58.

Serjeant, R.B. (1962b), 'Historians and Historiography of Hadramaut', *Bulletin of the School of Oriental and African Studies*, vol.25, pp.239-261.

Serjeant, R.B. (1964), 'Some Irrigation Systems in Hadramaut', *Bulletin of the School of Oriental and African Studies*, vol.27, pp.33-76.

Serjeant, R.B. (1974), *The Portuguese off the South Arabian Coast: Hadrami Chronicles*, Beirut, Librairie du Liban.

Shahid, I. (1971), *The Martyrs of Najran*, Brussels, Société des Bollandistes.

Smith, S. (1954), 'Events in Arabia in the 6th Century A.D.', *Bulletin of the School of Oriental and African Studies*, vol.16, pp.425-468.

Sprenger, A. (1864), *Die Post- und Reiserouten des Orients*, Leipzig, Brockhaus.

Stark, F. (1936), *The Southern Gates of Arabia: A Journey in the Hadhramaut*, New York, E.P. Dutton.

Steensgaard, N. (1973), *The Asian Trade Revolution of the Seventeenth Century: The East India Companies and the Decline of the Caravan Trade*, Chicago, University of Chicago Press.

Stookey, R.W. (1978), *Yemen: The Politics of the Yemen Arab Republic*, Boulder, Westview.

Toussaint, A. (1966), *History of the Indian Ocean*, Chicago, University of Chicago.

Trimingham, J.S. (1975), 'The Arab Geographers and the East African Coast', in H.N. Chittick and R.I. Rotberg (eds.), *East Africa and the Orient: Cultural Syntheses in Pre-colonial Times*, New York, Africana, pp.115-146.

Tufnell, O. (1961), 'These were the Potters... Notes on the Craft in Southern Arabia', *Annual of the Leeds Oriental Society*, vol.2, pp.26-36.

Van Beek, G.W., Cole, G.H., and Jamme, A. (1964), 'An Archaeological Reconnaissance in Hadhramaut, South Arabia – A Preliminary Report', *Smithsonian Report for 1963*, pp.521-545.

van den Berg, L.W.C. (1886), *Le Hadhramaut et les colonies arabes dans l'archipel Indien*, Batavia, Imprimerie du Gouvernement.

Van der Meulen, D. (1947), *Aden to the Hadhramaut: A Journey in South Arabia*, London, J. Murray.

Waddington, H. (1946), 'Adilabad, a part of the "fourth" Delhi', *Ancient India*, vol.1, pp.60-76.

Weir, S. (1975), 'Some Observations on Pottery and Weaving in the Yemen Arab Republic', *Proceedings of the Seminar for Arabian Studies*, vol.5, pp.65-76.

Wheatley, P. (1959), 'Geographical Notes on some Commodities involved in Sung Maritime Trade', *Journal of the Malayan*

Branch of the Royal Asatic Society, vol.32, pp.5-140.

Whitcomb, D.S. (1975), 'The Archaeology of Oman: A Preliminary Discussion of the Islamic Periods', *Journal of Oman Studies*, vol.1, pp.123-157.

Whitcomb, D.S. (1978), 'The Archaeology of Al-Ḥasā' Oasis in the Islamic Period', *Atlal*, vol.2, pp.95-113.

Whitcomb, D.S. (1983), 'Islamic Glass from Quseir al-Qadim, Egypt', *Journal of Glass Studies*, vol.25, pp.101-108.

Whitcomb, D.S. and Johnson, J.H. (1979), *Quseir al-Qadim 1978: Preliminary Report*, Cairo, American Research Center in Egypt.

Whitcomb, D.S. and Johnson, J.H. (1982), *Quseir al-Qadim 1980: Preliminary Report*, American Research Center in Egypt Reports, vol.7, Malibu, Undena.

Whitehouse, D. (1969), 'Excavations at Siraf: Second Interim Report', *Iran*, vol.7, pp.39-62.

Whitehouse, D. (1979), 'Islamic Glazed Pottery in Iraq and the Persian Gulf: The Ninth and Tenth Centuries', *Annali dell'Istituto Orientale di Napoli*, vol.39, pp.45-61.

Wilkinson, T.J. (1982), 'The Definition of Ancient Manured Zones by Means of Extensive Sherd-Sampling Techniques', *Journal of Field Archaeology*, vol.9, pp.323-334.

Wissmann, H. von and Höfner, M. (1952), *Beiträge zur historischen Geographie des vorislamischen Südarabien*, Wiesbaden, Franz Steiner.

Zarins, J. et al. (1979), 'Preliminary Report on the Third Phase of the Comprehensive Archaeological Survey Program – The Central Province', *Atlal*, vol.3, pp.9-42.

Branch of the Royal Asatic Society, vol.32, pp.5-140.
Whitcomb, D.S. (1975), 'The Archaeology of Oman: A Preliminary Discussion of the Islamic Periods', *Journal of Oman Studies*, vol.1, pp.123-157.
Whitcomb, D.S. (1978), 'The Archaeology of Al-Ḥasā' Oasis in the Islamic Period', *Atlal*, vol.2, pp.95-113.
Whitcomb, D.S. (1983), 'Islamic Glass from Quseir al-Qadim, Egypt', *Journal of Glass Studies*, vol.25, pp.101-108.
Whitcomb, D.S. and Johnson, J.H. (1979), *Quseir al-Qadim 1978: Preliminary Report*, Cairo, American Research Center in Egypt.
Whitcomb, D.S. and Johnson, J.H. (1982), *Quseir al-Qadim 1980: Preliminary Report*, American Research Center in Egypt Reports, vol.7, Malibu, Undena.
Whitehouse, D. (1969), 'Excavations at Siraf: Second Interim Report', *Iran*, vol.7, pp.39-62.
Whitehouse, D. (1979), 'Islamic Glazed Pottery in Iraq and the Persian Gulf: The Ninth and Tenth Centuries', *Annali dell'Istituto Orientale di Napoli*, vol.39, pp.45-61.
Wilkinson, T.J. (1982), 'The Definition of Ancient Manured Zones by Means of Extensive Sherd-Sampling Techniques', *Journal of Field Archaeology*, vol.9, pp.323-334.
Wissmann, H. von and Höfner, M. (1952), *Beiträge zur historischen Geographie des vorislamischen Südarabien*, Wiesbaden, Franz Steiner.
Zarins, J. et al. (1979), 'Preliminary Report on the Third Phase of the Comprehensive Archaeological Survey Program – The Central Province', *Atlal*, vol.3, pp.9-42.

List of Contributors

JEFFREY A. BLAKELY	The University Museum University of Pennsylvania, Philadelphia, Pa., USA
BEATRICE DE CARDI	London, UK
CHRISTOPHER EDENS	Department of Anthropology Harvard University, Cambridge, Ma., USA
PIERRE LOMBARD	Maison de l'Orient University of Lyon II, Lyon, France
H.A. McCLURE	Geology Department Arabian American Oil Company, Dhahran, Saudi Arabia
PETER J. PARR	Institute of Archaeology University of London, London, UK
D.T. POTTS	Carsten Niebuhr Institute of Ancient Near Eastern Studies, University of Copenhagen, Copenhagen, Denmark
CHRISTIAN ROBIN	Centre National de la Recherche Scientifique, Aix-en-Provence, France
JAMES A. SAUER	The University Museum University of Pennsylvania, Philadelphia, Pa., USA
DONALD S. WHITCOMB	The Oriental Institute University of Chicago, Chicago, Illinois, USA